GCE AS Level

D1647039

Liverpool Community College

AS Level for Edexcel

Applied Business

Rob Dransfield • Dave Needham

www.heinemann.co.uk
✓ Free online support
✓ Useful weblinks
✓ 24 hour online ordering

01865 888058

Heinemann

Inspiring generations

Heinemann Educational Publishers
Halley Court, Jordan Hill, Oxford OX2 8EJ
Part of Harcourt Education

Heinemann is a registered trademark of
Harcourt Education Limited

Text © Rob Dransfield, Dave Needham 2005

First published 2005

10 09 08 07 06 05
10 9 8 7 6 5 4 3 2 1

British Library Cataloguing in Publication Data is available
from the British Library on request.

10-digit ISBN 0 435 401149
13-digit ISBN 978 0 435 401 14 6

Edited by Mick Watson
Designed by Lorraine Inglis
Typeset by Saxon Graphics Ltd, Derby
Original illustrations © Harcourt Education Limited 2005
Cover design by Wooden Ark Studios
Printed by Bath Colourbooks
Cover photo © Alamy
Picture research by Bea Ray

Websites
There are links to relevant websites in this book. In order to ensure that the
links are up-to-date, that the links work, and that the sites aren't inadvertently
linked to sites that could be considered offensive, we have made the links
available on the Heinemann website at www.heinemann.co.uk/hotlinks. When
you access the site, the express code is 1149P.

Contents

Introduction

Welcome to your Edexcel GCE Applied Business course. The term 'Applied Business' is used to describe your course because it is focused not just upon learning about business organisations but also upon finding out and investigating how people within such organisations behave and make decisions. The Edexcel qualification is designed to 'provide you with a broad introduction to a vocational area and help you to apply knowledge in a variety of work-related situations' by 'exploring the world of business in a highly practical way'.

Edexcel places considerable emphasis upon getting you to learn within realistic business contexts. Your course will involve using theory as part or your learning and finding out how that theory relates to all of the decisions and activities that are undertaken by people within organisations at a variety of different levels. You will also undertake a range of investigative coursework activities which provide you with a first-hand opportunity to learn within and outside a classroom about many of the important activities and functions of business by undertaking many of these functions yourself. In this way your course is closely 'work related' and is designed to give you a much deeper and meaningful understanding of the sort of activities that people in business are involved with, so that you gain both knowledge and experience.

The Edexcel Applied Business qualification is flexible because it provides you with a real choice about which parts of the qualification you want to undertake. Just like the more traditional A levels, the Applied GCE adopts the AS and A2 structure of GCEs.

For the Edexcel *AS Double Award* you must take Units 1, 2, 3 and 6 plus two others from units 4, 5 and 7. All these units are covered in this book and they are:

Unit 1: Investigating People at Work (Externally Assessed)
Unit 2: Investigating Business (Internally Assessed)
Unit 3: Investigating Marketing (Internally Assessed).
Unit 4: Investigating Electronic Business (Internally Assessed)
Unit 5: Investigating Customer Service (Internally Assessed)
Unit 6: Investigating Promotion (Externally Assessed)
Unit 7: Investigating Enterprise (Internally Assessed).

In this course you will complete both external and internal assessments. The external assessments will relate to a business scenario to provide an appropriate context for the vocational element of your studies. For the internally-based assessments you will be asked to undertake realistic activities that relate to a vocational scenario, each of which you will be able to undertake in tandem with your learning within each unit. You will be assessed within 3 bands, the lowest of which is Mark Band 1 and the highest Mark Band 3. Your assessment criteria for each activity will identify all that you have to do to achieve the outcomes within each banded activity. Although some suggestions are given in this book about how to get higher marks, teachers should refer to the Edexcel specifications for full details of the marking and assessment criteria.

Throughout this book key words or concepts are highlighted in bold or italic. Many of those in bold are explained further in the glossary at the back of the book.

Enjoy your Applied Business course. By succeeding with your course you are opening up avenues so that you can either go into the workplace or go into higher education following your course.

Rob Dransfield
Dave Needham

Acknowledgements

The authors and publishers are grateful to those who have given permission to reproduce material.

Every effort has been made to contact copyright holders of material reproduced in this book. Any omissions or errors will be rectified in subsequent printings if notice is given to the publishers.

The publisher would like to thank David Floyd for acting as a consultant for this publication.

Text acknowledgements

Amazon, amazon.co.uk – page 123

Assael, H., *Marketing Principles and Strategy*, London: The Dryden Press, 1993 – page 132

Broadcasters' Audience Research Board (BARB) – page 157

Buy.co.uk screenshot, courtesy of www.buy.co.uk – page 203

CACI Ltd – page 148

Call Centre Association – page 271

Cannon, Tom, *Basic Marketing: Principles and Practice*, London: Cassel, 1997 – page 145

Cook, Sarah, *Customer Care: How to Create an Effective Customer Focus, London*: Kogan Page, 2000 – pages 241, 243, 256

Dibb, Sally et al., *Marketing Concepts and Strategies*, Boston: Houghton Mifflin, 2001 – pages 150, 172, 250

Drucker, Peter, *The Executive in Action: Managing for Results, Innovation and Entrepreneurship*, New York: Harper, New York – page 238

Ebay – page 304

EU, quote © European Communities, 1995-2005

FA, quote © The Football Association Limited 2002-04. All Rights Reserved – page 265

Friends of the Earth (England, Wales & Northern Ireland) – page 50

Dr Gelder, quote from www.biopsychology.com – page 261

Google screenshot © 2005 Google – page 224

Kotler, Philip, *Principles of Marketing*, Englewood Cliffs: Prentice Hall, 1996 – page 143

Lexus – page 252

Manchester United – pages 49, 218

Microsoft product screen shots reprinted with permission from Microsoft Corporation – pages 116, 118, 119, 226–9

Reg Millichamp www.archivist.f2s.com/bsu/Military/gordons/album/gs-memories.htm – page 254

Napster – page 213

National Readership Survey – pages 149, 335

Next – page 195

Nielsen Media Research – pages 159, 182, 220

Ofcom, quote © Ofcom copyright 2004 – page 303

Office of National Statistics – page 148

PIMS Study – page 136

P&O screenshot, courtesy of P&O Ferries – page 219

Popcorn, Faith, *The Popcorn Report: Faith Popcorn on the Future of Your Company, Your World, Your Life*, New York: Doubleday, 1992 – page 245

Peppers, D., and Rogers, M., *Managing Customers' Relationships: A Strategic Framework*, Chichester: Wiley, 2004 – page 245

Research Machines – page 175

Sainsbury's – page 318

Schumpeter, Joseph, *Capitalism, Socialism and Democracy*, New York: Harper and Row, 1974 – page 127

Shipley, D., *Pricing Objectives in British Manufacturing Industry*, Journal of Industrial Economics, vol. 29, no. 4 – page 169

Stewart, Rosemary, *Managers and Their Jobs*, Nuffield Foundation, 1965 – pages 70–71

TDC Ltd – page 276

Tesco – pages 198, 274, 296

TREE AID – page 4

Vodafone – page 269

World Advertising Research Center/DIMS – page 183

World Advertising Research Center (www.warc.com) – pages 295, 319

Wrangler © copyright 2005, VF Europe BVBA – page 199

Crown copyright material is reproduced under Class Licence No. C02W0005419 with the permission of the Controller of HMSO and the Queen's Printer for Scotland.

Photo and logo acknowledgements

3Com – page 232

Alamy – pages 8, 57(a), 60(b), 69, 76, 125, 322, 341

BBC – page 14

The Body Shop – page 2, 13

Coca-Cola – page 306

Corbis – page 38(a), 204, 287, 337, 345, 374

Dyson – page 60(a)

Empics – page 38(e),(h), 70(a), 344

The European Union – page 278

Friends of the Earth – page 50

Getty – pages 1, 38(b),(c),(g), 59(a), 235, 317, 341, 348

Holmes Place Health Clubs – page 308

Investors in People – page 40

Livewire – page 63

Nescafé – page 306

Nestlé – pages 2, 40

Nokia – page 221

Oxfam – page 3

P&O – page 85

Patak's Foods Lt – page 345

Rex Features – pages 5, 10, 38(d),(f), 43, 59(b), 70(b), 196

Rosabeth Moss Kanter – page 47

Sainsbury's – page 237

Shell – page 2

Tesco – pages 2, 13

Virgin Atlantic – pages 2, 57(b)

UNIT 1

Investigating people at work

This unit contains four parts:

1.1   Business aims, objectives and organisation

1.2   How businesses obtain employees

1.3   How businesses motivate employees

1.4   How people are influenced at work

Introduction

Businesses need to have a sense of direction. Therefore they need to define their aims, i.e. the ends that they seek to achieve. Having created a general aim for the organisation it is then possible to set out more specific objectives which provide guidance for the people who work for the organisation. Businesses also need to be structured in such a way that they are well organised to achieve their aims and objectives.

To provide goods and services, businesses rely on the people who work for them. It is therefore important to have an understanding of how and why people work in business, and what influences them at work.

What you will learn in this unit

* Why businesses have aims and objectives
* Typical aims of business organisations such as survival, growth and making a profit
* Different types of business organisations and how this affects the way they operate

FIGURE 1.1 *Motivated employees enjoy their work and help businesses to achieve their objectives*

* The functions and structures of business organisations
* How businesses obtain employees
* Effective ways of recruiting, selecting, and training employees
* How businesses motivate their employees
* How businesses can use theories of motivation in the workplace
* How external issues, such as environmental issues, influence people at work.

1.1 Business aims, objectives and organisation

Businesses are decision-making units that have been designed to make goods and provide services. A **good** is anything that a customer is prepared to buy because they believe that it will make them (or the person they buy the good for) better off. For example, you will probably have bought a mobile phone, computer game, or CD because you believed that it would give you more enjoyment.

A distinction is often made between a physical good, such as a sandwich, motor car or lawn mower, and **services**, which are benefits provided for consumers to enjoy but they do not have anything to take home with them (except for the benefit they have enjoyed). Examples of services include window cleaning, hairdressing or a visit to the cinema.

The term **product** refers to something offering a benefit that we can touch and see, for example a tube of Smarties or a compact disc. Production refers to the process of making these products, for example on a production line. However, the term product is also often used today for things such

PHYSICAL GOODS	SERVICES
Tangible goods (you can feel and see them)	Intangible services
A razor	Being given a shave by a barber
A packet of sandwiches	Being served in a restaurant
A piano	Listening to a musical concert

FIGURE 1.2 *Goods and services*

as insurance policies and other types of service outputs – the product is the complete article which a company sells to you as a discrete item.

There are many different types of business with their own particular purposes. An important distinction can be made between businesses that seek to make a profit and 'not for profit' businesses.

For profit businesses are ones that are owned by:

* individuals, such as **sole trader** (one owner) businesses

* a group of **partners** working together

* **shareholders**. A shareholder owned business is called a company.

Private companies are owned by private shareholders, and shares in them can only be bought privately with the permission of the **Board of Directors**. Anyone can buy shares in a **public company** (PLC). Shares in PLCs are traded on the **Stock Exchange**.

For profit businesses set out to make a profit. The profit can be used in the following ways:

1 For further expansion of the business

2 To be distributed among the owners. In the case of a company the owners are the shareholders and their share of the profit is given to them in the form of a dividend. For example, if they have 100 £1 shares in the company, and the company pays a dividend of 5p a share, then the shareholder will receive £5 worth of dividends.

Not-for-profit organisations come in two forms:

* Charities
* Voluntary organisations.

A **charity** is set up for a specific charitable purpose, e.g. Oxfam is a charity that is best-known for providing famine relief. Other charities have aims related to education, or providing sports and leisure activities to the community. Charities do not make profits. Instead they can make a surplus which is where the costs of running the charity are less than the proceeds in a given year.

FIGURE 1.4 *Oxfam – a charity providing famine relief*

Another form of not-for-profit organisation is a **voluntary organisation**. A voluntary organisation like the Women's Royal Voluntary Service (WRVS) is staffed by unpaid volunteers, whereas people who work for a charity are often paid.

Carry out research in your local town to find out the name of six for profit organisations and six not-for-profit organisations. Share out the task in your group of finding out the stated objectives of the six not-for-profit organisations.

The aims businesses have

Aims and **objectives** are the ends that you seek to achieve when you carry out a particular task.

The aim can be seen as the general end that you are working towards while objectives are sub-components of that aim. Often objectives can be **quantified**, i.e. numbers can be attached to them.

Many businesses today create what is termed a **mission statement** setting out the general aim or purpose of their organisation. Typically, missions are short statements such as Oxfam's mission 'Oxfam works with others to overcome

CHARITY LIKE OXFAM	COMPANY LIKE SHELL
When the revenues of Oxfam are greater than the costs of running the business a surplus is made which goes back into running the charity the next year	When the revenues of Shell are greater than the costs of running the business a profit is made which can be ploughed back into the business or distributed in dividends to shareholders

FIGURE 1.5 *Distinction between a for profit and a not-for-profit organisation*

CASE STUDY

Charities need to be business-like

Today charities have to operate in a business-like way if they are to be efficient.

Miranda Spitteler, the chief executive of the small development charity TREE AID, says:

'...passion for the cause is vital but it's not enough. People need to offer professional skills and experience. They'll be expected to work as hard and to meet as many targets and deadlines as in any commercial company. We're under more scrutiny than ever before, so we have to perform in order to survive.'

Rob Farace, the head of recruitment at Cancer Research UK, says that if anything charities have to be meaner and keener than commercial companies as they have to be accountable both to their donors and to the people they are helping. 'We have to be even slicker as we know how hard people have worked to collect our money.'

Identify three charities and state their key objectives. Research your answer by entering the name of the charity as an internet search.

Typically mission statements set out:

* Why a company exists

* What the company believes in

* What makes the company special

* How the company behaves

Carry out an internet search using the key words mission and the name of a company you are interested in.

1 To what extent is their mission clear?

2 To what extent does the mission communicate the four points listed above?

FIGURE 1.6 *Ryanair is a low-cost airline*

poverty and suffering'. You can see that this gives a sense of mission or purpose to everyone that works for the organisation and tells everyone outside the organisation what it stands for. The mission of leading supermarket chains typically involve statements such as 'To provide unbeatable value for our customers, while providing first class careers for our employees'. Often mission statements also mention the importance of creating growth for shareholders and building an excellent reputation in the community.

The mission of well-known organisations can typically be broken down into discrete objectives.

For example, the aim of Ryanair is to be 'Europe's leading low cost airline'.

To achieve this aim, there are a number of supporting objectives, such as:

* To undercut the fares of rivals

* To take over other airlines

* To increase sales each year.

Ryanair will want to quantify some of these objectives, e.g. to increase sales by x% in 2005, to sell tickets at y% less than rivals this year, etc.

In order to achieve aims and objectives an organisation will need to create plans which help it to achieve the desired ends.

The table illustrates the relationship between plans and aims and objectives for a company.

AIM	BUSINESS PLANS
To be Europe's Number 1 low-cost airline	Plans to raise finance e.g. by selling shares and borrowing.
Objectives (examples)	Plan to recruit and train high quality friendly staff
To operate efficiently at low cost, achieving sales and profit figures of x per cent in a given time period.	Marketing and operating plans
To fly to new destinations	Promotional plans
(aims and objectives are the ends to be worked towards)	(business plans are the means to achieve the ends)

A business plan will include details such as how the business will raise the finance it needs, who are the customers that make up its market, the type of people that it will need to employ, and so on.

SMART objectives

In business we often say that a good set of objectives is a **SMART** set of objectives. The term SMART stands for:

* **S**pecific
* **M**easurable
* **A**chievable
* **R**ealistic
* **T**ime-related.

For example, Manchester United Football Club set itself the target for the 2004–2005 season to win the European Champions League, and one major trophy in this country.

This was SMART because:

* This objective is clearly specific, it is easy to understand and everyone will know whether

they have been successful in achieving the objective.

* The objective is also measurable – if they won the Champions League and a major trophy in this country they would have achieved the required measure.

* The objective is also achievable. Manchester United started the season in a position where they could easily qualify for the Champions League, and they were already well placed in the Premier League in this country.

* The objective was realistic. Manchester United had been this country's most successful football team over the previous decade and had the players and manager to achieve success.

* The objective was also time related – it related to the 2004–2005 season.

Learning activity

Carry out a research activity to evaluate whether the objectives of a business are SMART or not by either:

* Interviewing a local business owner to find out what their objectives are. You can then assess these objectives by using the SMART criteria.

* Carrying out a piece of internet research. Use the search facility of your computer and enter the following terms:

1 The name of an organisation of your choice.

2 The term objectives or business objectives.

If you don't succeed in your first search, try the search again using the name of a different organisation.

FIGURE 1.7 *Objectives should be SMART*

✳ DID YOU KNOW?

The Times 100 website provides lots of useful information and case studies about companies as well as a good theory section. Search for it at www.heinemann.co.uk/hotlinks (express code 1149P, then go to Unit 1).

Why objectives apply to certain businesses

One of Ryanair's main aims in recent years has been that of growth – to expand into new routes and to attract more customers. However, growth is not the only aim of a business.

The main aims are:

1 Survival

2 Meeting stakeholder needs

3 Maximising sales revenue (income)

4 Maximising profit (surplus)

5 Growth.

1 Survival

Walk down any High Street and you will find a selection of businesses that have been there a long time – they have survived. Some of the survivors like Marks & Spencer or WH Smith may have seen better days. At one time it would have been unthinkable that Marks & Spencer would have to struggle to survive. Up until the 1990s Marks & Spencer went from strength to strength and represented the very best of British quality. It was said that you could walk into any room where people were gathered together and know with certainty that the majority of women would be wearing Marks & Spencer underwear.

However, by the 1990s many other new stores were springing up and there was a rapid change in consumers' tastes and the desire to become more fashionable. M&S were left behind and their profits started to suffer. Fortunately M&S woke up to the problem and in recent years they have completely revamped many of their stores and employed state of the art designers to make their clothing desirable. However, today M&S is engaged in a real battle for survival in an intensely competitive market place. For example, in recent times ASDA have started selling cut-price school uniforms to threaten M&S's hold in this area. At the same time companies like WH Smith have had to fight hard to survive faced by competition from internet-based booksellers (e.g. by setting up their own online bookstore).

We can therefore say that the prime objective of any business in the modern world is that of survival.

2 Meeting stakeholder needs

A business does not just serve the needs of its owners such as shareholders. Rather it must serve the needs of a range of **stakeholders** who are individuals and groups with an interest in how that business runs. Of course the shareholders are a very important interest group and so they have a lot of influence over decision making.

> **Learning activity**
>
> Choose a business that you are familiar with, e.g. a retail or manufacturing outlet in your area. Put the name of the business at the centre of a chart, and then draw a series of bubbles to represent different stakeholder groupings in the business. Explain what the interest of each of these stakeholder groupings is. Identify if there will be any clashes between the interests of each of the stakeholder groups. Explain how the organisation could succeed in meeting the needs of its various stakeholder groupings.

3 Maximising sales revenue (income)

The term **sales revenue** refers to the income that a business receives from selling goods or services. In accounts it is also referred to as turnover.

Many businesses will seek to steadily increase their turnover in order to win a larger share of the total market. In business there is a saying that if you win the lion's share of the market then the profits will follow. This makes sense. For example, if a business has 51% of the market its nearest rival can only gain 49%. The firm that sells in bulk is able to reduce its costs through a process known as **economies of scale**. Economies of scale are the advantages of producing on a grand scale which enable a firm to reduce the cost of producing and selling each unit of output.

The way in which firms seek to maximise sales revenue is illustrated by the mobile phone market where there are a number of competitors such as Nokia, Orange, and O_2. In the industry today the battle is well and truly on to grab and keep those

CASE STUDY
A multiplex cinema

FIGURE 1.8 *A multiplex cinema*

The case of a multiplex cinema provides a good example of an organisation with a variety of stakeholders as illustrated by the table below:

STAKEHOLDER	INTEREST AND INFLUENCE
Shareholders	The major owners of the multiplex. Some of them will be individuals while others will be **institutional investors** (i.e. large organisations that invest in shares, e.g. pension funds). The shareholders want the business to make a profit so that their dividends are high and the share price increases.
Employees	Managers and staff at the multiplex want to see it being successful because their job security and pay depends on it.
Customers	Customers want the multiplex to show interesting and enjoyable films at value for money prices.
The government	The government benefits from the taxes paid by the cinema. The government also regulates the types of films that can be shown, and makes sure that the premises meet regulations such as health and safety requirements.
The local community	People in the local community benefit from having entertainment on their doorstep. However, they may not be happy about the noise and congestion caused by the cinema complex.
Other businesses	Other businesses may be able to make a profit from setting up around the multiplex, e.g. cafés and restaurants.
Competitors	Competitors have an interest in how the business is run. They will complain if they feel that the multiplex is gaining an edge over them, for example if the local council allows the multiplex to stay open longer or to engage in new activities.

Organisations will seek to meet the needs of their various stakeholder groupings and failure to attend to the needs of any of these groupings may have enormous consequences for the business. For example, failure to keep the local community happy may lead to protest and adverse publicity. **For an organisation of your choice, outline five key stakeholders and their interests.**

FIGURE 1.9 *Arsenal Football Club is sponsored by O₂*

	1999	2000	2001	2002	2003
Sales revenue of O₂ (£000)	2,618	3,200	4,276	4,874	5,324

customers who will pay to download games, send photos, pictures and e-mail.

O₂, the sponsors of Arsenal football club, have been particularly effective in the mobile telephone market with about one-third of the text messaging market.

4 Maximising profit/surplus

A lot of people believe that the main objective of businesses is to maximise the profits they make. Although businesses probably seek to achieve high profits in the longer term they may have different short-term objectives. For example, in order to gain market leadership a firm may have to invest heavily in the short period so that short-term profits fall. By sacrificing short-term profit maximising a firm can secure its long-term survival or long-term profitability.

5 Growth

Earlier we stated that growth is an important business objective, and that Ryanair is a good example of this process. Ryanair has come a long way since it started in 1985. Its first route was

CASE STUDY

Corus

Corus was formed by the joining together of British Steel and the major Dutch steel manufacturing company Hoogovens in 2000. Steel manufacturing is intensely competitive and there were too many steel plants in Europe. Corus therefore made the tough decision to sack nearly 10,000 workers and to cut back some of its loss-making plant.

Fortunately for the company the world price of steel soared in 2004 as a result of surging demand from China which continued throughout 2004. The combination of falling costs and rising prices (and hence revenues) has helped to turn round the losses made by the company into profits, as shown below:

CORUS (OPERATING PROFITS £)	
2000	-133m
2001	-389m
2002	-400m
2003	-66m
2004	+340m

Corus is a good example of a company that has cut costs in order to increase its long-term ability to make profits. In a similar way, as we saw earlier, Marks & Spencer have invested heavily in updating the look of their stores, in retraining staff, and in creating new and attractive stock, as well as supporting these changes through exciting advertising campaigns. Manchester United is a business that pays careful attention to controlling costs. One of its cost objectives is to keep costs at under 50% of turnover (the value of sales). For example:

TARGET TO KEEP COSTS AT UNDER 50% OF TURNOVER		
Year	Costs as % of turnover	Profit change since previous year
2003	46	Up
2004	45	Up

Why do Corus and Manchester United seek to control costs?

Learning activity

Using examples from your own experience and newspaper and internet research identify an industry in which:

✳ some businesses are growing

✳ others are cutting back.

1 What are the advantages of having a growth strategy in that industry?

2 What are the potential drawbacks of the growth strategy?

from Waterford in Ireland to London, but it grew quickly, adding routes from Dublin to a number of European cities.

It made heavy losses until, under Michael O'Leary, who became chief executive in 1994, it embraced the low-cost model typified by America's Southwest Airlines.

The company has not looked back. It quickly grew to dominate Anglo-Irish services, and went public in 1997. It operates almost 100 aircraft, but if it continued to grow at its current rate, it would have 1,000 aircraft in 20 years – more than double the number operated by British Airways.

6 Non-profit objectives

Not-for-profit organisations may have different objectives from for profit ones. We have already seen that charity organisations have a range of objectives and purposes.

For example, an important objective of a number of organisations in this sector is to care for the environment, e.g. Friends of the Earth, Greenpeace, The Woodland Trust, etc.

Today the objectives of a charity which are recognised as being lawful include:

✳ the prevention and relief of poverty

FIGURE 1.10 *Band Aid is a not-for-profit organisation*

Learning activity

Carry out an internet search using the terms environmental protection and either charity or voluntary organisation. What are the key objectives of the organisations that your search reveals? Why do you think that these organisations have these not-for-profit objectives?

✳ the advancement of education

✳ the advancement of health

✳ the advancement of culture, arts and heritage

✳ the advancement of amateur sport

✳ the advancement of environmental protection and improvement.

How the way a business operates is influenced by ownership, control and financing

The owners of a business are the people the business belongs to. For example, Fred's corner store may be owned by Fred on his own. In contrast Makepeace, Patel and Amin the solicitors is a partnership.

Sole trader and partnership businesses are not only owned by the owners, they are also controlled by them. Control refers to decision making. Fred makes his own decisions about what he sells, who he employs and when he opens and shuts his shop.

In companies, however, there is a distinction between the ownership and the control of the business. Companies are owned by shareholders, but it is often managers who make decisions and hence control the business.

Different types of business are also financed in different ways. Typically large public companies have access to a much wider range of finance than small sole trader businesses.

A **sole trader** business is owned and controlled by one person. It is the most common form of business and is found in a wide range of activities (e.g. window cleaning, plumbing, electrical work, busking). No complicated work is required to set up a sole trader business. Decisions can be made quickly and close contact can be kept with customers and employees. All profits go to the sole trader, who also has the satisfaction of building up his or her own business.

But there are disadvantages. As a sole trader you have to make all the decisions yourself, and you may have to work long hours (what do you do if you are ill or want a holiday?). Another disadvantage is that you don't have the legal protection of **limited liability**. What this means is that should the business run up debts these debts become the responsibility of the business owner. The debts are unlimited and the owner may be forced to sell their house and other personal possessions to pay off their business debts.

The sole trader typically provides much of their own finance, although they may also borrow from a bank, or friends. As a sole trader you need to be a jack-of-all-trades, and just because you are a good hairdresser does not necessarily mean that you have a head for business!

A **partnership** is usually formed by signing a **Deed of Partnership** with the paperwork being supervised by a solicitor. Partnerships are typically found in professional work, e.g. a medical or dental practice, a group of accountants or solicitors. People in business partnerships can share skills and the workload, and it may be easier to raise the capital needed.

FIGURE 1.11 *A sole trader business is owned and controlled by one person*

FIGURE 1.12 *Partners can share the workload and decision-making*

For example, a group of vets is able to pool knowledge about different diseases and groups of animals, and two or three vets working together may be able to operate a 24-hour service. When one of the vets is ill or goes on holiday, the business can cope.

The **Deed of Partnership** sets out how profits will be shared and the different responsibilities and payments to partners.

The main disadvantages of partnerships are that people can fall out (she doesn't work as hard as me!), ordinary partnerships don't have limited liability, and partnerships can rarely borrow or raise large amounts of capital. Business decisions may be more difficult to make (and slower) because of the need to consult all the partners. There may be disagreements about how things should be done. A further disadvantage is that profits will be shared.

A **company** has to be registered before it can start to operate, but once all the paperwork is completed and approved the company becomes recognised as a legal body. The owners of

the company are its shareholders. They elect **directors** to represent their interests. A managing director is the senior director on the Board. The Board consists of executive directors who make the major ongoing policy decisions about the business. The Board will also have some non-executive directors in its membership. Non-executives are there to provide specialist advice and because of their links with other businesses.

Shareholders are able to have a say about the way the company is run when they attend an Annual General Meeting each year. At the Annual General Meeting highlights of the company's report will be presented to shareholders as well as the annual accounts. At this time the shareholders

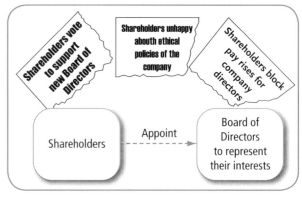

FIGURE 1.13 *Company directors have to satisfy shareholders*

are able to question company policy and can vote out the directors and take actions such as refusing to approve pay rises for directors.

Shareholders put funds into a company by buying shares. New shares are often sold in face values of £1 per share, but this is not always the case. Some shareholders will only have a few hundred pounds' worth of shares, whereas others may have thousands of pounds' worth.

The promoter or directors of the company can apply to the **Registrar of Companies** for permission to issue new shares. The amount that the Registrar agrees to is called the **authorised capital**.

The **issued capital** is the value of the shares that are actually sold to shareholders. A company may choose not to issue the full value of its authorised capital: it may hold back a certain amount for future issue.

Private companies tend to be smaller than public ones (discussed below) and are often family businesses. There must be at least two shareholders but there is no maximum number. Shares in private companies cannot be traded on the Stock Exchange, and often shares can only be bought with the permission of the board of directors.

Private companies may find it possible to raise more cash (by selling shares) than unlimited-liability businesses. The shareholders can also have the protection of limited liability.

The main disadvantage compared with unlimited liability businesses are that they have to share out profits among shareholders and that they cannot make decisions so quickly. They cost more to set up.

A public company has its shares bought and sold on the Stock Exchange. The main advantage of being a public company is that large amounts of capital can be raised very quickly. One

FIGURE 1.14 *Companies have shareholders and directors*

disadvantage is that control of a business can be lost by the original shareholders if large quantities of shares are purchased as part of a 'takeover bid'. It is also costly to have shares quoted on the Stock Exchange.

In order to create a public company the directors must apply to the Stock Exchange Council, which will carefully check the accounts. A business wanting to 'go public' will then arrange for one of the merchant banks to handle the paperwork. Selling new shares is quite a risky business. The Stock Exchange has 'good days' (when a lot of people want to buy shares) and 'bad days' (when a lot of people want to sell). If the issue of new shares coincides with a bad day a company can find itself in difficulties. For example, if it hopes to sell a million new shares at £1 each and all goes well, it will raise £1 million, but on a bad day it might only be able to sell half its shares at this price. When a company is up and running, a cheaper way of selling is to contact existing shareholders inviting them to buy new shares. This is called a rights issue.

Sole traders, partnerships, and companies are in the **private sector** where the objective is generally to make a profit, although we have seen that other objectives such as high sales, growth and survival are important.

The other sector of the economy is the public sector. The **public sector** consists of organisations that the government is involved in on behalf of the people.

Public sector organisations have somewhat different objectives to private sector ones.

A **government department** like the Inland Revenue operates on behalf of the government and is staffed by civil servants known as revenue officers. Their job is to collect income and other taxes on behalf of the government, to collect repayments on student loans, and to make payments known as tax credits. Rather than

FIGURE 1.15 *The BBC is a public corporation*

seeking to make a profit they will want to collect taxes efficiently and make sure that taxpayers get a fair deal.

A **municipal enterprise** is a government enterprise on a local scale. It may have responsibility for looking after the local parks, or street lighting. The prime task is to provide an efficient local service to serve the local community.

A third type of public sector enterprise is the **public corporation**. There are not many of these left now but a good example is the BBC (British Broadcasting Corporation). The BBC has the task of providing a high quality news, information and entertainment service for the people of this country. It is currently funded by people paying television licences but this funding is under review. A government minister appoints the Chair of the BBC who then has a responsibility for making sure that the BBC acts independently and fairly in broadcasting programmes. A public corporation is concerned not only to run on business lines but also to provide a public service. This public service emphasis often conflicts with the objective of profit maximisation. The main differences between a public company and a public corporation are set out in the table opposite.

> ✳ **DID YOU KNOW?**
>
> When you go to university and receive a student loan you will eventually have to pay this off bit by bit (provided that your income is more than a given threshold). Repayments are collected by the Inland Revenue.

PRIVATE SECTOR	PUBLIC SECTOR
Sole traders, partnerships, companies	Government departments, public corporations, municipal enterprises
Public/private partnerships (organisations that have both government and private funds and objectives)	

CONTRASTING PUBLIC CORPORATIONS WITH PUBLIC COMPANIES	
PUBLIC CORPORATION	**PUBLIC COMPANY**
Set up by Act of Parliament	Set up by issuing prospectus inviting public to buy shares
Owned by the government	Owned by shareholders
Run by chairperson and managers appointed by government	Run by management team chosen by directors representing shareholders
Aims to provide a public service as well as having profit-making objectives	Profit-making objectives

The range of functions carried out by businesses, and the part these functions play

When you start to work for a business you will usually find that you start off in a particular area of specialism which is termed a **function**. For example, working in a shoe shop you are most likely to work in the sales function. This will be the most important function in the shop, but there will be other functions such as the accounts department. If you work in a supermarket you may be involved in the sales function but you could also have a job in warehousing and packing. There will be a training department etc.

Some of the most important functions of a business are:

1 Production – responsible for making goods. This department is responsible for planning production schedules and for ensuring high quality standards.

2 Marketing – finds out what customers want through market research and then plans marketing activities such as advertising to attract customers.

3 Sales – whereas marketing is concerned with finding out what customers want, the emphasis in sales is on convincing the customer that products meet their needs and requirements.

CASE STUDY

Functions at McDonald's

Here is a list of business functions advertised by the McDonald's organisation:

* Administrative
* Accounting
* Air Travel
* Architecture/Construction
* Communications
* Corporate Tax
* Customer Satisfaction
* Distribution/Logistics
* Engineering
* Environmental Affairs
* Facilities Systems

* Franchising
* Government Relations
* Human Resources
* Information Services
* Insurance
* Legal
* Marketing
* Media Relations
* Product Development
* Purchasing
* Quality Assurance
* Real Estate
* Restaurant Operations
* Treasury

Outline the main functions of another organisation.

4   Finance and accounts – responsible for preparing budgets (financial plans), and for calculating the profit or loss made by various parts of the business, and the business as a whole. Creates financial reports such as the balance sheet showing the financial health of the business at a particular time, e.g. the end of the year.

5   Administration – responsible for creating and managing systems for keeping the business running smoothly.

6   Human Resources – responsible for people management in the company including hiring, firing and motivating.

7   Information Technology – creates the information systems that keep the business running smoothly, e.g. the development of a company website and intranet.

Until the late 1980s organisations relied very heavily on having large functional departments. This created tall organisational structures with lots of layers. Nowadays it is more common for organisations to concentrate on the functions which are most central to the organisations' activities, e.g. marketing in a marketing company,

Learning activity

Either by interviewing someone that works for a local business organisation, or using your own work experience, identify the main functions at your workplace.

production in a manufacturing company. Much of the work in non-core functions is then contracted out to other companies.

Today it is common practice for the various functions of a business to be more integrated. Often people are organised into **cross-functional teams**, so that it is possible to share experience, e.g. sales and marketing ideas, the accountant can explain budget implications of various decisions etc.

Organisation structures

An organisational chart is a way of illustrating how an organisation is organised. For example, Figure 1.17 shows how a printing firm producing textbooks might be organised.

There are other ways of structuring organisations, for example:

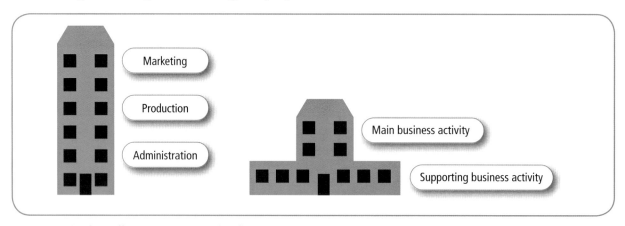

FIGURE 1.16 *The tall organisation v the flatter organisation*

Find out...

Using your own work experience or that of a friend or family member, provide an example of where you or they have worked in a cross-functional team. What were the benefits of working in this way?

1 By product or service

An organisation can be divided up according to the products supplied (e.g. in a supermarket into breakfast cereals, fruit and vegetables, toiletries) or the service (such as your local council's division into environmental services, parks, housing etc).

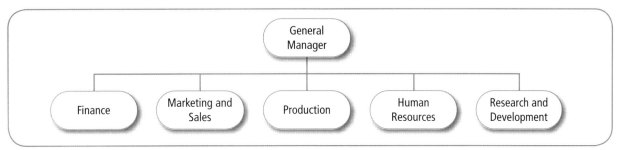

FIGURE 1.17 *The traditional organisation structure*

2 By customer

Often businesses are divided up to deal with different types of customers. For example, in banking there may be a department that deals specifically with business customers, and another with the general public.

3 By process or equipment

This is common practice in manufacturing in which a work area may be divided up into different types of machinery and activity. For example, in a printing company one department may be responsible for printing business catalogues, and another for magazines.

4 Matrix structures

A popular form of organisation structure today is the **matrix** which involves people working together on projects working as a team. A person working on a project may be accountable to more than one team leader – the team leader of the department in which they work, and the project team leader.

The following grid shows a situation in which John Smith is working both on project 1 in a cross-functional team as well as in his own department (production).

Of course, we can add many more dimensions to the matrix structure according to the number of projects an individual is working on.

✱ DID YOU KNOW?

Henry Ford – the founder of the Ford motor car company – saw his organisation as a giant machine. Ford was at the head driving the machine and his workers were simply expected to follow instructions. His organisation had a top down model with Ford at the top.

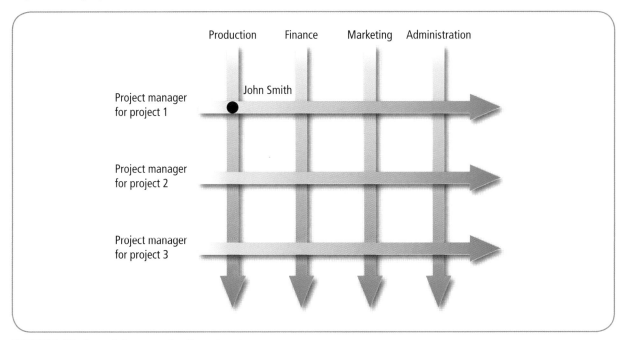

FIGURE 1.18 *A matrix organisation structure*

The roles of managers/supervisors and employees

Within an organisation there are various levels of management and supervision.

A **manager** is someone with responsibility – usually for others, for making various decisions, and for managing various resources.

For example, the job description of a marketing manager in a company might state that they:

* are *accountable* to their marketing director

* are *responsible* for staff in the market research function of the company

* are *responsible* for planning, organising and delivering market research campaigns

* have to create a market research budget and monitor that budget each month

* are *responsible* for making sure that the company keeps in tune with the changing needs of its customers.

You can see that management involves responsibility. The level of responsibility depends on the level of management.

Senior managers are responsible for long-term decisions made in a company, and major resources.

Middle managers are responsible for some medium-term decisions, and some important resources.

Junior managers are responsible for short-term decisions and have some responsibility for resources.

Supervisors also have an important role to play in an organisation and their responsibilities are often blurred with those of junior managers. Supervisors have responsibility for supervising a particular task or group of people.

Supervisors will often work with fairly tight boundaries. They have responsibility for making sure that:

* the right standards are met

* time deadlines are met

* people and other resources are supervised in an appropriate way.

Just because an employee is not a manager or employee does not mean that their work is any less important. Most employees have the potential to become supervisors and managers. Employees have a responsibility to meet legal requirements, and the responsibilities of the job set out in a job description. Today many employees are given additional responsibilities because managers recognise that individuals work best when trusted to do fulfilling work.

1.2 How businesses obtain employees

Businesses must plan to make sure that they have the right number of suitable employees for their needs.

The different qualities that business people look for

Examine the job advertisement below:

Superior Industries Ltd

ADMIN ASSISTANT

Due to expansion Superior Industries require an administrative assistant to help in their Customer Service department.

The successful applicant will possess excellent PC literacy and data entry skills and will be responsible for the management of customer orders for the business.

With an excellent telephone manner, you will be reliable and enthusiastic, well organised and a self starter and play a pivotal role in the day-to-day running of this busy but friendly department.

For further information and an application form please call xxxxx.

FIGURE 1.19 *A job advertisement*

Although this post is not at a high level in the organisation it immediately becomes obvious that the company is looking for a number of qualities:

Existing skills: PC literate, database skills.

Personal qualities: Excellent telephone manner, reliable, enthusiastic, well-organised, self starter, willingness to take on responsibility.

Businesses need to be clear about the sorts of qualities that they are looking for when recruiting employees in order to attract the most suitable applicants.

They will need to consider carefully the sorts of:

* Competencies that they are looking for – i.e. what they expect applicants to already be able to do
* Knowledge required – what should applicants already know
* Skills required
* Attitudes required.

Learning activity

Select a job that you are familiar with. Make a list of the competencies, knowledge, skills and attitudes that you would expect someone to have to be appointed to work at that job in your business.

Reasons for recruiting staff

Superior Industries (advertisement shown in Figure 1.19) were looking to recruit because their business was growing. There are a number of reasons for recruiting new staff:

1 The growth of the business

For example, in recent years many companies have moved into e-commerce buying and selling through the Internet. They have therefore needed to recruit web page designers and other IT specialists.

2 Filling vacancies caused by job leavers

All businesses have a turnover of staff. For example, supermarket chains like ASDA and Sainsbury's constantly need to recruit checkout staff, car park attendants and other employees. There will be a regular stream of people leaving their jobs, e.g. to go to college or university, who will need to be replaced.

3 Changing job roles

Modern work is constantly changing. Next year's jobs will require different skills to those that are required today. Businesses will therefore constantly create new opportunities and new jobs requiring new people.

4 Internal promotion

Most companies encourage their staff to take on more demanding and better paid posts within the business. New employees are required to replace those moving up the ladder.

Job descriptions, person specifications and advertisements for new staff

Organisations need to attract, recruit and retain the best possible people to fill the posts required and thus help a business to achieve its objectives.

Job descriptions

A **job description** will set out how a particular employee is to fit into the organisation. It will therefore need to set out:

* The title of the job
* To whom the employee is responsible
* For whom the employee is responsible
* A simple description of the role and duties of the employee within the organisation.

A job description could be used as a job indicator for applicants. Alternatively, it could be used as a guideline for an employee and/or line manager as to his or her role and responsibility within the organisation.

Job descriptions can be used by organisations to provide information for use in drafting a situations vacant advertisement and for briefing interviewers.

Job title

One of the most important parts of a job description is the job title. The job title should

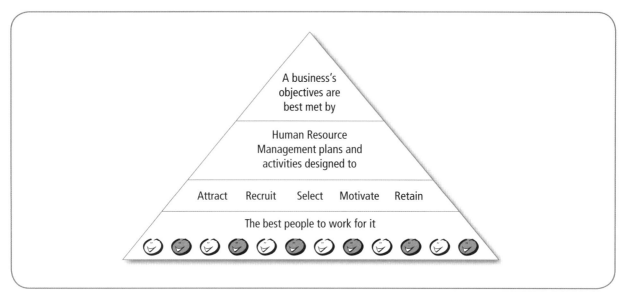

FIGURE 1.20 *Organisations seek the best people to achieve their objectives*

give a good indication of what the job entails. For example, you may hear people in organisations make statements such as: 'She's supposed to be the Managing Director, let her make the decision,' or 'Leave the word-processing of letters to the administrator, that's not your job.' I heard a conversation between a lecturer and a porter concerning the carrying of boxes which ended up with the remark: 'You're supposed to be a porter – get porting!'

When looking through job advertisements the first thing that job applicants will look for (apart from the salary) will be the job title.

From time to time job titles will change, often to give a slightly different feel to some jobs or to confer new status – the Principal of a college may become a 'Chief Executive', a dustbin man may become a 'Disposal services officer', a petrol pump cashier may become a 'Forecourt executive' and so on.

FIGURE 1.21 *A job title may be chosen to confer status*

Position within organisation structure

A job description will often establish where an individual stands in a particular organisation structure. This will mean that it can be clearly set out who the post-holder is accountable to, and who is accountable to him or her.

The position within an organisation will also give a clear idea of responsibilities. Job applicants will be interested to locate their position in order to work out whether their previous experience will be broad enough and to assess the kind of commitment they will be expected to make to the organisation.

Duties and responsibilities

A further important aspect of the job description will be that which sets out the duties and responsibilities of job holders.

Prior to setting out a job description an organisation may carry out an **analysis of the tasks** which need to be performed by a job-holder, and of the skills and qualities required.

If this is done carefully, then organisational planners will have a clear picture of how particular jobs fit in with all the other jobs carried on in an organisation. It also helps job applicants to get a clear picture of what is expected of them, and it helps job-holders to understand the priorities of their work (see Figure 1.22).

A **job analysis** is a study of the tasks that are required to do a particular job. Job analysis is very important in creating a clear job description. For example, the job of a trainee manager in a supermarket could be described under the following key headings:

* Title of post

* Prime objectives of the position

* Supervisory/managerial responsibilities

* Source(s) of supervision and guidance

* Range of decision making

* Responsibilities for assets, materials, etc.

FIGURE 1.22 *A job description helps the individual and the organisation*

One of ASDA's central values is to cut out waste of any kind. This value is stressed in job descriptions in which employees are instructed, for example, to 'Look for opportunities to reduce waste and put forward your ideas' and to 'Ensure stock is rotated correctly at all times'.

Learning activity

A large supermarket chain near to you (e.g. Sainsbury's, Morrisons, ASDA, Tesco) currently does not have enough shop assistants to meet the demands of customers, particularly at weekends. There are long queues at the tills, and it has become impossible to stack shelves neatly or to price all items accurately.

Set out a job analysis for a shop assistant, by answering the following questions:

1 What tasks need to be performed?

2 What skills and qualities are required?

3 How can the skills be acquired?

Person specifications

A person specification should do what the title suggests – specify (set out clearly) what attributes an individual needs to have to do a particular job well. The person specification goes beyond a simple description of the job, by highlighting the mental, physical and other attributes required of a job holder. For example, a recent Prison Service advertisement specified the following: 'At every level your task will call for a lot more than simple efficiency. It takes humanity, flexibility, enthusiasm, total commitment and, of course, a sense of humour.'

Armed with this sort of specification, those responsible for recruiting and selecting someone to do a particular job have a much clearer idea of the ideal candidate. At the same time those applying for a job have a much clearer idea of what is expected of them and whether they have the attributes.

The Human Resources department may therefore set out, for its own use, a 'person specification', using a layout similar to that shown in Figure 1.23.

Summary of job			
Attributes	Essential	Desirable	How identified
Physical			
Qualifications			
Experience			
Training			
Special knowledge			
Personal circumstances			
Attitudes			
Practical and intellectual skills			

FIGURE 1.23 *Layout for a person specification*

For example, a person specification for police recruits might include physical attributes related to the standard of physical fitness, qualifications including Advanced level or equivalents, etc.

The person specification can be used to:

✱ make sure that a job advertisement conveys the qualities that prospective candidates should have.

✱ check that candidates for a job have the right qualities.

Learning activity

Examine two job descriptions produced by an organisation (perhaps by the organisation that you work for or where you carried out your work experience).Explain how successful these job descriptions seem to have been in matching applicants with vacancies.

Create a person specification that would be suitable for selecting candidates for a job that you are familiar with.

Personal attributes and achievements

A person specification is concerned with identifying those people who have the right qualities to fit the jobs you are offering. For example, personal attributes for a member of the Paratroop Regiment might include physical toughness and alertness. The personal attributes of a teacher may include the ability to work well with others and to find out about the learning needs of pupils. The personal attributes of a shop assistant might include punctuality and smartness of appearance.

Personal achievements give a good indication of the existing abilities of given individuals. For example, someone who has achieved the Duke of Edinburgh Awards shows qualities of enterprise and initiative. Personal achievements can be good indicators of qualities such as the ability to work in a team, to help others, to persevere, etc.

Qualifications

Qualifications are another important ingredient in person specifications. For example, when recruiting a new Human Resources lecturer it would be essential to appoint someone with formal teaching qualifications, and some experience of work at an appropriate level in Human Resource management.

Qualifications are a good measure of prior learning. This has been simplified in recent years by the development of nationally recognised qualifications such as Applied Business courses.

The idea of a qualification is that it prepares you to do a particular job or activity. In creating job specifications, organisations will therefore need to consider the level of qualification required by a job holder.

Experience

There is a well-known saying that there is no substitute for experience. Someone with experience in carrying out a particular post or who has had particular responsibilities should be able to draw on that experience in new situations.

For example, an experienced lecturer has already taught, assessed, administered and carried out a variety of other duties in a college. A new lecturer has not had the same advantages.

We talk about the learning curve which results from experience. The implication is that the good learner will learn at a progressively faster rate as they draw on their experience. A person specification should therefore set out the required experience for a job-holder.

Competence

Competence is a word that is widely used today. Competence implies that a person has sufficient knowledge or skill to carry out particular tasks or activities. Most people would rather visit a competent than an incompetent doctor, or be taught by a competent rather than an incompetent teacher.

Person specifications should set out levels of competence required by a particular job-holder. Hairdressers, for example, need to show competence in a range of performance criteria that make up the elements of hairdressing work. A hairdresser would be foolish to take on a new stylist for dyeing purposes who had not first exhibited competence in mixing and applying hair dye.

FIGURE 1.24 *Competence is vital*

Job applications and curriculum vitae

We are now in a position to look at **job applications** and **interviewing**. First examine the two flow charts shown below which show the selection process for a job (a) from the employer's point of view, and (b) from the applicant's point of view:

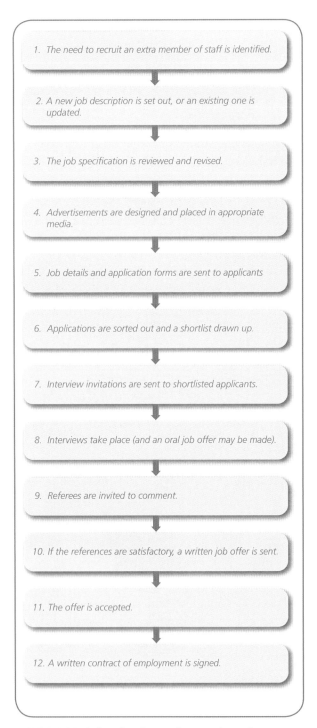

1. The need to recruit an extra member of staff is identified.
2. A new job description is set out, or an existing one is updated.
3. The job specification is reviewed and revised.
4. Advertisements are designed and placed in appropriate media.
5. Job details and application forms are sent to applicants
6. Applications are sorted out and a shortlist drawn up.
7. Interview invitations are sent to shortlisted applicants.
8. Interviews take place (and an oral job offer may be made).
9. Referees are invited to comment.
10. If the references are satisfactory, a written job offer is sent.
11. The offer is accepted.
12. A written contract of employment is signed.

FIGURE 1.25 *Job selection – the employer's schedule*

1. Evaluate different career choices, and narrow down your options.
2. Produce and update your curriculum vitae.
3. Ask three people to act as referees.
4. Photocopy your examination and other certificates.
5. See an interesting job advertisement and send for details.
6. Find out more about the organisation.
7. Send a short letter or e-mail asking for an application form.
8. Fill in the form and write a short letter supporting your application. Send copies of certificates and CV. Keep copies of all these documents.
9. If invited for interview, immediately telephone to confirm the arrangements.
10. Verbal acceptance of job.
11. Write a letter of acceptance and return the contract.
12. Make sure you know when and where you are expected to be on the first day.

FIGURE 1.26 *Job selection – the applicant's view*

Job applications

The following comments relate to how you should go about writing job applications. They are equally relevant in examining what businesses are looking for when they come to choose applicants. All students who are following this course will need at some stage to produce letters of application for jobs. It is important that you get this process right. Over the years we have seen many students applying for jobs. It is surprising how often there are two students who are almost identical in terms of qualifications, appearance and ability, but one is offered many interviews while the other receives only a few. Usually the difference is in the quality of their letters of application.

A letter should have a clear structure, with a beginning, a middle and an ending. It should state:

* your reasons for applying for the job
* the contribution you can make to the organisation
* how you have developed your capabilities through training and education
* the skills and knowledge you have acquired that would help you to do the job well.

The letter needs to be interesting – you are writing about (i.e. selling) yourself. It should contain just enough information to support your application form and CV (see below), highlighting the most relevant evidence. You will know that you are writing effective letters if they lead to interviews.

Here are some important rules to remember.

* Use good English with accurate spelling. Always check in a dictionary if you are unsure of the spelling of a word (use the spell checker on your computer)
* Use your own words rather than copying those in the advertisement
* Do not try to be too clever by using long words
* Keep the paragraphs short
* Try not to use 'I' too much
* Word process your work

* Follow the correct convention of addressing people. A letter beginning 'Dear Sir/ Madam' should be ended with 'Yours faithfully', whereas one that begins 'Dear Mr Chanderpaul' should be ended with 'Yours sincerely'
* Keep a copy of what you have written.

Curriculum vitae

A **curriculum vitae** (usually called simply a CV) is a summary of your career to date. There are three stages you should follow when setting out your CV.

* assemble all the facts about yourself
* draft the CV
* edit the document several times

Applying for a post

The following letter was sent by an applicant for the post of trainee accountant with Great Western Trains.

1 What strengths and weaknesses can you spot?
2 If you were to advise Charles Lawson on how he could improve his letter what comments would you make?

21 Wade Park Avenue
Market Deeping
Peterborough
PE6 8JL

20th February 2005

Great Western Trains Finance Manager,
Room 109
East Side Offices
Bristol
BS3 9HL

Dear Sir/Madam,

I noticed in a national paper that you have a job available for a junior accountant. I am very interested in the post because I see it as presenting a good opportunity for me. I have always been very interested in rail accounts. I am also studing accounts at collage. I understand that on your accountancy training scheme there will be good opportunities for promotion. I am also studing a course in Applied Business. This is a very interesting course and I have had good reports from all my tutors on the course. As part of the course I am sing accounts. I have found the accounts to be the most exciting and interesting parts. I am also interested in train spotting.

I am working at the Anglia Co-operative Society. This is a part time post but it involves a lot of responsibility. I have to check the stock and make sure the shelves are well organised. I also have had EPOS training.

I am currently working on my cv and will send it to you next week. Many thanks for your interest in my application.

Yours Sincerely,

Charles Lawson

FIGURE 1.27 *Job application letter*

Curriculum Vitae

Name	Prakesh Patel
Date of birth	1.3.1986
Address	50 Palmerston Road, Reading, RG31 9HL
Telephone	01604 76321
Education and training	Waingels' Copse School Reading, Sept 1998 – July 2004
Qualifications (GCSEs)	Mathematics (B)
	English (B)
	Business Studies (A)
	French (B)
	Geography (B)
	German (A)
	History (B)
	Technology (B)
	All 2004
Interests and activities	Captain of school football team, house captain and prefect (2002–2004) Venture Scout, Gold Award Duke of Edinburgh. Member of Woodley Chess Club.

Referees:		
	Mr I. Marks	Rev R. Babbage
	Waingels' Copse School	St Jude's
	Denmark Avenue	Church Street
	Woodley	Reading
	Reading RG3 8SL	Reading RG4 7QZ

FIGURE 1.28 *An outline curriculum vitae (CV)*

Try to create a favourable impression (but always be truthful). Leave out negative statements about yourself. Do not be vague.

Always use a word-processing package with an impressive, yet conservative, font.

Assembling the facts

At the initial stage you are trying to get together as many relevant facts as possible about your career to date. It does not matter if you put down too many to start with – make a list of all your educational, work-based and leisure achievements, as well as training activities and courses you have been on. Make brief notes about each of these as well as about projects and assignments you have been involved in.

Drafting the CV

A CV should be divided into suitable headings and sub-headings, for example:

1 Name

2 Date of birth

3 Address

Produce your own up-to-date CV. Ask someone else to evaluate your CV against the following checklist:

* Have you given a good impression of your skills, knowledge, experience and personality?

* Are these set out in a concise and readable fashion?

* Do significant achievements stand out?

* Have you eliminated confusing terms, jargon and obscure abbreviations?

* Are all words spelt accurately, have you used correct grammar, and is the layout clear and organised?

* Does your CV have a good feel?

* Would the person reading it understand it easily?

4 Telephone number

5 Education and training

6 Qualifications

7 Other relevant achievements

8 Interests

9 References.

Remember that the key part of the CV is the career history, so the sections that go before should not be too long. For example, when dealing with training, list only the most important and relevant training courses, and then if necessary include some of the others under 'other information'.

When you set out your responsibilities and achievements, decide whether it is necessary to put some of them under sub-headings. It is normal practice to start your career history with your most recent job and work backwards in time, because employers are usually more interested in your recent experience.

If some of your experience is of a technical nature, try to present it in a way that can be read easily by the general reader (rather than only by a specialist).

Try to use dynamic words in your CV. Here are some good examples:

accomplished	achieved	conducted
completed	created	decided
delivered	developed	designed
directed	established	expanded
finished	generated	implemented
improved	increased	introduced
launched	performed	pioneered
planned	promoted	redesigned
reorganised	set up	solved
succeeded	trained	widened
won	work	wrote

The main legal and ethical responsibilities relating to discrimination and equal opportunities

There are a number of legal and ethical requirements which businesses must meet when obtaining employees to work for them. The Sex Discrimination Act (1975 and 1986) and the Race Relations Act (1976 and 2000) sought to encourage equal treatment of people and respect for people in the workplace.

The **Sex Discrimination Act** set out rights for both men and women. Unlawful discrimination means giving less favourable treatment to someone because of their sex or because they are married or single, and can be either direct or indirect. **Direct sex discrimination** means being treated less favourably than a person of the opposite sex would be treated in similar circumstances. For example, a policy to appoint only men to management positions is clearly illegal. Direct marriage discrimination means being treated less favourably than an unmarried person of the same sex. **Indirect sex discrimination** is less easy to identify. It means being unable to comply with a requirement which on the face of it applies equally to both men and women, but which in practice can be met by a much smaller proportion of one sex. For example, an organisation may be indirectly discriminating against women if access to certain jobs is restricted to particular grades which in practice are held only by men.

The Race Relations Act makes it unlawful to discriminate against a person, directly or indirectly, in the field of employment on the basis of race, colour or national origin. Direct discrimination means treating a person on racial grounds less favourably than others are or would be treated in the same or similar circumstances. Segregating a person from others on racial grounds constitutes less favourable treatment. Indirect discrimination consists of applying a requirement or conditions which, although applied equally to persons of all racial groups, is such that a considerably smaller proportion of a particular racial group can comply with it. Examples are:

✳ a rule about clothing or uniforms which disproportionately disadvantages a racial group and cannot be justified

✳ an employer who requires higher language standards than are needed for safe and effective performance of the job.

These laws seek to prevent discrimination in areas such as the recruitment and selection of staff. The European Union Equal Treatment Directive now makes it unlawful to discriminate on grounds of sexual orientation and religion or other belief. By 2006 age discrimination will also be unlawful.

In addition to the bare essentials of legal requirements organisations need to consider the ethical side of their recruitment and selection policies. **Ethics** is about doing the right thing consistently rather than compromising sometimes. What this means in effect is that good employers will go beyond the letter of the law to provide excellent opportunities for all their people.

Learning activity

Which of the following would be inappropriate questions to ask in an interview from an equal opportunities angle?

'Mrs Smith, I see you are married. Do you intend to start a family soon?'

'What will happen when your children are ill or on school holidays? Who will look after them?'

'Your hair is very long, Mr Smith. If offered the job are you prepared to have it cut?'

'Mr Smith, as you are 55 do you think it's worth us employing you?'

'Miss Smith, as a woman do you think you are capable of doing the job?'

'Do you think your disability will affect your performance in the job?'

'How do you feel about working with people from a different ethnic background from yourself?'

'As a man, Mr Smith, you will be working in a department consisting mainly of women. Are you easily distracted?'

'Miss Smith, don't you think your skirt is rather short?'

Find out...

The Equal Opportunities Commission site contains case studies and other materials on areas such as employment practice, equal pay and discrimination. Find it at www.heinemann. co.uk/hotlinks (express code 1149P, then go to Unit 1).

Types of interviews

There are a number of different types of interviews that take place in work situations that you need to be familiar with. The main types are:

1 **Job interviews**. These take place when an organisation is seeking to find the right person to fill a particular post. These interviews are discussed in the next section.

FIGURE 1.29 *Personal objectives and organisational objectives*

2 **Appraisal interviews** are an important means of bringing into line the objectives of the organisation and the individual personal objectives of the individuals that work for the organisation.

3 **Exit interviews** are used when people leave the organisation.

Appraisal interviews

Most organisations today operate some form of staff appraisal or staff development scheme.

Common stages of staff appraisal are as follows:

1 The line manager meets with the job holder to discuss what is expected. The agreed expectations may be expressed in terms of targets, performance standards, or required job behaviour.

2 The outcome of the interview is recorded and usually signed by both parties.

3 The job holder performs the job for a period of six months or a year.

4 At the end of the period, the job holder and line manager or team leader meet again to review and discuss progress made. They draw up new action plans to deal with identified problems and agree targets and standards for the next period.

Exit interviews

Exit interviews involve situations where an employee is leaving an organisation because:

* they are being made redundant, i.e. the job no longer exists

* they are being fired for disciplinary reasons

* they are retiring or have resigned.

One aspect can be to find out why the employee has decided to move on. This enables the firm to understand why employees are leaving and, where appropriate, adjust their activities to retain employees better.

An organisation that cares about its people will want to conduct such interviews in a way that maximises the development potential of the individual concerned.

CASE STUDY
Advice for holding an appraisal interview

The following advice was given to members of staff carrying out appraisal interviews in a large UK company:

1 Give the appraisee a copy of the company's objectives, and a record of the previous year's appraisal at least two weeks before an appraisal takes place.

2 Ask the appraisee to provide you with details of their aims, aspirations and targets in written form at least one week before the interview to provide a basis for discussion.

3 Start the meeting by outlining the company objectives, and ask the appraisee to evaluate their own performance in meeting targets set in the previous year.

4 Don't make judgements. Use prompts like 'What do you see as being your major achievements?' 'How successful do you think you have been in meeting your targets?' 'What new targets do you have for the coming year?' 'What do you see as being your major training and development needs?'

5 Once the appraisee has outlined answers to the questions above, focus them on establishing new targets. Ask whether these targets are manageable. Ask them to consider how their personal aspirations fit with the objectives of the company.

1 **Why do you think that appraisors were asked to carry out the appraisal using the format described above?**

2 **What do you see as being the main strengths and weaknesses of the format outlined above? What improvements would you like to see?**

SUITABLE CANDIDATES	POSSIBLE CANDIDATES	REJECTS
Those that meet all or most of the relevant criteria.	Those that meet some of the relevant criteria and may show some exciting characteristics that could make them worth a chance.	Those that meet very few of the criteria.

FIGURE 1.30 *Sorting candidates for a shortlist*

Shortlisting procedures, job interviews and assessment methods

Shortlisting

Shortlisting involves drawing up a list of the most suitable applicants from those that have applied for a post with an organisation. Usually a small group of people will be trusted with the task of drawing up this list. Armed with a job specification, and other sets of criteria, it is possible to reject candidates who do not meet the required criteria.

It is helpful to sort applications into three piles – suitable, possible and rejects (see Figure 1.30).

A basic principle of equal opportunities is that clear criteria should be set up prior to selection, and that these criteria should be used in the first instance to select those candidates that are suitable to interview.

Learning activity

As part of your studies you should practise being the interviewer and the interviewee using the outline set out below. Record interviews using video recording equipment, and discuss in a group what makes a good interviewee/interviewer, and what makes a good job interview. Useful things to look out for are:

✳ the effective use of body language, and eye contact,

✳ the completeness of answers given to questions (rather than answering 'Yes' or 'No')

✳ whether interviewees listened to questions and gave appropriate responses.

Planning and carrying out job interviews

Carrying out practice job interviews is a helpful way for students to understand the dynamics of interview situations, what firms are looking for when carrying out interviews, and the characteristics of a good interviewer/interviewee.

Opening the interview

Generally speaking, interviewers should try to make the interviewee feel relaxed. For example, they might ask the interviewee about his or her journey to the interview on that day: 'Where have you come from?' 'Did you find it easy to get here today?', etc.

Of course, there are exceptional times when interviewers deliberately set out to make the interviewees feel uncomfortable to see how they react, for example by putting them on a wobbly chair or placing them at a lower height than the interviewer's chair.

However, the important thing to remember is that modern business organisations are not run like some sort of secret police. Generally the interviewer should find some means of making the interviewee feel comfortable, so that the interviewee can show his or her best side.

When there are several interviewers a starting point might be to introduce the interviewee to each of the panel in turn.

Asking questions

The next stage is to ask the interviewee a set of predetermined questions. The questions asked

Learning activity

Create a score sheet to be used in an interview situation. Relate the requirements to the job specification.

Post: Junior Retail Manager		
Candidate's name: Linda Booth		
Requirements	Score 1–5 *1 = Poor 5 = Excellent*	Notes
Tidy appearance	*3*	*Untidy hair*
Intelligence	*5*	*Answered questions quickly and with good attention to detail.*
Punctuality	*1*	*Turned up 2 minutes late for interview.*
Etc	etc	etc

FIGURE 1.31 *Part of an interviewer's score sheet*

should relate to the person specification and job description. Remember that you are looking for a candidate who is best able to meet the organisation's requirements. The interviewer will have a copy of the candidate's application form and curriculum vitae. Interviewers will normally want to make notes to check how each interviewee meets the job requirements.

For example, they may have a sheet like that shown as Figure 1.31 in front of them. By setting out a score-sheet it is possible to compare candidates' responses to questions and behaviour in the interview situation.

Interviewing requires a considerable amount of intelligence and inventiveness. When candidates answer your questions you may feel that you need to ask them a little bit more in order to get a more complete answer. Follow on questions are very important here. Some follow on questions may be planned in advance, while others may need to be developed on the spur of the moment.

For example, an interview for the job of a shelf stacker in a supermarket may proceed as follows:

Interviewer: Have you had experience of shelf stacking in a supermarket before?
Interviewee: Yes, I worked at Waitrose doing it for three months.
Interviewer: (Follow on question). Can you tell me exactly what you were responsible for doing in your shelf stacking job? (And why you left it!)

Without follow on questions an interview can pass very quickly with little being found out about the true strengths (and weaknesses) of job applicants.

Using body language

People do not communicate with each other just through words. They also communicate through their **body language**. An interviewer who wants to draw the best out of candidates for a job will use appropriate body language. The interviewer should be seated at the same height as the interviewee with a good frontal or open posture. The interviewer should not cross his or her arms or make threatening gestures such as pointing a finger or banging a fist down on the table. He or she should smile and use clear eye contact.

Closing the interview

The usual way of closing an interview is that, when the interviewer or interviewing panel have finished their list of questions, they will ask the interviewee if there is anything he or she would like to ask. When this is completed the interviewer will say something like: 'Thank you very much for coming to the interview, I hope you have a safe journey back. You will be hearing from us by...' The interviewer will clarify the procedures through which the interviewee will be informed of arrangements, and explain how any administrative task such as claiming for expenses should be done.

Giving feedback

Often candidates for a post will be given feedback on how they performed in the interview situation. They should be told about their strengths and weaknesses and the reasons why they were or were not chosen for the post. This feedback should be seen as a positive process concerned with the ongoing development of the interviewee.

Interviewee techniques

Interviews can be nerve-racking. In a short space of time the candidate must convince the interviewer that he or she is the person the organisation needs.

FIGURE 1.32 *Wear appropriate clothes for an interview*

INTERVIEW ASSESSMENT						
Factors	Rating					Remarks
	A	B	C	D	E	
Appearance Personality Manner Health						
Intelligence Understanding of questions						
Skills Special skills Work experience						
Interests Hobbies Sports						
Academic						
Motivation						
Circumstances Mobility Hours Limitations						
OVERALL						

A = Exceptional   B = Above average   C = Satisfactory
D = Below average   E = Unsuitable

FIGURE 1.33 *Interview assessment form*

Preparing

Both the interviewer and the candidate need to be prepared. The candidate can prepare by practising answers to the questions likely to be asked, possibly with the help of a friend who takes the role of the interviewer.

It must be remembered that interviews are a two-way activity. The candidate has a chance to ask questions and find out if the organisation and the job are suitable. Questions can, for example, be asked about training, promotion prospects and social facilities.

There are all sorts of things that you can prepare before an interview. For example, you may want to try out the clothes that you will wear to the interview beforehand, perhaps by wearing them to some sort of public occasion.

There is nothing worse than feeling uncomfortable in the clothes you have chosen for an interview. Many people like to plan the route they will take to get to the interview, even doing a dummy run beforehand.

You may like to prepare yourself by thinking about the kinds of things that interviewers will be look for in you. Figure 1.33 shows an interview

DO	DON'T
Find out about the firm before the interview	Be late
Dress smartly but comfortably	Smoke unless invited to
Speak clearly and with confidence	Chew gum or eat sweets
Look at the interviewer when speaking	Answer all questions 'yes', 'no' or 'I don't know'
Be positive about yourself	Be afraid to ask for clarification if anything is unclear
Be ready to ask questions	Say things which are obviously untrue or insincere

FIGURE 1.34 *Interview checklist*

assessment form that gives you some useful indications of the qualities that are looked for in many job holders.

The checklist shown in Figure 1.34 should also be helpful in giving you some useful preparatory advice for interviews.

Showing confidence

It is important for interviewees to appear confident but not over-confident. You should be confident in your own abilities. One of the most important attributes to have in the interview situation is enthusiasm. An enthusiastic person will tend to radiate confidence. Candidates who appear hangdog and timid will be viewed in a poor light, particularly for posts that require some degree of responsibility and initiative.

Body language

At an interview it is important for you to adopt the right body language. Look alert and eager. Look the questioner in the eye. Avoid nervous movements, and try not to cross your arms in a defensive position. Try not to threaten the interviewer by pointing your finger or making violent movements. Sit up straight and try to look

FIGURE 1.35 *Appropriate body language*

Learning activity

Study the following pictures which show a person who turned up for an interview for a part-time shelf filler's post.

In each case explain why the body language is inappropriate.

FIGURE 1.36 *Inappropriate body language*

confident and at ease – not apathetic and too laid back.

Do not give brief one-line answers, but try to expand on your answers so that the interviewer can see you at your best. Smile, and at all times try to appear interested and enthusiastic about what is being discussed. You do not have to let yourself be pushed around by an aggressive interviewer – be assertive by standing up for yourself, without taking it to the extreme by becoming heated and argumentative.

Listening to questions

When you are being interviewed, listen carefully to the questions that you are asked. If you do not understand a question or have not heard it clearly, it may be helpful to say, 'Please could you repeat that question?'

Responding to questions

When answering questions you will need to expand on points rather than giving a simple yes/no or a short answer. Try to give detailed and

Learning activity

It is often the first few minutes of an interview that the panel make up their minds about which candidate to appoint. A recent study reported that the person who is first on the interviewer's list is three times less likely to be hired than the last name on the list.

In groups, carry out mock interviews for one of the following posts.

1 A post that you are familiar with from work experience.

2 A post as a part-time shelf filler for Marks & Spencer.

3 An alternative post that members of your group agree on because you have sufficient knowledge of the post, and can get hold of materials such as job descriptions, job specifications etc.

Before the interviews take place the interviewing panel will need to establish the qualities they are looking for in the successful applicant. The interviewing panel will also need to establish a set of questions. The same questions need to be asked of each applicant if the interviews are to be fair.

The applicants will each need to produce a CV and a written application. They will also need to research the nature of the organisation and the post.

After the interviews, all interviewers and interviewees should fill in an evaluation sheet containing the following questions:

✱ How did you feel about the interview?

✱ How do you consider the interview went?

✱ What impression do you think that you gave?

✱ What do you think of the interviewers'/ interviewees':

  ✱ planning and organisation

  ✱ preparation for the interview

  ✱ performance at the interview?

Individual students should prepare an appraisal form for analysing their own strengths and weaknesses in the interview situation. This should be a very helpful process because it encourages you to be objective in your self-criticism. You can then use the form to reflect on your performance. Prepare the form before the interview takes place either by watching a video showing you interviewing or being interviewed, or simply by recalling your thoughts and feelings.

Aspect of performance	Rating				
	Very good	Good	Fair	Weak	Very weak
Eye contact					
Body language					
Appearing confident					
Answering questions					

FIGURE 1.37 *A self-appraisal form*

clear responses. Remember that the inverviewers are judging you against certain criteria. Try to think about what those criteria might be and prepare full answers which enable them to give you high scores.

Asking questions

When given the opportunity ask a small number of relevant questions. Don't ask questions that simply involve the repetition of what you have already been told. If you are not sure whether you want the job or not, ask questions that will help you to make an informed choice.

Be clear and concise

Good verbal communication involves asking and answering questions in a clear and concise way. The person who is straightforward, interesting and direct will often sway an interview in a positive way.

Other assessment methods

Many jobs today involves some form of **psychometric or aptitude testing** to find out whether individuals have the right sorts of personalities or dispositions to carry out particular types of work. A psychometric test is a way of assessing an individual's personality, drives and motivations, often by means of a paper and pencil questionnaire – or online test.

For example, one of the dimensions the psychometric test might draw out is an individual's willingness or ability to work in a team situation, or to handle stress.

A number of organisations place a great deal of emphasis on these tests because they believe they are reliable indicators of the sociability/personality of individuals, and that they are useful predictors of whether individuals will fit into the organisation.

> **Learning activity**
>
> Obtain a psychometric test that is used for selection purposes. Try out the test. What does it claim to show about your personality and disposition? Do you agree?

Evaluating recruitment and selection processes

Recruitment and selection can be a very costly process for a business. It takes a great deal of time to set up the process – involving deciding on what the jobs that are to be recruited for will entail, advertising, sifting through applications, checking which applications best meet the criteria set down for the post, interviewing candidates and, finally, selecting the best candidate for the post.

There is considerable scope along the way for waste and inefficiency. For example, when a job advertisement attracts 100 applicants there will be considerable waste when reducing the list down to six. If you get your procedures wrong you may eliminate some of the best candidates right from the start and end up with six who are barely

> **Learning activity**
>
> Produce an attractively laid out four-page booklet setting out good practice for recruiting and selecting applicants to fill posts in a specific organisation. You may want to base the work on the organisation in which you have carried out your work experience or had a part-time job. Alternatively relate your work to recruiting part-time shelf fillers at your local Marks & Spencer store.
>
> The booklet should consider:
>
> 1 Creating an effective person specification, and job descriptions.
>
> 2 Creating job advertisements.
>
> 3 Complying with the legal and ethical requirements, e.g. Equal Opportunities laws.
>
> 4 Shortlisting.
>
> 5 Interviewing to get the best candidates.
>
> 6 Any other areas that you consider relevant.
>
> Once you have developed your material you will be well placed to evaluate the recruitment and selection processes in different businesses. Using your own experience of being recruited and selected to work in a particular job, how did the process you experienced compare with the good practice guidelines that you have drawn up?

satisfactory. If you end up choosing an unsuitable candidate for the job, the company will suffer from having a poorly motivated person, who may make mischief within the organisation before walking out on the job and leaving the company to go through the expense of replacing him or her yet again.

Training staff

Training includes all forms of planned learning experiences and activities designed to make positive changes to performance and other behaviour. You can train an individual to develop new:

* knowledge
* skills
* beliefs
* values
* attitudes.

Learning is generally defined as 'a relatively permanent change in behaviour that occurs as a result of practice or experience'.

There are a number of training methods and activities which are described below.

Induction

Induction is the process of introducing new employees to their place of work, job, new surroundings and the people they will be working with. Induction also provides information to help new employees start work and generally 'fit in'.

As well as following naturally from recruitment and selection, induction should also consider the initial training needs either on joining a new organisation or on taking on a new function within it. As well as dealing with the initial knowledge and skills needed to do the job, in the case of a new organisation, it should also

FIGURE 1.38 *An induction pack*

deal with the structure, culture and activities in the organisation. The new recruit will typically be given an induction pack that introduces him or her to the organisation.

Mentoring

Mentoring involves a trainee being 'paired' with a more experienced employee. The trainee carries out the job but uses the 'mentor' to discuss problems that may occur and how best to solve them.

This approach is used in many lines of work. For example, it is common practice for trainee teachers to work with a mentor who is responsible for their early training and development. The student teacher will watch the mentor teach before starting his or her own teaching. The mentor will then give ongoing guidance to the student teacher on how best to improve his or her performance. The mentee will take any problems

and difficulties he or she is facing to the mentor to seek advice.

Coaching

Coaching involves providing individuals with personal coaches in the workplace. The person who is going to take on the coaching role will need, first, to develop coaching skills and will also need to have the time slots for the coaching to take place. The coach and the individual being coached will need to identify development opportunities that they can work on together – ways of tackling jobs, ways of improving performance, etc. The coach will provide continuous feedback on performance and how this is progressing.

Of course, coaching does not just benefit the person being coached; it also aids the coach's own personal development. It is particularly important in a coaching system that:

Learning activity

Study the pictures below and see if you can match the coach and the person they helped to develop.

FIGURE 1.39 *Can you match the coach with the star?*

* the coach wants to coach the person and has the necessary coaching skills

* the person being coached wants to be coached and has the necessary listening and learning skills

* sufficient time is given to the coaching process

* the organisation places sufficient value on the coaching process.

Some of the best sportspeople in this country have improved their skills and abilities by working closely with a coach they respect (Figure 1.39).

Apprenticeships

One of the great strengths of the British industrial system was the existence of a range of apprenticeship schemes, many of which no longer exist. With the apprenticeship scheme, the apprentice learnt by working for a more skilled craftsperson. The apprentices had to work for a number of years to master their trades.

Apprenticeships were once widespread in skilled work and, when the apprentices had learnt their trades, they were able to set up on their own and so bring in higher wages, employing apprentices on their own. During the early years of the apprenticeship wages might be quite low, and then rise as the apprentice became more skilled.

In recent years, the government has developed a Modern Apprenticeship scheme that enables young people to combine learning on the job with college-based courses. These schemes are subsidised by the government, which gives employers a greater incentive to take on apprentices. A modern apprenticeship is made up of a:

* A National Vocational Qualification (i.e. nationally recognised job-related qualification)

* Key skills

* A technical certificate.

Provided an individual starts the Modern Apprenticeship before they are 25 they will receive government funds. The length of time to complete the apprenticeship varies and the qualification is at both a Foundation and Advanced level.

In-house training and external training

In-house training is where an organisation has its own training department. External training is where employees are sent on external courses, or are trained in other ways, away from the organisation. In-house training can take place on the job or off the job within the company, but external training always takes place off the job.

CASE STUDY
Apprenticeship at Audi
Audi the car manufacturer has a well-organised apprenticeship and training scheme in this country to develop high quality people. Audi training centres are designed to develop the right skills. The following chart shows progression for technicians at Audi.

1 What other fields that you are familiar with provide the opportunity for apprenticeships?
2 What might attract an individual to take a Modern Apprenticeship?
3 Carry out a web search to find out the range of Modern Apprenticeships on offer.

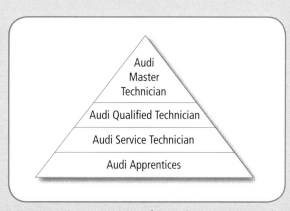

FIGURE 1.40 *Progression for technicians at Audi*

Nestlé provides two kinds of OJT. The first is for trainees. These training sessions are generally short and are geared towards new arrivals and those starting a job within a company.

The other is for current employees. Every Nestlé employee continues to receive training throughout his or her time with the company. The process is a constant and systematic communication of knowledge from executive levels down, and includes every level of management.

1 Why do new trainees require OJT ?
2 Why do existing employees need OJT?
3 Why is management important in delivering this training?

On-the-job training

On-the-job training (OJT) takes place when employees are trained while they are carrying out an activity, often at their place of work. There are four main advantages to this approach:

1 Participants can gain a thorough knowledge of the organisation.

2 There can be no substitute for hands-on experience in developing skills.

3 It allows the trainee to engage in productive, paid work and it can be carried out without the need for structured, permanent training facilities.

4 OJT is also a useful means of testing a trainee's knowledge and competence for any given task.

Off-the-job training

Off-the-job training, as its name suggests, takes place away from the job. This can be either internally within a company or externally using outside trainers. Many large companies will engage in a great deal of both off-the-job and on-the-job training.

Nationally recognised training structures

Most businesses take advantage of nationally recognised training schemes and qualifications. For example, **Modern Apprenticeships** allow young people to combine further education with on-the-job training. **Local Education Councils (LECs)** help to provide training for people in a particular area, to make the unemployed and others more employable.

Investors in People

Many organisations in all sectors now pride themselves in meeting the **Investors in People Standard**.

To achieve the Standard, an organisation needs to demonstrate that it does the following:

INVESTORS IN PEOPLE

FIGURE 1.41 *Investors in People is a nationally recognised standard*

Plan – develop strategies to improve the performance of the organisation, from business goals to leadership strategies.

Do – implement those strategies, taking action to improve the performance of the organisation.

Review – evaluate and adjust those strategies, measuring their impact on the performance of the organisation.

Being an Investor in People means that the organisation is likely to be seen more favourably by prospective employees, customers and other stakeholders. To achieve the Standard, an organisation is assessed by an independent assessor who gathers evidence (verbal, written and observed) that all requirements of the Standard are met. The assessor's recommendations are approved by a panel of business peers and the organisation is recognised as an Investor in People.

Learning activity

Interview someone who has been involved in setting up the systems that have enabled an organisation to gain Investors in People status. What were the main policies and practices that needed to be put in place to meet the standards?

Find out...

To find out more about Investors in People go to www.heinemann.co.uk/hotlinks (express code 1149P, then go to Unit 1).

Individual Learning Accounts

The current government's **'New Deal'** for the unemployed provides subsidised employment and support for young people to continue in full-time education and training. The creation of **Individual Learning Accounts** encourages individuals to save towards the costs of additional training.

Individual Learning Accounts are part of government policy to encourage everyone to engage in lifelong learning. An individual puts up a small sum of money towards a training or education course. The LEC then puts up a much larger sum of money towards the scheme. The Learning Account is then opened, and the trainee can go to a registered trainee with their account and sign on for training. The scheme is available for anyone in the 18–65 age range.

1.3 How businesses motivate employees

Having obtained and trained their staff, businesses will seek to keep these staff happy in their work.

Legislation that protects the well-being of employees

As a bare minimum, employees will need to comply with legislation about:

* **Hours of work:** As a member state in the European Union the UK must comply with EU regulations. The **Working Time Regulations** set out that workers aged 18 and over are entitled to four weeks' holiday a year, to work no more than six days out of every seven, to have a 20-minute break every six hours, and to work no more than an average of 48 hours a week.

* The **Employment Act 2002** provides employees with the right to leave from work in line with EU regulations. Employees are entitled to maternity and paternity (two weeks) leave before, during, and after the birth of a child. Employees who adopt a child are also eligible to 26 weeks' paid leave followed by 26 weeks' unpaid leave.

Learning activity

Carry out an internet search using the key words 'maternity leave', 'UK' and the current year, e.g. 2005. What are the latest entitlements of mothers in this respect?

Carry out another search using the key words 'Minimum Wage' 'UK' and the current year to find out what the present level is.

* **Minimum wage**: Before the minimum wage was introduced, well over a million workers were employed in jobs which paid less than the rate set. Many of these workers would have been young people in part-time or casual jobs with no permanent contact. The minimum wage is raised from time to time to guarantee a fair return for the most disadvantaged.

Pay and non-financial incentives

From a management view, a payment system should:

1 Be effective in recruiting the right quantity and quality of labour.

2 Be effective in retaining labour over the required period of time – it is expensive to have to keep advertising for and training new employees.

3 Keep labour costs as low as possible in order to maintain the competitiveness of a business.

4 Help to motivate staff and encourage effort. Careful thought needs to be applied to structuring pay systems in a way that encourages motivation and performance.

5 Be designed to allow for additional rewards and benefits.

The sum paid for a normal working week is termed a **basic wage** or **salary**. Many employees receive other benefits in addition to their basic wage, either in a money or non-money form. The main ways of calculating pay are outlined below. Sometimes elements of these methods are combined.

Flat rate

This is a set rate of weekly or monthly pay, based on a set number of hours. It is easy to calculate and administer but does not provide an incentive to employees to work harder.

Time rate

Under this scheme, workers receive a set rate per hour. Any hours worked above a set number are paid at an 'overtime rate'.

Piece rate

This system is sometimes used in the textile and electronics industries, among others. Payment is made for each item produced that meets given quality standards. The advantage of this is that it encourages effort. However, it is not suitable for jobs that require time and care. Also, many jobs particularly in the service sector produce 'outputs' that are impossible to measure.

Bonus

A bonus is paid as an added encouragement to employees. It can be paid out of additional profits earned by the employer as a result of the employee's effort and hard work, or as an incentive to workers at times when they might be inclined to slacken effort, e.g. at Christmas and summer holiday times.

Commission

This is a payment made as a percentage of the sales a salesperson has made.

Output-related payment schemes

Output-related schemes are the most common method used to reward manual workers. Most schemes involve an element of time-rates plus a bonus or other incentive.

> **Learning activity**
>
> The wages department of a large manufacturing organisation is deciding on the most appropriate payment systems in the following situations. What advice would you give them? If you have done work experience in a manufacturing company you may want to relate the reward system outlined to the company where you did your placement.
>
> They want to provide a financial reward system:
>
> 1 For sales people that rewards them according to the number of sales they make.
>
> 2 For production line staff that encourages them to be careful in their work.
>
> 3 For production line staff that discourages them from slacking off just before the Christmas period.

CASE STUDY
Performance-related pay

FIGURE 1.42 *Is the police force a suitable case for performance-related pay?*

In recent years the emphasis in a number of organisations has shifted towards performance-related pay. Based on performance appraisal techniques, such schemes have been adopted in a wide range of occupations, including the police force, universities, insurance and banking. Evidence indicates that up to three-quarters of all employers are now using some form of performance appraisal to set pay levels.

Managerial jobs are most affected by performance-related pay. Today managers' performance is increasingly assessed against working objectives. Individual objectives can be set by reference to company goals. An individual may be set broad objectives known as accountabilities. Shorter-term goals may be attached to each objective. Scoring systems are then worked out to assess performance against objectives, and these distinguish levels of attainment, e.g. high, medium or low.

One way of rewarding performance is to give a bonus if certain targets are met. Another is to give increments as targets are met, with the employee progressing up an incremental ladder each year.

1 Give a brief definition of performance-related pay.
2 Do you think it is appropriate to use performance-related pay in the police force? How would performance be measured?
3 Give examples of jobs where performance-related pay might be appropriate and ones where it definitely would not be appropriate.

Standards are set in many ways, varying from casual assessment to detailed work study based on method study and work measurement.

* **Method study** sets out to determine what is the most effective way of carrying out particular tasks.

* **Work measurement** takes place in three stages:

1 The time taken to perform a task is measured.
2 The effort of an individual worker or work-group is rated.
3 The work carried out is assessed and compared with the standard rate.

A standard allowable time is set according to the two stages. The worker's pay is then determined according to the success of the third stage.

Non-financial rewards

In addition to financial rewards so-called **fringe benefits** are provided including:

* Pension schemes
* Subsidised meals or canteen services
* Educational courses
* Opportunities for foreign travel
* Holiday entitlements
* Crèches
* Assistance with housing and relocation packages
* Discount and company purchase plans (i.e. cheap purchases of company products)
* Telephone costs
* Discounts on insurance costs

* Private healthcare, dental treatment, etc.

* Time off (sabbatical)

* Sports, leisure and social facilities.

There are a number of reasons for giving non-financial rewards including:

1 They can often be provided to employees free of tax, which benefits both the employer and the employee.

2 Some benefits can be provided cheaply through economies of scale, e.g. a works canteen offering cheap meals.

3 Some benefits are needed to improve employee performance, e.g. healthcare and hairdressing on site.

4 Some companies may be able to offer discounts on their own products and thus at the same time increase their sales.

5 The provision of certain benefits may help to create long-term commitment to the company, e.g. a crèche on site, a company pension scheme, company cars, etc.

Conditions of work and internal promotion

When you start work an important determinant of how happy you are in your job is the conditions in the workplace. One aspect of the conditions is the physical environment, for example:

* are you working in a bright, clean and well-lit environment?

* is the temperature suitable for work (not too hot or too cold)?

* is the workplace safe?

* other physical conditions.

The other important aspect is the 'culture' of the organisation. The culture relates to the relationships and typical ways of interacting and

✱ DID YOU KNOW?

The term HR refers to Human Resource management. This is an approach which involves welcoming the contribution that people can make to an organisation. However, some people are cynical about this approach particularly when HR managers end up sacking people. In these cases HR is said to stand for Human Remains!

✱ DID YOU KNOW?

From the 1970s right through to the 1990s when Liverpool Football Club was so successful, many of its managers were former backroom staff. This encouraged the backroom staff to be loyal to the club with excellent results.

doing things in the organisation. Different types of organisations have different cultures.

Promoting people within an organisation (internally) is another good motivating tool, because employees then see that they can develop themselves within the organisation.

The importance of motivating individuals

Motivation is the strength of commitment that individuals have to what they are doing. There are several theories which help us to think about motivation.

Maslow's hierarchy of needs

Maslow identified a hierarchy of needs split into five broad categories. He suggested that, although it is difficult, if not impossible, to analyse

FAVOURABLE CULTURES	UNFAVOURABLE CULTURES
Warm and welcoming	Unfriendly
Encouraging	Discouraging and based on fear
Welcomes initiative	Have to do what you are told

FIGURE 1.43 *Organisational cultures*

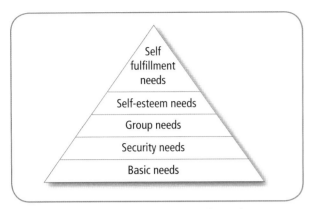

FIGURE 1.44 *Maslow's 'hierarchy of needs'*

individual needs, it is possible to develop a hierarchical picture of needs, split into categories.

Basic needs

Basic needs are for reasonable standards of food, shelter and clothing, and those other items that are considered the norm to meet the needs of the body and for physical survival. This base level of need will be attained at work from receiving a basic wage packet that helps the employee to survive – for example by receiving the minimum wage.

Security needs

Security needs are also concerned with physical survival. In the workplace, these needs could include safety, security of employment, adequate rest periods, pension and sick schemes, and protection from unfair treatment.

Group needs

Group needs are concerned with an individual's need for love and affection (within a group). In groups there are always some people who are strong enough and happy to keep apart. However, the majority of people want to feel that they belong to a group. In small and medium-sized organisations (up to 200 people) it is relatively easy to give each member of the group a feeling of belonging. However, in large organisations individuals can lose their group identify, becoming just another number, a face in the crowd. Managers therefore need to think about how they can organise their people into teams so as to meet group needs.

Self-esteem needs

Self-esteem needs are based on an individual's desire for self-respect and the respect of others.

Employees have a need to be recognised as individuals of some importance, to receive praise for their work and to have their efforts noticed and rewarded.

Maslow placed self-fulfillment at the top of the hierarchy of needs. Self-fulfillment is concerned with full personal development and individual creativity. In order to meet this need, it is important for individuals to be able to use their talents and abilities fully.

Maslow argued that individuals first have to have their lower-level needs met; however, if

> **✳ DID YOU KNOW?**
>
> The Chinese philosopher Confucius said that 'The person that finds a job they like never does a day's work in their life.'

Learning activity

Which of Maslow's needs do you think the following are looking to satisfy at work? How might managers go about seeking to meet these needs?

1 Simon is working part time in a supermarket to save up enough money to go back to university with. He is prepared to work long hours, providing his total pay is good. He is not interested in taking on responsibilities, but wants to work in a safe environment.

2 Pritesh is a graphic designer who recently graduated from art college. Ideally he would like to do something which allows him to express his artistic talent. He feels that his current job working in an advertising agency does not allow him to express himself. He works in a junior role in the company copying work that has been created by senior designers.

3 Gillian has recently been promoted to the post of supervisor in the food processing plant where she works. This has meant a rise in salary enabling her to take out a mortgage to buy a house and put down a deposit on a new car. The supervisor's post gives her the status she desires and she likes her working environment and the relationship she has with colleagues.

they are not to experience frustration it is also important for their higher level needs to be met. Frustrated employees are likely either to develop a 'couldn't care less approach' or to become antagonistic to working life. If employees are to become committed to work these higher level needs must be met. Self-fulfillment at work creates the complete employee, the person who enjoys work and feels a direct involvement in it.

Herzberg's theory of motivators and dissatisfiers

Herzberg carried out research on 200 engineers to find out what motivated them at work. He made a distinction between things that move people, which he referred to as KITA (kick in the ass), and factors that motivate people.

He argued that if he kicked his dog, this would get the dog to move (out of fear), but it would not motivate the animal.

When we are motivated we do something because we want to do it. In other words it provides an intrinsic (internal) reward.

Herzberg identified nine factors which he referred to as 'dissatisfiers' and when these factors reached a certain level they would cause employee absenteeism, poor levels of output, resistance to change, obstruction, and other negative actions.

The **'dissatisfiers'** are:

* dominating or unpredictable company policy and administration
* low pay
* poor working conditions
* confrontational relationships between different levels in the organisation
* unfriendly relationships within the chain of command
* unfair management and supervision
* unfair treatment of employees
* feelings of inadequacy
* impossibility for development of the individual.

Learning activity

From your own experience of working life, identify situations in which you felt highly motivated. How did these motivating factors relate to Herzberg's satisfiers?

By reducing these dissatisfiers you can reduce negative feelings but they are not the real motivating drives.

In contrast, Herzberg identified five motivating factors which relate to the content of jobs. He called these 'satisfiers'.

The **'satisfiers'** are:

* recognition of effort and performance
* the nature of the job itself – does it provide the employees with appropriate challenges?
* sense of achievement
* assumption of responsibility
* opportunity for promotion.

Herzberg suggested that jobs could be given more meaning if they included elements of responsibility and a more creative use of an individual's ability, as well as opportunities to achieve.

McGregor's Theory X v Theory Y

Douglas McGregor divided managers into two main types.

Theory X managers tend to have the view that:

* The average person naturally dislikes work and so will avoid it when possible. Management therefore needs to emphasise high levels of production, incentive schemes to encourage effort, and to discourage time wasting.

* Because people naturally dislike work, they need to be pushed, threatened and driven to get things done.

* The average person likes to be told what to do and to avoid responsibility; they have little ambition, and therefore require 'managing'.

Theory Y managers have a contrasting view, and believe in trusting employees to take on responsibilities. The Theory Y manager believes that:

* Work is a natural activity which people can enjoy. Managers need to create the right conditions in which work is enjoyable.

* External control is not the only way to manage people. Employees who identify with the organisation's objectives will be motivated to work hard.

* The most significant reward that will motivate people is self-fulfillment (see Maslow). Managers therefore need to identify opportunities for employees to fulfill themselves while working to meet company objectives.

* The average human being learns, when given the opportunity, to accept and to seek responsibility.

* Many people can contribute to a business's objectives when given the chance.

* People's potential is rarely achieved in the workplace.

McGregor saw the potential to make organisations far more effective by unleashing the people who work for them.

Moss Kanter's ideas on empowerment

Rosabeth Moss Kanter argues that we can empower people by giving them greater responsibility in the organisation.

FIGURE 1.45 *Rosabeth Moss Kanter*

Learning activity

Study one organisation to find out about how it motivates its people. This can be done by:

1 Using your own work experience.

2 Interviewing a Human Resources manager.

3 Looking at the human resources section of a company website.

✱ DID YOU KNOW?

Employees at Rank Xerox are allowed to reward each other. Under a scheme called 'You deserve an X today' any employee can give an X certificate to another employee. The X certificate is worth up to 50 dollars and is given for 'excellent support, excellent attendance, extra work or excellent co-operation.'

Empowerment involves passing power and responsibility down in the organisation, so that good ideas can bubble up to the surface from below. Empowered individuals enable an organisation to be more successful by coming up with lots of good ideas. In turn empowered people are motivated people.

1.4 How people are influenced at work

Managers and employees are affected not only by internal issues such as the conditions of work and levels of motivation, but also by external issues.

Environmental issues

Today we are more aware than every before of **environmental issues**. The Rio Treaty of 1992 marked a turning point in which governments, businesses and other groups recognised that we have a joint responsibility for our common environment.

The Kyoto Climate Change Treaty of 1997 recognised that businesses and governments should work together to limit harmful effects that are caused by pollution and environmental

Treaty to fight global warming – what is the Kyoto Protocol?

It is a treaty agreed by governments at a 1997 UN conference in Kyoto, Japan, to reduce emissions of the so-called greenhouse gases such as carbon dioxide from cars and power stations.

What are the reductions and who has to make them?

In the Treaty's first period to 2012, only the 39 major industrialised countries (including Britain) are required to make cuts. The developed nations as a whole have to cut their emissions to 5.2% below their 1990 levels during the five-year period 2008–2012. The EU as a whole has to cut its emissions to 8 per cent below, Britain to 12.5 per cent below, and the US to 7 per cent below.

Most countries are lagging behind their targets under Kyoto; only Britain and Sweden are currently on track in the European Union.

How is Britain's commitment to Kyoto likely to affect business costs?

Learning activity

Kyoto provides a useful topic for discussion. Currently Britain is on track to meet its targets. The United States has not signed up to the Treaty and is currently producing more pollution than the rest of the world put together. Developing countries like India and China do not have to abide by the Treaty. Is this fair? Should Britain comply with a treaty that the world's biggest polluters are ignoring?

---

degradation. The Treaty set out that governments should work together to limit the creation of greenhouse gases.

Treaties like Rio and Kyoto put pressure on business and the individuals that work for businesses. For example, the Rio Treaty set out Agenda 21 which is a list of actions for the 21st century. Part of Agenda 21 was the creation of Local Agenda 21s in which groups of businesses and local government in different parts of the country set out environmental action plans. For example, local councils have targets for recycling glass, paper, cardboard and other wastes.

The government has created a series of laws governing how businesses must operate, for example in how they handle waste. For example, dangerous wastes should not be put in waste containers with ordinary waste. Businesses must use special drains for clearing away harmful liquids which must not be mixed with other liquids such as rain water.

People who work for businesses are trained in methods of waste disposal. Wherever possible materials should be reused and **recycled** rather than being disposed of.

Many businesses have created environmental management systems. These systems involve:

* Auditing (listing) all business activities that have an environmental impact.
* Creating plans and policies for environmental management.
* Creating systems for environmental management.
* Training staff to manage these systems.
* Setting targets for environmental improvement.
* Creating reports which monitor the success of the business in meeting these targets.

Every employee in a business has a responsibility for environmental management, and must be familiar with guidelines and good practice in:

* Recycling
* Disposing of wastes
* Caring for the environment.

Social and ethical issues

Business organisations need at all times to do the 'right' thing rather than to get involved in questionable activities. Business **ethics** is concerned with behaving in a moral way.

CASE STUDY

Corporate social responsibility at Manchester United

Corporate social responsibility is the process of organisations taking responsibility for the wider community. Manchester United recognise that the success of the organisation is not only based on success on the field of play and profitability but also the impact the business has on the quality of life in communities and in the environment. Manchester United focuses its efforts on three main areas:

* sport
* health
* education.

Internationally Manchester United joined forces with UNICEF, the United Nations children's charity, in a partnership aimed at improving the lives of disadvantaged children in the world's poorest countries. Over a million pounds has already been raised. In addition the club works with the charity to raise awareness of children's issues such as the exploitation of children in the workplace.

Nationally the club supports a range of charities such as the Prince's Trust, designed to help 15–25 year olds to develop new skills.

The club works with unemployed people to get them back to work through education and training. It collaborates with Kick It Out (KIO) to nominate one game per season as Anti-Racism Day of Action.

Locally the club supports a number of initiatives. For example, the Football in the Community scheme offers coaching sessions to children and youngsters throughout the Manchester area. The club arranges educational-based activities in conjunction with schools and the local education authority.

In addition the club works to improve the local environment by:

* increasing the percentage of rubbish sent for recycling
* using more green supplies
* more environmentally friendly marketing material.

Of course, cynics might argue that businesses' commitment to social responsibility is partly fuelled by a desire to gain a good reputation which is good for their business. The more people who think that Manchester United is a great club, the more they are likely to buy the shirts and merchandise and go to matches.

1 Why is it important for business organisations to show a commitment to wider communities?
2 Explain how another organisation meets its commitment to international, national, and local communities as well as the environment.
3 Do you think that businesses have a genuine commitment to corporate social responsibility or is this a smokescreen for making as much profit as they can?
4 Can you give examples of situations in which what appears to be corporate social responsibility is really profiteering?

FIGURE 1.46 *Manchester United supports the KIO initiative against racism*

In responding to social and ethical issues organisations need to take account of industry **codes of practice** setting out good standards of behaviour. In addition it is also important to listen to stakeholder groupings.

For example, stakeholder groupings that help to shape Manchester United's social and ethical policies include:

* The government, which seeks a more responsible football industry

* The Premier League

* Supporters Associations

* The local community

* The shareholders.

Another important area to recognise is organised pressure groups, who campaign on specific or several related issues.

For example, Friends of the Earth claims to be 'the UK's most effective environment group'.

Another good example of pressure group activity is the work of children's charities in lobbying mobile phone companies to create controls which bar access of children to 'adult content' such as pornography and gambling on mobile phones and through internet connections.

Legal and self-regulatory constraints and issues

There are a number of other influences that determine the sorts of decisions that managers, supervisors and other employees are able to make in the workplace.

Some of these influences are legal, i.e. they results from laws made by the European Union or by government in this country. Other influences are self-regulatory, i.e. an industry creates its

CASE STUDY

Friends of the Earth

An advertisement from Friends of the Earth reveals how the organisation works:

Friends of the Earth

'Who really makes the big decisions about our future? Too often, it's the fat cats and the faceless business executives. In the search for ever bigger profits, many companies just don't think about the terrible side-effects of what they are doing.

Support Friends of the Earth and we'll work hard getting government to pass laws to make sure the likes of Shell, Asda Wal-Mart and the Royal Bank of Scotland get their filthy hands off our future.

We're not anti-business and we're only too happy to give praise where it's due. But Friends of the Earth believe passionately that a healthy, unpolluted world is too precious to squander for quick profits.

If you agree, please support us today with a regular gift of just £3 a month. We really are only as powerful as the people who support us.'

1 What do you see as the important messages here for businesses?

2 How do you think that socially responsible businesses should respond to these criticisms?

own rules about how firms should behave in the industry.

Competition law

A number of laws have been passed in this country to seek to ensure that firms compete fairly with each other. The Office of Fair Trading (OFT) is an independent organisation set up by the government and is responsible for making sure that markets work well for customers. Markets operate well when businesses work in open and vigorous competition with each other. The OFT's powers come from consumer and competition legislation, e.g. The Competition Act 1998, designed to ensure that businesses compete fairly; it outlaws certain types of anti-competitive behaviour. The OFT has strong powers to investigate businesses suspected of anti-competitive behaviour, and can impose tough penalties on wrong doers.

Find out...

Search for the OFT website at www.heinemann.co.uk/hotlinks (express code 1149P, then go to Unit 1) to see the range of OFT activities.

Consumer protection

There is a wealth of consumer protection law designed to protect the consumer from unfair business dealing, including laws concerning trades descriptions, sale of goods, food safety, weights and measures.

Trade Descriptions Acts, 1968 and 1972

These laws make it illegal to give false or misleading descriptions of goods, services, accommodation or facilities.

The Sale of Goods Act, 1979

This law sets out that:

* the seller must have the right to sell their goods (i.e. it is not stolen property)
* the goods must fit the description provided
* the goods should be of satisfactory quality

* the goods should be fit for the buyer's purpose (e.g. a bed should not break when you are sleeping on it)
* when a sample is provided the remainder of the goods should be the same as the sample.

Supply of Goods and Services Act, 1982

There are provisions so that:

* the supplier must carry out the service with reasonable care and skill
* the service must be performed within a reasonable time
* a reasonable price must be charged.

Food Safety Act, 1990

This sets out that businesses which handle food must take all reasonable precautions when manufacturing, transporting, storing, preparing and selling food items. In 1999 the government set up the Food Standards Agency to monitor the food industry.

Consumer Protection Act, 1987

This sets out regulations for certain potentially harmful products such as flammable items and poisonous substances.

Weights and Measures Act, 1985

This requires traders to provide standard measures of fluids and weights of substances. It has been followed up by legislation requiring information about weights and measures to be displayed on packaging.

The work of trade unions

Today many unions see themselves as working in partnership with government, employers and workers towards common goals, including a safe, secure, harmonious working environment for all employees regardless of their differences. There are a number of benefits to being a member of a trade union.

In a unionised workplace:

1 Average earnings are around 8% higher.
2 The average trade union member receives 29 days annual holiday compared with 23 days for non-unionised workers.

3 Unionised workplaces have health and safety officers to ensure employers keep work safe.

4 Unions help workers to gain compensation for injuries, illness at work and other matters.

5 Unionised workplaces are more likely to have in place parental policies that are more generous than the legal minimum.

6 Workers in unionised workplaces are more likely to receive job-related training.

7 Workers in unionised workplaces are more likely to have an equal opportunities policy in place.

8 Trade union members are only half as likely to be dismissed as non-union ones.

9 Black and Asian trade union members earn 32% more than their non-unionised colleagues from similar ethnic backgrounds.

10 Trade unions support each other.

Unions are involved in negotiating the best possible working conditions for their members and for workers in general. Sometimes trade unions will work together to negotiate with management on behalf of a whole category of workers within an organisation. This is known as collective bargaining. This gives a great deal of power to the union. Unions typically prefer to solve disputes by negotiation. However, when all else fails the action taken is known as industrial action and includes:

* a strike involving all members

* selective strike action

* action short of strike action such as just working to the rules of the job

* refusing to work overtime or unsociable hours.

Trade unions are not just concerned with resolving conflict and disputes, they also help to provide lots of benefits for members such as educational courses, pension and insurance schemes, and many other benefits.

Employment protection

The **Employment Act of 2002** set out a number of rights of employees in the workplace to modify previous Employment Acts. Employees are entitled to receive a written statement of the main terms in their contract of employment within two months of starting work.

The terms which must be included are:

* The names of the employer and employee

* The date employment began

* Pay, hours, overtime, holiday and sick pay entitlements

* Pension terms

* Workplace and mobility clauses (circumstances in which workers may be required to change their location and / or do different work)

* Job title and description of duties

* Notice entitlement for both parties

* Disciplinary and grievance procedures.

Employees are also entitled to an itemised pay slip setting out deductions, and are also entitled to the minimum wage.

* Conditions for handling the dismissal and discipline of workers must be set out in every contract of employment, and there is a clear code as to how such matters should be handled.

* Rules are set out for handling employee grievances.

* Maternity leave has been improved. Fathers are also entitled to a period of parental leave.

* There is a statutory period of leave allowed for employees who adopt a child.

* Flexible working conditions apply to parents with a child under the age of 6 or a disabled child under 18 and who have been continuously working for over 6 months. They can apply for flexible working conditions to help with child care arrangements.

Health and safety

Employers are required by law to provide a safe and healthy working environment for their employees. In addition employees are required to work in a safe and responsible manner. Employers are required to provide appropriate health and safety training and information to employees. The Management of Health and Safety at Work Regulations require the employer to do a risk assessment to identify the best way to make premises safe. There needs to be a written health and safety policy setting out the systems and procedures that have to be in place for ensuring the health and safety of employees, visitors and customers of a business.

The BusinessLink and Health and Safety Executive (HSE) websites will help you to carry out a health and safety risk assessment in a workplace and to draw up a health and safety policy. Search for them at www.heinemann.co.uk/hotlinks (express code 1149P, then go to Unit 1).

UNIT ASSESSMENT

INVESTIGATING PEOPLE AT WORK

Specimen paper

Answer all the questions

To find a boyfriend/ bet on the next Rooney hat-trick/ play games with friends elsewhere in the country, press the red button on your remote now. The rise of interactive TV means that people increasingly have the option of dating, gambling and gaming without leaving the couch.

YooMedia, which owns Dateline and a string of other services in these areas, is expert at expanding them as offerings on interactive TV platforms such as Sky. It has also positioned itself to win government contracts to put health advice on interactive television if the technology really catches on. However, YooMedia might well find that people don't take to interactive TV as fast as it hopes, or that, if they do, competition will suddenly flare up.

You can buy shares on the Stock Exchange in YooMedia. Many of its services are profitable so it seems like a good stock to buy for investors interested in high-tech shares.

1 Describe one business objective that YooMedia might have. Describe another business objective of a business that you have studied during your course. (4 marks)

2 Explain why a particular stakeholder grouping would support the objective you identified for YooMedia. Contrast this with why another stakeholder grouping might support the objective you identified for an organisation you have studied. (4 marks)

3 Who are the owners of YooMedia? (1 mark)

4 What benefits is YooMedia likely to have from being a public company? (5 marks)

5 How would a company like YooMedia raise money for expansion? Compare these methods with those of another organisation that you have studied as part of your business course. (10 marks)

6 How does YooMedia stand to benefit from its public sector contracts? (3 marks)

7 Why would it be important for YooMedia to have a strong marketing function? (3 marks)

Total for this section: 30 marks

YooMedia is looking to recruit a new junior sales manager with responsibility for winning international custom. The sales manager will be responsible for a small sales team of 10 staff operating initially in European Union member countries. The sales manager will need to have had previous selling experience in an international field. This is a new post.

8 What sort of details would you expect to find in the job description for the new sales manager? (4 marks)

9 How do these details differ from those included in a job description for a business organisation that you studied as part of your course? (4 marks)

10 What purposes might the job description be used for in the organisation that you studied as part of your course? (4 marks)

11 Why might YooMedia also create a person specification for the post? (4 marks)

12 Explain one piece of legislation designed to prevent discrimination that would be taken account of by Human Resource managers when designing a job advertisement. (5 marks)

13 How might psychometric testing be helpful in the selection process for the sales manager at YooMedia? What sorts of characteristics might the psychometric testing be looking for? (6 marks)

14 Why might YooMedia choose to train the sales person externally rather than in-house? (4 marks)

15 Explain how either coaching or training has benefited a specific individual or group of employees in an organisation you studied as part of your course. (4 marks)

Total for this section: 35 marks

YooMedia is a new and exciting company to work for. The management team is determined to attract and retain high quality employees with appropriate skills such as good IT skills, the ability to communicate well with others and to operate in team situations.

16 Describe one possible payment method that the company might use to encourage sales staff to work hard. Contrast this method with payment schemes that you have come across in organisations that you studied during the course. (6 marks)

17 Explain one non-financial incentive that you are familiar with from studying another business and which YooMedia might offer its employees. Explain how this would work. (5 marks)

18 Senior managers believe that it is important to motivate staff at YooMedia.
   i   What is meant by motivation? (2 marks)
   ii Use the work of one important motivational theorist to explain how managers might be able to achieve high levels of motivation at work. Illustrate your answer by reference to an organisation you studied during the course. (7 marks)

Total for this section: 20 marks

Employees are affected not only by internal issues such as the conditions of work and levels of motivation, but also by external issues.

19 What initiatives might managers take to make sure that employees are aware of the importance of reducing waste? Illustrate your answer by reference to an organisation that you have studied. (5 marks)

20 How might managers seek to motivate employees to give a high priority to reducing waste? (5 marks)

21 Identify one pressure group and explain how its actions might affect YooMedia. (5 marks)

22 Why might employees working for YooMedia seek to join a trade union? (5 marks)

23 Describe one piece of consumer protection legislation that will limit the actions of YooMedia. (5 marks)

Total for this section: 25 marks

Total for paper: 110 marks.

The following marking scheme provides you with examples of how you can develop your answers to score high marks. However, there are many other ways of answering questions that will help you to meet the criteria. Please note that while you can score marks for describing and identifying points, higher marks are achieved for relating your answers to the context of the case study, and for using higher order skills such as analysis and evaluation. The mark shown for each question is the maximum that can be achieved.

1   For describing a business objective of YooMedia you can score up to 2 marks. One for naming the objective, the second for further description. E.g. An objective of YooMedia might be to make a profit (1 mark) e.g. by seeking to sell services such as Dateline by achieving revenues in excess of costs (1 mark). (Other objectives might include to be the market leader, to increase sales, to develop an international presence etc.) Naming a business objective of a business where you did your work experience will enable you to score 1 mark (e.g. to increase sales, to build up a brand image etc). You score a further mark for describing this objective in greater detail.

2   Here you score 1 mark for naming a stakeholder group (e.g. shareholders, employees, customers, etc). You score a second mark for explaining why it would support the objective you identified in question 1. E.g. shareholders would support the objective of making a profit because this enables them to benefit from increased dividends. You can then score a further 2 marks for naming another stakeholder group that would support the business objective that you identified for the company that you did work experience in (1 mark) and for showing that this is a different motive from the one you identified for the stakeholder grouping for YooMedia (1 mark).

3   1 mark for listing this as the shareholders.

4   Here you will score up to 3 marks for identifying and explaining a benefit. E.g., as a public limited company YooMedia will be able to raise more capital (1 mark) by selling shares that are traded on the Stock Market (1 mark) enabling it to put more capital into advertising, marketing, and other aspects of expansion (1 mark). You can score up to 3 marks for developing other benefits such as having limited liability, developing a wider market presence, being able to employ specialist managers and directors, etc.

5   Here you can score up to 6 marks for identifying sources of capital that would be appropriate for YooMedia. (If you simply make a list of sources of capital without relating them to YooMedia the most you will be able to score is 3 marks). E.g. YooMedia could sell shares in their company (1 mark) giving them access to a pool of capital to develop the YooMedia brand. (1 mark) they could take out a loan from a bank (1 mark) enabling it to use these funds to buy capital equipment with interest being paid back on the loan (1 mark), etc. You can score up to 4 other marks for showing how a business where you did work experience raised money for expansion. If you simply list these you can score up to 2 marks only. However, if you compare these with YooMedia's sources of capital, and explain how these sources of capital relate specifically to your organisation you can score all 4 marks.

6   Here you can score 1 mark for explaining what a public sector contract is, namely a contract from a government owned or funded organisation. You can then score up to 2 marks for developing a reason why YooMedia can benefit from these contracts. E.g. you can show that the government is a widespread user of information channels (1 mark) so that government contracts are worth a lot of money through repeat and new contracts (1 mark).

7   You will score 1 mark for describing the benefits of having a good marketing function e.g. marketing helps a company to find out what customers want and need and then to provide them with it. You will score a further 2 marks for explaining the importance of marketing in the context of YooMedia e.g. it is important to find out what users of Dateline and other services are looking for (1 mark), in order to create the right sorts of facilities for them to access at the right times and in the right places (1 mark).

8   Up to 2 marks for each appropriate point that would appear on a job description e.g. who they are responsible to, who and what they are responsible for, etc. An additional 2 marks for aspects of a description that relate to the job of a sales manager for YooMedia e.g. description of where YooMedia salesperson would be working from and what countries they would be responsible for, and description of how their work would fit into YooMedia's sales operation (2 marks).

9   In answering this question you will get up to 2 marks for each developed explanation of how details of the job description for a sales manager differed from those in an organisation that you studied as part of your course. E.g. the description of a sales manager might include an outline of the materials and resources that they would be responsible for, whereas a job description that you might have studied for an assembly line worker might have included much less responsibility.

10 Up to 2 marks for describing appropriate purposes in the context of an organisation that you worked for. E.g. the description of a supervisor at Marks & Spencer was used as part of the recruitment process being sent out to job applicants (1 mark) so they knew what the job entailed (1 mark). Or the supervisor was able to use the job description when they had a dispute with managers (1 mark) about what their responsibilities involved (1 mark).

11 Here you can score up to 4 marks for explaining reasons why YooMedia might additionally create a person spec as well as a job description. You score 1 mark for answering in the context of YooMedia, 1 mark for explaining in the context of the salesperson's job. You could then score additional marks for showing that e.g. the person specification is more useful in job interviewing than the job description, by setting out essential and desired qualities (1 mark) which can be checked off by YooMedia interviewers to get the best person for the post (1 mark).

12 To answer this question you need to choose an appropriate piece of legislation e.g. Race, Sex, or Disability Discrimination Acts. You score 1 mark for naming the Act. You can score up to 2 marks for each developed point relating to how HR managers would take account of the Act when designing a job advertisement. E.g. the Sex Discrimination Act sets out that job advertisements must not indicate or imply (1 mark) that members of a particular gender group (1 mark) will be unfairly disadvantaged or treated less favourably (1 mark) as a result of the way a job is described or offered in a media advertisement (1 mark).

13 You can score 1 mark for explaining what a psychometric test is, i.e. a test to identify personality traits of an individual that are relevant to an organisation like YooMedia. You can score up to 3 marks for developing an argument as to why YooMedia would want to use psychometric testing, e.g. a psychometric test will enable Yoomedia to recruit and select with greater accuracy (1 mark) individuals who have appropriate personality characteristics for working in a dynamic enterprise (1 mark) and help to weed out unsuitable candidates (1 mark) You can score up to 2 marks for identifying personality characteristics that would be appropriate for YooMedia e.g. the ability to work in a team, the ability to think outside the box etc.

14 Here you can score 1 mark for explaining the difference between training on-the-job or in some other inhouse approach at YooMedia, and through external off-the-job training with an external agency. You can then score up to 2 points for each benefit to YooMedia that would encourage them to train externally, e.g. it enables the individual to draw on a wider range of skill/knowledge than available within YooMedia (1 mark), and that external training gives the individual a break from their work which acts as a motivating incentive, (1 mark) etc.

15 Here you can score up to 2 marks for describing the benefits of either coaching or training within the context of your work organisation e.g. training enabled individuals to learn new skills (1 mark) which enabled them to take on more responsibility (1 mark). You can score up to a further 2 marks for evaluating the benefits, e.g. the training and coaching acted as a motivational tool (1 mark) and was seen as a way in which they could develop their careers (1 mark).

16 You can score up to 3 marks for describing a payment method that YooMedia could use to encourage sales staff to work hard. You can only score 1 mark for describing a payment method. You can score 3 marks for doing so in the context of YooMedia. E.g. YooMedia could offer sales staff a bonus based on the sale of a new service to a new client. (1 mark). The bonus would act as an incentive to encourage staff to go out and sell (1 mark), it would also be a means of rewarding the most effective staff (1 mark). You can score up to 3 marks for contrasting this with another organisation that you've studied. E.g. you could show that another organisation uses a reward system linked to appraisal (1 mark). This approach may be seen as more effective because targets are agreed between the salesperson and the sales manager (1 mark) so that sales targets can be set which are seen as being reachable and appropriate (1 mark).

17 You can score up to 2 marks for describing a non-financial incentive in the context of an organisation you have studied. E.g. you may show that a well known retailing organisation rewards loyal employees by offering them the opportunity to be promoted to supervisors' positions (1 mark) where they would be given more responsibility within the organisation (1 mark). You can then score up to an additional 3 marks for evaluating the merits of such an approach in showing how it would work. E.g. promotion to a supervisor's position gives an individual something to strive for (1 mark) that would give them more personal fulfilment (1 mark) enabling them to achieve some of the higher levels of personal satisfaction that Maslow and Herzberg alluded to (1 mark).

18 i Here you can score up to 2 marks for providing an appropriate definition of motivation and expanding on it. E.g. you might argue that motivation is something that comes from inside the individual (1 mark) and is based on a desire and willingness to achieve given goals at work and elsewhere (1 mark).

ii Here you need to identify one motivational theorist e.g. Herzberg, Maslow or McGregor (1 mark). You can score a further 2 marks for describing key features of their work accurately. (2 marks) However, to score an additional 4 marks you will need to show how these theories can be applied to a specific organisation in order to create a high performance workplace. Each developed point will be worth 2 marks.

19 You can score up to 2 marks for listing initiatives that managers might employ for minimising waste, e.g. by publicising the costs of wastes through company communications on noticeboards (1 mark), and by developing work practices that seek to eliminate waste (1 mark). To score an additional 2 marks you will have to relate these initiatives to an organisation that you studied on your course.

20 You can score up to 3 marks for each well-developed argument as to how managers can motivate employees to reduce waste. Each answer must combine the concept of motivation with that of waste reduction. E.g. managers might develop training courses about waste management which identify the benefits to the individual, and the company (1 mark) this would enable employees to appreciate that waste reduction at work will lead to greater company profits and hence wages (1 mark), a more prosperous and efficient business would be able to offer a more securing working future for individual employees.

21 Here you can score 1 mark for identifying a pressure group and then up to 2 marks for developing arguments which show how the actions of this group may impact on YooMedia. E.g. you might show that a children's charity like Childline may be worried about the activities of companies like YooMedia. They may be worried that children may be exposed to dangers resulting from access to the Internet and exploitation by unscrupulous adults. Childline may then put pressure on the government (1 mark) to pass legislation that limits the activities of YooMedia in terms of who they can offer their services to. (1 mark) Childline could also alert the media to some of YooMedia's activities (1 mark) leading to adverse publicity for the company (1 mark).

22 You can score 1 mark for explaining what a trade union is – ie an association of employees who by joining together in a union are able to put pressure for their collective and individual interests to be looked after. You can then score a further four marks for identifying individual benefits of a trade union. E.g. It puts pressure on employers to provide better wages (1 mark) and improved working conditions (1 mark). The union will represent individual members in disputes (1 mark). A union also provides benefits such as subsidised health care, insurance, and discounts on shopping with various companies (1 mark)

23 You can score 1 mark for identifying a piece of consumer legislation. (e.g. Trade Descriptions Act), up to 2 marks for describing the limitations of this Act, and a further 2 marks for describing the limitations in the context of YooMedia.

UNIT 2

Investigating business

This unit contains four parts:

2.1 Business planning

2.2 Managing business activities

2.3 Financial management in business

2.4 The use of software to aid decision-making

Introduction

In this unit, you will find out about how businesses are planned and managed. An important part of this process is the management of people and other resources. Managers need to develop systems which enable them to control the business and its activities. Managers will need to check the performance of the business in meeting objectives. By regularly checking business performance, managers are able to take appropriate steps to keep the business on track. You will find out about the importance of financial management in obtaining the right sorts of short-, medium- and long-term finance for the business as well as how to check the solvency and profitability of the organisation.

As part of your learning, you will obtain, use and assess information drawn from businesses.

What you will learn in this unit

* Why businesses plan and the importance of planning
* Important steps in setting up a business
* Planning to acquire resources and to monitor performance

FIGURE 2.1 *Richard Branson's Virgin PLC is well known for detailed planning and for efficiently bringing together a range of suitable resources to deliver good business results. Virgin uses modern ICT and e-commerce applications.*

* The relationship between planning and business objectives
* Key elements in business planning such as marketing, finance and production
* The types of resources used in business
* The importance of quality control, quality assurance and total quality management
* The importance of monitoring and reviewing business performance
* The need to manage and measure financial performance
* Ways of measuring the 'financial health' of a business
* Key financial statements (balance sheet and profit and loss account), cash flow forecasts, budgets, and break-even analysis
* The use of software to aid decision-making
* The use of spreadsheets, word processing and database software
* Specialist software and the use of the Internet
* The importance of e-commerce
* The main legal and corporate issues associated with using ICT in a business environment.

2.1 Business planning

Central to the work of any business – large or small, existing or newly set up, in the public or private sector – is planning. Without planning there is no way to judge if the business is likely to achieve its objectives. In this chapter we are concerned with how and why businesses plan.

There are a number of key reasons why organisations produce a business plan:

1 To provide a clear sense of direction for owners and managers so they know where they are going

2 To provide a means for managers and other interested parties to check on progress in meeting targets

3 To provide a means of controlling the business, i.e. keeping to plan

4 To help raise finance. Outside parties such as banks need to be able to see that an organisation is well planned if they are to have confidence in it (e.g. to provide loans).

The importance of enterprise and innovation to business

When people say 'enterprise' or 'individual initiative' they automatically think of a small business, usually a service or creative business. Big companies, particularly those engaged in manufacturing, are just 'there' – no-one quite knows how.

The fact is that with very few exceptions, every big company began as a small company, often with one enterprising individual at its head.

William Morris began by mending bicycles in a back street garage in Oxford, and built up a major motor manufacturing company.

William Lever started work in the family shop when he was sixteen, and then decided that he could make soap as well as anyone else. Result... Unilever is now one of the world's great companies.

> ## ✱ DID YOU KNOW?
>
> One of George Bush's famous 'foot in mouth' quotes is 'The problem with the French is that they don't have a word for entrepreneur' – of course, the word entrepreneur is a French one!

Surviving by the seat of your pants

FIGURE 2.2 *Jack Cohen (the founder of Tesco) did not believe in detailed planning*

Use www.heinemann.co.uk/hotlinks (express code 1149P, then go to Unit 2) to look at the websites of well-known organisations like Tesco, Oxfam and Nestlé.

You will find that the organisations have a clear set of objectives backed up by a well-formulated plan. This contrasts with the early days of some of the business pioneers in this country. For example, Sir Jack Cohen the founder of Tesco was notorious for keeping all of his plans in his head. He set up in business as a market trader and kept his accounts on the back of an envelope. It was only once the business became established and moved to the supermarket format that Cohen started to employ professional managers who created systems and plans which enabled the business to grow. There is no way that Tesco could have been successful if it had not moved towards professional planning.

1 Why do you think Jack Cohen's business was able to flourish despite the lack of a documented business plan?
2 Why wouldn't such a business last long in the modern world?

More recently, Anita Roddick started up The Body Shop from a small shop in Brighton and went on to pioneer one of the great 'alternative businesses' of the modern age.

Patak's, the leading supplier of authentic Indian foodstuffs worldwide, was set up by L.G. Patak on his arrival from Kenya in this country. He started out by selling samosas from home to raise sufficient capital to buy his first small shop in north London. The business expanded with the introduction of other products, including pickles and chutneys, as orders from small shops, housewives and students flooded in and Patak's fame spread.

Small may be beautiful, but in business the great thing about being small is that one day you may become big, as illustrated by Patak's and The Body Shop.

Enterprise does not stop once a business starts. No business can begin without enterprise but no matter how big it becomes, no business can continue without enterprise. Nor, for that matter, can any other kind of human activity, commercial or charitable.

Being enterprising involves the following characteristics:

* Coming up with original ideas (e.g. Anita Roddick's natural products)
* Willingness to take a risk (e.g. Jack Cohen investing most of his money in buying stocks to resell on his market store)
* Being energetic and willing to work hard (e.g. L.G. Patak who worked long hours to build his business).

All of the above characteristics help to get a business off the ground. However, many small

FIGURE 2.3 *Anita Roddick – an enterprising business woman who started a great company from small beginnings*

businesses do not flourish because they have not planned effectively. For example, they:

* have failed to secure the finance required to ensure the development of the business

* have not carried out enough market research to find out what consumers want

* have not planned carefully when cash will come into the business to cover outgoings

* have failed to look at the legal requirements which are essential to setting up in business

* had other planning failures – can you think of some?

We use the term entrepreneur to describe someone who brings together the various resources required to run a business, and takes a risk in doing so. Patak, Roddick, Morris and Cohen were all entrepreneurs and in recent years have been joined by new names such as Martha Lane Fox and Brent Hoberman – the founders of LastMinute.Com which will provide you with a range of last minute services including tickets to a Norah Jones concert or a last minute holiday in the sun.

Innovation is another important aspect of setting up in business. Innovation is all about producing new solutions to problems. A good example of an innovative idea is Google, the Internet search engine that was recently developed by entrepreneurs Larry Page and Sergey Brin working from a garage. Google's major innovation was searching out web pages according to their popularity and interrelationship, not just according to key words. The results are therefore more likely to be what the customer wants. However, Google and LastMinute.Com would not have survived without careful business planning and detailed

organisation, enabling them to dominate their respective market places.

Another example of innovation is Dyson. James Dyson is an enterprising and energetic designer. One of his first innovations was the ball barrow as an improvement on the traditional

FIGURE 2.4 *The ballbarrow and the dual cyclone are winning innovations*

Learning activity

Carry out some research into local examples of enterprise. Methods of doing the research include: studying the local paper to find examples of new businesses that have recently set up with an interesting or innovative idea, or talking to friends and relatives to see if they can suggest an example of a local person or group that has come up with an enterprising idea. For example, at the University where the authors work a researcher came up with the original idea of putting flavourings into crisps.

If you can identify a local exciting entrepreneur, then why not arrange to interview them to find out how they first developed their idea and what were the biggest hurdles they had to overcome to turn their good idea into a working business.

✳ DID YOU KNOW?

In 2003, 300,000 people set up their own businesses in this country. This figure exactly accounted for the growth of employment in that year indicating that self-employment is a key factor in our economy.

wheelbarrow. Later he hit upon the idea of creating a dual cyclone vacuum cleaner. The idea came to him when he was visiting a factory and saw an industrial cyclone in operation. He realised that if he could reduce the scale of the cyclone it would provide a brilliant way of vacuuming up dirt and other materials in the home. He tried hundreds of prototypes before perfecting the Dyson Dual Cyclone. Today everyone is familiar with the product which comes in a range of attractive designs.

The legal implications of starting in business

There are a number of legal implications involved in planning to set up in business:

1 Choosing a business name

A business that is a private company must have Ltd after its name. If it is a public company, like Marks & Spencer, it must be followed by PLC. The registrar of companies will not register a business name if it is already registered. A business name will not be registered if it is offensive or implies the provision of sexual services.

2 Setting up a business

A sole trader can simply set up by choosing an appropriate name and registering for VAT if the annual turnover exceeds a set limit. Partnerships are typically set up by registering a Deed of Partnership with a solicitor. Setting up a company is more regulated.

A private limited company must:

* have at least two members, one of whom must be a director
* have at least £1 worth of capital
* obtain a certificate of incorporation before starting trading
* produce a set of audited accounts within 10 months of the end of its financial year.

A public limited company must:

* obtain a certificate of incorporation and a certificate to trade before starting trading

* have a minimum starting capital of £50,000
* produce a set of audited accounts within seven months of the end of its financial year
* register a memorandum of association stating that it is a PLC
* have at least two directors and two members
* have a qualified company secretary.

Companies must be registered by law. Registration involves filing two documents.

The Memorandum of Association outlines:

* The name of the company
* The address of the registered office of the company
* The amount of the liability of the members
* The authorised capital
* The company objectives.

The Articles of Association concern the internal administration of the company and cover:

* Rules about meetings
* Voting rights of shareholders.

The Articles also include a list of directors and information on other internal matters. A shareholder might want to examine the Articles to find out how their company is run.

A company must have a Board of Directors. These directors may be fee-paid trustees who represent the shareholders, or senior executives who work full-time for the company. There must be at least one executive in a company but usually there are several, e.g. a company accountant, a marketing executive etc.

Companies are not required by law to have a chairperson but most do because they need someone to run the annual meeting. The managing director is the senior executive director of a company.

Directors owe a duty of care to the company not to act negligently when managing its affairs. Directors are typically experts in a particular field such as accountancy or law, and so a high standard of care is expected of them.

Other legal implications of setting up in business are that the business will need to:

* Abide by health and safety legislation.

* Comply with equal opportunities legislation. For example, it must give equal pay to work of equal value. It must also comply with legislation preventing discrimination.

* Abide by employment legislation related to hours worked, payment of the minimum wage, contracts of employment and dismissal and redundancy matters.

* Have appropriate insurances, e.g. employer's liability in case of accidents involving employees, public liability to protect against accidents involving customers and members of the general public on company premises, and product and other forms of liability insurance.

* Abide by consumer protection and competition legislation.

* Comply with other legal requirements.

Learning activity

Interview a senior business manager or owner of a small business. What are the main areas of legislation that they must keep on top of in running the day-to-day activities of the business?

* DID YOU KNOW?

In December 2004 the BT Group was found to have unlawfully misused confidential customer information to try to stop its customers leaving for competitors. The part of BT that runs telephone networks was warning BT retailing when customers intended to switch. This allowed BT Retail to try to 'save' the customer by offering them new deals. The case illustrates the way in which legal requirements seek to create a level playing field for businesses to compete (in this case, rivals of BT Retail were being unfairly disadvantaged).

Sources of advice and support for business

There are a number of sources of advice for people wishing to set up in business. Some of these are government sources, while others are private sources.

Government sources

Currently the government's Department of Trade and Industry provides a range of support for business through grants, loan guarantees and subsidised consultancy.

Grants are sums of money provided by the government for specific activities, e.g. for research purposes.

Loan guarantees are where the government will guarantee to pay back certain loans that a business might take out.

Subsidised consultancy is where the government provides part of the sum of money a business has to pay out for advice from third parties.

Typical areas of government support include:

* Succeeding through innovation: providing practical support for the key stages of innovation or research and development into new products

* Achieving best practice: helping businesses to become more efficient, competitive and profitable

* Regional investment: encouraging investment in specific areas of the country to promote economic regeneration.

The Small Business Council advises the government on small business issues. It is made up of 24 members, 22 of whom are small business owners.

Unemployed people can find out about setting up a small business from their local Jobcentre. Young people can get further help with starting a business under the New Deal. Parts of the UK have been designated as 'Employment Zones' and in these areas people can get advice on getting a business off the ground from the Department of Work and Pensions.

The government has created a new fund to encourage entrepreneurship in disadvantaged communities and groups.

The Ethnic Minority Business Forum advises the government on the needs of ethnic minority businesses.

New businesses (particularly those using new technology) can get help with premises and management from the UK Business Incubation Centre or from one of the 50 UK Science parks.

There are regional schemes to help small businesses, supported by the European Structural Funds. They are normally administered by government offices and delivered through organisations such as local Business Links (and their equivalents).

Private sources

There are also many private sources of aid for business. Most banks have arrangements to help customers in new and small businesses. You can also get business advice from professional accountants, solicitors and independent advisors.

Young people wanting to set up a business can find advice and guidance from the Prince's Trust and 'Livewire' sponsored by Shell UK Ltd.

To find out more, search for these useful websites at www.heinemann.co.uk/hotlinks (express code 1149P, then go to Unit 2):

* The Federation of Small Businesses
* Young Enterprise UK
* Business Link – practical help and advice for business
* Young entrepreneur site
* Scottish Enterprise
* The Prince's Trust
* Shell LiveWire

FIGURE 2.5 *Livewire helps young people setting up in business*

Learning activity

Produce a short brochure using a desktop publishing package. Research the work of an organisation that supports young people in setting up a new enterprise of their own. The brochure should outline the work of this organisation and give a case study of a young person who has been able to benefit from the support of this organisation.

The importance of planning

If a business is to acquire the resources that it needs to carry out ongoing activities then it will need to show clear evidence of good planning. Having created plans, the business is then able to monitor how well it is doing and identify any corrections that need to be made.

When you create a business plan, you need to be able to show that:

* You have a clear sense of where you are going. We call this direction – hence the term 'directors of a company'. A short mission statement will set out the purpose of the organisation.

* You have clear targets and objectives to work towards

* You have created structured plans to enable you to get where you want to go

* In business the concept of focus is an important one. A plan should not be vague it should be focused. Managers need to

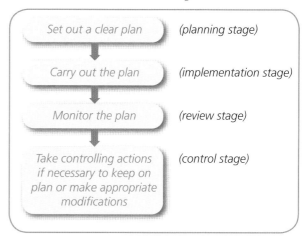

FIGURE 2.6 *Creating and using a business plan*

understand the plan and communicate it in a focused way

* A master plan can be broken down into a number of sub-plans. These plans should all be carefully integrated and well focused.

A business plan is very important in helping the organisation to gain resources because:

* Providers of capital, e.g. shareholders, have more confidence in a well-planned business

* Banks and other providers of finance will often want to examine plans to make sure that they are well structured and based on accurate calculations

* By having a well-organised plan it is also possible to monitor performance. For example, one part of a business plan will be budgets. Budgets are plans for the future that are set out in numbers.

FIGURE 2.7 *The Chief Executive and the bank manager both appreciate a business plan*

Learning activity

Working in a small group, identify a good idea for a business.

Establish an appropriate mission for the organisation and a set of objectives. Then identify six areas of the business that it would be appropriate to create plans for (you do not need to produce these plans at this stage).

For example, Superior Holidays might budget to make the following sales over the next twelve months. The budgeted costs of making the sales, e.g. supplying catalogues, answering phone calls, etc. are shown (see Figure 2.8).

However, in the real world events don't always turn out as planned. For example, sales may be less than expected in the first three months of the year. Costs may be higher than expected, for example:

	Jan	Feb	Mar
Sales (000s)	18	20	23
Cost of sales (000s)	17	21	21

FIGURE 2.9 *Superior Holidays actual sales and costs*

By examining the plan, managers are able to take actions to try and improve performance. For example, to improve sales they can increase advertising activities or lower prices. To reduce costs they may lay off staff or produce fewer brochures.

Planning therefore supports a cycle of monitoring and improvement, as shown in Figure 2.11.

The process of monitoring can be applied to any form of plan. For example, an action plan is a very useful method of planning. It sets out actions that need to be taken, by who, and by what time (see Figure 2.10).

BUDGET: SALES AND COSTS OF MAKING SALES FOR SUPERIOR HOLIDAYS

	Jan	Feb	Mar	Apr	May	Jun	Jul	Aug	Sep	Oct	Nov	Dec
Sales (000s)	20	25	25	30	35	40	40	45	40	35	30	55
Cost of sales (000s)	15	20	20	25	30	30	30	40	30	30	25	45

FIGURE 2.8 *Superior Holidays sales and costs budget*

ADVERTISING ACTION PLAN FOR SUPERIOR HOLIDAYS

ACTION POINT	WHO RESPONSIBLE	DATE OF COMPLETION
Decide on budget	John Christopher	1st March
Discuss creative brief with client	Rupinder Kaur, Meenum Mandal	15th March
Create designs	Meenum Mandal, John Francis	30th March
Show designs to client	John Francis, Rupinder Kaur	1st April
Client to provide feedback	Client to liaise with Rupinder Kaur	10th April
Create final designs	Meenum Mandal	21st April

FIGURE 2.10 *An advertising action plan for Superior Holidays*

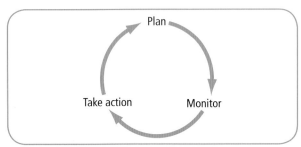

FIGURE 2.11 *The process of monitoring*

Business objectives and planning

A business plan should be seen as the means by which a business achieves its objectives.

For example, supposing that a business has established the following objectives for next year:

1 To increase its share of the market from 10% to 15%

2 To improve staff IT skills

3 To increase profit margins from 20% to 25%.

A well-organised plan can be developed to achieve these targets. The plan should:

* provide a clear strategy, setting out the steps that need to be taken

* the strategy should be easy to communicate by means of the plan

* the achievement of the plan should be able to be checked by an ongoing monitoring process

* a master plan should be able to be broken down into sub-plans for various functions and operating units within the organisation.

We can show how the overall plan can be broken down into relevant components. For example, a marketing plan should set out how the marketing objective will be met, e.g. through advertising and promotional activities. The IT skills objective can be achieved through a human resources and training plan setting out how and when training activities will be carried out to make sure that all staff are given the required training opportunities.

Budgets can be set out planning how the profit objective will be achieved, e.g. by setting out budgeted sales and costs.

Key elements in business planning

A well-constructed business plan will help a business owner:

* to manage and control a business well

* obtain finance (e.g. from a bank)

* make accurate forecasts of future cash flows and profits.

Cash flow forecasts set out the timing of cash flows into a business and cash payments made by the business. It is essential that the business has enough cash flowing into the business to meet pressing needs for cash e.g. to pay bills, wages, etc.

Profit forecasts set out how much profit the business expects to make and when. It is essential that a business makes a profit to cover the risk of running that business. The business that only just covers its costs is taking too big a risk.

The means (business plans) ⟶ The ends (objectives)

FIGURE 2.12 *Business plans and objectives*

The contents of the business plan

A business plan (for a small business) should be clearly set out under the following headings:

1 Contents page	A contents page is useful in any kind of report that is more than two or three pages long.
2 The owner	This section should give some information about the owner (or owners), including their educational background, what jobs they have done, and their interests. This section should include the names and addresses of two referees – people of some status who will vouch for the character of the business owner.
3 The business	This should set out the name and address of the business. There should then be a detailed description of the product or service being offered, how and where it will be sold, who is likely to buy it, and in what quantities.
4 Business aims and objectives	It is important to set out aims and objectives so that those reading the plan can see how well focused the business is.
5 A SWOT analysis	A brief analysis setting out the internal strengths and weaknesses of the business and the external opportunities and threats. This section should show how the business is seeking to build on its strength, minimize weaknesses, take advantages of opportunities and reduce the threats.
6 The market	This section will describe the market research that has been carried out and what it has revealed. It should give details of prospective customers – how many there are, how much they are prepared to buy, and what price they are willing to pay. It should also give details of the competition. It is useful to draw a few charts showing details such as the total size of the market and the expected market share of the new business.
7 Advertising and promotion	This section should give information about how the business will be publicised to potential customers. It should also give details of likely advertising costs.
8 Premises and equipment	This section should show that the owners have considered a range of locations before choosing the best site. It should also give details of planning regulations (if appropriate). Costs of premises and the equipment needed should also be set out.
9 Business organisation	This should state whether the enterprise will take the form of sole trader, partnership, private or public company.
10 Costings	A guide to the cost of producing the product or service should be set out and the prices that will be charged to cover these costs. A calculation of gross profit can be calculated by taking away the cost of sales from sales revenue.
11 Profit forecasts	Profit forecasts should be set out for the first year in detail, as well as expected profits for the first five years.
12 Cash flow forecasts	This should set out the expected incoming and outgoings over the first year. These will be approximate figures.
13 The finance	This should set out details of how the finance for the business is going to be raised. How much will come from savings? How much needs to be borrowed?
14 Expansion	This final section gives an indication of future plans. Does the business want to keep on producing a steady output or is a dramatic expansion possible? Will the business increase its product range? What kind of competition is likely to emerge and how will the business deal with it?

Key elements of the business plan are the marketing, finance, and production plans.

The marketing plan should set out:

* Marketing objectives related to such aspects as market share, awareness of brands and products by consumers, growth of the market etc.

* The marketing environment, e.g. plans to compete against rivals, plans to manage changing social trends and so on.

* Market research – to find out what customers want and need and then to develop plans to give them what they want.

* The marketing mix, i.e. the mix of product, price, promotions, and place (i.e. distribution channels).

For example, a young entrepreneur offering a web design service to local businesses may have the objective of becoming the web designer of choice for at least 50% of the main local business areas in a town. A further marketing objective might be to increase the size of the total market by 10% a year. The plan would set out who the main rivals are and their key selling points. The plan would show how the web design business would offer a better product and service than the competition. The marketing mix would examine aspects of:

* details of the product/service

* prices charged

* how the business would be advertised and promoted

* where the business's activities would be bought and sold, e.g. by working directly at clients' premises.

The financial plan would set out:

1 A forecasted profit and loss statement

2 Break-even calculation

3 Cash flow forecast.

The profit forecast shows expected profit after the running costs of the business are deducted from the value of sales.

The break-even is the point where income from sales covers all costs. It shows the number of items the business has to sell to cover costs. These items can be products or services e.g. sandwiches (products) or cinema film viewings (services).

The cash flow forecast sets out the sums of money the business expects to come in and go out of the bank account each month.

The production plan should be closely tied to the marketing and financial plans.

The production plan needs to be created so as to enable the organisation to satisfy customers. Marketing-oriented production involves making the types of goods that customers want, when they want them. Production methods are therefore designed with the consumer in mind. Production and marketing departments will work with financial budgets which will be regularly monitored. Efficient production techniques will enable the business to go well beyond the break-even point to produce profit forecasts which yield high returns to business owners.

MARKETING PLAN	FINANCIAL PLAN	PRODUCTION PLAN
Study the market environment	Set out profit forecasts	Decide what to produce
Carry out market research	Identify the break-even	Decide how to produce
Clarify your marketing objectives	Set out a cash flow forecast	Decide when to produce
Set out a marketing mix	Set out marketing and production budgets	

FIGURE 2.13 *Marketing, financial and production plans should be closely tied together*

2.2 Managing business activities

Having made plans, businesses must check
whether their actual performance is meeting their
planned performance. To do this, managers and
staff will monitor, review and control the activities
of their business.

FIGURE 2.14 *Managing business activities*

The role of the manager

There are a number of ways of looking at management, three of which are described below.

Management through people

Management has been described as 'getting things done by other people'. Although this sounds like the manager is avoiding responsibility, this misses the point about good management. A good manager is someone who motivates others and gives them clear guidelines to work to. For example, Anita Roddick – the founder of The Body Shop – is often quoted as someone with good management skills. She set up a business with a focus on natural ingredients, waste minimization and recycling in cosmetics. She was then able to inspire lots of independent business owners who worked on a franchise system to work hard for the brand.

Arsene Wenger, the Arsenal manager, is another example of someone who 'gets things done by others'. He provides inspiration and the systems for his team to work to.

Management – what managers do

Another way of examining management is in terms of what managers do. For example the mnemonic 'POSDCORB' is often used to describe what managers do:

P   Planning – creating paper-based and other plans with objectives, actions and measurements for checking that the business is on target

O   Organising – creating systems and deciding who does what in an organisation and how plans will be put into practice

S   Staffing – placing the right people in the right posts at the right time

D   Decision-making – deciding what will be done and communicating these decisions clearly

C   Co-ordinating – co-ordination involves
O   bringing together in the right sequence and
R   at the right time the appropriate resources and parts of the plan. Co-ordination lies at the heart of successful management.

B   Budgeting – making plans which involve the use of numbers (often financial plans) and then controlling the budget to keep it to plan.

Management of resources

Another way of looking at management is in terms of the resources that need to be managed, which include:

* People

* Finance

* Time

* Physical resources, e.g. plant, machinery, and materials

* Information.

In her famous book *Managers and their jobs*, Rosemary Stewart identified the following work that is carried out by managers. It was based on studying managers at work. Managers typically:

FIGURE 2.16 *Wenger and Roddick are good at getting things done by others – are you?*

Study the work of a manager e.g. within your school/college or at work.

1 To what extent does the manager 'get things done through other people'?

2 Analyse the work of the manager in terms of POSDCORB.

3. What are the key resources that the manager manages?

* Work long hours. The number of hours worked increases with seniority and with more general rather than specific functional responsibilities.

* Are highly interactive. A typical day contains several hundred brief interactions. Working on one item for more than half an hour is very rare. As rank increases, the number of interactions increases, but the fragmented nature of the job remains.

* Have to cope with highly variable tasks. Managers have to cope equally well with paperwork, meetings, telephone calls, visits, ceremonial functions etc.

* Communicate mostly by word of mouth. About three-quarters of communication is verbal. Many managers actually prefer verbal data such as hearsay, gossip or general feelings. Such data are immediate, accessible and can be acted upon before it is too late and gossip becomes fact. Information by post or written reports comes very much in second place in informing the manager what is going on (note that Stewart's work was carried out before the age of e-mail).

* Use lots of contact points to gather information. Managers continually exchange verbal information with others. Most of this occurs within the organisation although as rank increases the number of verbal information points outside the organisation also increases. Information is traded across all levels of the hierarchy, with superiors, peers and subordinates.

Types of resources used by businesses

We can now look at some of the main resources managed by managers – human resources, physical resources and financial resources.

Human resources

The prime concern of people management at work was at one time 'manpower planning'. This involved getting the right number of people in the right number of jobs at the right time.

In the early nineteenth century people were seen as a resource to be manipulated. Frederick Winslow Taylor developed an approach to managing people known as 'scientific management'. This involved trying to find the best way of getting people to work efficiently, e.g. by studying their movements at work to cut out waste.

The Ford Motor Company's approach characterised scientific management, where the production line ran like a giant machine. The workers had simply to keep up with the machine.

However, in the 1920s experiments were carried out in America which identified a 'human relations' approach to work. A team of experimenters at the Hawthorne Electrical Company, led by Elton Mayo, had been trying scientific approaches to improving work efficiency, for example, turning the lights up and down to find the best lighting to get the highest output. However, they found out that whatever they did to the lights work levels increased. They discovered that the workers were responding to

> **✱ DID YOU KNOW?**
>
> F.W. Taylor was known as 'speedy Taylor' because he set out to speed up the rate at which work was completed. He thought that he could create a science of work to find out the single best way that particular tasks could be carried out. Some companies today use a sort of scientific management approach in which they have studied all the processes involved in carrying out a particular operation to make it as simple and quick as possible. For example, it is argued that Quick Service Restaurants are based on a scientific management approach.

Learning activity

The following figures relate to a confectionery plant that employs two types of production line employees – skilled employees and unskilled employees.

The firm currently employs 10,000 employees – 8,000 of them are skilled and 2,000 are unskilled. The manpower planners have created an employment budget for the next four years.

YEAR	2005	2006	2007	2008
Required number of skilled employees	8,000	8,500	8,500	8,800
Required number of unskilled employees	2,000	2,200	2,400	2,200

The firm has calculated that each year it will lose the following numbers of employees:

Year	2005	2006	2007	2008
Skilled leaving the company	500	520	540	560
Unskilled leaving the company	600	650	650	700
Unskilled graduating into the skilled category	400	420	420	420

FIGURE 2.17 *Employment budget for a confectionery plant*

1 Using the figures given above calculate:

  * The number of new skilled employees that will need to be recruited externally in each year.
  * The number of unskilled employees that will need to be recruited externally each year.

2 An external consultant has suggested that the company spends more money on training its unskilled workforce. What do you think of this suggestion?

Whilst manpower planning is very important, it is the part of people management that is very mechanical (machine-like). What is more important in managing people at work is the human side of things – hence the term Human Resource Management (HRM).

1	Scientific Management	Early 19th century. Involved treating employees as part of the machine. Looked for the best way of maximising their output.
2	Human Relations	1920s onwards. Understanding that if you take an interest in your employees they will work harder for you.
3	Personnel management	Up to the 1990s. Approach which valued people and looked for ways of encouraging them to help an organisation to meet its objectives.
4	Human Resource Management	Modern approach in which managers seek to find out what motivates and drives employees. It involves identifying the needs and aspirations of employees so that employees can fulfil themselves in their work while at the same time working to help the organisation meet its objectives.

FIGURE 2.18 *The development of Human Resource Management (HRM)*

the interest shown in them by the researchers. They hit upon the idea that if workers were made to feel important and valued then their motivation would increase. Since that time the new human resource approach has dominated thinking.

Indeed, in the modern world Human Resource Management has gone one step further, as illustrated in Figure 2.18.

There are a number of ways in which managers can help to motivate people using an HRM approach, including:

1 Appraisal – regular performance reviews at which the employee is given the opportunity to discuss their hopes, aspirations and training needs and in which the appraiser can clarify the objectives of the organisation or a relevant part of that organisation. Appraisal makes it possible to review current performance and to establish future targets.

2 Job enrichment – identifying ways in which employees' work can be made more rewarding and interesting.

3 Job enlargement – giving employees a wider selection of responsibilities and activities to carry out.

4 Employee involvement (EI) – providing more opportunities for employees to become involved in decision making processes.

5 Linking pay and rewards to performance.

Management of physical resources

Physical resource management includes the management of premises, machinery and equipment, materials and other stocks.

While these activities are particularly important in manufacturing plants they are also relevant in services.

Learning activity

Which of the activities in Figure 2.19 do you see as fitting more closely with a scientific management or a human resource management approach?

FIGURE 2.19 *Scientific Management or Human Resource Management?*

FIGURE 2.20 *Managing business activities*

The manager of a fish-and-chip shop needs to make sure that the premises are in an appropriate location for customer parking. The premises must meet health and safety and fire regulations. The premises need to be kept clean and well decorated. The fish and potato frying equipment must be to industry standard and be regularly cleaned, with proper electrical testing. The potatoes and fish which are the basic ingredients must be bought regularly and waste handled in an appropriate way. The right sort of packaging material needs to be used (newspaper is no longer acceptable). It is essential to keep appropriate stocks to meet customer demand.

Managing a hairdressing business has very similar requirements. There must be ease of access to the premises, which must meet fire regulations and health and safety checks. Appliances such as hairdryers and dyeing equipment must meet industry standards. It is essential to regularly re-order new chemicals, shampoos etc.

What are the main similarities and the main differences in managing a fish-and-chip shop and a hairdressing salon?

The management of the production process can be broken down into the 'five Ps of production':

* product
* plant
* process
* programme
* people

1 The product

It is essential to provide a good or service that clearly meets the needs of consumers and that can be provided at the right place, at the right time and for the most attractive price.

2 The plant

The location, size, design, safety and layout of the plant are all important. Managers need to think carefully about how parts and materials are to be delivered and how finished goods will be transported away from the plant. The layout should make it easy to co-ordinate the various activities that will take place there. Time and costs involved in transferring goods, materials, information and people should be kept to a minimum.

Managers must also make sure that plant and equipment are properly maintained. A maintenance department may include electricians, plumbers and joiners, as well as many other skilled workers. The effectiveness of the maintenance department can be judged by the number of breakdowns and accidents at work. Safety is vitally important.

3 The process

Different organisations will have different sets of operations depending on the nature of the product they make, the type of plant and equipment employed and many other factors. Process management sets out to:

✱ Identify the key processes of business activity. If these are carried out properly it will be possible to maximise customer satisfaction thus leading to better financial performance.

✱ Develop a detailed understanding of how processes work.

✱ Identify who in the organisation is involved in these processes.

✱ Seek ongoing improvements in the management of these processes.

✱ Put in motion an ongoing cycle of continuous process improvement.

4 The programme

Programming is mainly concerned with timetabling the use of resources. To meet orders successfully, the organisation will need to plan and control activities carefully. Successful programming involves purchasing, stock control and quality control.

5 The people

The success of any production process will depend on the people involved. The quality of people depends on how much is invested in them and how motivated they are. Training and development are vital.

Stock control

In an ideal world, in which businesses know demand well in advance and suppliers always meet delivery dates, there would be little need for stocks. In practice, demand varies and suppliers are often late, so stocks act as a protection against unpredictable events.

Organisations hold stocks in a variety of forms:

✱ raw materials

✱ work-in-progress

✱ finished goods

✱ plant and machinery spares.

The aim of any stock control system is to provide stocks that cater for uncertainties but are at minimum levels thus making sure that costs are kept low without reducing service to customers.

CASE STUDY

Lean production

Lean production is a means of organising people and physical resources in a highly efficient way. It is an approach that has been used widely in Japan and is today used in a lot of British manufacturing plants such as the Jaguar plant near Birmingham.

Lean thinking involves identifying exactly what your customers want and then providing them with it in the most efficient way. The objective is not just to reduce costs but also to simplify processes. Lean thinking focuses on what the customer needs at a specific price at a specific time.

In order to create value, the next step is to identify the value stream or to set out all the actions required to bring a particular product from concept to completion. By doing this many types of 'muda' (waste) will be identified.

By cutting out 'muda' you can concentrate simply on those activities that create value. Organisations can be re-organised into product teams which focus on the customer. This enables companies to let customers pull the product from them as they need it, rather than pushing products on to a market that does not necessarily want them.

For example, at Castle Bromwich, the Jaguar production line runs at the speed which enables finished cars to come off the line just in time to meet customer demand. All along the production line, teams of workers work in problem-solving circles to identify 'muda' and to cut it out. What this means is that the employees work smarter rather than harder. By working smart they work at value-creating activities rather than wasting time on muda. The physical layout of the factory has been reorganised to cut out all those activities that are wasteful. For example, supplies and stores are kept away from the manufacturing area as much as possible because they get in the way. Parts and supplies are brought in when they are needed by a worker pressing a buzzer to call for them.

FIGURE 2.21 *Jaguar uses lean techniques to manage resources*

PROBLEMS OF LOW STOCKS	PROBLEMS OF HIGH STOCKS
Difficult to meet orders	Increased risk of stock going out of date
Possible loss of business	Increased risk of stock theft and other loss
Loss of goodwill	High storage costs
Ordering needs to be frequent and handling costs rise	Stocks tie up money

FIGURE 2.22 *Problems caused by incorrect stock levels*

Balancing stock levels is essential. Having too little or too much stock can be harmful to a business. High stock levels mean that cash isn't being generated quickly enough through sales, whereas low stock levels might result in not being able to meet orders.

Figure 2.22 shows the impact of having the wrong stock levels and the modern approach is 'Just-in-time'.

In contrast to a Just-in-time approach, we can have a 'Just-in-case' approach where an organisation holds a buffer stock.

This approach can be helpful to make sure there are large enough stocks.

A minimum stock level is established – stocks should not fall below this.

Stocks are re-ordered when the existing stock falls to the re-order level.

When new stocks arrive this will take the stock situation back to the maximum stock level.

The re-order quantity is the quantity that will be supplied when stocks have fallen to the minimum level and brings the stock level back up to the maximum stock level.

CASE STUDY

Just-in-time (JIT)

Just-in-time approaches to holding stock are very important in modern industry. Just-in-time is a very simple idea:

* Finished goods are produced just in time for them to be sold, rather than weeks or months ahead.
* The parts that go into a finished product arrive just in time to be put together to make the final product, rather than being stored (at some cost) in a warehouse. With a JIT system, a factory or other workplace is re-organised so that people are grouped together around the products they produce.

1 What do you see as being the main benefit of a JIT system?
2 Can you see any potential drawbacks?

Try out the following activity. Divide the class into two equal groups. One group of students should be given 20 car templates (see Figure 2.23) and some glue. The job of the group is to make 20 completed cars. They must be of a high quality.

The other group of students must be divided into four: one group to assemble the final car using glue, one group to cut out windows, one group to distribute parts to final assembly and one group to cut out wheels. The final assemblers must call for parts just in time to assemble them. When the activity is completed the quality of the cars produced by both groups and the time taken to make them must be assessed. An analysis should be carried out of the efficiency of the Just-in-time approach.

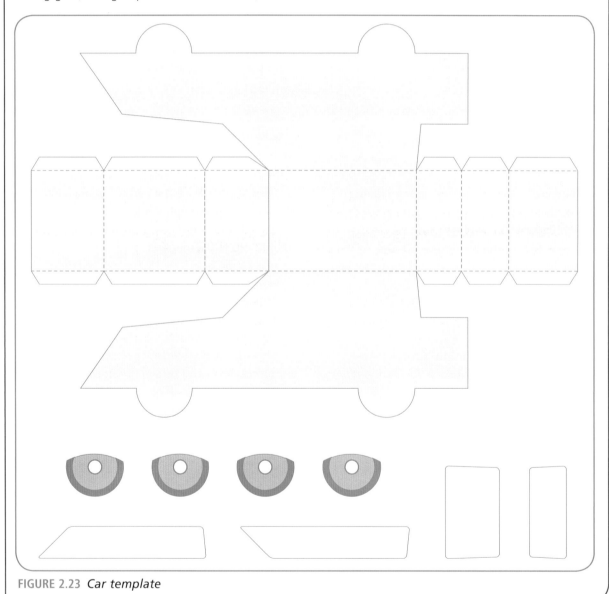

FIGURE 2.23 *Car template*

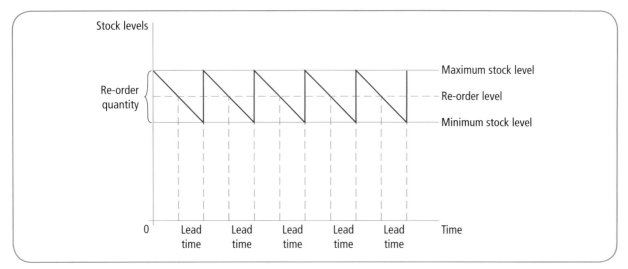

FIGURE 2.24 *Lead time*

The lead time is the time that is taken between the re-ordering of the stock and the arrival of this new stock (see Figure 2.24).

Managing financial resources

Another important managerial responsibility is that of obtaining finance for a business or part of a business. Each year individual managers will need to bid for funds. Typically this involves arguing the case for levels of funding that are appropriate to the activities that need to be carried out. For example:

* a course manager in a school or college will need funds to manage a course

* a production manager in a factory will need to bid for funds to buy new machinery and equipment and to purchase stocks of raw materials.

At an organisation-wide level, financial managers will have responsibility for securing funds for the business to enable it to operate well.

Learning activity

What other examples of needs for funds can you think of? Use your work experience and part-time job experience to generate ideas.

Organisations have available to them a number of sources of finance, including:

* individuals
* organisations providing venture capital
* banks and other financial institutions
* suppliers
* government
* profits retained in the business.

In deciding what types of finance to draw on financial managers need to consider:

* the length of time for which they need the finance
* the cost of raising the finance in one way rather than another.

ORGANISATIONS MAY NEED:	
Long-term finance	e.g. to purchase other businesses or buildings
Medium-term finance	e.g. to update machinery, equipment and fittings
Short-term finance	e.g. to buy new stocks, to pay wages etc

FIGURE 2.25 *Types of finance*

Owner's capital

This is raised from individual owners of a business, from partners or shareholders. This type of capital is raised when starting up a new business venture or when expanding a business.

When issuing shares, careful consideration needs to be given to the need to pay a dividend (share of the profit) to shareholders. The amount of dividend paid is decided by the Board of Directors of the company. A good thing about raising finance from shareholders is that the company is not legally obliged to pay a set return each year (as it has to with loans). However, if the company keeps asking shareholders for more funds they will lose confidence in the company.

Venture capital

Venture capital companies such as 3i provide finance in return for an equity (ordinary) shareholding in the company and an element of control. This is a quick and relatively cheap way for a new business to raise capital but it may not want to lose some control to the venture capitalist.

Profit retention

One of the most important sources of finance for a business is from profits that have been put back in. Initially, profits are subject to corporation tax, payable to the Inland Revenue. Then a proportion of what is left is distributed to shareholders as dividends. Finally profits can be ploughed back into expansion.

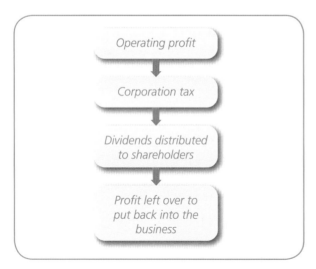

FIGURE 2.26 *Profits are an important source of finance for a business*

Borrowing

The charge made for borrowing money is termed interest. The longer the business borrows money the greater the rate of interest charged.

1 Bank loans are taken out for a fixed period, repayments either being in instalments or in full at the end of the term. Banks generally provide funds on a short- to medium-term basis, with relatively few loans over more than ten years in duration. As well as the interest payment there may be an arrangement fee.

2 Debentures are certificates issued by companies acknowledging their debt. The debt is paid at a fixed rate of interest and the certificate sets out the term of repayment at the end of the period of debts. Debentures can usually be traded on the Stock Exchange.

3 Bank overdrafts are the most frequently used form of short-term bank finance and they are used to ease cash flow problems. Arrangements are made between the customer and the bank to include an agreed limit on an account beyond which the customer will not draw. Interest is calculated on the level of the overdraft on a daily basis. Often a bank will make a special charge for arranging an overdraft. A bank can take away the customer's right to use an overdraft if they think it is being abused.

Hire-purchase

Hire-purchase (HP) allows a business to use an asset (e.g. photocopier, computer) without having to find the money immediately. A finance house buys the asset from the supplier and retains ownership of it during the period of the hire-purchase agreement. The business pays a deposit and then further payments to the finance house, as set out in the agreement. At the end of the HP agreement, ownership of the asset is passed to the business. The repayments made by the business are in excess of the cash price of the item. The difference is the finance charge to the finance house.

Leasing

Leasing an asset provides similar benefits to hire-purchase, in that a leasing agreement with a finance house (lessor) allows the business (lessee) to use an asset without having to buy it outright. However, leasing does not give an automatic right to eventual ownership of the asset. It is a very popular form of finance for company vehicles, office equipment and factory machinery.

The lessee benefits from not having to put up large sums of capital to be able to use assets and they can exchange the asset for a more modern version when technology changes. The lessor is also usually responsible for the maintenance of the item.

Mortgages

A commercial mortgage is a loan secured on land and buildings and can either be used to finance the purchase of the property or to provide security for a loan applied to some other purpose. It is a long-term financing arrangement typically from 10 to 30 years. Repayments include a considerable interest rate.

Sale and leaseback

This involves a firm selling its freehold property to an investment company and then leasing it back over a long period of time. This releases funds for other purposes.

Suppliers

Suppliers are a valuable source of finance for many businesses. Just as the business may give credit to its own customers, the firm may be able to negotiate credit terms with its suppliers. Credit terms are typically 30 days from date of supply or the end of the month following a delivery, i.e. 30 to 60 days.

Factoring

When a business is owed money and needs cash urgently it can sell off part or all of this debt for collection by a third party – a factoring company.

Government loans

Businesses can acquire loans and grants from the government for various purposes depending on circumstances. Some of these grants and loans may come from European Union sources, others from UK national government, and others from local government. National Lottery funds can be obtained in some circumstances. Typical purposes might be funds for helping with government schemes such as Modern Apprenticeships and job creation schemes. Other grants may be for building development and machinery purchase, particularly in areas of economic decline.

> ### Learning activity
>
> You are the financial manager of an organisation that is opening a petrol station on a new city bypass. Refer to Figure 2.27 and match the organisation's financial needs with the possible sources of finance available.

NEEDS	POSSIBLE SOURCES OF FINANCE
✳ Land and buildings: £500,000	✳ Hire-purchase or leasing
✳ Shopfittings: £50,000	✳ Bank loan for two years
✳ Petrol pumps: £100,000	✳ Commercial mortgage
✳ Stocks of petrol and retail items: £75,000	✳ Bank overdraft
✳ Computer terminal: £6,000	✳ Trade credit
✳ First few weeks' wages: £8,000	✳ Owner's capital: £100,000

FIGURE 2.27 *Finance needs and sources*

We have seen that business organisations use a range of methods of finance. If you are a financial manager in the following organisations what type of finance would you use in each case?

1 A school wishes to replace its existing photocopier with a more elaborate version which they want to pay for over a period of time.

2 The Queen's Medical Centre wishes to build a new hospital wing on vacant land close to its existing site in Nottingham.

3 Prakesh Patel needs a new computer system costing £7,500 for his business. Identify two ways of financing the purchase and state the circumstances in which either would be most appropriate.

4 A medium-sized company wants to expand its factory building. The cost will be £1m. Identify two ways of financing the expansion and state the circumstance in which either would be more appropriate.

5 A small firm is temporarily having problems with its cash flow. Identify two ways of financing any shortfall it might currently have in its cash requirements and state the circumstances in which either would be more appropriate.

The role of quality control, quality assurance and total quality management

Quality can be defined as:

* continually meeting agreed customer needs
* what it takes to satisfy the customer
* fitness for purpose.

Consumers make purchases when they feel that their need for quality is being met.

There have been three main stages in the development of quality in business, as shown in Figure 2.28.

Quality control

Quality control is an old idea. It is concerned with detecting and cutting out components or final products which fall below set standards. This process takes place after these products have been made. It may involve considerable waste as defect products are scrapped. Quality control is carried out by Quality Control Inspectors. Inspection and testing are the most common methods of carrying out quality control.

Quality assurance

Quality assurance occurs both during and after the event and is concerned with trying to stop faults from happening in the first place. Quality assurance is concerned with making sure that products are produced to predetermined standards. The aim is to produce goods with 'zero defects'.

Quality assurance is the responsibility of the workforce, working in cells or teams, rather than an inspector (although inspection will take place). Quality standards should be maintained by following steps set out in a quality assurance system.

Total Quality Management (TQM)

Total Quality Management (TQM) goes beyond quality assurance. It is concerned with creating a

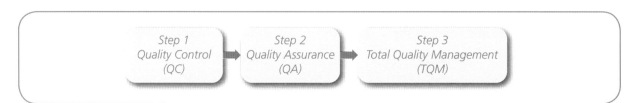

FIGURE 2.28 *The evolution of quality in business*

Can you think of examples of businesses that operate with a Total Quality Management approach:

* in the hotel business

* in providing air travel

* in retailing

* in the entertainment industry

* elsewhere.

quality culture so that every employee will seek to delight customers. The customer is at the centre of the production process.

A company that believes in TQM will seek to provide customers:

* with what they want

* when they want it

* how they want it.

TQM involves moving with changing customer requirements and fashions to design products and services which meet and exceed their requirements. Delighted customers will pass the message on to their friends.

Quality Circles

A lot of the early work on the development of Quality was done by Dr W. Edwards Deming working as a consultant to Japanese companies after the Second World War. In a total quality system, TQM takes place at every stage of an organisation's operations and is the responsibility of all employees. Emphasis is placed on quality chains, i.e. links between groups and individuals involved in operations. The concept of 'customer' extends to include the 'internal' customer. Internal customers are people inside the company receiving products (usually unfinished) or services from their colleagues also in the company.

Deming developed the idea of the Quality Circle. Quality Circles are made up of small groups of employees engaged in any sort of problem

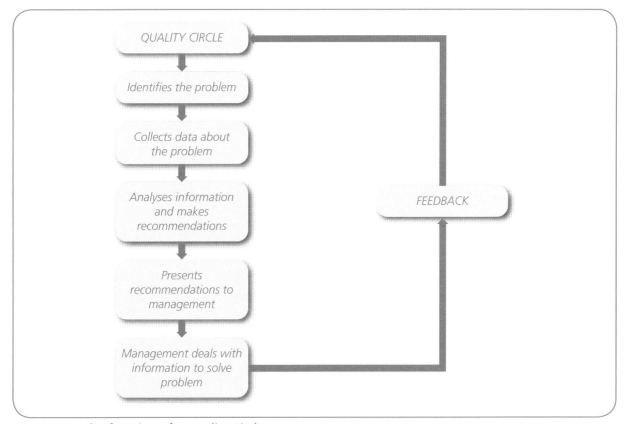

FIGURE 2.29 *The function of a Quality Circle*

Learning activity

How was quality managed in an organisation in which you carried out work experience or in which you have a part time job?

affecting their working environment, for example, safety, production methods, efficiency. They are a means for employees to improve their working life by putting forward their points of view on day-to-day quality issues. Quality Circles may meet once a week or more frequently. Each circle has a leader and operates as shown in Figure 2.29.

A great benefit of Quality Circles is that an organisation can use specialists who know and understand their jobs and problems related to them to solve problems without having to call in management consultants. Because these circles are supported by top managers, the members of them feel that they are trusted and valued. This increases motivation and the links between managers and employees.

The importance of monitoring and reviewing business performance

Managers need to monitor and review the performance of a business in order to make improvements. The act of monitoring and reviewing performance gives the manager control, as illustrated in Figure 2.30.

Control involves the measurement and correction of performance. Control and planning should go hand in hand. Many writers on management theory argue that the two cannot be separated. They can be seen as the twin blades of a pair of scissors.

FIGURE 2.31 *Planning and control should always go together*

In order to monitor and review business performance it is necessary to have standards against which to judge this performance.

Such standards include:

1 The solvency of a business

2 Profitability

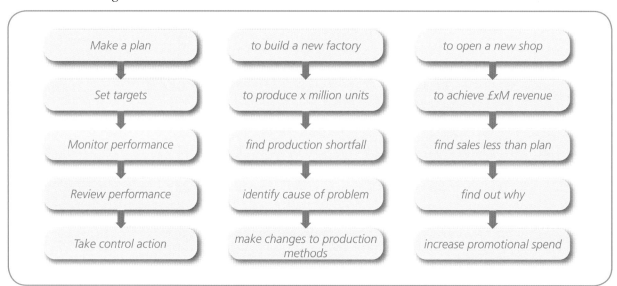

Make a plan	to build a new factory	to open a new shop
Set targets	to produce x million units	to achieve £xM revenue
Monitor performance	find production shortfall	find sales less than plan
Review performance	identify cause of problem	find out why
Take control action	make changes to production methods	increase promotional spend

FIGURE 2.30 *Management control by monitoring and reviewing performance*

FIGURE 2.32 *The cross-channel business is very competitive*

In the period 2003–2004 the cross channel ferry section of P&O carried 10 million passengers but it still made a loss of £25 million in the first half of 2004. These losses seemed likely to increase. After reviewing this situation managers decided to take the following actions:

* Cut 1,200 jobs
* Sell off one third of the fleet
* Reduce the number of routes from 11 to 7.

1 Can you identify a news story where a company has taken management control actions after reviewing its profit performance?
2 What had happened to profits?
3 What control actions were taken?

---

3 Complying with laws

4 Identifying areas for improvement.

1 The solvency of a business

Solvency is concerned with whether a business has access to enough cash to pay outstanding demands. For example, if a business knows that in any quarter it will have to pay out £10,000 for wages, raw materials and other short-term costs, it must make sure that it can quickly get hold of £10,000 to meet these demands. A solvent business is one that can always meet demands for short-term payments. Cash flow forecasting is an important management tool for controlling solvency. It involves forecasting cash incomings and outgoings from a business.

2 Profitability

Businesses need to make a profit if they are to survive. Managers will therefore establish profit targets for coming periods. Actions can be taken to make sure these profits are achieved, e.g. by creating an appropriate pricing or advertising policy as well as having a quality product. If profits fall short of expectations then managers will need to take appropriate control actions as illustrated by the P&O case study.

Learning activity

Identify one situation where there is a legal change that affects business. Identify the sorts of actions that managers might need to take in this situation to make sure that the business complies with the law.

3 Complying with laws

Managers also have responsibility for making sure that their business complies with relevant laws, e.g. with regard to Health and Safety at Work, Equal Opportunities, Environmental Protection, Competition Policy, Data Protection etc.

4 Identifying areas for improvement

Managers have a general responsibility for identifying all areas where there is room for improvement in business performance.

* DID YOU KNOW?

There are around 460 loss-making companies listed on the London Stock Exchange and some of these are fairly well-known companies. Some organisations make losses because of a sudden change in their business environment. For example, the events of 11th September 2001 suddenly hit the aviation industry.

Record sales for Tesco this year

Price of petrol hits record high

£1 in every £3 of grocery retail sales is made by Tesco

Manchester United continue to lead British football clubs in the profit stakes

Manchester United keep players' wage costs at under 50% of the value of sales

Oil giants BP and Shell make record profits in the history of British companies

FIGURE 2:33 *The kind of headlines you might see in the financial pages of a newspaper*

2.3 Financial management in business

Look at the financial pages of any newspaper and you will see the extent to which external confidence in the management of a large business is determined by its financial performance. Shareholders and other external stakeholders keenly await information on financial performance of the business. If you are working for the business, your work will contribute to this financial performance and you may have a role in recording the financial transactions of the business. Even the smallest transaction will be audited so that the final accounts accurately represent what the business has been doing during the year. Public confidence in a business and the confidence of all employees will rely upon good accounts.

Every business has to meet internal and external reporting requirements to show its financial health and to meet legal and other requirements. The following people need financial information about the performance of a business:

* Internal users – groups within the organisation, such as managers.
* External users – groups outside the organisation, such as shareholders and creditors.

Every business environment is competitive, which by its very nature means that in this rapidly changing world in which organisations exist, some will inevitably perform better than others. Where a business does well, there are many rewards and benefits for individuals and organisations affected by its actions. On the other hand, if a business has a bad year or does not do well, there is a similar knock-on effect with a range of consequences for individuals and organisations that may be affected in a range of ways by its poor performance.

Every individual or organisation likely to be affected through the successes, failures or actions of a business will therefore have their own areas of concern. To clarify their concerns, they will have information needs and requirements. They will want facts, knowledge and understanding about how the actions of that organisation affect either their own circumstances or the circumstances of the organisation for which they work.

The importance of profitability and liquidity (solvency)

Profitability

Some businesses make losses over a considerable time as it is difficult to generate revenues to cover expenses. For example, with new high-tech companies or drug companies it may take years to generate revenues.

Despite their lack of profits, many investors like loss-makers, mainly because there is always a chance of a turnaround and the shares may be cheap.

Why do we assume that all businesses will be profitable?

Is it possible to identify a sector in which few businesses are profitable?

Why might an investor wish to buy shares in unprofitable companies?

In order to make judgements about business activities, individuals require accounting information from an accounting system. Accounting acts as an information system by processing business data so that those parties either interested in or affected by the business can be provided with the means to find out how well or badly the organisation is performing.

Business data are the inputs for the accounting system. The output is financial information. Financial information can then be fed to those who require such information.

Accounting information may be used both within and outside an organisation. It involves providing important data that may form the basis for decisions. In order to clarify what we mean by accounting information, it is perhaps best to explain what we mean by accounting:

Accounting is concerned with identifying, measuring, recording and reporting information relating to the activities of an organisation.

We can break each of these activities down into the following:

* Identifying – This involves capturing all the financial data within a business related to how it is performing. For example, this would include all information about the sales of goods to customers, data about the payment of expenses (such as wages and rent) and also information about the purchase of any stock, as well as data about the purchase of new vehicles and machinery.

* Measuring – Money, in the form of pounds and pence, is used as the form of measurement of economic transactions. In the future, the form of measurement might change to become euros. For accounting purposes, instead of saying a business had sold 10 cars in a week, which may be meaningless if you do not know the value of the cars, it may be useful to specify the value of the cars. For example, 10 cars valued at £15,000 would mean a turnover during the week of £150,000.

* Recording – Accounting data and information must be recorded into either handwritten accounting books or into a suitable computer package, such as a specialised accounting package or a spreadsheet.

* Communicating – The reporting of financial information may take a variety of different forms. For example, although some financial information may be required and extracted from the accounts weekly, such as sales totals, there are standard financial statements (such as profit and loss accounts and balance sheets) that have a set format for reporting the activities of organisations.

It is important that throughout this accounting process the accounting information is:

* Reliable – free from errors and bias
* Comparable – accounting information should be comparable with information from other organisations
* Relevant – accounting information should relate to many of the decisions that have to be made about the business
* Understandable – information should be capable of being understood by those at whom it is targeted.

Financial and management accounting

The process of accounting can be divided into two broad areas: financial accounting and management accounting.

Financial accounting

This is concerned with the recording of financial transactions and the preparation of financial reports to communicate past financial performance.

Subject to accounting regulations, financial accounting ensures:

* that reports/statements follow a standard approach
* a broad overview of the whole business using totals
* information to a particular date
* general statements and reports
* information in monetary terms and values.

Management accounting

Management accounting involves looking to the future using a knowledge of past performance, where relevant, to aid the management of the business.

In management accounting reports are only for internal use so no restrictions are necessary. This sector of accounting:

* uses information extracted from parts of the organisation where it is used to help with a particular decision

* will look at future performance as well as at past perfomance
* produces reports with a specific decision in mind
* may have non-financial information such as stocks.

Following the financial reports in any newspaper will reveal that one of the key newsworthy areas constantly emphasised by the press is profits. For example, 'Eurostar' might be 'rocked by profit warnings' or 'Somerfield to retreat to the high street'. Profits are a key indicator when judging business performance. It is the first point of reference for many organisational stakeholders.

It is all very well saying that sales have risen, productivity is soaring and the organisation is growing. However, shareholders and providers of capital will always ask the question: 'But have you been making a profit?'

Learning activity

Which of the following would fall into the realms of financial accounting and which would be management accounting?

* Recording transactions from source documentation.
* Calculating what the profit is likely to be over a range of outputs for the launch of a new product.
* Producing financial statements to show what has happened to the business during the past year.
* Advising a business on its tax liability.
* Creating a budgetary system to improve control over the costs within a business.
* Setting the prices of products or services.

* DID YOU KNOW?

The UK insurance industry is the largest in Europe and the third largest in the world.

Liquidity (solvency)

The words 'liquidity' or 'solvency' mean 'to be able to meet financial obligations'. A business becomes 'technically insolvent' when it has sufficient assets to meet all its financial obligations but insufficient time to convert these assets into cash. It is 'legally insolvent' if it is in a situation of permanent cash shortage.

A number of users of accounting information will want to check regularly on the solvency of business organisations. For example, owners and shareholders will want to know their money is 'safe'. In this respect they will want to look at the distribution of assets and liabilities a company has. In other words they will want to know what a business owns and what a business owes. For example, the company may have money coming in at 'some time in the future'. However, unless it has money coming in now, tomorrow and the next day, it may face cash flow problems that make it 'technically insolvent'.

Lenders of money to organisations want to know their loans will be repaid and that interest will be paid at regular intervals. Employees and other stakeholders in organisations will want the security of knowing the organisation is solvent.

Managers will want to know the extent of solvency so that they can restructure assets and liabilities into an appropriate form. For example, they will want to manage their assets in a way that enables them to pay bills as and when they arrive in the organisation, without being too liquid and having too much cash or cash not doing anything. Solvency is a base-line for ongoing business operations.

When auditors carry out a periodic audit of an organisation's accounts, one of the key areas they would need to emphasise would be how solvent the organisation is.

Assets, liabilities, expenses and revenues

Assets

Assets are things that an organisation owns, as well as other items that may be owed to the business. The word 'asset' appears frequently in a balance sheet, which provides a statement of what an organisation owns and owes at any fixed point in time. Assets in a balance sheet are normally set out in what is called an inverse order of liquidity. This means items that may be easy to convert into cash quickly, and are therefore liquid, appear at the bottom of the list of assets. By looking down the order it is possible to gauge the ease with which successive assets can be converted to cash, until we come to the most liquid asset of all, cash itself.

Assets can be divided into fixed assets and current assets.

Fixed assets tend to have a life-span of more than one year. They comprise items that are purchased and generally kept for a long period of time. Examples of fixed assets would be premises, machinery and motor vehicles. When a business buys fixed assets it does so by incurring capital expenditure.

Current assets are sometimes called 'circulating assets' because the form they take is constantly

Learning activity

Explain what the word 'asset' means.

A small bakery has the following assets. Try to put them into an inverse order of liquidity, with the least liquid at the top and the most liquid at the bottom:

✱ cash in the tills

✱ bread in the shops

✱ a bakery van

✱ the baker's oven

✱ supplies of flour

✱ money in the bakery's bank account

✱ money owed to the bakery by firms

✱ the baker's premises.

changing. Examples of current assets are stocks, debtors, money in the bank and cash in hand.

For example, a manufacturing business holds stocks of finished goods in readiness to satisfy the demands of the market. When a credit transaction takes place, stocks are reduced and the business gains debtors. These debtors have bought goods on credit and therefore owe the business money; after a reasonable credit period payment will be expected. Payments will have to be made on further stocks so that the business has a cash cycle. 'Cash' or 'bank' changes to 'stock' then to 'debtors', back to 'cash' or 'bank' and then to 'stock' again.

Liabilities

Liabilities include anything that an organisation owes and are usually set out either as current liabilities or long-term liabilities, depending upon their duration.

Current liabilities are debts a business needs to repay within a short period of time (normally a year). These liabilities include creditors, who are suppliers of goods on credit for which the business has been invoiced but not yet paid. They may also include a bank overdraft that is arranged up to a limit over a time period and is, technically, repayable on demand. Other current liabilities may include any short-term loans and any taxes owed.

Working capital is always an important calculation for an organisation as it shows how easily the business can pay its short-term debts. Working capital is the ratio of current assets to current liabilities.

It is important for an organisation to maintain a sensible ratio. The level of ratio depends on the type of business and the likelihood that funds will be required quickly to meet liabilities (e.g. creditors demanding quick repayment). For most businesses a ratio of 2:1 is regarded as a sign of careful management, but some businesses have lower ratios.

Working capital is important because it provides a buffer: to 'keep the wolf from the door'. Many businesses have suffered the consequences of having too many of their assets tied up in liquid assets.

A long-term liability is sometimes called a deferred liability as it is not due for payment until some time in the future. By convention, in a set of accounts this means longer than one year. Examples for a sole trader could include a bank loan or mortgage.

As we saw earlier, capital is provided by the owner of the business and is therefore deemed to be owed to the owner by the business. The balance sheet keeps an updated record of the amount owed by the business to the owner.

During a year's trading the owner's capital may be increased by the inflows of profits (profits for the period) and decreased by outflows of drawings (money or other assets taken out of the business for personal use). Having taken these into consideration, a new capital figure is calculated at the end of the year. So the balance sheet shows how the capital has increased (or decreased!) since the last balance sheet was prepared. For a company, capital will appear as shares and the profits are called dividends.

Expenses

Almost all business activities involve some element of cost and most managers have to deal with costs on a day-to-day basis. Expenses are fundamental, from the early development of a business, through to the controlling and monitoring of expenditures. Information about expenses and costs help an organisation to:

* create short-term, medium-term and long-term plans
* control an organisation's activities
* decide between alternative strategies.

Every organisation incurs expenses and a range of overheads. These might include:

Rent of premises
Gas
Electricity
Stationery
Cleaning costs
Insurance
Business rates
Depreciation (loss in value of an asset through wear and tear)
Bad debts (people owing the business money who fail to pay)
Interest on loans
Advertising costs
Sundry expenses
Motor expenses
Accountancy and legal fees.

Revenues

Most revenue for a business organisation will come either from sales or from fees charged to customers. The sales figure can be derived by looking at the selling price of the units sold, against the number of units sold. Some organisations receive income from sources other than sales. This is known as non-operating income. This may include rents received on any

CASE STUDY

Understanding how to manage working capital

Working capital is often considered to be the portion of the capital that 'oils the wheels' of business. It provides the stocks from which the fixed assets help to produce the finished goods. It allows the salesforce to offer attractive credit and terms to customers, which creates debtors.

Organisations that do not have sufficient working capital lack the funds to buy stocks and to produce and create debtors.

The dangers of insufficient working capital are therefore clear to see:

* A business with limited working capital will not be able to buy in bulk and could miss out on any opportunities to obtain trade discounts.
* Cash discounts will be lost as the business will avoid paying creditors until the last possible opportunity.
* It will become more difficult to offer extensive credit facilities for customers. By shortening the credit period, customers may well go to alternative suppliers.
* The business will be unable to innovate. Limited finances will hinder its ability to develop new products or improve production techniques.
* The business's financial reputation as a good payer may be lost.
* Creditors may well take action. As capital becomes squeezed, a business will be forced to finance its activities by overdrafts and trade credit. A point could well be reached where its future is dependent upon the actions of creditors.
* Overtrading could take place. This is where a larger volume of production or orders take place, without sufficient working capital to support it. This then leads to a complete imbalance in the working capital ratio.

As a result of problems with working capital, there are a number of options. These may include the following:

* Reducing the period between the time cash is paid out for raw materials and the time

cash is received from sales. This helps to provide funds for regeneration. However, although the improved efficiency of the cash cycle may improve working capital, actions taken may be unpopular with creditors.

* Fixed assets (such as land and buildings) may not be fully utilised, or space may be used for unprofitable purposes. Space could be rented, sold or allowed to house a more profitable operation so that cash flow could be improved. A business's cash flow might be improved by selling assets and leasing them back, although this may commit an organisation to heavy leasing fees.

* A company could review its stock levels to see if these could be subject to economy measures. If the stock of raw materials is divided by the average weekly issue, the number of weeks' raw materials held in stock can be calculated. The problem with this is the business might then lose out on trade discounts or have problems obtaining supplies.

* Many businesses employ a credit controller to manage cash flow and control the debtors. A credit controller will vet new customers and set them a credit limit, ensure that credit limits are not exceeded and encourage debtors to pay on time. Credit controllers are often caught in a conflict with sales staff, who wish to offer attractive credit terms, and the accounts department, who want debtors to pay quickly and so increase their working capital.

* As we have seen, the use of cash budgets can be an important control mechanism that can be used to predict the effects of future transactions on the cash balance of a company. Cash flow forecasting or cash budgeting can help an organisation to take actions to ensure cash is available when required.

* A number of short-term solutions are available to increase working capital. Companies might extend their overdraft or bring in a factoring company to buy some of their debtors and so provide them with instant finance. It might be possible to delay the payment of bills, although this obviously displeases creditors.

When a business can no longer pay its debts it may go into liquidation. This may be ordered by a court, usually on behalf of a creditor. This may then be followed by receivership, where independent accountants supervise the sale of the different parts of the business. But, sometimes, while struggling to survive and meet the demands of creditors, a white knight appears on the scene to launch a rescue bid and save the business.

1 **Why do organisations have to manage their working capital?**
2 **Describe one problem that arises if an organisation fails to manage its working capital properly.**
3 **What are the likely effects upon the business of insufficient working capital?**

properties that the business owns, profits from the sale of assets such as cars, as well as income from other areas such as investments.

Constructing financial statements

Final accounts are usually produced once a year by a firm of outside auditors or accountants. As well as helping the owners of a business to revise and fine-tune their business strategies, they provide a broad picture of how an organisation is performing and may be presented to the Inland Revenue and lenders of money, such as banks.

Profit and loss account

As the trading account is usually linked together with the profit and loss account, with the trading account appearing above, they are sometimes collectively called 'the profit and loss account'.

The trading account can be likened to a video giving ongoing pictures of an organisation's trading activities. For many business organisations, trading involves buying and selling stock. The difference between the value of the stock sold (sales) and the cost of producing those sales (which may be the production costs of manufactured goods for a manufacturing company or the cost of purchasing the supplies for a trading company) is known as the gross profit.

The trading account simply shows how gross profit is arrived at:

Net sales − Cost of sales   = Gross profit

The trading account includes *only the items in which an organisation trades*. For example, if a small supermarket buys baked beans and sells them to its customers, then the cost of purchasing these and the amounts received from selling them will appear in the trading account. However, if the supermarket's owner decided to sell the business's van, this would not be included in the trading account as he or she is not in the second-hand vehicle business.

Sales

Sales are often described as turnover. As we have seen earlier, sometimes goods which have been sold are returned inwards as sales returns. We obviously do not want to include these in the sales figures because they have come back to us. Net sales, which is the final sales figure, is therefore:

Sales − Returns inwards (sales returns)   = Net sales

Purchases

As with sales, some purchases may have been returned but, in this instance, the returns will have been outwards as purchases returns. Purchases may also include the cost of transporting the goods to the organisation, which must be added to the cost of buying goods, known, as we saw earlier, as carriage inwards. Net purchases, where there is carriage inwards and purchases returns, could therefore be:

Purchases + Carriage inwards − Returns outward
(purchases returns)
= Net purchases

Stocks

The final sales figure must take into account the value of stocks. Opening stock is effectively a purchase as these will be sold in the current trading period. On the other hand, closing stock must be deducted from the purchases as these will be sold next year.

Cost of sales

The calculation for cost of sales, including a full set of adjustments to purchases and stocks, would therefore be:

Opening stock + Purchases + Carriage inwards
− Returns outwards − Closing stock
= Cost of sales

We can show all these with an example:

The trading account of D. Gough for the year ended 31 December 2004

	£	£	£
Sales			21,000
Less: Returns inwards			1,000
Net sales			20,000
Opening stock (1 January 2001)		4,500	
Purchases	12,100		
Carriage inwards	300		
	12,400		
Less: Returns outwards	500		
Net purchases		11,900	
		16,400	
Less: Closing stock (31 December 2001)		3,700	
Cost of sales		12,700	
Gross profit		£7,300	

So far, and with all the organisations we have looked at, we have assumed a gross profit is made. This may not always be the case! If the cost of sales is greater than the net sales figure, an organisation may make a gross loss.

The profit and loss account may be drawn up beneath the trading account and covers the same period of trading. The gross profit (or gross loss)

Prepare accounts for each of the following sets of figures:

1 M. Patel on 31 December 2004. His figures are as follows: closing stock 4,100, returns outwards 700, carriage inwards 400, purchases 15,300, returns inwards 500, opening stock 3,900 and sales 34,800.

2 J. Gallian on 31 December 2004. Her figures are as follows: closing stock 3,200, returns outwards 550, carriage inwards 324, purchases 10,125, returns inwards 650, opening stock 4,789 and sales 15,000.

figure becomes the starting point for the profit and loss account.

Some organisations receive income from sources other than sales. These may be rents received, commission received or profits on the sales of assets. As these are extra income, they are added to the gross profit.

In addition, every organisation incurs expenses and a range of overheads, and these are deducted to show the true net profit (or loss) of the business. These expenses might, for example, include:

* rent of premises

* discount allowed

* gas

* electricity

* stationery

* cleaning costs

* insurances

* business rates

* depreciation

* bad debts

* interest on loans

* sundry expenses

* motor expenses

* accountancy and legal fees.

$$\text{Net profit} = \frac{\text{Gross profit} + \text{Income from other sources} - \text{Expenses}}{}$$

Net profit is the final profit in the business and will belong to the owner.

The trading and profit and loss account of D. Gough for the year ended 31 December 2004

	£	£	£
Sales			21,000
Less: Returns inwards			1,000
Net sales			20,000
Opening stock			
(1 January 2001)		4,500	
Purchases	12,100		
Less: Returns outwards	500		
Net purchases		11,600	
		16,100	
Less: Closing stock			
(31 December 2001)		3,700	
Cost of sales			12,400
Gross profit			7,600
Add other income:			
Discount received			2,000
			9,600
	£	£	£
Less expenses:			
Electricity		510	
Stationery		125	
Business rate		756	
Interest on loans		159	
Advertising		745	
Depreciation – motor vehicles	1,000		
Insurances	545		
Sundry expenses	124		
Total expenses			3,964
Net profit			£5,636

It is important to note that trading accounts will apply only to organisations who *trade* in goods or who are involved in the process of manufacturing. Service sector businesses (such as a dentist, estate agent or solicitor) will not require a trading account because they are not buying and selling goods. Instead, their final accounts will consist simply of a profit and loss account and a balance sheet. Instead of starting with gross profit, their profit and loss account will start by listing the various forms of income, such as fees received:

The profit and loss account of P. Franks for the year ended 31 December 2001		
	£	£
Income from clients		4,100
Add other income:		
Rent received		1,400
		5,500
Less expenses:		
Electricity	412	
Insurances	124	
Sundry expenses	415	
Travel expenses	147	
Total expenses		1,098
Net profit		£4,402

The balance sheet

Whereas the trading account provides an ongoing picture, a balance sheet is a snapshot of what an organisation owns and owes on a particular date.

A balance sheet is a clear statement of the assets, liabilities and capital of a business at a particular moment in time (normally at the end of an accounting period, e.g. quarter, year, etc.).

Looking at the balance sheet can thus provide valuable information because it summarises a business's financial position at that instant in time.

The balance sheet balances because the accounts record every transaction twice. For example, if you lend me £100 we can say that:

✳ I owe you £100 (a liability or debt)

✳ I now have £100 (an asset, something I own).

Look at the balance sheet of D. Bicknell. As you can see, a balance sheet is represented by a simple formula that underlies all accounting activity:

Assets = Liabilities + Capital

At the end of a trading period a business will have a number of assets and liabilities. Some of these will be for short periods of time while others will be for longer periods. Whatever the nature of the individual assets and liabilities, the balance sheet will balance.

Learning activity

Make a list of six assets and six liabilities you would expect a small corner-shop to have. Do the same for a public house.

As you work through this section, look at the balance sheet illustrated below:

The balance sheet of D. Bicknell as at 31 December 2004			
	£	£	£
Fixed assets			
Land and buildings			80,000
Machinery			13,200
Motor vehicles			8,700
			101,900
Current assets			
Stocks		9,700	
Debtors		3,750	
Bank		2,100	
Cash		970	
		16,520	
Less: Current liabilities			
Creditors	8,000		
Value Added Tax owing	1,000	9,000	
Working capital/net current assets			7,520
			109,420
Less: Long-term liabilities			
Bank loan	9,000		
Mortgage	30,000		
			39,000
Net assets			£70,420
Financed by:			
Capital		70,000	
Add: Net profit		5,286	
		75,286	
Less: Drawings		4,866	
			£70,420

Every balance sheet will have a heading containing the name of the organisation as well as the date upon which the snapshot is taken.

Final accounts of a limited company

So far, our analysis of accounts has centred on those of a sole trader. Before looking further at how to interpret and analyse financial information, we are going to look at another type of business organisation, that of a company. Accounts of a company are prepared on a similar basis to those for a sole trader, but there are some important differences in the appropriation of profit and in the organisation's capital structure.

As we have seen, a limited company has:

✳ A legal identity separate from that of its owners.

✳ Owners who are known as shareholders and who have limited liability.

* A management that is delegated to a board of directors, who may or may not be shareholders.

* A commitment to pay Corporation Tax on any profits made.

Companies must comply with the Companies Acts, and the Companies Registration Office controls their formation. There are two types of limited companies:

* Public, which have their shares traded on the Stock Exchange

* Private, for which there are restrictions on the trading in their shares.

One clause of the Memorandum of Association states the share capital of the company and indicates how it is to be divided into separate shares. Authorised share capital is the amount the shareholders have authorised the directors to issue. Issued share capital is the amount that has actually been issued by the directors.

Using www.heinemann.co.uk/hotlinks (express code 1149P, then go to Unit 2), visit the London Stock Exchange website and you will see there are a number of types of securities. These may include:

* Ordinary shares – dividends/profits for these are normally expressed as a percentage of the nominal value of the shares or as a monetary value per share

* Preference shares – these carry a preferential right to receive a dividend

* Debentures – these are split into units in the same way as shares but are, in effect, loans to the company that may be secured on specific assets.

A company's capital is split into shares that are recorded at a nominal value. Nominal values might be at 5p, 10p, 25p, 50p or £1. For example, a company with 10,000 shares issued at a nominal value of £0.50 has a share capital of £5,000, and this would be disclosed in the capital section of the balance sheet. The difference between the issue price paid by the shareholder and the nominal value is called the share premium.

Limited companies rarely distribute all their profits. A proportion is usually retained in the form of reserves. There are two forms of reserves:

* Revenue reserves – These are usually left as the balance of the 'profit and loss account' or 'retained profits'. To give shareholders confidence in the funding of the business, directors may decide to transfer some of the profit and loss account balance into a general reserve.

* Capital reserves – They may include revaluation reserves that occur when property is revalued and also share premium, the value of the higher amount than the nominal value of shares.

The trading account of a limited company is similar to the trading account of any other type of organisation. However, in the profit and loss account:

* Directors' fees or salaries may be included, because these people are employed by the company and their fees and salaries are an expense.

* Debenture payments, being the same as loan interest, may also appear as an expense.

Beneath the profit and loss account of a company will appear the appropriation account. This is designed to show what happens to any profit and how it is divided. An appropriation account for a company with a net profit of £250,000 would look like this:

	£	£
Net profit		250,000
Less: Corporation Tax		100,000
Profit after taxation		150,000
Less: Proposed dividends		
Ordinary shares	70,000	
Preference shares	20,000	90,000
		60,000
Less: Transfer to general reserve		40,000
		20,000
Add: Retained profit from previous year		30,000
Balance of retained profit carried forward		50,000

Corporation tax is the first charge on profits and has to be paid to the Inland Revenue. Proposed dividends are the portion of the profits paid to the shareholders. After dividends have been paid, it is possible to allocate profits to reserves. Any profit left over at the end of the year, after taxes and shareholders of all kinds have been paid, is added to the balance of profit from the previous year to give the new retained profit:

Balance of profit at end of year =
Net profit from current year +
Retained profits from previous years
− Corporation Tax − Transfers to reserves − Dividends

In the balance sheet of a company, the fixed and current assets are presented in the same way as in any other balance sheet.

The current liabilities are the liabilities due to be paid within 12 months of the date of the balance sheet. In addition to those which normally appear in this section, limited companies also have to show Corporation Tax that is due to be paid during the next 12 months, as well as ordinary and preference share dividends to be paid. Long-term liabilities may include debentures.

At the beginning of the 'Financed by' section of the balance sheet, details will appear of the authorised capital, specifying the type, value and number of shares the company is authorised to issue. These are in the balance sheet for interest only and their value is excluded from the totals. 'Issued capital' contains details of the classes and numbers of shares that have been issued (obviously, the issued share capital cannot exceed the authorised).

Reserves are shown beneath the capital. Reserves and retained profits are the amounts the

The balance sheet of Wargrave Ltd as at 31 December 2004

	£	£	£
Fixed assets			
Land and buildings			320,000
Machinery			24,000
Motor vehicles			12,000
			356,000
Current assets			
Stocks		12,250	
Debtors		7,100	
Bank		23,200	
Cash		500	
		43,050	
Less: Current liabilities			
Creditors		500	
Proposed dividends:			
Ordinary shares	12,000		
Preference shares	10,000		
Corporation Tax	10,350	32,850	
Working capital/			
net current assets			10,200
			366,200
Less: Long-term liabilities			
Bank loan		10,000	
10% debentures		8,000	
			18,000
Net assets			348,200
Financed by			
Authorised share capital			
400,000 ordinary shares of £1			400,000
100,000 10% preference			
shares of £1			100,000
			500,000
Issued share capital			
200,000 ordinary shares			
of £1 fully paid			200,000
100,000 10% preference			
shares of £1 fully paid			100,000
			300,000
Reserves			
General reserve		6,000	
Balance of retained profit		42,200	
		48,200	
Shareholders' funds			348,200

directors and shareholders decide to keep within the company. Shareholders' funds comprise the total of share capital plus reserves.

Cash flow forecasting

Whereas profit is a surplus from trading activities, cash is a liquid asset that enables an organisation to buy the goods and services it requires in order to add value to them, trade and make profits. It is therefore possible for an organisation to be profitable while, at the same time, creditors have not been paid and liquid resources have not been properly accounted for.

On the other hand, an organisation must look carefully to see that its use of cash is to its best advantage. For example, if it holds too much cash in the bank, it might be sacrificing the potential to earn greater income.

An organisation must therefore ensure it has sufficient cash to carry out its plans and that the cash coming in is sufficient to cover the cash going out. At the same time it must take into account any cash surpluses it might have in the bank.

Looking carefully at the availability of liquid funds is essential to the smooth running of any organisation. With cash planning or budgeting it is possible to forecast the flows into and out of an organisation's bank account so that any surpluses or deficits can be highlighted and any necessary action can be taken promptly. For example, overdraft facilities may be arranged in good time so funds are available when required.

The cash flow forecast is an extremely important tool within an organisation and has a number of clear purposes. For example:

✱ The forecast can be used to highlight the timing consequences of different expenditures, ensuring that facilities, such as an overdraft, can be set up to pay bills.

✱ The cash flow forecast (see example in Figure 2.34) is an essential document for the compilation of the business plan. It will help to show whether the organisation is capable of achieving the objectives it sets. This is very important if the business applies for finance, where the lender will almost certainly want to know about the ability of the applicant to keep on top of the cash flow and meet the proposed payment schedules.

✱ The cash flow forecast will help to boost the lender's confidence and the owner's confidence. By looking into the future it will provide them with the reassurance they

	JULY	AUG	SEPT	OCT	NOV	DEC
Receipts						
Sales	900	1,125	1,350	825	2,100	1,950
Total receipts	900	1,125	1,350	825	2,100	1,950
Payments						
Raw materials	520	600	580	640	680	640
Direct labour	400	650	650	750	725	800
Variable expenses	300	420	520	560	590	610
Fixed expenses	50	50	50	50	50	50
Total payments	1,270	1,720	1,800	2,000	2,045	2,100
Receipts – payments	(370)	(595)	(450)	(1,175)	55	(150)
Balance b/f	4,500	4,130	3,535	3,085	1,910	1,965
Balance c/f	4,130	3,535	3,085	1,910	1,965	1,815

FIGURE 2.34 *Example of a cash flow forecast*

require that their plans are going according to schedule.

* It will also help with the monitoring of performance. The cash flow forecast sets benchmarks against which the business is expected to perform. If the organisation actually performs differently from these benchmarks, the cash flow forecast may have highlighted an area for investigation. As we have seen, investigating differences between forecast figures and actual figures is known as variance analysis.

To prepare a cash flow forecast you need to know what receipts and payments are likely to take place in the future and exactly when they will occur. It is important to know the length of the lead-time between incurring an expense and paying for it, as well as the time lag between making a sale and collecting the money from debtors. The art of successful forecasting is being able to calculate receipts and expenditures accurately.

When working though a cash flow forecast, it is important to look carefully at the timing of every entry.

For example, C. Moon Ltd has £500 in the bank on 1 January. The owner, Christine Moon, anticipates that her receipts over the next six months are likely to be:

JAN	FEB	MARCH	APRIL	MAY	JUNE
£2,300	£1,400	£5,300	£6,100	£4,700	£1,400

She has also worked out what her payments are likely to be over the next six months:

JAN	FEB	MARCH	APRIL	MAY	JUNE
£1,400	£4,100	£5,600	£5,000	£3,100	£900

Christine Moon is concerned about whether she needs an overdraft facility and, if so, when she is likely to use it. Construct a cash flow forecast and advise her on her financial requirements.

The forecast shows that C. Moon Ltd needs to set up an overdraft facility between the months of February and April.

	JAN £	FEB £	MAR £	APR £	JUNE £	JULY £
Balance	500	1,400	(1,300)	(1,600)	(500)	1,100
Receipts	2,300	1,400	5,300	6,100	4,700	1,400
	2,800	2,800	4,000	4,500	4,200	2,500
Payments	1,400	4,100	5,600	5,000	3,100	900
	1,400	(1,300)	(1,600)	(500)	1,100	1,600

Learning activity

Prepare the cash flow forecast of S. Huang Ltd. The business has £250 in the bank and the owner anticipates his receipts over the next six months are likely to be as follows:

JAN	FEB	MARCH	APRIL	MAY	JUNE
£1,400	£1,600	£1,500	£1,000	£900	£700

He has also worked out his payments and expects these to be:

JAN	FEB	MARCH	APRIL	MAY	JUNE
£1,100	£700	£900	£1,400	£1,000	£900

Prepare S. Huang Ltd's cash flow forecast for the next six months.

Budgeting

As well as recording financial information and making judgements about the effectiveness of the information, businesses need to manage their finances. The two main elements of financial management are budgeting and cash flow.

Budgets help businesses to plan, set targets and control expenditure. To understand how budgets are used you need to know what they are, how they work and their particular purposes. You will need to be able to identify and interpret variance and explain the benefits of budgeting to businesses.

Businesses need to control their working capital. To understand how they can do this you need to know what working capital is and how businesses manage their cash. You also need to know that businesses may have cash flow problems and that they need to be solved. This

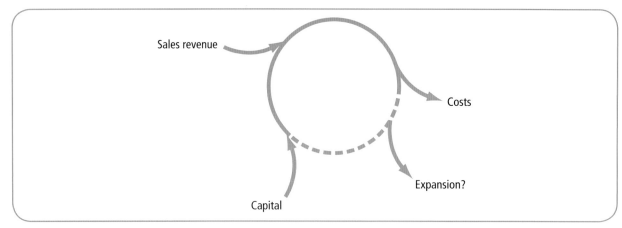

FIGURE 2.35 *The 'money-go-round'*

involves examining credit control and other methods businesses use to maintain their working capital.

Financial planning involves defining objectives and then developing ways to achieve them. To be able to do this, a financial manager must have a realistic understanding of what is happening and what is likely to happen within the organisation – for example, when is money going to come in, what is it needed for and would it be possible to use some of it for expansion and development? In the 'money-go-round' (see Figure 2.35), capital and sales revenue come into a business, but is there enough left over, after paying all the costs, for expansion and development?

Looking into their future helps all organisations to plan their activities so that what they anticipate and want to happen can actually happen. This process of financial planning is known as budgeting. It is considered to be a system of responsibility accounting because it puts

an onus on budgeted areas to perform in a way that has been outlined for them, and its success will depend upon the quality of information provided. Businesses that do not budget may not be pleased when they view their final accounts. Budgeting helps the financial manager to develop an understanding of how the business is likely to perform in the future.

We all budget to a greater or lesser extent. Our short-term budget may relate to how we are going to get through the coming week and do all the things we want to do. Our slightly longer-term budget may involve being able to afford

Learning activity

Identify a range of activities in which you participate that you think could be helped by some form of budgeting. For example, these may include your personal finances or some club responsibility. Explain how in each instance.

CASE STUDY

Managing Student Finances

One of the big problems for most students today is how to manage their finances effectively. In order to be able to spread their income and student loan across all of their financial responsibilities students need to be both sensible and resourceful. Students have many different financial commitments and yet for many of them, it is the first time away

from home in a different environment and a situation where they have to manage money for the first time. Some of the consequences of not managing their money can be quite serious.

1 **Why is it important for students to budget?**
2 **What practical steps could they take to budget?**

Christmas presents in two months' time. Our longest-term budget could involve the planning necessary to afford the car tax, MOT and motor insurance, which are all due ten months from now. Also, when can we afford in the longer term to replace the car?

In exactly the same way, businesses try to see far into the future. The problem is that, the further one looks into the future, the more difficult it is to see it accurately.

A budget is a financial plan developed for the future. Many businesses appoint a budget controller whose sole task is to co-ordinate budgetary activities. A short-term budget would be for up to one year, a medium-term budget would be for anything from one year to five years and a budget for a longer period than this would be a long-term budget.

Wherever budgeting takes place, it is important to draw upon the collective experience of people throughout the business. A budgeting team might consist of representatives from various areas of activity. The team will consider the objectives of the budgeting process, obtain and provide relevant information, make decisions, prepare budgets and then use these budgets to help to control the business.

Budgeting provides a valuable benchmark against which to measure and judge the actual performance of key areas of business activity. There are therefore many benefits of budgeting:

* It helps to predict what the organisation thinks will happen. Given the experience within the organisation, budgets help to show what is likely to take place in the future.

* Budgets create opportunities to appraise alternative courses of action. Information created for budgeting purposes forms the basis of decisions that have to be taken. The research necessary for budgeting will look at alternative ways of achieving the organisation's objectives.

* Budgets set targets. If communicated to people throughout the organisation, the budgets will help them to work towards the targets that have been set.

* They help to monitor and control performance. This can be done by studying actual results,

comparing these to budgeted results and then finding out why differences (known as variances) may have occurred. Sometimes variances are bad, while at other times they may be good. Whatever the causes of the variances, they are a useful starting point for dealing with issues within the business.

* Budgets are fundamental to the process of business planning. They provide a series of quantitative guidelines that can be used for co-ordination and then followed in order to achieve the organisation's business objectives.

* They can be used as a source of motivation. As part of the consultation process, budgets help to keep people involved. They also help to create goal congruence, so that the aims and objectives of the individual are the same as those for the organisation.

* Budgets are a form of communication. They enable employees from across the organisation to be aware of performance expectations with regard to their individual work area.

Budgeting may also have some useful spin-offs. Every year the business is reviewed and this gives members of the various departments a better understanding of the working of the organisation as a whole. In fact, by participating in the budgetary process they feel their experience is contributing to policy decisions.

It also increases co-operation between departments and lowers departmental barriers. In this way members of one department can become aware of the difficulties facing another department. By being involved in the budgetary process, non-accountants also appreciate the importance of costs.

In reality, budgeting may take place in almost all parts of an organisation. Budgeting should also be viewed as something that is going on all the time and as a source of useful information and guidance for managers.

The process of budget setting

The process of setting budgets has to be seen within the context of the longer-term objectives and strategies at the highest level of management of any organisation. The administration of the budgeting process will usually be the responsibility of the accounts department. Many organisations set up a budget committee to oversee the process.

The budgetary process is usually governed by a formal budget timetable. This helps to link the budget in with all other aspects of business planning (see Figure 2.36).

The accounts department is involved at all stages of the budgeting process, and an effective accounts team will provide a range of advice to managers as the exercise develops. Spreadsheets are an effective 'what-if' tool that are often used to help within the budgeting process.

Setting up a system of 'responsibility accounting' such as budgeting involves breaking down an organisation into a series of 'control centres'. Each individual manager then has the responsibility for managing the budget relating to his or her particular control centre.

Budgetary reports, therefore, reflect the assigned responsibility at each level of the organisation. As all organisations have a structure of control, it is important the budgetary system fits around this. The reports should be designed to reflect the different levels within the organisation and the responsibilities of each of the managers concerned.

If the budgeting process reflects the different levels of control, managers will be kept informed not just of their own performance but also of that of other budget holders for whom they are responsible. They will also know that managers above them will be assessing their performance. This system can be reviewed regularly at meetings attended by all the individual managers concerned (see Figure 2.37).

Although it could be claimed that they are mechanistic, budget models formalise the inter-relationships between departments and provide

Learning activity

Find out more about the budgeting process within your school or college. For example, how are budgets set, what processes take place and who are the budget holders? What happens if budget holders overspend?

BUDGET TIMETABLE FOR YEAR 1 APRIL 2005 TO 31 MARCH 2006		
Date	*Narrative*	*Responsibility*
1 Sept	Board of directors to review long-term objectives and strategies and specify short term goals for the year	Directors
22 Sept	Budget guidelines and standard forms issued to line managers	Accounts
6 Oct	Actual results for year are issued to line management, so that comparisons can be made with current budget and last year's actual results	Accounts
20 Oct	Budget submissions are made to the management accountant	Line management
27 Oct	First draft of the master budget is issued	Accounts
3 Nov	First draft of the budget is reviewed for results and consistency – line managers to justify their submissions	MD and individual directors
7 Nov	New assumptions and guidelines issued to line management	Accounts
10 Nov	Budgets revised and resubmitted	Line management
21 Nov	Second draft of master budget issued	Accounts
28 Nov	Final review of the draft budget	Managing Director and financial director
1 Dec	Final amendments	Accounts
12 Dec	Submission to the board for their approval	Financial director

FIGURE 2.36 *A budget timetable*

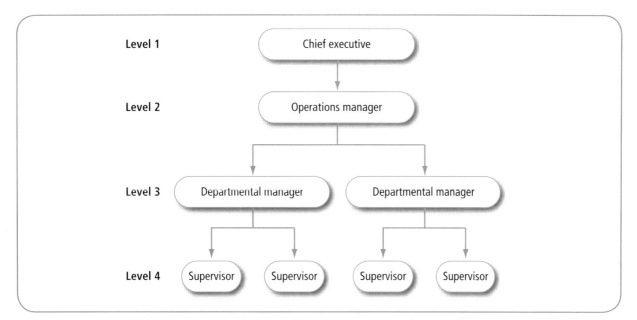

FIGURE 2.37 *A reporting hierarchy*

a basic understanding of work flows within business organisations.

The overall budget as a plan will have real value only if the performance levels set through the budget are realistic. Budgets based upon ideal conditions are unlikely to be met and will result in departments failing to meet their targets. For example, the sales department may fail to achieve their sales budget, which may result in goods remaining unsold. Budgets can be motivating only if they are pitched at a realistic level.

There are two approaches to budget setting. The top-down approach involves senior managers specifying what the best performance indicators are for the business across all departments and budgeted areas. The bottom-up approach builds up the organisational master budget on the basis of the submissions of individual line managers and supervisors, based upon their own views of their requirements. In practice most organisations use a mixture of both methods (see Figure 2.38).

Budget setting should be based upon realistic predictions of future sales and costs. Many organisations base future predictions solely on past figures, with adjustments for forecast growth and inflation rates. Although the main advantage of this approach is that budgets are based upon actual data, future conditions may not mirror past ones.

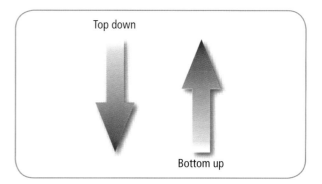

FIGURE 2.38 *Approaches to budget setting*

One of the dangers of budgeting is that, if actual results are dramatically different from the budgeting ones, the process could lose its credibility as a means of control. Following a budget too rigidly may also restrict a business's activities. For example, if the budget for entertainment has been exceeded and subsequent visiting customers are not treated with the usual hospitality, orders may be lost. On the other hand, if managers realise that towards the end of the year a department has underspent, they may decide to go on a spending spree.

Budgeting is a routine annual event for many different types of organisations. The process may start in the middle of the financial year, with a revision of the current year's budget and with first drafts of the budget for the coming year. Some organisations plan further ahead with an outline plan for 3–5 years.

Using budgetary control variances

Budgets provide an opportunity for everyone to play a part in either the strategic or tactical development of the organisation. As the activities following the budgetary process unfold, they provide a benchmark against which actual performance can be measured and judged.

As a result, an essential feature of the budgetary control system is the feedback of actual results. The process of measuring the difference between budgeted (intended) and actual outcomes is known as variance analysis. Variance analysis makes it possible to detect problems. Reasons can be sought for variances and speedy action can be taken to improve performance.

Budgeting should be viewed as something that is going on all the time and as a source of useful information and guidance for managers.

Creating budgets

In practice, budgeting may take place in almost all parts of an organisation. The money values attached to budgets are often linked to quantities, such as units, weights and other forms of measurement. This also helps to tie the budgeting process in with operational activities so that the budget can be used as a management tool. We shall discuss three key areas of budgetary forecasts:

* *The capital budget* The word 'capital' refers to the buying of fixed assets. Do we plan now for the money we will need in the future to buy another machine? The capital budget is a simple statement of intent or forecast, which specifies the planned purchase of assets, the date of intended purchase and the expected cost of purchase.

* *The cash budget or cash flow forecast* This forecast looks at the cash coming in to the organisation as well as the cash going out. It is a prediction by a business of how much money it thinks it will receive and how much it thinks it will pay out over a specified time. By forecasting cash flow, managers will know what their future

financial requirements will be and will be able to take action beforehand if they need an overdraft or some form of loan.

* *Subsidiary budgets and the master budget* Functional budgets for different business activities and budgets for individual balance sheet items are called subsidiary budgets. The exact nature of subsidiary budgets will depend on the organisational structure and the operational processes of an organisation. The term 'master budget' includes the budgeted profit and loss account, balance sheet and cash budget.

The capital budget

Capital expenditure refers to the acquisition of fixed assets. Capital budgets are prepared to plan for the purchase of fixed assets.

The capital budget is prepared after reviewing fixed asset needs for the budget period. This will be done in the light of business objectives and planned strategy for the next budget period. The next step is to consider the condition and capacity of existing fixed assets. For example, a planned expansion into new markets will require a review of existing assets to ensure sufficient business capacity is available. Capital expenditure may also be required to renew existing assets, such as worn-out equipment. In recognising that more fixed assets are required, it is necessary to plan their purchase, including the time and cost of acquisition.

It follows from the nature of this type of expenditure that some years will require more capital expenditure than others. Together with the fact that, for many businesses, the value of fixed assets used is significant, it is important capital budgets are prepared to ensure adequate finance is planned.

Classifications of capital expenditure will follow those you are already familiar with from constructing the fixed assets section of the balance sheet. Typically they include:

* land and buildings
* factory plant and machinery
* office fixtures and fittings

* computer equipment

* motor vehicles.

Expenditure may be further analysed into assets required for:

* expansion of existing product ranges

* expansion into new products

* replacement of existing assets

* satisfying health and safety requirements.

In this way information is provided as to whether the business is expanding or just maintaining its productive capacity. It may also indicate whether items of capital expenditure are essential or merely desirable.

Look at the capital budget of Jason Robards (see Figure 2.39). The forecast shows that, over the year, £50,000 is needed for a CNC machine, £20,000 for two motor vans, £5,500 for a new computer, £50,000 for a new building extension, £40,000 for improving the production line and £9,500 for installing a new air conditioning system. The capital budget quickly provides an indication that £175,000 is needed for capital purchases for the year and then itemises amounts required month by month.

When evaluating expenditure on capital items, the business managers will consider the likely returns on making the investment and the associated risk of not reaping the hoped-for benefits. The cost of purchasing assets should be evaluated against a range of benefits such as increased sales or reduced costs. In many cases it is necessary to perform a cost–benefit analysis to recognise the more qualitative aspects of the proposal. For example, expenditure on welfare facilities (such as employee social clubs and catering facilities) will be evaluated for the

Learning activity

Whitehills Leisure Centre provides customers with a gym, swimming pool and team sports hall. The centre's management is reviewing capital expenditure needs for 2006. They intend to expand facilities during the year with four squash courts and more equipment for the gym. The squash courts will be built in May at a cost of £75,000. The additional gym equipment will comprise three exercise bikes costing £1,000 in March, a rowing machine costing £1,200 in July and weight-lifting equipment costing £2,000 in November.

The receptionist has been complaining about the number of repair visits required recently for the computerised cash till, and so it has been decided to replace this in January at a cost of £1,600.

The floor surface around the swimming pool is too slippery when wet and so the management have decided this should be replaced in January at a cost of £5,000 to minimise the risk of accidents. It has also been decided to refurbish the changing rooms. New lockers and benches will cost £5,000 in June.

Prepare a capital budget for Whitehills Leisure Centre for the year ended 31 December 2006, with separate sections for expansion, replacement and health and safety.

	Jan £	Feb £	March £	April £	May £	June £	July £	Aug £	Sept £	Oct £	Nov £	Dec £	Total £
Replacement													
CNC machine						50,000							50,000
2 motor vans								20,000					20,000
Computer			5,500										5,500
Expansion													
Building extension									50,000				50,000
Production line										40,000			40,000
Health and safety													
Air conditioning		9,500											9,500
Total	0	9,500	5,500	0	0	50,000	0	20,000	50,000	40,000	0	0	175,000

FIGURE 2.39 *A budget timetable for Jason Robards*

goodwill and lower staff turnover such facilities may encourage.

Remember that, even though we are looking at the capital budget and the cash budget individually, all budgets are linked to the master budget. Once prepared, the details from the capital budget are incorporated into the cash budget.

Subsidiary budgets and the master budget

Subsidiary budgets include all parts of a business organisation. When put together they are used to produce the master budget, which includes the profit and loss account, balance sheet and cash budget, all of which help to map the future of a business organisation for the next accounting period.

A key feature of the budgeting process is the feedback it provides for individuals and groups throughout an organisation. Feedback should reflect the information needs of each level of the organisation, with each level of reporting being inter-related with levels above and below. For example, a budget holder will wish to be

---

Learning activity

The Premier Christmas Pudding Co. require you to prepare their budget statements for the seven months to January 2006. You have been given the following information:

* The sales forecast for 1 kg puddings is as follows:

July	Aug	Sept	Oct	Nov	Dec	Total
100	100	500	1,300	10,000	20,000	32,000

* No sales of puddings have been made in the previous six months.

* Each 1 kg pudding sells for £2.50.

* Customers are mainly retailers and wholesalers who take one month to pay for puddings received.

* It is company policy to hold a minimum stock of puddings each month that is equivalent to the next month's forecast sales. After December, sales are not forecast until July of the next year. The requisite minimum stock would be held at the end of June, valued at £1.20 per pudding.

* Sufficient dry fruits are held in stock to cover the next month's forecast production. Other ingredients are purchased in the month of use.

* All suppliers are paid on delivery.

* Production capacity is limited to 10,000 kg per month.

* Direct labour is employed on a piece-work rate of £0.20 per kg of pudding.

* Costs for a 100 kg batch are as follows:

	kg	£
Dried fruit	50	60
Other	50	30
Packaging		10
Distribution		20

* The whole period's packaging materials will be received from the printers at the beginning of July. The packaging is of a special design to celebrate the firm's 50th anniversary. In case sales exceed forecast, sufficient packaging for 35,000 puddings has been ordered. Excess packaging is to be disposed of in December.

* Administration overhead is fixed at £3,000 per month and is payable up to the end of January 2006.

* The bank balance at the end of June 2005 is forecast to be £15,930.

* No losses are assumed in the production process.

For each of the seven months up to 31 January 2006, prepare:

1 The sales budget

2 The finished stock and production budget

3 The raw materials stock and purchases budget (separate for mixed fruit, packaging and other)

4 The direct labour budget

5 The cash budget

6 The forecast trading and profit and loss account.

---

informed of his or her own performance as well as that of the budget holders for whom he or she is responsible.

Variance analysis

Earlier in this chapter we looked at the construction of budgets related to functional aspects of an organisation for the control and monitoring of performance. The key benefit of the budgeting process is to analyse how closely actual performance relates to budgeted performance. Wherever actual differs from budgeted performance a variance takes place. The process of analysing the difference between actual performance and budgeted performance is called variance analysis.

Variances are recorded as being either adverse (A) or favourable (F), depending upon whether actual expenditure is more or less than budget. For example, if actual expenditure is less than budgeted expenditure, the variance would be favourable. On the other hand, if actual expenditure is more than budgeted expenditure, the variance is adverse.

Figure 2.40 shows that managers cannot be answerable for cost over-runs if they occur in areas where they have no control. For example, whereas expenditure on machine maintenance may be controlled, this is not true of depreciation, which is outside the manager's control.

Understanding variances

Variances may arise for a number of reasons. These include:

* *Random deviations which are uncontrollable* As we saw above, these are outside the control of individual managers.

* *An incorrectly set budget* This may require further research and management action.

* *Failure to meet an agreed budget* This would be because a manager has failed to meet the appropriate figures and deadlines.

Problems of the budgetary process

Budgetary and control systems vary from one organisation to another. They are found both in the private sector and the public sector, and in all sorts of organisations from the very small

MACHINE SHOP OVERHEAD REPORT FOR OCTOBER 2004			
	Budget £	Actual £	Variance £
Controllable			
Indirect wages	8,000	8,200	200 A
Machine maintenance	2,250	1,900	350 F
Consumable materials	500	550	50 A
Total controllable costs	10,750	10,650	100 F
Uncontrollable			
Depreciation	5,700	6,000	300 A
Property cost apportionment	8,500	9,000	500 A
Total uncontrollable costs	14,200	15,000	800 A
Total cost centre overhead	24,950	25,650	700 A
A = Adverse			
F = Favourable			

FIGURE 2.40 *Controllable and uncontrollable costs*

to the very large. Given the different aims of organisations, budgetary systems reflect the context in which they are put to use. There are, however, certain problems associated with budgeting processes that have to be recognised.

First, reliance upon budgeting and its processes is no substitute for good management. Budgeting should simply be viewed as one tool among many for managers to use. If forecasting is poor or inadequate allowances are made, the process may create unnecessary pressure upon managers to perform in a particular way. This may be stressful and cause antagonism and resentment within the organisation.

The creation of rigid financial plans that are 'cast in stone' may cause inertia in certain parts of a business and reduce its ability to adapt to change. Budgets may also not reflect the realities of the business environment and act simply as a straitjacket upon the performance of managers and decision-makers. It has also been argued that delays and time lags can make it difficult to compare budgeted and actual results.

Break-even analysis

Before looking at break-even analysis we need a basic understanding of costs. One method of classifying costs is according to changes in output. This identifies costs as either fixed or variable.

Fixed costs are costs that do not increase as total output increases. For example, if an organisation has the capacity needed it might increase its production from 25,000 units to 30,000 units. However its fixed costs such as rent, rates, heating and lighting will be the same, since they also had to be paid when the organisation was producing 25,000 units.

In contrast variable costs are those costs that increase as total output increases because more of these factors need to be employed as inputs in order to increase outputs. For example, if you produce more items you need more raw materials.

The **break-even point** is the point at which sales levels are high enough not to make a loss, but not high enough to make a profit.

The concept of break-even is a development from the principles of *marginal costing*. Marginal costing is a commonly employed technique that uses costs to forecast profits from the production and sales levels expected in future periods. The benefit of marginal costing over other costing methods is that it overcomes the problem of allocating fixed costs – only variable costs are allocated as we shall see.

The difference between an item's selling price and the variable costs needed to produce that item is know as *contribution*.

$$\text{Contribution} = \begin{array}{l} \text{Selling price per unit} \\ \textit{less } \text{variable costs per unit} \end{array}$$

By producing and selling enough units to produce a total contribution that is in excess of *fixed costs*, an organisation will make a profit.

For example, Penzance Toys Ltd manufactures plastic train sets for young children. They anticipate that next year they will sell 8,000 units at £12 per unit. Their variable costs are £5 per unit and their fixed costs are £9,000. From the above formula we can deduce that the contribution is £12 minus £5, which is £7 per unit. Therefore, for each unit made, £7 will go towards paying the fixed costs. We can also see this using totals to show how much profit will be made if the company sells 8,000 units. The problem can also be looked at by constructing a table, as follows:

	Fixed	Variable	Total	Revenue	Profit
Units of production	costs (£)	costs (£)	costs (£)	(£)	(loss) (£)
1,000	9,000	5,000	14,000	12,000	(2,000)
2,000	9,000	10,000	19,000	24,000	5,000
3,000	9,000	15,000	24,000	36,000	12,000
4,000	9,000	20,000	29,000	48,000	19,000
5,000	9,000	25,000	34,000	60,000	26,000
6,000	9,000	30,000	39,000	72,000	33,000
7,000	9,000	35,000	44,000	84,000	40,000
8,000	9,000	40,000	49,000	96,000	47,000
9,000	9,000	45,000	54,000	108,000	54,000
10,000	9,000	50,000	59,000	120,000	61,000

FIGURE 2.41 *Profit increases as the units of production increase*

	£
Sales revenue (8000 x £12)	96,000
Less: Marginal costs (8000 x £5)	40,000
Total contribution	56,000
Less: Fixed costs	9,000
Net profit	47,000

Learning activity

Rovers Medallions Ltd produce a standard size trophy for sports shops and clubs. They hope to sell 2,000 trophies next year at £9 per unit. Their variable costs are £5 per unit and their fixed costs are £4,000.

Draw up a profit statement to show how much profit they will make in the year. Also construct a table to show how much profit they will make at each 500 units of production up to 3,000 units.

How break-even analysis helps monitor business performance

Marginal costing is particularly useful for making short-term decisions – for example, helping to set the selling price of a product, or deciding whether or not to accept an order. It might also help an organisation to decide whether to buy in a component or whether to produce it themselves.

Break-even analysis is a concept that is central to the process of marginal costing. Breaking even is the unique point at which an organisation neither makes profit or loss. If sales go beyond the break-even point, profits are made, and if they are below the break-even point, losses are made. In marginal costing terms, it is the *point at which the contribution equals the fixed costs.*

Calculating and interpreting break-even charts

To calculate the break-even point there are two stages:

Calculate the unit contribution (selling price less variable cost per unit)

Divide the fixed costs by the unit contribution:

$$\text{Break-even point} = \frac{\text{Fixed costs}}{\text{Unit contribution}}$$

For example, in Penzance Toys Ltd the contribution per unit is £7 and the fixed costs are £9,000. The break-even point would therefore be:

$$\frac{9,000}{7} = 1,286 \text{ units (to nearest unit)}$$

The *sales value* at the break-even point can be calculated by multiplying the number of units by the selling price per unit. For Penzance Toys this would be:

$$1,286 \times £12 = £15,432$$

Hussey and family Ltd is a small business selling hives to local beekeepers. Each hive is sold for £25. Fixed costs are £18,000 and variable costs are £13 per unit. The company wishes to achieve a profit of £18,000. Calculate the break-even point in both units and sales value. Calculate both the units and sales value necessary to achieve the selected operating profit.

Penzance Toys have covered their costs (fixed and variable) and broken even with a sales value of £15,432. Anything sold in excess of this will provide them with profits.

If an organisation has a *profit target* or selecting operating point to aim at, break-even analysis can be used to calculate the number of units that need to be sold and the value of sales required to achieve that target.

For example, we can image that Penzance Toys wish to achieve a target of £15,000 profit. By adding this £15,000 to the fixed costs and dividing by the contribution, the number of units can be found that need to be sold to meet this target. Thus:

£9,000 + £15,000 = 3,429 units (to nearest unit)

The difference between the break-even point and the selected level of activity designed to achieve the profit target is known as the *margin of safety*.

A break-even chart can be used to show changes in the relationship between costs, production volumes and various levels of sales activity. The following is the procedure to construct a break-even chart:

* Label the horizontal axis for units of production and sales
* Label the vertical axis to represent the values of sales and costs
* Plot fixed costs. Fixed costs will remain the same over all levels of production, so plot this as a straight line parallel to the horizontal axis
* Plot the total costs (variable and fixed costs). This will be a line rising from where the fixed cost line touches the vertical axis. It is plotted by calculating the total costs at two or three random levels of production

* Sales are then plotted by taking two or three random levels of turnover. The line will rise from the intersection of the two axes.

The break-even point will be where the total cost line and the sales line intersect. The area to the *left* of the break-even point between the sales and total cost lines will represent *losses*, and the area to the *right* of the break-even point between these lines will represent *profit*.

For example, Eddie Bowen plans to set up a small restaurant. In doing so he knows he will immediately incur annual fixed costs of £10,000. He is concerned about how many meals he will have to sell to break even. Extensive market research indicates a typical customer will pay £8 for a meal, and Eddie knows that variable costs (such as cooking ingredients and the costs of serving customers) will amount to about £3. Eddie has set himself a profit target of £14,000 for the first year of operation. Our task is to advise Eddie on the number of meals he has to sell and to indicate to him his margin of safety.

Eddie's *unit contribution* is:

£8 − £3 (Selling price − Variable cost) = £5 per meal

His *break-even point* in units will be:

£10,000 (Fixed costs) divided by £5 unit contribution = 2,000 meals

The *sales value* of the meals will be:

2,000 meals x £8 (Selling price) = £16,000

His *profit target* will be achieved by:

$$\frac{£10,000 \text{ (Fixed costs)} + £14,000 \text{ (Profit Target)}}{£5 \text{ (Unit contribution)}} = 4,800 \text{ meals}$$

The *margin of safety* will be the difference between the selected level of activity and the break-even point. It will be between 4,800 meals with a turnover of £38,400 and 2,000 meals with a turnover of £16,000.

The three random levels of variable costs and sales chosen for the purpose of plotting the break-even chart are at 1,000 meals, 3,000 meals and 5,000 meals. They are:

	1,000 MEALS £	3,000 MEALS £	5,000 MEALS £
Variable costs (£3 per meal)	3,000	9,000	15,000
Fixed costs	10,000	10,000	10,000
Total costs	13,000	19,000	25,000
Sales	8,000	24,000	40,000

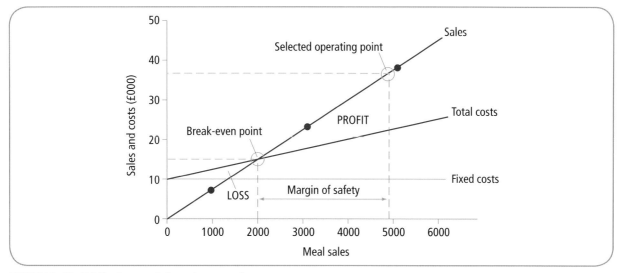

FIGURE 2.42 *Eddie Bowen's break-even chart*

We can now plot the break-even chart (Figure 2.42) which shows graphically the break-even point of 2,000 meals with a sales revenue of £16,000. The margin of safety can be seen on the chart if we identify the selected level of profit (at 4,800 meals) and the targeted turnover (of £38,400), and compare this point with the break-even point.

The break-even chart is a simple visual tool enabling managers to anticipate the effects of changes in production and sales upon the profitability of an organisation's activities. It emphasises the importance of earning revenue and is particularly helpful for those who are unused to interpreting accounting information.

How changes in variables such as fixed costs affect break-even

The break-even chart can be used to explore changes in a number of key variables. These may include:

* *Sales volume and value* By looking at the chart it is possible to predict the effects of changes in

sales trends. For example, a sudden fall in sales may lead to a loss and a sudden increase may improve profitability.

* *Profits or losses at a given level of production* The break-even chart enables a business to monitor levels of production. By doing this, important decisions can be made if changes take place.

* *Prices* It is possible to use the break-even chart to analyse different business scenarios. For example, given market research information, what would happen if we reduced the price by £2.

* *Costs* The effects of any sudden change in costs can be plotted on the break-even chart.

Any of the above may affect an organisation's ability to achieve its selected operating point and margin of safety. The break-even chart is thus a useful management tool upon which to base action that enables an organisation to achieve its plans.

John Smith had a visit from an aged relative who wanted advice. For many years she had run a small hotel in a market town in the Thames Valley. After careful consideration she had decided to 'call it a day' and retire, but she was keen to see the business continue and wished to retain her ownership in it.

John is interested in a proposition she has put forward, which involves running the hotel on her behalf. The hotel has been allowed to deteriorate over the years and, in John's opinion, it is obvious that extensive refurbishment is necessary before he could realistically consider her proposal. The hotel is, however, in a prime spot, was extensively used little more than ten years ago, and John feels that, with hard work, it has the potential to become successful again.

He has arranged a number of quotations to be made for the building work. The most favourable received was for £180,000, which involved extensive interior redecoration and refurbishment as well as completely reorganising the reception and kitchen areas.

John's intention is that the finance for the building work should come from a five-year bank loan with a fixed annual interest rate of 10%, payable each calendar month, and based upon the original sum. The loan principal would be paid back in five equal annual instalments. He has estimated the following fixed and variable costs:

Fixed

✱ Annual loan repayment   £36,000

✱ Annual interest on loan   £18,000

✱ Business rate and water
   rates   £7,000 per annum

✱ Insurance   £4,500 per annum

✱ Electricity   £1,300 per quarter

✱ Staff salaries   £37,000 per annum.

Variable

These include direct labour (such as cleaners and bar staff), as well as the cost of food, bar stocks, etc. After careful research John has estimated these to be £2,000 for each 100 customers who visit the hotel.

John has had a local agency conduct an extensive market research survey and feels confident that the hotel will attract about 100 customers per week, who will each spend on average (including accommodation, food and drinks) about £70 in the hotel.

Work out the break-even point for the hotel in both numbers of customers and value.

Work out the numbers of customers required to make a gross profit of £35,000.

Draw a break-even chart showing the break-even point, the profit target and the margin of safety.

What other information might John Smith require before deciding to go ahead with the project?

The limitations of break-even analysis

Break-even analysis is often considered by some to oversimplify organisational behaviour by reducing it to an equation: how to generate sufficient contribution to cover fixed costs and provide a surplus (profits).

The limitations are as follows:

✱ It can be argued that, in real situations, fixed costs actually vary with different levels of activity, and so a stepped fixed cost line would provide a more accurate guide.

✱ Many organisations fail to break even because of a limiting factor restricting their ability to do so (e.g. a shortage of space, labour or orders).

✱ The variable cost and sales lines are unlikely to be linear (i.e. straight). Discounts, special contracts and overtime payments mean the cost line is more likely to be curved.

✱ Break-even charts depict short-term relationships, and forecasts are therefore unrealistic when the proposals cover a number of years.

Theme Holidays Ltd is a private company that specialises in providing holidays for adults and children who require a unique form of entertainment. All their holidays involve overseas packages based upon a theme. Half the packages are based upon Disneyland Parks, while the other half are based upon theme destinations in the USA.

Theme Holidays are currently reviewing their profitability for 2006. They anticipate fixed overheads will be £450,000 for the year. With the Disneyland Paris packages, a quarter of the variable costs will go in travel costs, at an average of £30 per package. They anticipate selling packages at an average of £160 per holiday in 2006.

The American holidays are sold at an average price of £650 per holiday. Travel costs of £200 for the American holidays comprise half the variable costs of the holiday.

Market research has revealed that, during 2006, Theme Holidays expect to sell 400 holidays.

Work out the contribution for both the European and American holidays.

Calculate the company's profit for the year before tax and interest.

Market research also revealed that, if Theme Holidays reduced their prices by 10%, they could sell 300 more holidays per year. Calculate how this would affect profitability and advise accordingly.

Theme Holidays are aware of the size of their fixed overheads. How would a 10% reduction in fixed overheads through cost-cutting measures affect both of the above?

---

* Break-even analysis is (like all other methods) dependent upon the accuracy of forecasts made about costs and revenues. Changes in the market and in the cost of raw materials could affect the success of this technique.

2.4 The use of software to aid decision-making

The success of business organisations depends in large measure on the efficient and accurate production of goods or services. But its survival also depends on the rapid and accurate processing and distribution of information.

In today's business environment this process is almost totally dependent upon new technology. This is because:

* The scale of many large organisations makes it impossible for every meeting to be conducted face-to-face

* Many organisations are geographically spread out, and require communication links between interrelated plants and offices

* Modern business decision-making frequently requires up-to-date information from a variety of sources

* Competition between business organisations is more fierce

* The pace of industrial development has increased. Organisations must therefore be quicker in responding to factors such as technological change, market forces and competition from rivals.

List the different ways you communicate with friends in a typical day. How many of these different forms of communication such as MSN Messenger and the telephone are dependent upon technologies. Describe how such technologies are transforming the ways in which individuals communicate.

Over the last ten years the modern office workplace has changed dramatically. Paper may still be around in many of these offices, but it is usual for almost every employee to have access to a computer terminal and the expectation is that, where employees use computers, they have the capability to use the many different software applications relevant for their particular jobs. For example, when using computers individuals may be required to use a range of applications such as databases, spreadsheets, word processing packages, the Internet, e-mail, and so on.

In nearly all cases, these computers will be networked. Networking involves linking together two or more computers to allow facilities and information to be shared. This has the effect of decentralising information and communications so that managers and employees have more information upon which to base their decisions. A computer network may be specially developed for almost any type of organisation or application. Terminals may be just a few metres apart or they may exist in completely different parts of the world.

A local area network (LAN) may be used to connect computers within a single room, building or group of buildings on the same site, without the use of telecommunications links. LANs may be linked to a file server, which is a permanent data store that provides files and software for other PCs and also acts as a storage base (see Figure 2.43). Using a form of device such as a hub that links computers, it is relatively easy to connect computers to provide some form of network. Computer gamers often connect their machines together using a hub, so that they can compete with each other in the same room or the same house.

A wide area network (WAN) may be used to connect computers on different sites by making use of telecommunications. The great benefit is that WAN networks extend the use of the computer beyond the office by using a modem (modulator/demodulator), which converts computer signals for transmission over the telephone lines before reconverting them again.

Modems are used because telephone lines are primarily used for speech transmissions and not for use by computers. Waves travelling along lines are analogue waves, where sounds and images are converted into corresponding variations in electrical voltages or currents. However, the digital revolution has seen the creation of new formats that enable the transmission of video and voice signals.

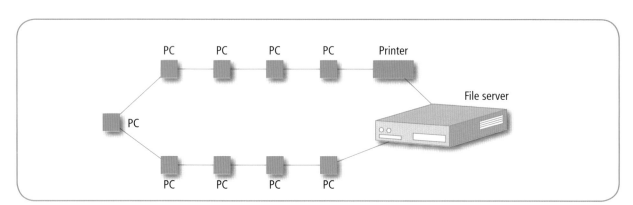

FIGURE 2.43 *Examples of a local area network (LAN)*

One of the hottest talking points at the moment when it comes to both home comforts and for businesses is the emergence of 'broadband'. Broadband is a way of accessing the internet with higher bandwidth with transmission and downloading times more than 40 times faster than that of a standard telephone line. Broadband can be delivered either over an existing telephone line or using cable and wireless networks.

Broadband has the potential to transform how people and businesses operate. With broadband, users are on line all of the time, which saves time and does not involve constantly dialing up and logging on. Broadband users have high-speed access to digital information. For businesses this involves:

* Being able to develop business opportunities electronically over the Internet and the world wide web
* Developing e-commerce services such as on-line ordering and payment systems

* Systems are developed to include all parts of an organisation wherever they are, so that information can be shared
* Possibilities to take goods and services on-line to a global marketplace
* Creating different ways for people to work, providing them with the opportunity to access information quickly, even from home.

How is broadband delivered?

Broadband services can be delivered in different ways – over an ordinary telephone line or private network, via a cable connection or across mobile and wireless networks. BT offers ADSL broadband services over a customer's existing BT telephone line, separating voice and data signals so you can continue to make calls when you are online.

1 **Why might businesses want to have broadband?**
2 **How might broadband create new opportunities for organisations, sometimes irrespective of size?**

Spreadsheets

A spreadsheet is a table of numbers which can be organised and altered on a computer according to preset formulae. Spreadsheets, as we will see, are particularly useful for forecasting and financial modelling, as they show the effects of financial decisions without the need to repeat the calculations manually.

For example, a firm will make a forecast of all the money coming in and going out over a twelve-month period. The spreadsheet can alter the inputs to calculate the effect, for example, of lowering a heating bill by a certain amount each month. The computer will automatically recalculate the columns to change the heating figures, total cost figures and cash flows for each month. In this way a manager, accountant or other user of a spreadsheet can quickly carry out business calculations such as introducing and finding out the effect of minor changes of variables.

As we can see in Figure 2.44 a spreadsheet presents the user with a series of rows and columns. Above each column are letters of the alphabet and the rows are each numbered. The box created where a column meets a row is called a cell and the cell reference is made up from its column letter and row number. So, B3 would be in the second column on the third row down.

	A	B	C
1	A1	B1	C1
2	A2	B2	C2

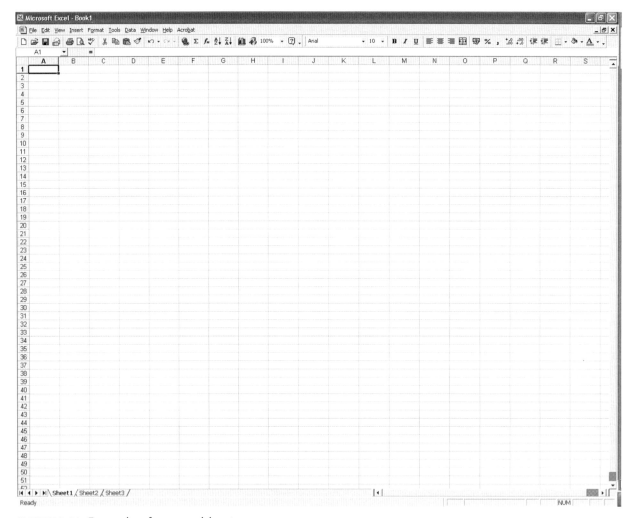

FIGURE 2.44 *Example of a spreadsheet screen*

Cells in a spreadsheet may contain:

* *Text* This may be used to provide column titles or labels that help the spreadsheet user to understand the significance of other data.

* *Numbers* These are at the very heart of spreadsheet use, and numbers are sometimes called values. For example, they could appear as a currency or be a percentage.

* *Formulas* The way in which spreadsheets work depends upon formulas. It is the formulas that enable spreadsheets to make calculations. For example A1 + B2 will add together the values found in these two cells. A formula expressed as A2+B3*C3/D1 will tell the spreadsheet to add the values of A2 and B3, having multipled cell B3 by C3 and then having divided cell C3 by D1.

One term used within the spreadsheet is one called *function*. The SUM function adds up all of the values between two cells. By putting three values into a box and then by highlighting the three cells as well as pressing the SUM function represented by Σ it is possible to add the three

Learning activity

Put 3 values into separate boxes within a spreadsheet C3, C4 and C5. Add the contents of the three cells. What formula was put into cell C6?

The way in which the cell addresses change when the formula is developed is called relative referencing, as the address changes according to whether it is copied. When rows are highlighted and copied the row number will change rather than the column letter.

Simple cash budget

Date	Jan	Feb	March	April	May	June	July	Aug	Sept	Oct	Nov	Dec
Opening balance	100	105	115	115	115	127	136	141	146	151	151	146
Receipts												
cash sales	20	30	30	30	30	30	30	25	25	25	20	25
credit sales	40	45	40	40	45	40	40	40	40	30	30	35
Total	60	75	70	70	75	70	70	65	65	55	50	60
Payments												
materials	25	35	35	35	33	30	35	30	25	25	25	25
overheads	20	20	25	25	20	21	20	20	25	20	20	21
wages	10	10	10	10	10	10	10	10	10	10	10	10
Total	55	65	70	70	63	61	65	60	60	55	55	56
overall +/-	5	10	0	0	12	9	5	5	5	0	-5	4
Closing balance	105	115	115	115	127	136	141	146	151	151	146	150

FIGURE 2.45 *A simple cash budget, prepared manually*

cells together. If the columns are C1, C2 and C3 you can see that the spreadsheet has added them together and this is represented by the SUM(C1: C3).

Cash flow, budgeting and profit forecasting

One of the benefits of using a spreadsheet is that, having developed and entered the formulas, it is possible to change figures and predict different outcomes.

Simple cash budget

The example shown in Figure 2.46 was prepared in a spreadsheet.

The receipts simply involved totalling two boxes to produce total receipts which in this instance involved the sum of B7+B8.

The total for payments involved totalling materials, overheads and wages which came out at B12+B13+B14.

Overall +/- was B9−B16 and the closing balance was B4+B9−B16. The closing balance has to become the opening balance for the next period and so C4, the opening balance on the second column, is now shown to =B18. By highlighting, these decisions can be extended across the page.

Spreadsheets like this that forecast either cash or profits are relatively simple to construct and easy to change. By simply changing the opening balance at the beginning of the spreadsheet all of the other calculations instantly change.

Break-even analysis

Entering figures into a spreadsheet can also be used for break-even analysis. The great benefit of doing this is that spreadsheets such as Excel are linked to charting tools and the spreadsheet can be used as a basis for producing a break-even chart shown in Figure 2.47. In the example the Fixed costs are £40,000, Variable cost per unit £10 and Sales price per unit £20. Output is then calculated at various levels from 1,000 units to 8,000 units. These are then highlighted and an appropriate line chart is chosen.

Word processing

At its most basic the function of a word processor is to manipulate text. Its great advantage is that it allows the user to make unlimited changes to text on screen before the final document is printed out.

Word processors make life easier for the writer in a number of ways:

Learning activity

If fixed costs are £30,000, variable costs per unit are £5 and sales price per unit is £40, construct a spreadsheet at each 2,000 sales of units and then use the spreadsheet to draw a break-even chart.

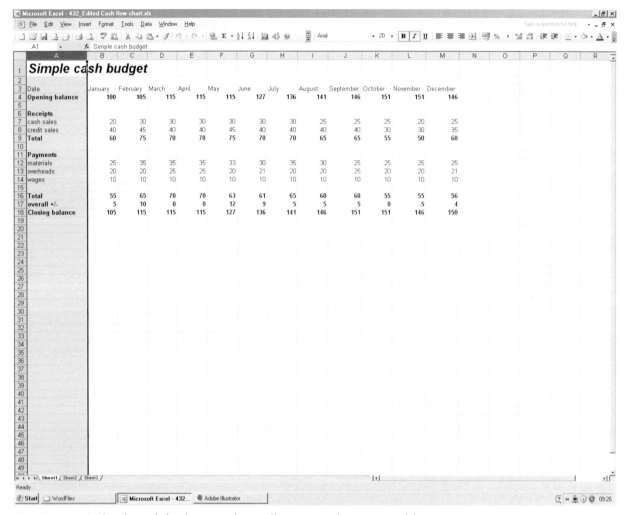

FIGURE 2.46 *A simple cash budget can be easily prepared as a spreadsheet*

* New text can be put on screen while existing text moves to create space for it

* Blocks of text can be moved around on the document that is being created

* The text can be spaced out to fill the whole line

* A word or phrase can be searched for, and can be removed or replaced by another word or phrase. A spelling mistake which is repeated throughout the document can be corrected in a single operation

* A header or footer can be added to the top or bottom of the document.

There are, of course many other functions, many of which you will be familiar with. For example, you can use different styles and fonts, insert graphics into text, use a spell-checker, thesaurus,

bullets, borders, tables, numbers, word count and even auto summarise.

Databases

A database is a store of information held on a computer. Examples might include anything from a list of customer accounts held by a bank or building society to a record of members of a church congregation and their addresses held by a parish priest. Another use might be to record tickets sold by a football club for various matches.

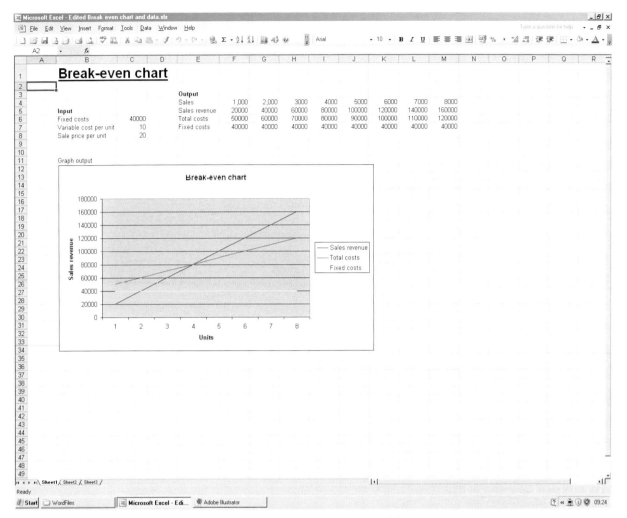

FIGURE 2.47 *A break-even analysis and chart, prepared as a spreadsheet*

In the university in which this author works, the database is the fundamental way in which the institution tracks the activities of students and the courses they register for.

The essence of a database is that data can be accessed and analysed in a number of different ways, depending upon the needs of the user. For example, suppose that Amin Stores wishes to record the account details of all of its customers. It would store the information in a number of fields – addressee, value of goods supplied, payments received and balance of account. If a customer rings up asking for the state of their account, Amin can simply order the computer to produce the appropriate information and display it on screen.

Accounting software

The widespread use of computers by all types of organisations has seen many organisations opt to computerise their book-keeping systems.

Computerised accounting systems simply incorporate manual-based theories using customised packages.

There are a number of advantages of using computerised accounting packages:

* Computers help to improve the control of funds coming into and going out of an organisation and make this control more effective.

* They improve accuracy, particularly where large amounts of data are entering into accounts (i.e. they take away much of the tedium of data entry into double-entry accounts).

CASE STUDY

Sage Line 50

You can reach the Sage Line 50 website through www.heinemann.co.uk/hotlinks (express code 1149P, then go to Unit 2).

Sage Line 50 is the UK's best-selling accounting software. It is an integrated package designed to provide users with the opportunity to make best use of their accounting data. The package makes all facts and figures readily available so that managers can quickly analyse their trading situation and solve problems or seize new opportunities. The package handles sales and purchases, stock control and order processing. It also generates invoices, produces statements, creates reports and can be used to create sales letters.

There are a number of elements to the system, including the following:

- *Sales Ledger* This shows who the customers are, what and when they buy and how much they owe and for how long.
- *Purchases Ledger* This enables the users to get the best value from their suppliers, enabling them to be in a strong position to get better discounts and higher credit levels.
- *Nominal Ledger* This brings together all the transactions and balances from other ledgers to create a chart of accounts to suit specific user requirements.
- *Financials* This enables Sage Line 50 to deal with management accounts, VAT returns and budget analysis.
- *Bank* The system manages accounts as well as transfers between accounts.
- *Fixed Assets Register* This enables the system to maintain records of all fixed assets and set up depreciation rates.
- *Stock* Sage Line 50 helps the user to achieve the right balance with reliable and up-to-date information on each stock item.

- *Invoicing* Prices, discounts and VAT are automatically calculated, with every invoice cross-referenced to ledgers.
- *Order processing* This provides a window into orders received and placed.
- *Report generator* This sets templates to allow the users to retrieve, sort and print out all of the information they require.

Sage Line 50 is easy to set up and use. Various forms, such as cheques, bank statements and invoices, are all created on screen and 'Wizards' take the user through various procedures. The real benefit of using this sort of package is speed and efficiency. Sage Line 50 has an automatic backup system, making it easy to spot and amend mistakes, and there is also password security access.

A key benefit of using Sage Line 50 is that it integrates with all other office software. For example, data from the system can be transferred into spreadsheets. Information can also be integrated into mail-merge and marketing databases.

There are single user or network versions of Sage Line 50. The networking option allows more than one user on to the system at any one time.

Although there are a variety of computerised accounting systems available, there are not many major differences between the packages. This is because all computerised accounting systems adhere to basic accounting concepts and practices.

1. Why does a package such as Sage Line 50 mirror the workings of a book-keeping system?
2. What are the advantages of using such a package?

* Accounting data is, by its very nature, arithmetical, which is well suited to being recorded and maintained by computer.

* Computerised book-keeping systems can supply reports and account balances much more quickly (such as trial balance, stock valuation, payroll analysis, VAT return, etc.).

* Many reports can be produced quickly and easily in a way that would not be possible in a manual system because of time and cost. For example, it would be easy to go through the sales ledger to find out all the customers (aged debtors) who have not paid their debts and send them reminders to do so.

* They help to provide managers with a readily accessible view of how the business organisation is functioning.

Computer programs for financial accounts usually follow the same system of ledger division into general and personal. In doing so the system provides an element of continuity with past practices. Commercially available accounting software is usually described as an 'integrated package', covering a range of accounting activities. For example, an accounting package would:

* update customer accounts in the sales ledger

* update supplier accounts in the purchases ledger

* record bank receipts and payments

* print out invoices

* make payments to suppliers and for expenses

* adjust records automatically.

Many packages offer more than just the control of each of the ledgers. Some may also provide for payroll, stock control production planning, electronic data interchange (EDI) and financial planning. These can be integrated with the rest of the accounting system.

An integrated accounting system means that, when a business transaction takes place and is input into the computer, it is recorded into a range of accounting records at the same time. For example, if a sales invoice is generated for a customer:

✳ DID YOU KNOW?

Passengers at Glasgow airport are expected to be the first in Scotland to use completely self-service check-in desks. The no-frills airline EasyJet plans to launch the automated kiosks as part of its move to the airport's new 'T2 Check in' building, adjacent to the terminal. Passengers will print out their own boarding passes and attach tags to their baggage, saving on staff costs.

---

* The customer's account will be adjusted with the invoice total.

* The sales account will increase and VAT will be applied.

* Stock records will change.

Project planning

At a time when increasingly people work in one or more project teams, an evolving application for computer software is in project planning. Computer programs allow projects to be broken down into a number of interrelated stages called activities. First the activities are defined and the time taken by each is estimated. Then the way in which the activities depend upon each other is defined. The computer calculates the total time for the project and shows the activities that must be completed on time in order for the project not to be delayed.

For example, in the case of a project to build a new office the activities and times might be as follows:

1	Prepare land and build foundations	30 days
2	Build walls	30 days
3	Build roof	15 days
4	Install equipment	30 days
5	Equip office	20 days

Activity 1 must be done first, then Activity 2, then Activity 3. However, Activities 4 and 5 – although they come after Activity 3 has finished – can be done at the same time. Therefore the total time for the project is only 105 days (30 + 30 + 15 + 30), not 125 days. The computer output will also show that Activity 5 is not critical: that is, it can start late or take longer than planned without delaying the project.

Many organisations use packages such as Microsoft Project that not only help to calculate the path (critical path) that should be used to finish the project on time, but also have charting tools that show how the project is progressing.

The Internet

The Internet came into being in the last quarter of the twentieth century. It was born in 1969, the year of the Apollo moon landings. For a number of years it was used mainly by computer buffs or 'Netties' who wallowed in their own brand of computer jargon but it has become widely accessible to a broader group of users.

Today, the Internet is providing a magnet for most of the world's major businesses, many of whom have spotted opportunities for advertising and communications to open up a whole new world of e-commerce. Net shopping is becoming increasingly important across a wide range of areas of buying and selling.

The Internet is also an excellent medium for sources of information.

Search engines such as Google can be used to search for a whole variety of topics simply by inserting helpful words or research terms. Try Google at www.heinemann.co.uk/hotlinks (express code 1149P, then go to Unit 2).

There are specialist engines for academics such as Google scholar that can be used to search for articles related to specialist education-related topics. Try Google scholar at www.heinemann.co.uk/hotlinks (express code 1149P, then go to Unit 2).

Organisations can use the Internet to search for information about competitors.

There are many specialist search engines, such as Emerald Fulltext, that provide business journals in fulltext format which saves having to deal with paper copies.

The Internet can be used as a form of market research in itself, so that those browsing a site can be asked to fill in and submit a questionnaire.

E-mail

As an alternative to written communications, the workplace is now characterised through electronic communications such as through e-mail. The sender simply forwards a document to a sender's e-mail address on their computer. When the receiver logs onto the system, he or she can see on screen that there is a message waiting which he or she can either read at the time or later. Anyone who is connected to the Internet has the capability to use e-mail. The advantages of using e-mail is that it is:

* Faster than ordinary mail
* The message does not have to be printed
* It is more environmentally friendly as less paper and energy are used.

One problem is that some people do not read their e-mails frequently enough. Another problem is that sometimes individuals get saturated by the sheer number of e-mails that they receive and the danger is that they may miss important ones.

E-commerce

Whereas e-business as a term refers to how organisations use information and communications technology (ICT) within their businesses to improve their operations, e-commerce refers more to how organisations use ICT for trading purposes.

According to many surveys, and despite what is happening to many economies around the world, the statistics tend to show that e-commerce is booming. For example, in the USA it was reported that e-commerce sales grew by 21.2 per cent over the same quarter in the previous year. In the same period, total retail sales increased by only 6.5 per cent.

You only have to look at a range of websites to see how organisations trade. There are now electronic banking facilities and a whole range of products and services can be purchased over the web, from a variety of different types of businesses, both large and small. e-Bay has been successful in allowing individuals to trade their own products and one of the most popular ways of buying books today is from Amazon.

Legal and corporate issues

Using IT in the business environment represents a whole new way of working. There have been a variety of issues associated with this. For example, some individuals find it difficult to spend all day

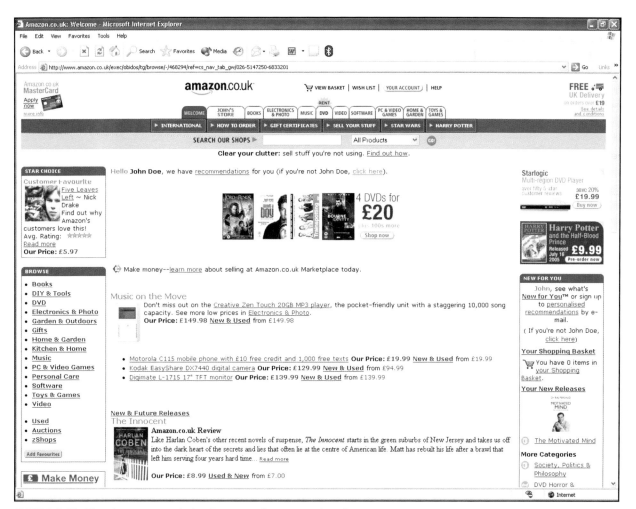

FIGURE 2.48 *The Amazon website is a popular example of e-commerce*

looking at a screen without getting a headache. Others have developed repetitive strain injuries (RSI). Clearly, organisations are finding that they have to develop different responsibilities to their employees based upon the use of technologies in the business environment.

With so much data around, an important element of dealing with it all is data protection. The Data Protection Act regulates the use of computerised information which relates to 'individuals' and the provision of services in respect of such 'information'.

The Act covers the holding of computer records only, and not manual records. The Act requires those using personal data to register with the Data Protection Registrar. Registered data users must then follow the eight principles of the Act:

✳ Data must be obtained and processed fairly and lawfully

✳ Data must be held only for specific lawful purposes which are described in the entry in the register

✳ Data should not be used in any other way than those related to such purposes

✳ Data should be adequate, relevant and not excessive for those purposes

✳ Personal data should be accurate and kept up-to-date

✳ Data should be held no longer than is required

✳ Individuals should be entitled to access their data and, if necessary, have it corrected or erased

✳ Data must be protected with appropriate security against unauthorised access or alteration.

There are a variety of exemptions from the Act, including information kept by government departments for reasons of national security. To ensure that data is held only for legitimate purposes many organisations appoint a data protection officer whose job it is to monitor the use of computerised information.

UNIT ASSESSMENT

You will investigate the setting up of a small business, which provides a service only in your local area.

Possible examples to choose include businesses:

* providing Desk Top Publishing (DTP)

* providing web design support for local business

* printing logos on to T shirts and other clothing

* running a school shop

* offering health food

* supplying sandwiches or food for special occasions

* providing health or gym facilities.

Each individual student's assessment evidence should consist of a presentation using ICT, to include:

1   A plan for the business covering the proposed legal form, main objectives and stakeholders of the business. Research and analysis of the market in which it will operate will also be provided.

2   An explanation of how the business will manage its activities, including the human, physical and financial resources needed and an analysis of how the business will manage these to provide a quality output.

3   Financial management information to include identification of and explanation of the main start-up and running costs for the business and consideration of how the business will monitor its performance, with particular reference to cash flow forecasts and break-even analysis using software where appropriate.

4   An explanation of how software can support the business including evidence of how it will help the business to operate efficiently.

Here is an outline of what you need to do to score high marks for this assignment.

* Show that you have detailed knowledge and understanding of key planning factors associated with starting a business. To be able to show this you need to provide evidence – by giving detailed explanations of each area that you research. These areas are the proposed legal form, the objectives of the business, the stakeholders and their stake in the business. In addition you will need to provide a good analysis of the market situation including consideration of areas such as pricing, the appropriateness of the product for the market, the suitability of advertising and other means of promotion, and the effectiveness of the distribution channels.

* Show that you have detailed knowledge and understanding of approaches to managing business activities. You can provide evidence of this by analysing practical issues such as the relevance and cost of the resources, and the approach that the business uses to managing quality.

* Show that you have detailed knowledge and understanding of financial management. You can provide evidence of this by providing an appropriate selection of start-up and running costs, and a well-structured and integrated assessment of monitoring performance by producing and evaluating cash flow forecasts and break-even calculations.

* Show that you have detailed knowledge and understanding of business software. You can show evidence of this by providing a clear analysis of how spreadsheets, word processing, and various pieces of software might help to improve the efficiency of the business that you have chosen to study.

UNIT 3

Investigating marketing

This unit contains four parts:

3.1   Identifying marketing aims and objectives

3.2   Using appropriate methods of market research

3.3   Choosing an appropriate marketing mix

3.4   Other factors influencing the marketing mix

Introduction

If you have been stopped in the shopping mall 'just to answer a few questions' or heard a TV advertisement which says 'nine out of ten customers preferred', you have seen some aspects of marketing. You may have wondered how a supermarket decides which products to promote or place on the top or bottom shelf. These are all very visible parts of a highly skilled and sophisticated marketing process which interacts with all the other functions of a business.

It is very easy to take our lifestyle and the sheer range of products and choices that we see or think about every day for granted. All around us we are blitzed by messages targeted at our needs. When we go into shops there are a huge variety of goods on view and we have to make a range of critical decisions that relate not just to our needs but also our income. At the same time, we are constantly offered a range of service opportunities to match our lifestyle. It is clear that all of the people and organisations offering so many different opportunities not only show a good understanding

FIGURE 3.1 *Marketing is important for any organisation*

of us as consumers and how our thoughts, perceptions and minds work, but they must also have carried out widespread and precise market research to find out about our needs.

What you will learn in this unit

* The importance of marketing as a strategic activity
* How marketing objectives direct an organisation
* The need for market segmentation
* How market research can inform business strategies
* An appreciation of each of the elements of the marketing mix.

3.1 Identifying marketing aims and objectives

Marketing is about understanding the customer and ensuring that products and services match existing and potential customer needs. Marketing is also about looking at ways of influencing the behaviour of customers. Perhaps the most useful way to think about marketing is to think about it as two main phases.

As we will see the passive phase involves finding out about customer needs though market research as well as understanding the behaviour of customers. Having done all of this 'finding out' organisations will then have to *decide who to focus upon and who to sell or deliver goods or services to*. Then comes the active phase. This

Learning activity

Think of a simple product concept such as a new shoe horn, a different type of baked bean, a new vegetarian concept or a form of men's grooming. Also consider the introduction and development of a new type of sport – possibly one from overseas such as Australian Rules Football, a more interesting nightclub concept or some type of service focused upon making household chores easier to undertake.

List the sort of questions that would have to be answered by using marketing research to find out more about the behaviour of consumers. Then, discuss the processes that could be used to satisfy customer needs.

phase involves putting together lots of plans and actions that meet customer needs. This is not just about advertising. It starts from the product itself, includes the price that is charged and then focuses upon the organisation doing everything it can to successfully meet and satisfy customer needs better than its competitors.

Understanding customer wants and needs

Marketing is essential to the success of any business. Its primary aim is to enable businesses to meet the needs of their actual and potential customers, whether for profit or not. You need to understand that, if a business's marketing is to be successful, it must:

The process that takes place before customer needs are addressed
THE PASSIVE PHASE

↓

The process that takes place to satisfy customer needs
THE ACTIVE PHASE

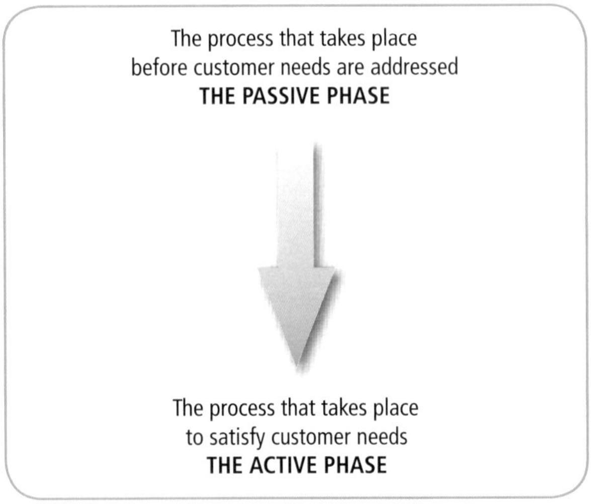

FIGURE 3.2 *The two phases of marketing*

Think about your own needs as a student for learning. What products and services are associated with such needs? For example, what services does your school or college provide for your needs and how could they be improved?

* understand customer needs

* understand and keep ahead of the competition

* communicate effectively with its customers to satisfy customer expectations

* co-ordinate its functions to achieve marketing aims

* be aware of constraints on marketing activities.

You need to understand how these criteria for successful marketing are related to the central aim of marketing – meeting actual and potential customer needs. You should also understand the importance to many businesses of developing and maintaining a relationship with the actual and potential customers and other stakeholders.

How easy it is to take all we have for granted! Wherever we look there are advertising messages bombarding us with images of goods or services designed to provide us with more choices and a better lifestyle. Shops, mail-order services and the Internet provide us with the opportunity to buy almost anything we want, as long as we have the 'filthy lucre'.

It was only in 1942 that Joseph Schumpeter, the great Austrian economist, wrote:

'Queen Elizabeth I owned silk stockings. The capitalist achievement does not typically consist of providing more silk stockings for queens, but in bringing them within the reach of factory girls in return for steadily decreasing amounts of effort.'

CASE STUDY

Using interactive TV to communicate with clients

A few years ago the first truly interactive TV advertisement appeared on the screens of the UK's homes. Chicken Tonight offered viewers willing to 'push the red button' money-off coupons for the tasty chicken treat in exchange for a couple of precious minutes of their time. The event was significant as it reminded everybody of the possibilities within a digital and interactive market.

Since then the digital media market has, to say the least, gone through turbulent times, with ITV Digital becoming Freeview, selling half a million set-top boxes in the first six months. With more viewers claiming to be interacting with their television, broadcasters are looking to interactive TV to reinvigorate their revenue streams.

By early 2005, 52.4% of income for digital channels came from channel subscription. Advertising accounted for 22.2%, and with sponsorship 1.3% the digital companies were looking to expand other income which stood at 24.1%.

ITV has already experimented with interactive versions of *Who Wants to be a Millionaire?* and the Brit Awards where viewers were invited to play along at home and vote for their favourite record or artist respectively for the chance to win cash or prizes. Plans are now being developed for more interactive advertising and promotions, particularly alongside Freeview where viewers are interacting all of the time, such as in programmes like *Big Brother* and *I'm a Celebrity, Get Me Out of Here*.

The potential for advertisers is there; 62% agreed that interactive advertising is a convenient way to get information about a product or service. Half of all digital viewers think that companies that use interactive are more innovative than their competitors and 58% think it stands out more than traditional TV ads.

1 **What is interactive advertising?**
2 **Why might companies wish to use it?**
3 **How might interactive advertising relate to your needs as a customer?**

Today we live in a *market economy*, in which many consumers have been able to enjoy the range of goods and services that were previously afforded by kings and queens only. The existence of a market makes it possible for consumers to express their preferences for the goods and services they would like, and prices act as signals to suppliers informing them which goods are in most demand.

In this marketplace, today's consumers indicate to suppliers through their purchases what should or should not be produced for the market. In effect they have become king or queen.

The Chartered Institute of Marketing defines marketing as:

'The management process responsible for identifying, anticipating and satisfying customer requirements profitably.'

This definition provides an important starting point to help you gain a clear picture of the major issues facing a market-focused organisation.

There are a number of key words in the above definition:

✳ *Management process* – the use of this term indicates the level of importance of marketing decisions. Successful marketing needs managerial input because it requires constant information gathering, as well as data analysis, in order for decisions to be made.

✳ *Identifying* involves answering questions such as 'how do we find out what the consumers' requirements are?' and 'how do we keep in touch with their thoughts and perceptions about our goods or service?'

✳ *Anticipating* takes into account that consumer requirements change all the time. For example, as people become richer they may seek a greater variety of goods and services. Anticipation involves looking at the future as well as at the present. What will be the Next Best Thing people will require tomorrow?

✳ *Satisfying* involves meeting consumer requirements. Customers seek particular benefits. They want the right goods, at the right price, at the right time and in the right place.

✳ *Profitability* is the margin of profit that *motivates* organisations to supply goods to consumers in a market. Of course, profit may be simply one motive for supplying goods to a market. Others may include market share or market leadership.

A recent major study of some 1,700 companies showed that marketing-orientated firms have enhanced profitability. In other words, good marketing helps managers to improve the performance of their part of the business and to meet the most basic of business objectives – profit.

Clearly, one of the key components of marketing is understanding customer wants and needs. Marketing is, therefore, the process through which Jaguar is able to identify the kinds of cars people will want to buy in the near future and the features that should be built into those cars. It helps Reebok anticipate changes in consumers' preferences for trainers, and digital television formats such as Freeview and Sky Television to identify the types of channels viewers will want to watch in the future.

In a relatively short period of time organisations have moved forward from *production orientation* to *sales orientation*, and, more recently, to *marketing orientation* (see Figure 3.3).

In a market dominated by production orientation, manufacturers feel they know what is best for customers. When there is little competition (for example, where there is only one supplier of telecommunications services in a particular geographical area or where there is only one producer of motor vehicles), organisations may not have to pay close attention to customer needs.

As consumer incomes began to rise after the Second World War, standards of living began to improve. During the 1950s and 1960s, emphasis was upon sales orientation. Prime Minister Harold Macmillan claimed that 'You've never had it so good!', and the focus was upon trying to persuade customers they needed the goods rather than attempting to find out about buyers' needs.

Marketing orientation is all about focusing the activities or organisations on meeting the needs of consumers. It means the consumer is the driving

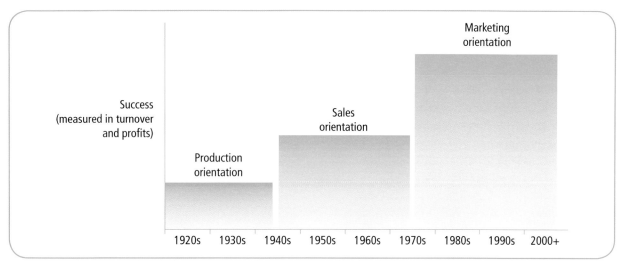

FIGURE 3.3 *Business orientation*

force behind everything an organisation does. No longer is marketing something that is simply added on to a number of company functions. Today, the customer drives all the activities of a market-focused organisation.

Learning activity

FIGURE 3.4 *Starbucks organisation chart*

Starbucks have 8,337 coffee bars throughout the world and yet the organisation has only been around since 1971 when the first coffee bar was opened in Seattle's Pike Place Market.

Look at the chart in Figure 3.4. What does it tell you about their orientation?

You can find the Starbucks website through www.heinemann.co.uk/hotlinks (express code 1149P, then go to Unit 3).

Learning activity

Use an example of an organisation known to you to describe how it anticipates market needs and opportunities.

Amazon, the world's biggest online bookseller (and CD supplier), provides a good example of marketing orientation. Amazon claim to provide 'the Earth's biggest selection'. The aim is to give consumers as much choice as possible using a consumer-focused, easy-to-use website. Amazon's approach represents the marketing-oriented view of e-commerce, i.e. that with a customer-focused website they are able to find new ways of delighting customers. This contrasts with the production appproaches of some other web users who have the view that if they have a website then customers will flock to them. They forget to find out how customers want the site to be structured and what they want from it.

It is, therefore, the ability to satisfy customers that marks the difference between a successful and unsuccessful organisation. This is why some schools are oversubscribed and have a huge demand for places while others have falling numbers. It is the reason why some supermarkets have people crowding the aisles whereas others are practically empty.

CASE STUDY

Virgin

The Virgin group is involved in planes, trains, finance, soft drinks, music, mobile phones, holidays, cars, wines, publishing, and even bridal wear, all of which amounts to over 200 companies worldwide, employing over 25,000 people with revenues exceeding £4 billion per annum.

Virgin began with a student magazine and a small mail order company in the 1970s. Since then the company has grown on the basis of developing good ideas where the organisation can offer something better, fresher and more exciting. The company often moves into areas where the customer has traditionally received a poor deal, and where the competition is complacent. With the growing e-commerce activities, Virgin is looking to deliver 'old' products and services in new ways.

For example, a recent venture for Virgin has been into online holidays. It is now possible to book a holiday with a couple of clicks of a mouse. Before making a booking decision, it is possible for the customer to experience aspects of their holiday from their armchair. This could include descending a piste in the Alps or looking at a 360° view from a campsite on the French Riviera.

One of the key ingredients of the success of Virgin has been its managers' ability to anticipate market needs. Successes include high-street record stores in the 1970s and cheap flights across the Atlantic during the 1980s, followed by contraceptives and Virgin Cola.

1 **What makes Virgin unique in their approach to markets?**
2 **Comment upon how well you feel they anticipate market needs.**

Learning activity

Discuss the following statement and relate the quote to two business organisations:

'Marketing, therefore, is concerned with attempting to reduce risk by applying formal techniques systematically to assess the situation and develop the company's response to it.'

At this stage it is important to emphasise that marketing is linked to planning, and that successfully meeting the objectives identified within these plans is crucial for business organisations. An organisation with a strategy knows where it is going because it is planning ahead. Marketing strategy is concerned with identifying and meeting the requirements of customers successfully so that the organisation can meet a range of objectives.

Marketing strategies are the means by which organisations attempt to find out exactly what their customers want, and then to influence customers in a way that is favourable to the organisation.

Marketing strategies require detailed research to find out:

* about the requirements of customers
* the right products to develop to meet customer needs
* how to position the product or service in relation to other products and services
* the right marketing mix.

It is important to be able to differentiate between marketing strategy and marketing tactics.

Learning activity

You have recently developed a revolutionary new type of seat that can be used in offices and would overcome any form of back pain. Working in groups, comment upon the sort of research you need to undertake before making a major investment in this product.

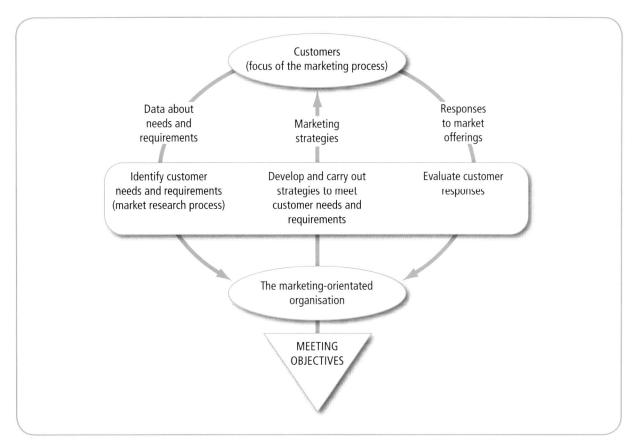

FIGURE 3.5 *The strategic process*

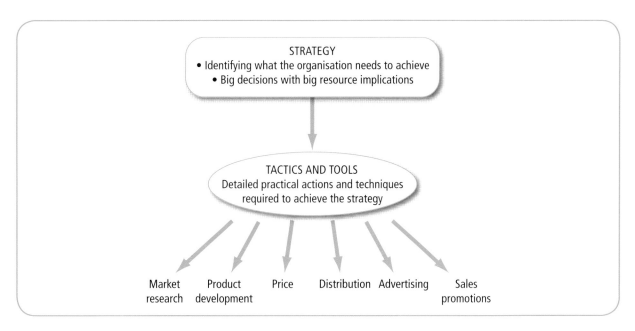

FIGURE 3.6 *Marketing strategy and tactics*

The terms 'strategy' and 'tactics' are of military origin. Military *strategy* is a general overview that involves the creation of clear aims and objectives and then deciding the key means to achieve these. Military *tactics* are the means used to win a particular campaign or battle.

Having established the marketing strategy, it is possible to decide on the tactics and tools to be used to make the strategy work. For example, this may involve carrying out some detailed market research, developing a product, working out the best price to charge, developing a distribution strategy, running an appropriate advertising campaign or engaging in sales promotional activity.

Planning is at the heart of marketing. It enables decision-makers within an organisation to plan for the present and for the future, and to learn from the past. The three main reasons for planning are to:

1   assess how well the organisation is doing in the various markets in which it operates

2   identify the strengths and weaknesses of the organisation in each of these markets

3   establish goals and objectives, so that resources can be used appropriately.

Assael defines a *marketing plan* as a document invented by marketing managers that:

∗ *'identifies marketing opportunities*

∗ *defines the target market that represents that opportunity*

∗ *develops a mix of strategies directed at this target*

∗ *guides the evaluation of the marketing effort.'*

Marketing objectives are an essential part of the marketing plan as they provide direction for activities to follow. Without clear objectives it is difficult to evaluate what a marketing plan is trying to achieve or whether a plan has been successful. It is usual to translate marketing objectives into quantifiable 'result areas', such as market share, market penetration or growth rate of sales. Some of these may be further broken down into specific sales volumes, value goals or geographical targets.

Marketing objectives may have a time frame and direction. They also provide a basis for evaluation. Marketing must ensure that organisational activities are co-ordinated in a way that marketing objectives are met.

Marketing objectives should therefore be:

1   *Achievable* They should be based on a practical analysis of an organisation's capabilities.

2   *Understandable* They need to be clear so that everyone knows what they are trying to achieve.

3   *Challenging* They should be something everyone has to strive for.

4   *Measurable* Quantification makes it possible to record progress and to make adjustments if marketing objectives are not being met.

We can also relate marketing objectives to the SMART approach used in Unit 1. This stands for:

Specific – objectives should specify what they want to achieve
Measurable – an organisation should measure whether they are meeting objectives or not.
Achievable – the objectives set must be achievable and attainable
Realistic – the objectives must be realistic give the resources used
Time-related – time should be allocated to achieve the objectives.

For example, if market research indicates that people who visit multiplex cinemas are unwilling to stand in the rain queuing for an hour for the last seat to be sold just in front of them, then it is essential for the organisation to find solutions. In Manchester, the UCI multiplex has a bank of 90 telephone operators at the end of a freephone number who take nationwide bookings. Customers can also say where they want to sit. The transaction takes on average 64 seconds. Marketing thus has a responsibility to ensure all aspects of the way in which an organisation operates are geared to meeting consumer requirements.

FIGURE 3.7 *Process of exchange between buyers and sellers*

Developing new products

Being human, all customers are different! But only a few businesses (a tailor, for example, or a firm of architects) can provide products *specifically designed* for each individual customer. Most marketing activities are therefore designed to meet the needs of groups of customers within a market.

A market is made up of actual or potential buyers of a product and the sellers who offer goods to meet buyers' needs. The market for computers is composed of existing owners and prospective buyers of computers, as well as companies such as Apple Macintosh who manufacture them, Microsoft who develop software and Time who distribute them within the marketplace. A market requires a process of exchange between buyers and sellers (see Figure 3.7).

Interaction between buyers and sellers is based upon the notion of the marketing mix. The marketing mix provides a useful way of looking at the marketplace for products. Organisations need to create a successful mix of:

* the right product or service
* sold in the right place
* at the right price
* using the most suitable form of promotion.

The first challenge for any organisation is to find a set of customers and to identify their needs so that appropriate goods and services can be developed. The first element in the marketing mix is the *product.* Once organisations have a product, then all the other elements in this marketing mix can be engaged to meet customer needs. These may

FIGURE 3.8 *The marketing mix*

Find out...

You can see the Next Directory and Knorr websites using www.heinemann.co.uk/hotlinks (express code 1149P, then go to Unit 3).

include developing the *pricing* for the product or service provided, working out how to *distribute* (*place*) goods to the customers, as well as how to *promote* them.

When Next identified a large group of potential customers who could be reached using

CASE STUDY

Falling behind the needs of the customer

For many years, Marks & Spencer (view the website through www.heinemann.co.uk/hotlinks – express code 1149P, then go to Unit 3) had been a British institution, supported by the blind faith of their customers. Their products were the fruits of endless compromises between buyers, managers and suppliers.

The products were a benchmark of British quality – dependable and decent – and stood as a British emblem. But people increasingly came to think that much of this merchandise was dull, and was out of touch with changing fashions. However, at the heart of these products' success was a strong bond between M&S and the British public.

During the 1980s, M&S were probably propped up by good fortune. Men's and women's fashions in the 1980s were based on the older styles of the 1940s and, as more women entered the workforce the ready-made meal became accepted as a comfort food. At the time the alternatives to M&S were probably not attractive enough, but then George at Asda and designers at Debenhams, Zara, IKEA and Gap changed the fashion world, with new merchandise every three weeks instead of M&S's twice-yearly collections. Fashion was also blown apart the moment Next arrived on the scene. Niche-ing, sub-branding and product clustering became the new buzz words. The most fashion conscious of women suddenly became those women in their thirties and forties. They had money, knew about fashion and wanted to make an effort.

During the 1990s M&S emphasised 'value' rather then price, and this provided them with an enviable position in the high street.

However, it was during this time they also got so hung up on quality they forgot about style and fashion. With inappropriate styles, sales fell and even their food halls lost customers. The unthinkable had happened . . . perhaps M&S was not so great after all. The disaffected customers went elsewhere.

In recent years M&S have got into branding, recently buying women's fashion brand Per Una from its creator George Davies for £125m.

Per Una was formed as a joint venture between M&S and Mr Davies. George Davies had a supplier relationship with M&S, but following the purchase the retailer will receive all revenues generated by the brand. The purchase of Per Una was just one of a number of measures unveiled by the new chief David Rose in July 2004 to defeat a potential £9.1bn takeover offer for M&S from retail tycoon Philip Green.

Today, M&S is ripe for acquisition. Valued at more than £9 billion, they have many sites that would be a valuable catch for a predator.

The future of M&S largely depends upon how well their designers are able to push through improvements to core products and win back the confidence of the British public. It is argued today that M&S's biggest problem is public perception and their solution to change such perceptions is through the process of branding.

1 To what extent were the problems encountered by M&S a failure to understand their customers?
2 How have M&S tried to make themselves more market-orientated?

the Next Directory, they identified a range of different mail order and electronic ways of reaching customers. When Unilever acquired the Knorr brand in 2000, it obtained an evolving family of brands that constantly develop new products based upon the strength of the brand that are sold in more than 87 countries.

In recent years we have seen increasing efforts to meet the individual wants and needs of customers – a process known as *customisation*. This has been particularly noticeable in service industries. Services such as delivering parcels, guarding property or maintaining equipment can be designed to suit a particular customer.

Improving profitability

One distinct objective allied to marketing processes for many organisations in the private sector is that of profitability. In the public sector income and maximising revenue may also be equally important. Shareholders and owners of organisations will inevitably be interested in profits as well as the value of their investment. The **dividend** they receive is a reward for the risk they take in buying shares.

It is probably wrong just to associate most shareholders with trying to make as much profit as possible. Many take a pride in the organisation in which they have invested as well as its reputation. Some of them may be employees or former employees. A number of shareholders will ask questions of their directors at the **annual general meeting** and in some cases may vote to remove certain directors from the board. Shareholders appoint the board of directors of a company, who in turn appoint the management team.

Many large organisations place considerable emphasis upon 'shareholder value' – that is, making sure that shareholders receive a good return on their investment. The organisation that fails to provide shareholder value will find that its shareholders sell off their shares.

Some customers are worth more to an organisation than others. If a well-established customer decides to shop elsewhere this can have a dire result upon an organisation. For example, when Marks & Spencer decided to source more products from overseas, companies like Courtaulds within the UK were badly affected, and this led to the closing down of factories. A key element therefore within marketing relationships is to appreciate the profitability attached to each customer. If employees understand how much each relationship contributes to an organisation, then they can link their actions to keep customers delighted with products and services in a way that further develops and builds other profitable relationships.

Improving market share

For many organisations their main business objective is to obtain a high market share, and some organisations deliberately set prices that allow them to build such a share. The Boston Consultancy Group argue that organisations with a high market share gain more experience and that such experience is a key asset enabling an organisation to reduce costs per unit and compete more efficiently than their competitors.

A programme of research in the USA produced another theory concerning factors that influence organisational competitiveness. This study was called 'Profit Impact of Marketing Strategies', and is usually referred to as PIMS. This study attempted to analyse the marketing factors that had the biggest impact upon profits. Though a number of conclusions were drawn, the study highlighted the close relationship between market share and profitability.

MARKET SHARE (%)	PROFITABILITY (%)
Under 7	9.6
7–14	12.0
14–22	13.5
22–36	17.9
Over 36	30.2

FIGURE 3.9 *The PIMS study*

The PIMS research showed that organisations with a larger market share were more likely to be profitable (see Figure 3.9). Research took this concept further by showing that high market share and increased performance were the results of moving along a 'learning curve', so that the more an organisation learnt about its position through market research, the better it would perform.

Learning activity

Working in small groups, think of a new product idea. If you were to commercialise this idea, what would your objectives be for the first year? How would you measure whether or not you would be achieving these objectives? Explain why market share is an important marketing objective for many organisations. Why might improving market share be easier in rapidly changing rather than static markets? Provide two examples of organisations that seem to have improved their market share in recent years.

Think of a new product idea that would be useful and relevant to your school or college. Discuss how you could use this idea to make it a commercial reality. What objectives would you have for your idea?

Why are organisations with a large market share likely to be more profitable? One reason is that with high market share and larger levels of output, firms benefit from larger production runs and, when unit costs are reduced, they benefit from increased margins. Though the PIMS study showed that the best competitive strategy for a business was to aim for higher market share, this theory has been criticised for only making weak links between two key variables.

Diversification

This is a strategy for growth which involves developing products or business areas which are outside the organisation's markets. For example, a jeans manufacturer might decide to further develop its labels and brand strengths by going into healthy foods. Some companies deliberately operate a policy of diversification by always trying to identify the most attractive and rapidly developing industries in which to engage. They feel that the best business strategy to guarantee success is to enter attractive and emerging industries, rather than stay in static and slow developing ones.

Whenever an organisation diversifies it is engaging in some activity which is different to its core activities. This can be very useful as a business or marketing objective as it allows the organisation to spread its business risks by entering other markets or delivering other products or services. So, for example, if one product market starts to lose sales, by diversifying this may not damage a business organisation too badly.

Firms might want to diversify if opportunities in new market areas seem attractive or when the organisation wishes to reduce the impact of a trend within an industry.

To diversify an organisation could engage in forward or backward integration whereby the outlets or sources of supplies are joined with the organisation. This is prevalent in the semiconductor businesses where manufacturers of microprocessors join forces with semiconductor producers to ensure a continuous supply.

Alternatively a firm can engage in a conglomerate diversification, which involves the organisation expanding into businesses that have no relationship to its current product, markets or technology. For example, Coca-Cola purchased a movie company as a strategic move to counter a possible decline in the customer segment for its products, such as the youth group.

CASE STUDY

News Corporation – a truly diversified company

It is easy to take the media for granted, but there are some huge media giants out there. One of these is News Corporation. Forever linked with the 'Murdoch' name, and owners of 20th Century Fox, News Corporation has released three of the top five best-performing motion pictures of all time: Star Wars, Star Wars Episode I: The Phantom Menace, and Titanic.

News Corporation is the world's leading publisher of English-language newspapers, with operations in the UK, Australia, Fiji, Papua New Guinea and the USA. Newspapers it publishes in the UK include *The Times*, *The Sun* and *The News of the World*. In the book industry it owns HarperCollins publishers.

News Corporation had total assets as of 30 June 2004 of approximately US$51 billion and total annual revenues of approximately US$21 billion. It is therefore a diversified international media and entertainment company with operations in eight industry segments: filmed entertainment; television; cable network programming; direct broadcast satellite television; magazines and inserts; newspapers; book publishing; and other. It has activities principally in the United States, Continental Europe, the United Kingdom, Australia, Asia and the Pacific Basin.

1 Describe News Corporation's marketing strategy.
2 What benefits do they gain from diversification?

Relaunching/launching a product

All business organisations have to make critical decisions about products from time to time. For example, if a product has been around for a long time, a decision may have to be made about whether to replace it, or inject life into it, or more crucially whether to let the product fade out of existence.

The life of a product is the period over which it appeals to customers. We can all think of goods that everyone wanted at one time but which have now gone out of fashion. Famous examples from the 60s include hotpants and beehive hairstyles.

The sales performance of any product rises from zero when the product is introduced to the market, reaches a peak and then goes into decline (see Figure 3.10). Most products are faced by a limited life-cycle. Initially the produce may flourish and grow, eventually the market will mature and finally the product will move towards decline and petrification. At each stage in the product life-cycle there is a close relationship between sales and profits so that as organisations or brands go into decline their profitability decreases.

The life-cycle can be broken down into distinct stages. In the *introductory* phase, growth is slow and volume is low because of limited awareness of the product's existence. Sales then rise rapidly during the period of *growth*. It is during this phase that the profit per unit sold usually reaches a maximum. Towards the end of this phase, competitors enter the market to promote their own products, which reduces the rate of growth of sales of the first product.

This period is known as *maturity*. Competitive jockeying – such as product differentiation in the form of new flavours, colours, sizes, etc. – will sift out the weaker brands. During *saturation*, some brands will drop out of the market. The product market may eventually decline and reach a stage when it becomes unprofitable.

The life-cycle may last for a few months or for hundreds of years. To prolong the life-cycle of a brand or a product, an organisation needs to readjust the ingredients of the marketing mix. Periodic injections of new ideas are needed – product improvements, line extensions or improved promotions. Figure 3.11 illustrates the process of injecting new life into a product.

A readjustment of the marketing mix might include:

* Changing or modifying the product, to keep up with or ahead of the competition

* Altering distribution patterns, to provide a more suitable place for the consumer to make purchases

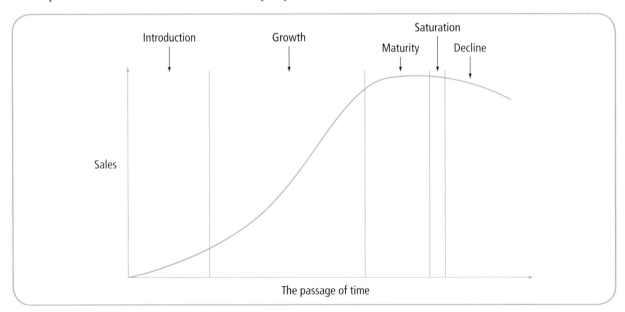

FIGURE 3.10 *Stages in the product life-cycle*

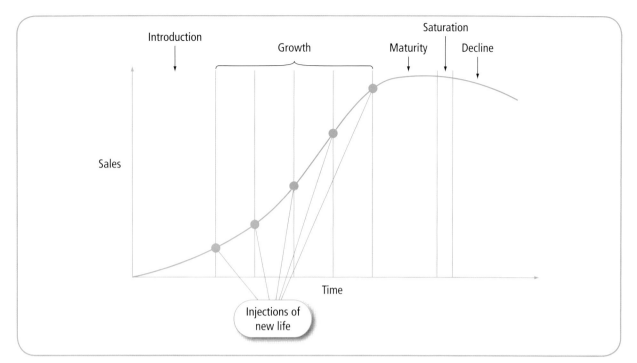

FIGURE 3.11 *Injecting new life into a product*

* Changing prices to reflect competitive activities
* Considering carefully the style of promotion.

Most large organisations produce a range of products, each with its own unique life-cycle. By using life-cycles, marketers can plan when to introduce new lines as old products go into decline. The collection of products that an organisation produces is known as its *product portfolio* (see Figure 3.12).

In Figure 3.12, T_1 represents a point in time. At that point product 1 is in decline, product 2 is in maturity, product 3 is in growth and product 4 has recently been introduced.

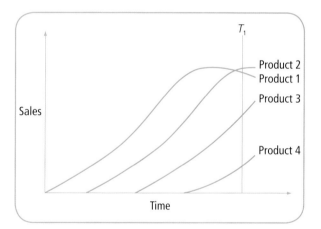

FIGURE 3.12 *A product portfolio*

Examining the life-cycle of a product helps us to appreciate that products go through various phases from infancy to decline. Markets and their structures are changing all of the time. In recent years 'niche marketing' has been popular, particularly with the emergence of branding. Today many organisations have spotted opportunities through the use of the Internet and other technologies to develop their markets.

Earlier we saw that market share is important for business organisations. The Boston Consultancy Group have argued that the faster the growth of a particular market the greater the

> **Learning activity**
>
> Look at the portfolio of products or services provided by one large organisation. It may be a car manufacturer who provide different models for different segments of the market. Alternatively, it could be a major retailer who use different forms of retailing to reach different groups of consumers. Look at where each of their products or services falls within the product life-cycle. Explain what their strategies are likely to be in the near future based upon your analysis.

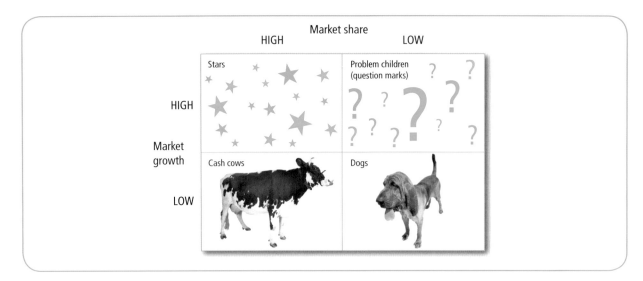

FIGURE 3.13 *The Boston Box or matrix*

cost necessary to maintain position. In a rapidly growing market, considerable expenditure will be required on investment in product lines, and to combat the threat posed by new firms and brands.

The Boston Group developed 'The Boston Box' or matrix, which relates closely to product life-cycles. They identify four types of products in an organisation's portfolio (Figure 3.13).

Problem children

Problem children are products that have just been launched. This is an appropriate name because many products fail to move beyond this phase. Such products are often referred to as *question marks*. Is it possible to develop these products and turn them into the *stars* and *cash cows* of the future? It might be, but first they will require a lot of financial support and this will represent a heavy financial commitment.

Stars

Stars are products that have successfully reached the growth stage in the life-cycle. Although these products too will require a lot of financial support, they will also provide high cash returns. On balance they will provide a neutral cash flow and are good prospects for the future.

Cash-cows

Cash-cows have reached the maturity stage in their product life-cycle and are now 'yielders'.

They have a high market share in markets that are no longer rapidly expanding. Because the market is relatively static, they require few fresh injections of capital, for example, advertising and promotion may be required to inject a little fresh life from time to time. However, the net effect is of a positive cash flow. Cash generated by the cash cows may be used to help the question marks.

Dogs

Dogs are products in decline. These have a low market share in a low-growing or a declining market. As they generate a negative cash flow, they will usually be disposed of.

In order to maintain an effective portfolio development, it is important to have a balance

Learning activity

Using your own experience of a product portfolio from an organisation, identify its:

❊ Question marks

❊ Stars

❊ Cash cows

❊ Dogs.

In each case explain what evidence you have for drawing the conclusions you make. Having done this, look at the portfolio of courses and products offered by your school and college, relating some to the categories above.

of products at any one time. An organisation will require a number of cash cows to provide its 'bread and butter'. At the same time, it is important to develop the cash cows of the future by investing in the question marks. Fortunately the stars should pay their own way. It is also important to identify the dogs and cut them out.

Products in the top half of the Boston Matrix are in the earlier stage of their product life-cycle and so are in high-growth markets. Those in the lower half of the box are in the later stages and so are in markets where growth will have slowed down or stopped.

Ansoff has developed this theory further by outlining a product-market mix. This looks not just at the management of a product portfolio but also more widely at market developments and opportunities. Ansoff's matrix matches existing and new product strategies with existing and new markets (Figure 3.14).

In this way, this matrix suggests five alternative marketing strategies which hinge upon whether the product is new or existing and whether the market is new or existing. These are:

* *Consolidation* implies a positive and active defence of existing products in existing markets.

* *Market penetration* suggests a further penetration of existing markets with existing products. This will involve a strategy of increasing market share within existing segments and markets.

* *Product development* involves developing new products for existing markets.

* *Market development* entails using existing products and finding new markets for them. Better targeting, market research and further segmentation will identify these new markets.

* *Diversification* will lead to a move away from core activities. This might involve some form of integration of production into related activities.

A new product may be one which:

* Replaces an old product

* Opens up a new market

* Broadens an existing market.

It may involve an innovation, a technological breakthrough or simply be a line extension based upon a modification. It is often said that only about 10% of new products are really new. In fact, it is often possible to turn old products into new products simply by finding a new market for them.

There are six distinct stages in the development process for new products. These are:

Step 1 Ideas

Step 2 Screening of ideas

Step 3 Marketing analysis

Step 4 Product development

Step 5 Testing

Step 6 Launch and commercialisation.

As new products go through each of these stages there is a mortality rate (see Figure 3.15).

Product / Market	Existing products		New products
Existing markets	Consolidation	Market penetration	Product development
New markets	Market development		Diversification

FIGURE 3.14 *Ansoff's product matrix*

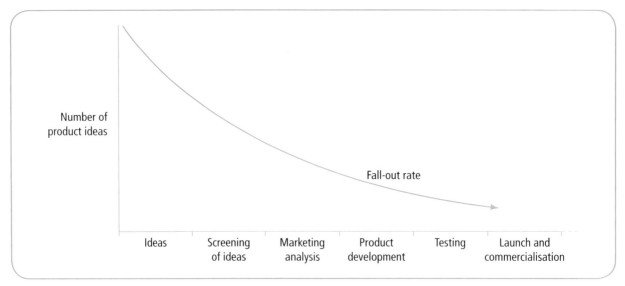

FIGURE 3.15 *Mortality (fall out) during the new product development process*

Step 1 *Ideas*

All new products start from ideas. These ideas may be completely new or simply be an update of an existing product. Ideas may come from:

Research and development – product development and market research working together. Technological breakthroughs and innovations from research are very important.

Mindstorming – involving a few people developing ideas from words and concepts.

Suggestions box – cash incentives may encourage employees to contribute their own ideas.

Sales force – working close to customers, the sales force understands their needs and requirements.

Forced relationships – sometimes one or more products can be joined together to form new product concepts. For example, shampoo and conditioner.

Competitors – monitoring the actions of competitors may provide a rich source of new ideas.

Step 2 *Screening of ideas*

Once ideas have been generated it is important to screen for the ideas likely to be successful and reject the rest. Considerations may include how well the product fits in with others in the product range, the unique elements of any idea that make it competitive, the likely demand for the product and whether or not it could be manufactured economically.

Step 3 *Marketing analysis*

Once the ideas have been screened, further marketing analysis begins. This involves a thorough analysis of the product's market potential. This type of research helps to identify the market volume (units that could be sold) as well as the value of sales expected. It may also help to identify market potential.

Step 4 *Product development*

Having come through the test of marketing analysis it is now time to translate the idea or product concept into a product. Design, innovation and the uses of technology are very important in product development. An assessment of packaging and branding may also be involved.

Step 5 *Testing*

Testing is a vital stage in the product development process. It may involve identifying valuable information through further market research which helps to fine-tune the venture. Test marketing may comprise testing on part of a consumer market or trialling the product to ensure that it meets the required standards.

Step 6 *Launch and commercialisation*

The launch is the most important day in the life of a product – it is finally revealed to customers. It may involve rolling from one TV region to another TV region. Today a common technique is to provide sneak glimpses of new products before they are launched.

Increasing brand awareness

A key marketing objective may be to develop brand awareness. A *brand* is a particular product or characteristic that identifies a particular producer.

Many mass-produced products are almost identical. For example, most washing powders are similar, as are different types of margarine. These goods tend to be produced by two or three large companies who encourage sales by creating a brand that differentiates the products in the minds of consumers.

A brand can be a name, a symbol or a design used to identify a specific product and differentiate it from its competitors. Brand names, designs, trademarks, symbols, slogans and even music can be used to distinguish one product from another and allow an organisation to distinguish its products from competing ones.

The business of creating a brand is a particularly important function of marketing. Often people will buy the brand name as much as the product itself. You will see people in supermarkets pick up an item (which they have not seen before) and say, 'this must be a good one because it is made by ....'.

Large organisations swear by the power of the brand. They will fight tooth and nail to raise the status of their brands, and be determined that nothing should affect the power of their brands.

✷ DID YOU KNOW?

Virgin Atlantic became locked in a furious row with airport bosses in Australia over Sir Richard Branson's celebratory stunt following its first flight to Sydney. On arrival, Sir Richard, climbed onto the wing of Virgin's Airbus jet holding a surfboard. He was joined by a group of swimwear models waving a Union flag and an Australian national flag.

There are three different types of brands. These are:

Manufacturer brands Examples of these include Kellogg's Cornflakes, Nescafé Coffee and Heinz Baked Beans. These manufacturer brands associate the producer with the specific product, and the producer will be heavily involved with the promotion of the product.

Own-label brands Examples of these include Tesco, St Michael (Marks & Spencer), Farm Foods (Asda), Sainsbury's own label, etc. These brands are owned and controlled by retailers, and therefore the producers or manufacturers are not associated with the products or involved in their promotion.

Generic brands Such products are extremely rare in the modern competitive market, and those that exist are usually at the lower end of the market with respect to price and quality. These products have no identifiable name or logo. Examples may include plain T-shirts or bin-liners if they have no branded packaging or labels attached that identify the originator.

Organisations seek to create a portfolio of individual products which support the image of a brand. Well-known brand names will therefore emphasise quality throughout the organisation.

A brand which is held in high esteem is worth a lot of money to an organisation. There is a well-

Learning activity

Identify two or three brands of products in a particular market. To what extent could these brands be further developed in a way that exemplifies the attributes of each brand?

known saying in business that, 'an organisation can afford to get rid of its other assets, but not its brand image!'

Market segmentation

Remember that the simplest and most important principle of marketing is that marketing and its related activities should be designed to serve the customers. Serving customers needs with goods and services that do so more precisely than those of competitors in a market-orientated society has today become more important than ever. Whereas in the past, in many markets, all customers were treated to a similar diet of goods and services, organisations now recognise that groups of consumers have different needs, wants and tastes.

Not every person likes the same make of motor car or has the same taste in clothes. Equally, if cost and production time were of no importance, manufacturers would make products to the exact specifications of each buyer. On the other hand, neither can a manufacturer serve all customers successfully if it groups all of their needs and wants together.

CASE STUDY

Special K

Special K is a brand with a unique heritage. Over many years it has evolved as a stand-alone product and Kellogg's have not attempted to create any variants or develop the product further. However, over a period of time products reach their maturity phase of the product life-cycle, and in order to keep the brand fresh it was necessary to revitalise it and extend the growth phase by looking for opportunities to do so.

The solution for Kellogg's was to invest in a series of variants that would support the values

of the brand and extend sales of the product. To do this Kellogg's launched cereal bars and also use berries and other variants to provide different taste opportunities for the core product. For Kellogg's this represented low risk and offered a good rate of return.

1 To whom does Special K appeal?
2 Why have Kellogg's invested in a series of variants?

Instead of trying to serve all customers equally, an organisation may focus its efforts on different parts of the total marketplace. Within the total marketplace it is possible to group customers with similar characteristics and divide the market into parts. This is known as market segmentation. Market segments are groups of customers with similar needs and characteristics. The task is to produce and supply different products to suit these segments.

Market segmentation is therefore a process of separating a total market into parts so that different strategies can be used for different sets of customers.

If you attempt to market a single product to the whole population, this is sometimes said to be like using a blunderbuss, firing shots to pepper the whole marketplace.

This is sometimes called *undifferentiated or mass marketing.* A single marketing mix is offered to the whole marketplace. In other words all potential customers are treated as if they have similar characteristics. This may be a relatively cheap way of tackling marketing, but its weakness is that it ignores individual differences.

Market segmentation, using differentiated marketing strategies, tailors separate product and market strategies to different sectors of the market. For example, the market for cars has many segments such as economy, off-road, MPV, luxury, high performance, etc. This approach

Learning activity

Does any market today exist where segmentation does not take place?

When it is not possible to satisfy all of its customers' needs with a uniform product, an organisation will use market segmentation to divide consumers into smaller segments consisting of buyers with similar needs or characteristics so that marketing becomes like firing a rifle instead of a blunderbuss. A rifle with an accurate sight will hit the target more efficiently without wasting ammunition.

recognises that in order to be successful and hit consumer needs, it is necessary to recognise the needs of different groups of consumers and meet them in different ways.

In fact some organisations simply exist to serve highly specialised market segments. They deliberately choose to compete in one segment and develop the most effective mix for that market. This is known as concentrated marketing. For example, Morgan serves the specific and highly esoteric needs of customers who like a car from the past. Jaguar cars are associated with luxury market segments. Similarly, quality fashion retailers today increasingly use brand names

FIGURE 3.16 *Marketing by blunderbuss*

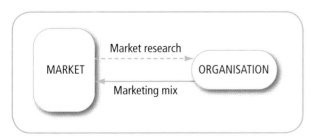

FIGURE 3.17 *Undifferentiated marketing*

FIGURE 3.18 *Marketing by rifle – hitting the target segment*

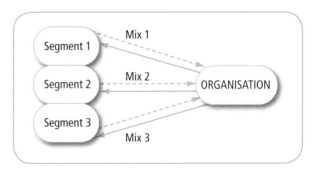

FIGURE 3.19 *Differentiated marketing*

The following diagram illustrates some of the main segments of the tea market, showing examples of teas sold in each segment.

Choose two of the segments and explain how you might use a slightly different marketing mix to appeal to consumers in these segments.

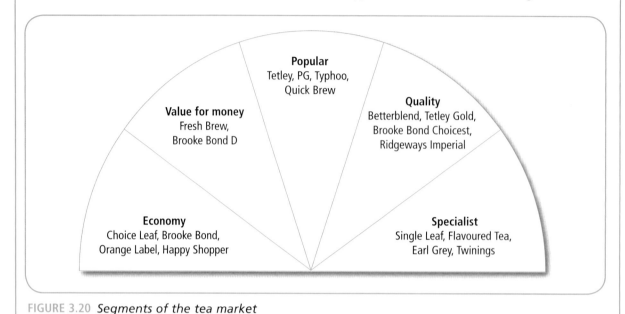

Popular
Tetley, PG, Typhoo, Quick Brew

Value for money
Fresh Brew, Brooke Bond D

Quality
Betterblend, Tetley Gold, Brooke Bond Choicest, Ridgeways Imperial

Economy
Choice Leaf, Brooke Bond, Orange Label, Happy Shopper

Specialist
Single Leaf, Flavoured Tea, Earl Grey, Twinings

FIGURE 3.20 *Segments of the tea market*

to position themselves in particular parts of a market. This is sometimes called niche marketing. A disadvantage is that if sales of a product decline in that segment, the lack of diversification means that this may affect the performance of the organisation.

There are three elements to segmentation – market segments, targeting and positioning.

Market segments

Market segments are groups of customers with similar needs and characteristics. The task is to produce and supply different products to suit these segments.

Targeting

Once segments have been identified, organisations have to identify one or more segments which has a need which can best be met by the organisation. This is known as targeting and may involve mass, undifferentiated marketing or concentrated marketing.

Positioning

Even though parts of the market are divided into segments, and organisations have worked out which ones to target, buyers within each segment will not have identical needs. Positioning involves developing a market strategy through the marketing mix that takes into account the thoughts and perceptions of customers about a product relative to other products and brands. The position is how the product is perceived in the minds of customers. Repositioning involves moving the product away from its current position in the market to another part of the market, where it might compete more effectively. Perhaps the most famous repositioning strategy in recent years is Skoda, who have moved away from a low cost, low reliability position in the market to become a well respected high value brand.

Look at two similar products. Comment upon the similarities and differences of their marketing mixes. To what extent are these due to positioning strategy?

Niche marketing

It could be argued that one of the great things about the World Wide Web is that it allows small organisations to identify and reach niche markets, sometimes almost as well as large organisations. Most marketers know that 20 percent of buyers consume 80 percent of product volume. If you could identify that key 20 percent and find others like them, you could sell much more product with much less effort. The web enables organisations to do this and makes it easier to enter markets that are well segmented.

Even large companies have embraced niche marketing, by continuing to refine and target their product offerings to more specific buyer groups. For example, we only have to look at the car market to see how many different models are offered by large organisations and the huge number of variants they offer both in terms of the extras they put on them as well as colours and options.

1 **How does the web provide business opportunities for smaller organisations?**
2 **What is niche marketing?**
3 **To what extent has marketing become increasingly focused upon niches?**

Bases for segmenting markets

Geographic segmentation

This form of segmentation assumes that consumers in different regions may be affected by similar climate, natural factors, population density and levels of income. By dividing markets into regions it is possible to recognise and cater for the needs of customers in the regions. For example, people living in certain countries are assumed to have common characteristics that influence buying attitudes.

Demographic segmentation

Demographic factors, which can be measured with relative precision, have helped many organisations to define a basis on which to segment their market. Because demographic variables can be closely related to customer needs and purchasing behaviour, this helps producers to target their products more effectively. Demographic segmentation may involve dividing the population into discrete segments – for example, by age for clothes retailing, by sex for cosmetics, by family size for different sized packages of breakfast cereals, or in many other ways.

Segmentation by age

Segmentation by age is widely applied. A good example is the way in which banks and building societies develop services for students, young children, elderly customers and so on. Many products are also segmented by gender – clothing, alcohol, cosmetics and cars are segmented in such a way.

Other segmentation

Marketers may also segment according to ethnic background particularly for clothes, food and music. Levels of education can be a segmentation variable – some products clearly appeal to people of higher intellectual ability such as those who read *New Scientist* or *The Economist*.

Geodemographic segmentation

The newest methods of segmentation combine geographic and demographic segmentation principles. These are based on the belief that similar households in a particular locality exhibit similar purchasing behaviour.

The best-known geodemographic method is provided by CACI ACORN in their profile of Great Britain (see Figure 3.21). ACORN stands for A Classification Of Residential Neighbourhoods.

Look at the data below illustrating demographic trends for males within the UK between 1981 and 2002. Comment upon the different sort of products that might follow some of these trends.

	UNDER 4	5–14	15–24	25–34	35–44	45–59	60–64	65–74	75+	ALL
GREAT BRITAIN										
MALES (000s)										
1981	1,706	4,039	4,455	3,933	3,322	4,603	1,345	2,214	1,038	**26,655**
1982	1,737	3,887	4,514	3,826	3,462	4,554	1,401	2,179	1,073	**26,633**
1983	1,769	3,759	4,560	3,793	3,559	4,532	1,463	2,117	1,108	**26,660**
1984	1,773	3,667	4,590	3,818	3,640	4,514	1,515	2,067	1,145	**26,729**
1985	1,781	3,608	4,594	3,866	3,705	4,501	1,462	2,117	1,176	**26,810**
1986	1,797	3,542	4,580	3,935	3,778	4,467	1,426	2,152	1,201	**26,878**
1987	1,818	3,494	4,532	4,025	3,820	4,459	1,395	2,175	1,245	**26,963**
1988	1,849	3,468	4,443	4,113	3,838	4,490	1,379	2,180	1,277	**27,037**
1989	1,882	3,477	4,347	4,257	3,854	4,530	1,372	2,193	1,301	**27,213**
1990	1,901	3,508	4,227	4,379	3,868	4,571	1,365	2,199	1,321	**27,339**
1991	1,928	3,555	4,095	4,473	3,887	4,614	1,358	2,219	1,337	**27,466**
1992	1,939	3,609	3,954	4,548	3,816	4,769	1,352	2,243	1,340	**27,570**
1993	1,926	3,673	3,836	4,599	3,801	4,893	1,341	2,279	1,330	**27,678**
1994	1,920	3,704	3,749	4,642	3,825	4,992	1,331	2,309	1,319	**27,791**
1995	1,900	3,726	3,694	4,668	3,879	5,073	1,325	2,276	1,381	**27,922**
1996	1,866	3,761	3,630	4,677	3,965	5,139	1,322	2,257	1,427	**28,044**
1997	1,841	3,796	3,582	4,650	4,070	5,193	1,327	2,244	1,466	**28,169**
1998	1,820	3,817	3,561	4,589	4,181	5,252	1,346	2,236	1,500	**28,302**
1999	1,796	3,844	3,571	4,512	4,309	5,316	1,366	2,230	1,526	**28,470**
2000	1,771	3,838	3,598	4,435	4,444	5,379	1,376	2,233	1,552	**28,627**
2001	1,727	3,771	3,516	3,976	4,214	5,362	1,374	2,245	1,574	**27,760**
2002	1,686	3,756	3,606	4,004	4,314	5,448	1,376	2,267	1,614	**28,072**

Source: Office for National Statistics

	ACORN CATEGORY A: THRIVING	POP PROJ 2004 19.9%
1.1	Wealthy suburbs, large detached houses	2.9
1.2	Villages with wealthy commuters	2.7
1.3	Mature affluent home-owning areas	2.8
1.4	Affluent suburbs, older families	3.8
1.5	Mature well-off suburbs	2.7
2.6	Agricultural villages, home-based workers	1.6
2.7	Holiday retreats, older people, home-based workers	0.7
3.8	Home-owning areas, well-off older residents	1.4
3.9	Private flats, elderly people	1.2

Source: 2001 Census Area Statistics © Crown Copyright 2001, © CACI Ltd, 2005

FIGURE 3.21 *Example of ACORN Thriving category*

Psychographic and behavioural segmentation

This form of segmentation divides different groups up on the basis of social class, lifestyle or personality. For example:

1 *Social class* is a socio-economic way of dividing a market according to people's purchasing power and habits. The socio-economic grouping is sometimes called social stratification and each class roughly indicates a pattern of behaviour or consumption habits. One of the best known classifications is the NRS Social Grade Definitions, shown in Figure 3.22.

2 *Lifestyle* influences many of the goods or services that we purchase. Increasingly many make purchases that reflect their various lifestyles. For example, the lifestyle of this author includes healthfood, a love for a particular type of motor car and the occasional glass of Chardonnay.

3 *Personality* is something that we all have. All marketers have to do is to develop goods and services that match the personalities of their consumers. For example, what does it say about someone if they drive an Astra convertible, wear colourful clothes and wear lots of make-up?

4 *Behavioural segmentation* looks at behaviour patterns such as frequent/infrequent purchase and loyalty to a product. For example, one segment of the market may always purchase a product while another may be made up of people who frequently switch between brands. An experienced drinker may stick with Guinness, while an inexperienced one may try out a range of stouts and beers.

3.2 Using appropriate methods of market research

Business activities, by their very nature, are competitive. Within a dynamic business environment producers may be constantly entering and leaving the market. At the same time, changing consumer preferences may provide signals for them to develop new strategies with different products and services. Whereas some organisations will succeed and achieve or surpass their marketing objectives, others will inevitably not perform as well.

Market research is that vital link in the chain between buyers and suppliers. It does this by enabling those who provide goods and services to keep in touch with the needs and wants of those who buy the goods and services.

The American Market Research Association defines market research as:

'The systematic gathering, recording and analysis of data about problems related to the marketing of goods and services.'

We can break this definition down into its various ingredients:

systematic – in other words using an organised and clear method or system

SOCIAL GRADE	SOCIAL STATUS	OCCUPATION
A	Upper middle class	Higher managerial, administrative or professional
B	Middle class	Intermediate managerial, administrative or professional
C1	Lower middle class	Supervisory or clerical, and junior managerial or professional
C2	Skilled working class	Skilled manual workers
D	Working class	Semi-skilled and unskilled workers
E	Those at the lowest level of subsistence	State pensioners or widows (no other earner), casual or low-grade worker

Source: National Readership Survey

FIGURE 3.22 *One form of socio-economic grouping*

It has been said that 'a problem well defined is a problem half solved'. How might this relate to the context of market research?

gathering – knowing what you are looking for, and collecting appropriate information

recording – keeping clear and organised records of what you find out

analysing – ordering and making sense of your information in order to draw out relevant trends and conclusions

problems related to marketing – finding out the answers to questions which will help you to understand better your customers and other details about the market-place.

All organisational activities take place in an environment where there is some element of risk. For example, last year a firm might have sold 40,000 fridges to a market in Italy. Who is to say that they will sell the 50,000 they plan to sell this year? They may suddenly find new competitors in this market with a much better product than they currently produce, which is being sold at a lower price. Italy may go through a cold spell – there may be problems in the economy that reduce the likelihood that people will change their fridge.

To reduce risk, market research provides an invaluable source of information to help organisations to make decisions and develop strategies for products. For example, it could help them to:

* identify their competitors
* improve their knowledge of consumers and competitors so that changing trends can be identified
* use trends to forecast activities
* monitor their market position and develop plans and strategies
* improve their competitive advantage.

Purpose of market research

All organisations require answers to key questions. Answers help decision-makers to understand the nature of the decisions they have to make about the products they provide and the markets in which they operate.

Questions may include:

How do we define the market? What are its features such as size and character, and what is the nature of competition?

What do customers require? At the heart of marketing should be the ongoing activities of satisfying the needs and aspirations of customers.

CASE STUDY

Connecting the washer to the web

Ariston have developed a washing machine that can communicate with the Internet using its own mobile phone. The margherita2000. com washing machine will be able to send breakdown reports for repair and download new washing cycles from its own website. The householder will also be able to control their washing machine remotely either by using a mobile phone or by logging onto the machine's own website.

The key achievement of this machine is that it is the first of a range of web-connected devices in the home that will be able to talk to each other using a new open communications system called WRAP – WebReady Appliances Protocol. In the first years of the new century, Ariston hope to follow up the launch of the washing machine with a dishwasher, fridge and then an oven.

1 To what sort of audience might the margherita2000 appeal?
2 What sort of market research questions might product planners ask before launching this type of product?

Who are the target groups and how do we reach them? The market may be made up of different groups and segments. Different distribution channels may be used to reach different groups of customers.

What strategies are used by our competitors? It is important to know and understand how the actions of competitors might influence the market.

How do we measure our performance? Market performance may be measured according to a number of key criteria, such as the value or volume of sales as well as brand or market share.

Where is our competitive position? An important feature of marketing analysis is an ongoing review of where the organisation is within the market, its competitive advantage and how changes in its actions might influence market shape and market share.

> *In short, the purpose of market research is to make the process of business scientific, by cutting out unsubstantiated guesswork and hunches!*

Some organisations are creative in their outlook to planning and research. These businesses may anticipate developments in markets and introduce new ideas and new methods to exploit opportunities or minimise problems. In doing this they may take risks to develop new ideas. In contrast other businesses will wait to see what their competitors do before reacting.

Some businesses therefore use market research to move ahead of the competition while others simply see it as a way of keeping up with their competitors. The first type of firm we would describe as being **proactive**, while the second we would describe as **reactive.**

The proactive business will be the first to come up with new ideas, and consequently well placed

to exploit their ideas in meeting adventurous marketing objectives such as brand leadership in a new market. Sony are famous for breaking new ground and taking risks through proactive planning and research.

The reactive business does not put itself at the mercy of such risk and can never be in a position to make the same sort of impact as a proactive firm. Equally, it does not fall foul of the mistakes made by proactive firms.

Working in small groups, make a list of:

* five proactive organisations, together with some of their products;

* five reactive organisations and their products.

One of the most important things to remember is that what comes out of market research is only as good as what goes in. Identifying the information required, successfully choosing the most suitable research method and then the type and nature of questioning should all be carefully considered before any project proceeds.

Primary research

Any information that is original and is obtained outside an organisation is referred to as primary data. It is obtained by research conducted by or on behalf of the organisation, is specific to its needs and will involve a range of methods such as discussions, questionnaires and surveys and testing through pilots and field trials.

Questionnaires

Many market research methods depend upon the use of a questionnaire. A questionnaire is a systematic list of questions designed to obtain information from people about:

* specific events

* their attitudes

* their values

* their beliefs.

The quality of the questionnaire is inextricably linked with the survey. A good questionnaire will result in a smooth interview, giving the interviewer a precise format to follow and

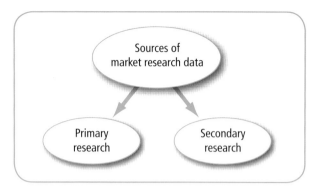

FIGURE 3.23 *Sources of research data*

ensuring that he or she obtains exactly the information required in a format that is easy for the researcher to analyse later.

Questionnaire design is critical. Although it is easy to make up questions, it is very difficult to produce a good questionnaire – and a badly designed questionnaire may lead to biased results.

Another problem may arise if very few completed forms are returned, or if those returned are only partially completed. In addition, if the questionnaire is being administered by a number of interviewers, there is always the danger that some may misinterpret questions and introduce their own personal bias in a way that prompts certain answers from respondents.

If you were asked to write a questionnaire, where would you start? The starting point would be to think about the focus of your questions. For example, what information do you require and why do you need it? You would also need to think about the target audience that you wish to examine. It would be important to question all of the people who are likely to have relevant opinions or information.

When people give up their own time to answer the questions on a questionnaire, it is useful to tell them who you are and why you are undertaking this research. This is not only polite but will also put the respondent at ease and may facilitate co-operation. The language used and the number of prompts and examples to support the points made within the questionnaire need to be considered.

A good questionnaire will:

✳ ask questions which relate directly to information needs

✳ not ask too many questions

✳ not ask leading or intimate questions

✳ fit questions into a logical sequence

✳ use the language of the target group

✳ not use questions that are confusing or ambiguous

✳ avoid questions relating to sexuality, politics and religion unless they are very relevant.

Sequencing the questions logically is very important. It may be useful to start with a few factual questions that are easy to respond to. Some form of multiple-choice questions may follow these up before introducing questions that require the respondent to think about some of the issues being researched. The questionnaire may be closed with 'filter questions' about the background of the respondent, which help to locate them in the sampling frame.

There is no point including questions that do not relate to the main purposes of the research. The questionnaire should be kept as short as practically possible. More than 40 questions could put off respondents or cause them to provide hasty replies to questions.

The questions in a questionnaire may be 'open' or 'closed'. *Open questions* allow the person answering to give an opinion and may encourage him or her to talk at length. You have to be careful though. Asking questions such as 'What type of music do you listen to?' could lead to such a variety of answers that analysing them would be very difficult. *Closed questions* usually require an answer picked from a range of options (which may be simply yes/no). Most questionnaires use closed questions, so that they can be answered quickly and efficiently, and the answers are easier to analyse (see Figure 3.24).

Sometimes it is necessary to judge the degree of the respondent's feelings on a subject. The best way to do this is to use a rating or response scale. There are various types:

Likert scales show how strongly the respondent agrees or disagrees with a statement (see Figure 3.25).

Rank order scale questions ask the respondent to put a number beside various items in order to

Please indicate with a tick which types of music you listen to regularly (tick all that apply):

- [ ] Classical
- [ ] Easy listening
- [ ] Jazz
- [ ] Blues
- [ ] Golden oldies
- [ ] Popular
- [ ] Heavy metal
- [ ] Punk
- [ ] Indie
- [ ] Rap
- [ ] Dance
- [ ] Swing
- [ ] Hip Hop
- [ ] Other (please specify) _____

FIGURE 3.24 *A closed question*

put them in some sort of order of preference, as shown in Figure 3.26.

An **intention-to-buy** asks respondents to indicate by ticking a box how likely it is that they will buy some items in the future (see Figure 3.27).

Semantic differential scales use two words describing the opposite ends of a scale, with a series of points highlighted between. The

These are all considerations when choosing where to buy a new computer. Put them in rank order with 1 by the most important, 2 by the second most important and so on down to 5 against the least important.

Wide choice	2
Helpful sales staff	3
Value for money	1
After-sales service	4
Quick delivery	5

FIGURE 3.26 *A rank order scale question*

If a textbook was available covering this unit/module, I would:

Definitely buy	Probably buy	Not sure	Probably not buy	Definitely not buy
1 ☐	2 ☐	3 ☐	4 ☐	5 ☐

FIGURE 3.27 *An intention-to-buy question*

respondents are asked to indicate where on the scale their opinion lies (see Figure 3.28).

Put a cross in the box that shows how strongly you agree or disagree with each of the following statements:

	Strongly agree	Agree	Neither agree nor disagree	Disagree	Strongly disagree
This AS course has prepared me well for work		X			
The lecturers at college are well prepared			X		
The lectures at college are interesting	X				
I was well prepared for my assignments				X	

FIGURE 3.25 *A Likert scale*

Frosty's ice creams are:

Good value									Poor value
Tasty									Tasteless
Well packaged									Poorly packaged
Satisfying									Unsatisfying

FIGURE 3.28 *A semantic differential scale*

Frosty's ice creams are:

1 2 3 4 5 6 7 8 9 10

Good value	X	Poor value
Tasty	X	Tasteless
Well packaged	X	Poorly packaged
Satisfying	X	Unsatisfying

FIGURE 3.29 *Comparing respondent replies*

Frosty and Polar ice creams are:

1 2 3 4 5 6 7 8 9

Good value	X X	Poor value
Tasty	X X	Tasteless
Well packaged	X X	Poorly packaged
Satisfying	X X	Unsatisfying

Polar   Frosty

FIGURE 3.30 *Comparing product strengths and weaknesses*

Once the respondent has completed such a question, the points can be joined up to produce a profile of that product. Comparing replies from a number of respondents provides a useful profile of how the product is viewed by customers (see Figure 3.29).

It is then possible to compare products or brands by superimposing two or more profiles on one scale, to identify the strengths and weaknesses of each. An example of this is shown in Figure 3.30.

The purpose of a closed question is to get people to commit themselves to a concrete answer. The problem with open questions is that

they are difficult to analyse. Closed questions tie respondents down so that they have to make a decision within a range of choices.

To help interviewers operate a questionnaire, a **prompt card** is sometimes used. This means that, if several or all of the questions in the questionnaire have the same range or set of answers, these can be numbered and then the respondents answers can be recorded as numbers (see Figure 3.31).

Some questionnaires are designed so that respondents can concentrate on the questions that are relevant, and the skip over the questions which do not relate to them (see Figure 3.32).

Dolland & Aitchison	01
Specsavers Optical Superstores	02
Boots Opticians	03
Vision Express	04
Rayner & Keeler	05
Optical Express	06
G. C. Bateman	07
Co-op	08
Scrivens	09
Others	10

FIGURE 3.31 *A prompt card*

Question 6 **Do you have a bank account?**

☐ YES

☐ NO

If your answer is **NO**, proceed to question 20

FIGURE 3.32 *A question that permits a respondent to skip to the next relevant part of a questionnaire*

Use the questionnaire below to discuss your feelings about one product which you regularly purchase (Product A):

Total performance of Product A (including product, sales, support, price, etc.):

Dissatisfied ☐ ☐ ☐ ☐ ☐ ☐ ☐ ☐ ☐ ☐ **Very satisfied**
　　　　　　　1　2　3　4　5　6　7　8　9　10

Compared to one year earlier, is Product A's total performance:

☐ Better　　☐ Worse　　☐ Same

Why?

What one thing can_____ do to improve the performance of Product A in meeting your total needs?

Explain how the answers you have provided for this brief questionnaire might be used.

What information has it provided?

Comment upon the structure of the questions.

How easy would it be to analyse and interpret the information it provided?

Observation

This involves looking at how consumers behave in the shopping environment. Information like this can help marketers to make decisions about packaging, or influence the choice of point-of-sale materials designed to attract the attention of shoppers. It may also help to make decisions about where to place particular products in a shop – the process of putting products in a store in the right place at the right time is known as **merchandising**. This is particularly important in the retail trade.

Today a number of electronic devices can be used to monitor customers' individual responses. For example:

* a psycho-galvanometer measures perspiration and this may be used for a variety of forms of testing

* an eye camera may record reactions such as visual stimulation

* a tachistoscope exposes material for a short period and then measures responses.

Product testing and test marketing

It is possible to use tests within the marketplace as a form of primary research. For example, an organisation may test a new product in a television region that is regarded as being representative of the wider market. One major problem with test marketing is that it alerts competitors to new ideas. However, at least it does help an organisation to anticipate the ways in which consumers will respond to a new product idea or concept.

In test marketing the organisation will need to decide upon the size and make-up of the sample it is using. They will also need to give consideration to the length of time that is appropriate for the test in order to provide valid and reliable results. Research indicates that the longer the period for which products are test marketed, the more accurate the forecasts that can be made about their likely success.

An alternative to test marketing is to use a consumer panel to find out consumer attitudes to a product or the strength of preferences.

Focus groups

Focus groups are an inexpensive method of obtaining useful qualitative information from consumers. For example, under the guidance of a chairperson, a group of users of the same product may be invited to provide opinions on its use. Members of a focus group might be members of the public who have opinions on certain products and services. They may be drawn from a certain market segment or from an industry. Focus groups are very good at testing customer reactions to product developments or proposals.

A good leader is essential for a focus group. He or she will introduce key topics for discussion, keep order and ensure that every group member has the opportunity to make a contribution. The main benefit of such groups is that new ideas and opinions can be 'bounced off' each group member to refine them and prompt further creative thought. A group requires a note taker. It may also be audio or video-taped.

Consumer panels

Another market research method is to set up panels of consumers, which consist of groups of consumers who agree to provide information about their attitudes or buying habits.

A consumer on a *home audit panel* will discuss consumer issues during a series of personal visits by a researcher. The great advantage is that this type of panel will supply information over a long period of time from a willing participant who may agree to sample, test or use a range of products or who is simply asked to respond to questions on consumer issues.

Another type of panel are those that involve the collection of electronically-generated information. For example, one such panel is provided by the Broadcasters' Audience Research Board which estimates the number of people watching TV programmes. Members of this panel are selected in a way that makes sure that they are representative of all television households. Once a prospective panel member agrees to join the panel, their television sets and video recorders are then monitored by a meter which collects information about their viewing habits. Members register their presence in a room by pressing a button on their peoplemeter handset when they enter a room and then the meter captures information related to their viewing.

According to BARB:

'The Broadcasters' Audience Research Board (BARB) is responsible for providing estimates of the number of people watching television. This includes which channels and programmes are being watched, at what time, and the type of people who are watching at any one time. BARB provides television audience data on a minute-by-minute basis for channels received within the UK. The data is available for reporting nationally and at ITV and BBC regional level and covers all analogue and digital platforms.

Viewing estimates are obtained from panels of television owning households representing the viewing behaviour of the 24+ million households within the UK. The panels are selected to be representative of each ITV and BBC region. The service covers viewing within private households only.

Panel homes are selected via a "multi-stage, stratified and unclustered" sample design. What this means is that the panel is fully representative of all television households across the whole of the UK.'

Set up your own consumer discussion panel. Provide respondents with a suitable form and then ask five people to monitor their purchases over a fortnight. Think of some appropriate questions and then interview each person to discuss their purchases. Record your results.

For more information on BARB, visit their website using www.heinemann.co.uk/hotlinks (express code 1149P, then go to Unit 3).

Organisations that buy Homescan information from Nielsen can understand exactly who their customers are. They find out about what products customers are buying day by day, so that they can tailor this knowledge to develop promotions and their advertising for the days when the right customers come in store. They can assess a new product launch. By using Homescan they can evaluate the retail distribution of a new product and understand the factors behind its build in volume and market share. It also provides an opportunity to track products to find out factors that might be undermining their performance. This all helps to measure the tactical and strategic objectives of a marketing campaign and to refine and develop precise elements of marketing strategies. For example, it might help to answer questions such as:

CASE STUDY

Waving the wand

A C Nielsen's electronic consumer panel is known as Homescan. It brings a new dimension to consumer analysis providing a powerful insight into the behaviour of customers. In a sophisticated and competitive marketing environment, this type of panel provides instant and precise data using barcode technology. Launched in June 1989, Homescan became the first panel in Europe to use in-home scanning.

See more about Homescan on A C Nielsen's website through www.heinemann.co.uk/hotlinks (express code 1149P, then go to Unit 3).

Households are chosen to mirror demographics within regions to provide accurate representations of purchasing across the country. Each household is equipped with a small hand-held scanner, referred to as a wand. After each shopping trip they record the date, the items bought, any promotional offers which applied, the price, the quantity and the store used.

The wand asks a series of questions to prompt the panellist. Scanning each product's barcode enables its 'fingerprint' to be recorded and provides A C Nielsen with a precise record of consumer purchasing. The information is then transferred directly, via telephone modem links, to Nielsen's host computer. Collecting daily purchasing data provides speed and precision to marketing.

Homescan includes all grocery purchases brought into the home from any outlet. The panel includes 10,500 households throughout the UK, including Northern Ireland.

1 What is the purpose of Homescan?
2 How might A C Nielsen use this data?

Has the relaunch succeeded in regaining lapsed buyers?
What is the best way to target mailing activity?
How does advertising expenditure help which brands?
Where do consumers buy?
How loyal are consumers?

In October 2004 A C Nielsen announced that it had completed the first phase of the expansion of its U.S. Homescan consumer panel, bringing the panel size up to 91,500 households creating a rich source of consumer insights.

As part of its *Homescan MegaPanel* initiative, A C Nielsen expanded the size of its Homescan panel from 61,500 households, with a second phase set to increase the size of the panel to 125,000 households by the end of 2005.

According to A C Nielsen, 'The expanded panel will allow for the development of specialty panels consisting of households with babies, households with teens, and others, all of which will help clients better serve specific niches and identify new ones. The *MegaPanel* will also allow for improved sales measurement within fast-growing retail channels such as mass merchandisers, dollar stores, warehouse clubs stores, and pet specialty stores.'

Trade audits

Sometimes the best and easiest form of market research is simply to discuss issues with customers to make sure that their experiences match their expectations. This is known as a trade audit. Trade audits involve an analysis of consumer experiences. For example, at the end of your course you may be asked to fill in a questionnaire so that you can provide feedback about each of your modules and discuss your experiences.

Marketing/trade auditing is used as a means of assessing past performance so that an assessment can be taken about future courses of action. As an internal audit it enables an organisation to understand how it stands in relation to its customers and where its strengths and weaknesses lie. David Mercer sets out the following list of key points of information that need to be collected for the marketing audit:

Who are the customers? What are their key characteristics and what differentiates them from other members of the population?
What are their needs and wants? What do they expect the product to do and what are their special requirements and perceptions?
What are their attitudes and what are their buying intentions?

Trade or marketing audits will therefore be concerned with:

* reviewing all of current marketing activity, focusing upon how well the marketing mix meets the needs of existing customers
* a review of marketing systems from the customers' standpoint to assess how well their needs are being catered for.

Secondary research

Secondary marketing information is effectively anything that has previously been published. It can be built from both *internal* and *external* sources.

Internal sources of secondary data

Internal information is information already held within the organisation, more often than not held in databases. A database is a large amount of information stored in a way that it can easily be found, processed and updated. Users may access the database across an organisation

Information on existing customers will form the core of the database, with sales invoices probably being the most valued source of data. The invoice is created for financial purposes but it contains a considerable amount of customer data that can be made immediately available for others. For example, it might contain information such as:

Customer title	gender, job description, other forms of identification
Customer surname	ethnic coding
Customer address	geographic coding
Date of sale	tracking purchase rates and repurchasing patterns
Items ordered	product category interests
Quantities ordered	heavy/medium/light users
Price	value of customer
Terms and conditions	customer service needs.

One way in which organisations in the retail industry keep and analyse data from customers is by the use of loyalty cards. It would be possible to match the postcode of the customer with the nature and type of purchases they might make, and then to use this information as a base for making product and merchandising decisions within a store.

External sources of secondary data

External data exists in the form of published materials collected by somebody else. It can provide a broader dimension to data previously collected.

For example, external information can be used to enhance existing knowledge. Postcodes may help to group customers geographically. By identifying and labelling certain characteristics of a customer, a company may be able to make assumptions about their needs. Two examples of useful external sources are:

Domestic socio-economic data Customers are classified according to their house type, the assumption being that a certain lifestyle is associated with that type of house.

Industrial classification Organisational customers can be classified according to the nature of their activities. Certain types of organisations can then be expected to have predictable demands for services.

External information can complement an organisation's own information by providing direct comparison with competitors, by putting performance within the context of the economy as a whole, and by identifying markets offering potential.

Learning activity

Imagine that you are the owner or manager of a small shop selling sports equipment in your local neighbourhood. What sort of information might give you a better understanding of the decisions you have to make?

Government statistics

The principal suppliers of government statistics in the UK are:

ONS (Office for National Statistics)
DTI (Department of Trade and Industry)
DfES (Department for Education and Skills)
GSS (Government Statistical Service)
OECD (Organisation for Economic Co-operation and Development)
Visit the websites of these organisations through www.heinemann.co.uk/hotlinks (express code 1149P, then go to Unit 3).

Some of the key publications include:

Monthly Digest of Statistics – summary information on many economic trends.
Regional Trends – regional profiles, households, labour, living standards, etc.
Labour Market Trends – topical articles, hours worked, sickness, training, vacancies, disputes, earnings and unemployment.
Social Trends – trends in labour markets, incomes, and spending by item and by region.
Family Spending – details on who earns and spends what.

New Earnings Survey – earnings listed by industry, area, occupation and others.
National Food Survey – expenditure on and consumption of food by income group and region.
Population Trends – family statistics including births, marriages and deaths, etc. in regions.
Annual Abstract of Statistics – population, social conditions, production, prices, employment.
Bank of England Quarterly Bulletin – articles on financial trends.
General Household Survey – social and socio-economic issues.
Retail Prices Index – changes in UK prices.
Census of Production – data about production by firms in all industries.
Eurostat Publications – a variety, covering economic, industrial and demographic changes across Europe.
Indicators of Industrial Activity - production, employment and prices across a variety of industries and compared worldwide.
Business Monitors – statistics concerning output in different business sectors. *The Retailing Monitor* is of particular interest, covering what is being bought by region.

Media and other sources

Another useful source of information is the *media*. Whilst unlikely to yield detailed data, the media may present a series of stories about key market sectors or larger organisations. Sources include:

Learning activity

Choose a product market or industry in which to research. Visit the reference section and the periodicals section of either your school or college library or your local public library. Identify which sources would help you with this research and produce a short report. Use the internet to support your final analysis.

There are many business **directories** that provide general information about industries and markets. These include Kompass Register, Who Owns Whom and Key British Enterprises.

Visit the Kompass website through www.heinemann.co.uk/hotlinks (express code 1149P, then go to Unit 3).

CASE STUDY

Applying to be a market researcher

Market researchers organise the collection of public and business opinion about products, services or organisations. They may also conduct market research interviews and test new questionnaires.

Tasks and duties

If you apply to be a market researcher you may be asked to:

Discuss information with clients

Design surveys and questionnaires

Organise and manage surveys

Liaise with field workers and their supervisors

Supervise survey staff

Conduct interviews

Undertake comprehensive secondary research and generally develop an understanding of how such knowledge could be used to support decision-making processes.

Skills

Market researchers need good research skills and the ability to think logically so that they can design good surveys and questionnaires. They need mathematical and statistical ability and computer skills, to analyse and interpret their data.

Organisational and time-management skills are important in this work. Market researchers should also have good written and oral communication skills and they should be good listeners. It is also important to have creative thinking ability to be able to find solutions to problems.

Knowledge

Market researchers should know about questionnaire design, survey methods and marketing techniques. They should also know how to interpret statistics. They should understand how humans behave and think, and they need to be aware of different sampling and interview methods.

It is important for market researchers to have some knowledge and understanding of the businesses or industries they research. Market researchers need an understanding of marketing, business or research methods.

Personal qualities

Market researchers need to be able to work well under pressure, and juggle many tasks within a project. Accuracy is important, and they should be culturally sensitive when designing questionnaires and managing survey projects. They should be team players and honest. The ability to manage tasks and take responsibility are important for this job. Market researchers must also be able to keep information private.

Appearance

As market researchers spend a lot of time dealing with people such as clients, respondents and other professionals outside the organisation, their appearance is important.

Write a list detailing your experiences of market research.

Newspapers – broadsheets such as *The Times* and *The Financial Times* are both authoritative sources. However, they do not take into account the value of local papers and local circumstances.

Magazines and trade journals – the obvious ones are *The Economist* and *The Grocer*.

TV and radio – these include specialist news and current affairs programmes.

Teletext – this provides a variety of current information across many topics.

Trade associations publish information for their members concerning their particular fields, and there are associations for almost all trades.

The Internet has rapidly become an invaluable research tool providing a rich resource for information from a multitude of sources. As a resource it is predicted to continue to grow rapidly and become much more central to the workings of organisations not just in terms

Using the case study, draft a person specification for a market research post.

Look at the requirements for market researchers. Think about how you might or might not fit the bill for such a post. Draft a letter of application for the post of a market researcher at an organisation you have some knowledge of or interest in.

Identify a product market which you feel has potential for growth. Explain briefly what sort of information would help you to analyse the changes taking place within that market. Present this in the form of a short report.

of 'Internet marketing' but also as a business resource. Try visiting MORI through www. heinemann.co.uk/hotlinks (express code 1149P, then go to Unit 3). Many organisations such as Boots or Nestlé have their own *intranet*. Unlike the Internet which is available to all, an intranet is a data sharing facility within an organisation.

There are a number of *commercial market research companies* offering a range of services and selling data that they acquire from a variety of sources. For example, Mintel is a commercial research organisation which, in return for a fee, provides a monthly journal containing reports on consumer markets – for example, bread, alcoholic drinks and financial services. Information includes areas such as market size, main competitors, projected growth, market share of main competitors, advertising spend of main competitors and other trends. Mintel also produces in-depth reports on certain markets and the website is available through www. heinemann.co.uk/hotlinks (express code 1149P, then go to Unit 3).

The types of reports produced by agencies include:

Retail Business Market Surveys These are published monthly and each carries details of certain industries. It is important for those involved in market research to be able to access those relevant to their particular field. Each copy will carry an index of industries investigated. There will be details on market size, market sectors, price trends, sales abroad, advertising and promotion, consumption, distribution, branding and prospects for the industry.

Key Note Reports carry even more information with specific information upon each industry.

Retail Audits Some organisations such as Retail Audits collect data of retail sales through supermarkets and larger chains and then sell the information to organisations wishing to buy it. These figures enable producers to work out the market shares of their markets, the sales of different products and the effects of any recent strategy such as a price change or a promotional campaign.

Quantitative and qualitative data

The information gathered through market research may be described as being either **qualitative** or **quantitative** in nature. Qualitative information informs the organisation about the opinions and preferences of individuals and cannot always be interpreted statistically. For example, in response to a qualitative interview about cakes one person might feel that the cake is too moist and rich, while another might think that

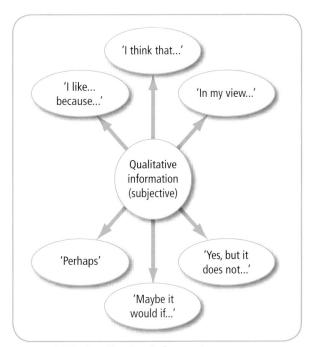

FIGURE 3.33 *Qualitative information*

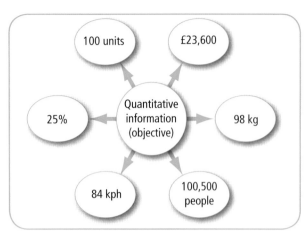

FIGURE 3.34 *Quantitative information*

FIGURE 3.35 *Supporting quantitative data by qualitative information*

it has a rich taste. Qualitative research is therefore about descriptions. This type of information is difficult to categorise and measure because it is based upon personal views deemed to be subjective.

On the other hand quantitative information is research that produces figures that can be examined statistically. For example, 15 out of 20 people might prefer one brand to another. As this is considered to be based upon hard facts, it is considered to be objective.

Many research methods supply both qualitative and quantitative information, and the two are closely interlinked. Qualitative information provides the context within which quantitative facts operate. The 'What do you think about…?' approach gives people the opportunity to offer a variety of opinions, reasons, motivations and influencing factors. A *group discussion*, for example, allows different opinions to be offered, which will frequently lead to a consensus, giving an idea of the popular view. People enjoy offering their opinions on subjects as diverse as the current political climate and the taste of a particular margarine, and what this gives the researcher is an overall view of that particular audience's reaction to a proposition.

Quantitative data helps to produce an idea of the size and overall shape of markets and the effects of strategies on the demand for goods and services. Qualitative data helps to take this process further to show how goods and services have met the needs of current and potential customers (Figure 3.35).

There are two broad areas in which market research can take place. If information does not already exist in an identifiable form it will have to be collected first-hand. This is known as **primary research**. Any information that is already published outside an organisation is known as **secondary research data.**

Validity, use and limitations

Planning the data collection process helps to ensure that data is reliable. In *primary research* it is important to think about what you are trying to achieve from the survey. If you are unclear about what you are trying to achieve, the results will be equally unclear. It is also important with this type of research to beware of vague objectives. Choosing the correct sampling method and research technique is particularly important.

Although there may be a ready availability of *secondary research* data, it has to be remembered that the information has been collected by someone else and will not be specific to the needs of a particular organisation. It may also be dated.

Whatever technique is used for collecting data, it is important to ensure that the research is both reliable and valid. A research technique is considered reliable if it produces almost identical results in successive or repeated trials. To have validity a research technique must measure what it is supposed to measure and not something else! A valid market research method provides data that can be used to test what is being sought.

As market research takes place, it provides a wealth of data that has to be collected, processed and analysed. Research may be carried out by the organisation's own market research staff or by staff from an agency. Alternatively secondary data may be bought in the form of reports. Clearly, primary collection of data is likely to be of greater cost than simply buying data. Data collection is not only expensive, but also subject to error. The process, therefore, has to be carefully monitored and managed.

The final stage in the market research process is to interpret the findings and draw conclusions. These are then reported back to managers and other decision-makers. Many different statistical techniques may be used to support this process. Clearly, if managers are to make decisions based upon the data they will want to know that the research process was carried out properly and that they can rely upon the data before deciding what action to take.

Interpretation and generalisation from data

The real benefit of market research information is determined by how much it improves the marketer's ability to make decisions. Good quality information will enable decisions to be made which satisfy the needs of the target market and also help the organisation to achieve its goals.

The use of market research represents a change from problem-solving by intuition to decision-making based on scientific gathering and analysis of information. The great advantage is that market research systematically provides information upon which managers may base product decisions.

Market analysis may, therefore, be used to identify:

❋ Changes in the markets for different products and businesses

❋ Profit opportunities

❋ The need to make changes to the product mix.

Changes in the markets for different products and businesses

The size and potential of any market must be constantly monitored for change. Analysis of sales trends as well as the size and potential of any market must be considered important. If the total size of the market is known, an organisation can thus work out what percentage of the market it has (market share) and then develop a strategy

Find out...

Check current developments in television from the Independent Television Commission through www.heinemann.co.uk/hotlinks (express code 1149P, then go to Unit 3).

FIGURE 3.36 *Market growth*

which helps it to increase its proportion of the market.

Market analysis may also be used to predict changes in the potential of the market both in the short- and long-term. Few markets are static and, as changes take place, it is important to understand about potential buyers as well as existing buyers.

There are three digital platforms of digital television. These are Terrestrial (DTT) with OnDigital, Digital Satellite Television currently served by BskyB and Digital Cable Television. Digital television currently has 9% penetration in UK homes. For example, for the marketers of digital television, it is important to know about the numbers of households who do not have digital set-top boxes as well as those who have them. They need to think about how long it will take to reach buyers who do not have digital services.

In high-growth markets it is usually easier to meet growth objectives, and these markets are often considered to be more profitable. Low-growth markets, by their very nature, are more static and may even be declining. As the market size approaches the market potential, growth slows and competition usually intensifies.

Profit opportunities

As products go through their product life-cycle, the profitability of different products changes.

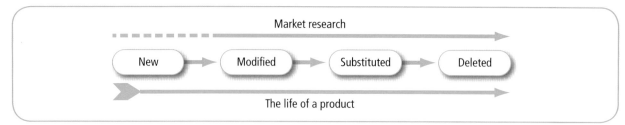

FIGURE 3.37 *Using research during the life of a product to make key product decisions*

Marketing analysis helps to direct an organisation towards those activities where profitability and other business objectives can best be satisfied.

The need to make changes to the product mix

The product mix comprises all of the products an organisation provides for its customers. Research will help managers to understand the sort of decisions they have to make about the product mix. For example, it might:

* identify opportunities for growth and development for new and existing products

* show how new products could replace existing products. This is known as *product substitution*

* show how some products are in decline – by modifying a product it may be possible to slow down its decline and sustain its profitability

* indicate that because a product is no longer satisfying a number of customers it ought to be deleted.

Changes in consumer behaviour

The process of buying a good or service is not as simple as it might appear. A customer does not usually make a purchase without thinking carefully about his or her requirements. Wherever there is choice, decisions are made and these are influenced by complex motives.

Market research will help an organisation to understand why customers make particular decisions, particularly through the analysis of buying patterns, who buys, what they buy, how they develop preferences and how they buy. Analysing these changes will help an organisation to cater more closely for customers' needs.

Changes in the activities of competitors

An organisation must at all times be aware of its competitors and the nature of what they are doing. Competition exists when two or more organisations act independently to sell their products to the same group of consumers. In some markets there may be a lot of competition, signified by an abundance of products and services so that consumers have a massive choice. These markets are characterised by promotional activities and price competition.

In other markets competition is limited and consumers are only able to choose from a limited range of products and services. In these circumstances consumers may feel that prices are too high – they are not getting value for money.

Direct competition exists where organisations produce similar products that appeal to the same group of consumers. *The Daily Star* competes directly with *The Sun*; and if you want to have a wall built, all the builders in your area looking for this type of work are in direct competition.

Even an organisation with no direct competition may face indirect competition as potential customers may consider different ways of meeting the same need. Instead of buying a motor car, they might buy a moped; instead of buying a box of chocolates on Mother's Day, they could buy a bunch of flowers – or send their mother a lottery ticket! See the National Lottery website through www.heinemann.co.uk/hotlinks (express code 1149P, then go to Unit 3).

Changes in the effectiveness of other marketing mix ingredients

Market research will also provide valuable information about the use of other marketing mix ingredients. For example, what are customers

Learning activity

Look at the market for one particular type of product. For example, it could be cars, electricity, confectionery or even beer. Comment upon how organisations within this market behave. What sorts of decisions have some of them recently made? What type of information would they have had available before they made these decisions?

perceptions of price, how effective is advertising, do distribution systems cater for customer requirements, what would be the effect on demand of changes in pricing policies?

3.3 Choosing an appropriate marketing mix

The marketing mix provides us with a useful way of looking at the marketing of products. Organisations need to create a successful mix of:

* the right *product* (or service)
* sold in the right *place*
* at the right *price*
* using the most suitable form of *promotion*.

As we have seen this simple mix is often referred to as the four Ps of product, price, place and promotion. This rather straightforward way of looking at what has become an increasingly complex business environment has at times been felt to be a little simplistic and limiting in terms of the real mix and what should be the fullness of our understanding. In recent times, therefore,

it has been expanded to include three more Ps to become a 7P mix with the additional elements of:

* *people*
* *provision* of customer service
* *process management*

People

People are widely recognised to be the greatest asset of the modern organisation. The governing principle, whether recognised or not, is that everybody who works for an organisation is a customer, either inside (the internal customer) or outside (the 'traditional customer') the company. Both kinds of customer expect to be supplied with the product or service they need, on time and as specified. This principle holds good for everyone in the company, whatever their level of skill and experience, whether their 'product' is answering a telephone or masterminding a major new project. It works to everyone's benefit. In doing so it provides the individual with genuine responsibility and scope for initiative, and it virtually guarantees that the organisation's performance will be improved.

Provision of customer service

Customer service has become increasingly important in a rapidly changing market-place. It has become more closely linked with the core product. Customer service is associated with developing bonds with customers in order to create long-term relationships that lead to advantages for all groups. It does not just happen. It is a process which involves pre-transaction, transaction and post-transaction considerations. Emphasis upon customer service will change from one product to another. For example, when manufacturing goods such as bread or shampoo customer service may involve developing strong customer relationships with many of the large retailers. In a pure service industry such as hairdressing or insurance, there are no tangible goods, and so customers will view nearly all of the benefits they get on the basis of the service they receive.

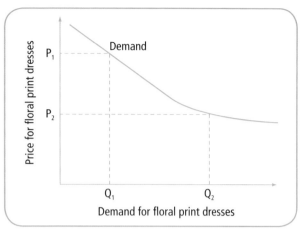

FIGURE 3.38 *Demand curve*

Process management

This involves all of the procedures, tasks, mechanisms and activities through which a product or service is delivered to a customer. It is clear that in a modern organisation processes are a key part of the marketing mix, involving developing priorities and ways of meeting customer needs. Processes might involve key decisions about customer involvement and employee discretion. In today's rapidly changing business environment, in order to meet consumer needs more closely, it is marketing that should determine the processes that link manufacturing with the customer.

The marketing mix is therefore a series of controllable variables that an organisation can use in order to best meet customer needs and ensure that an organisation is successful in the markets in which it serves.

Pricing and the techniques of pricing

The Oxford English Dictionary defines prices as the *'sum or consideration or sacrifice for which a thing may be bought or attained'*. Price is the only element of the marketing mix that directly generates incomes – other elements of the marketing mix are costs. The importance of price in the marketing mix varies. In low-cost, non-fashion markets price can be critical (for example, in the sale of white emulsion and gloss paint). In fashion markets, such as clothing, it can be one of the least relevant factors. Certain products are designed to suit a

particular segment (e.g. economy family cars), while others perform a specific function regardless of price (e.g. sports cars). For consumers with limited budgets, price is a key-purchasing criterion, while for those to whom 'money is no object' price is less important.

The first pricing task is to create an overall pricing goal for an organisation which is in line with the marketing strategy, and then determine objectives for each of the product lines.

The price charged for a product is associated with a given level of sales. We can illustrate this relationship by means of a demand curve (see Figure 3.38).

The curve in Figure 3.38 shows the levels of demand for a floral print dress sold at different market prices. As with most products, customers for floral dresses would be prepared to make more purchases at a lower than a higher price. The normal way to express customer sensitivity to price changes is through a measure known as **price elasticity of demand**. This is the measure of how much quantities purchased will alter in response to given price changes. Demand is said to be **elastic** if the change in quantity demanded is of a greater proportion than the change in price that initiated it.

For example, if the price of a particular brand of washing powder fell by 10 per cent and there was an increase in sales of 20 per cent, the demand for the product would be said to be elastic; the change in price led to more than proportionate response in quantity demanded.

Pricing objectives	Percentage of firms
Target profit or return on capital employed	67
Prices fair to firm and customers	13
Prices similar to those of competitors	8
Target sales volume	7
Stable sales volume	5
Target market share	2
Stable prices	2
Other	1

FIGURE 3.39 *Firms' pricing objectives*

$$\text{Price elasticity of demand} = \frac{\text{\% change in quantity demanded}}{\text{\% change in price}}$$

When a relative change in the quantity sold is less than the relative change in price, demand is said to be **inelastic**. For example, if a price increase of 10 per cent results in a 5 per cent fall in sales, price elasticity will be –0.5.

Price elasticities vary with the level of competition. The more competition in the market, the more likely it is that demand for a particular product line will be elastic. Price elasticity also varies during the product life-cycle. In the early days, when there is little competition, price inelasticity will be the rule within a sensible price range. However, as products mature, elasticity will increase in the competitive price range.

D. Shipley noted preferences among the principal set of pricing objectives of firms as shown in Figure 3.39.

Once pricing objectives have been established, organisations need to establish an appropriate pricing strategy.

Penetration pricing

Penetration pricing is appropriate when the seller knows that demand is likely to be elastic. A low price is therefore required to attract consumers to the product. Penetration pricing is normally associated with the launch of a new product for which the market needs to be penetrated (see Figure 3.40).

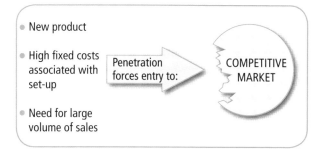

- New product
- High fixed costs associated with set-up
- Need for large volume of sales

Penetration forces entry to: → COMPETITIVE MARKET

FIGURE 3.40 *An environment appropriate for penetration pricing*

Because a price starts low, even though a product will be developing market share, the product may initially make a loss until consumer awareness is increased.

A typical example would be that of a new breakfast cereal or a product being launched in a new overseas market. Initially it would be launched with a relatively low price, coupled with discounts and special offers. As the product penetrates the market, sales and profitability increase. Prices then creep upwards.

Penetration pricing is particularly appropriate for products where economies of scale can be employed to produce large volumes at low unit costs. Products which are produced on a large scale are initially burdened by high fixed costs for research, development and purchases of plant and equipment. It is important to spread these fixed costs quickly over a large volume of output. Penetration pricing is also common when there is a strong possibility of competition from rival pricing.

Skimming

At the launch of a new product, there will frequently be little competition in the market, so that demand for the product may be relatively inelastic. Consumers will probably have little knowledge of the product. Skimming involves setting a reasonably high initial price in order to yield high initial returns from those consumers willing to buy the new product. Once the first group of customers has been satisfied, the seller can then lower prices in order to make sales to new groups of customers.

This process can be continued until a larger section of the total market has been catered for. By

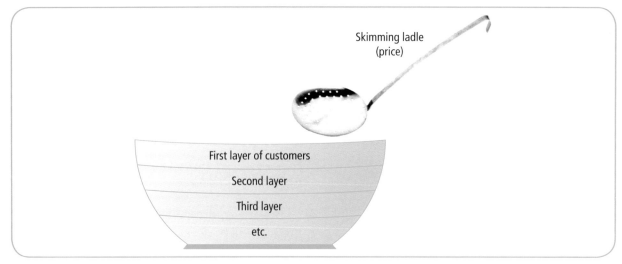

Skimming ladle
(price)

First layer of customers

Second layer

Third layer

etc.

FIGURE 3.41 *Skimming*

operating in this way, the business removes the risk of underpricing the product.

The name 'skimming' comes from the process of skimming the cream from the top of a milk product (Figure 3.41).

Cost-plus pricing

Any study of organisations in the real world shows that many businesses use no other basis than a **mark-up** on the cost of providing the product or service concerned. Information about costs is usually easier to piece together than information about other variables such as likely revenue. Firms will often therefore simply add a margin to the **unit cost.**

The unit cost is the average cost of each item produced. For example, if an organisation produces 800 units at a total cost of £24,000, the unit cost will be £30. Talk to many owners of small businesses and they will tell you that they 'cost out' each hour worked and then add a margin for profits; or they will simply mark-up each item sold by a certain percentage. For example, fashion items are frequently marked up by between 100 and 200 per cent.

The process of cost-plus pricing can best be illustrated in relation to large organisations where **economies of scale** can be spread over a considerable range of output.

For a large organisation, unit costs will fall rapidly at first as the overheads are spread over a larger output. It is therefore a relatively simple

calculation to add a fixed margin (e.g. 20 per cent) to the unit cost. The organisation is able to select an output to produce and to set a price that will be 20 per cent higher than the unit cost of production (see Figure 3.42).

Whilst cost-plus pricing is very popular, there are many dangers associated with it. If the price is set too high, sales may fall short of expectations; and if the price is set too low, then potential revenue is sacrificed. However, the greatest danger of cost-based pricing is that it indicates a *production-orientated approach to the market*. Emphasis on costs leads to tunnel vision that looks inwards at the company's product rather than outwards at the customers' perception of the product.

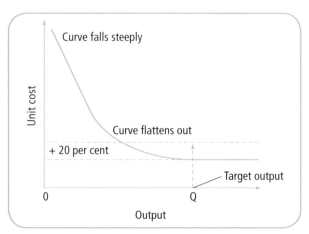

FIGURE 3.42 *Select a target output OQ and then add 20 per cent to the unit cost to get price*

Why is the margin for luxury goods such as designer goods and fashion accessories likely to be higher than for cigarettes or newspapers?

There is a strong link between value and price. **Delivery of value** is an important ingredient of an exchange. Marketing has been described as 'selling goods that don't come back to people who do'. If the seller does not provide customers with a significant value proposition, whatever the price, goods may be returned or customers will not come back.

In the longer term, the success of business organisations (and individuals) will depend on their ability to provide customers with **value for money** through the exchange process.

Most customers compare prices with the perceived quality or value provided by the goods and services they purchase – they are concerned with the value proposition provided by the organisation and its relationship to the price they have paid. For example, some customers are value orientated and want to pay low prices for acceptable quality; some buyers want high quality and are willing to pay more for it. Many of today's retailers are using emphasis upon 'value' as a form of competition. Instead of focusing simply upon price, they provide customers with a better value package – more for the same price – than other competitors in that segment of the market.

It is therefore important to price according to the nature of customers in the marketplace. On the one hand you may lose customers by charging too high a price – with a low value proposition if customers feel that they are not getting value for money. On the other hand you may lose custom from charging too low a price – potential customers may feel that the low price indicates lower quality than they are seeking.

Compare two products or services for which roughly similar prices are charged. Explain which product or service represents a better value proposition.

Competition-based pricing

In extremely competitive situations, costs have to be treated as a secondary consideration in short-term price determination. This is particularly true when competing products are almost identical, customers are well informed and where there are few suppliers.

The nature and extent of competition is frequently an important influence upon price. If a product is faced with direct competition, then it will compete against other very similar products in the marketplace. This will constrain pricing decisions so that price setting will need to be kept closely in line with rivals' actions. In contrast, when a product is faced by indirect competition (i.e. competition with products in different sectors of the market) then there will be more scope to vary price. This opens up the possibility for a number of strategies. For example, a firm might choose a high-price strategy to give a product a 'quality' feel. In contrast, it might charge a low price so that consumers see the product as a 'bargain'.

An individual organisation might try to insulate itself against price sensitivity by differentiating its products from those of rivals. Markets are sometimes classified according to the level of competition that applies. For example, an extreme level of competition is termed **perfect competition** (it exists in theory rather than in practice). The other extreme is **monopoly** where a single firm dominates a market. In the real world, most markets lie between these extremes and involve some level of imperfection.

If a perfect market could exist there would be no limitations to new firms entering the market, and buyers would know exactly what was on offer and would incur no costs in buying from one seller rather than another. Products would be almost identical. In a monopoly situation, only one firm exists and barriers prevent new firms from entering the market. The seller has considerable powers to control the market.

FIGURE 3.43 *Competition*

In imperfect markets, there may be few or many sellers. Products are usually **differentiated** and consumers do not have perfect information about the differences between products.

Where organisations seek to reduce competition and make their products better than their rivals, the development of monopolistic powers enables them to push up prices and make larger profits. The level of competition is thus a key determinant of price. Where there are many close competitors, there is little scope to charge a price which is above the market price. Organisations in such markets are *price takers.*

In a situation where there is no competition, the seller can often charge a relatively high price. In other words they are a *price maker.* However,

Learning activity

Categorise the following examples into:

Penetration pricing
Skimming
Cost plus pricing
Value-based competition
Competition-based pricing

In each instance explain why you have categorised the example in the way in which you have:

1 A new book comes onto the market in hardback form at £25, two months later it comes out in paperback at £15, the following year it comes out in a 2nd edition at £10.

2 In order to improve its competitive position in the high street, a major retailer creates a series of sub-brands designed to improve the ways in which its customers view its products.

3 A breakfast cereal manufacturer introduces a new type of cereal at a low price in order to attract customers to buy the product.

4 A garden centre sets a margin of 30 per cent on all of its stock.

5 A company launches a revolutionary piece of software.

6 In a fiercely competitive market, a business simply looks at the price charged by others before setting its own price.

Learning activity

Identify a number of products known to you and discuss the pricing strategies used by the product or service provider.

the seller cannot charge more than the consumer is prepared to pay. At the end of the day consumers can spend their income on alternative products. Between these two extremes, we find hundreds of different markets. In some the consumer has more power, in others it is the seller.

Product

The product is the most important element in an organisation's marketing mix. According to Sally Dibb et al (1994), 'A product is everything, both favourable and unfavourable, that is received in an exchange.' We shall see later that this is supported through the total product concept. That is, the product is the organisation itself, the brand and everything it does to satisfy customer needs including the very tangible item (physical product), if there is one, as well as all of the accompanying intangible benefits that are sometimes less obvious and more difficult to identify.

As we saw on page 143, *brand* is part of a particular product and includes characteristics that identify it with a particular producer. Brands are very important.

Product features, advantages and benefits

Customers as a rule do not buy features, they buy what those features can do for them – the problems they solve, the money or the time they save, etc. A product is really a bundle of benefits. A key aspect of marketing is to make sure that products create the benefits that a consumer desires in a particular product and that the product offering is better than those of competitors. Associated with this is the need to make sure that the market fully understands the range of benefits on offer, through strong communications.

When we understand the benefits that customers are looking for in a product, we are best placed to know why they will buy it – and hence focus our marketing accordingly. For example, in buying toothpaste the benefits that customers may be looking for include:

* Flavour and product appearance

* Brightness of teeth

* Decay prevention

* Price/value for money

* Appealing brand name and confidence in brand.

Knowing that these are the benefits the consumer requires enables the organisation to focus its efforts on creating products that will produce one or more of them, and then promotion can be used to highlight the organisation's ability to create these benefits.

There are often clear and *tangible features* (things you can touch and see) associated with a product. Tangible features might include shape, design, colour, packaging and size.

Intangible features are not so obvious. These include the reputation of an organisation, the brand image, after sales service, availability of spare parts, service centres and so on.

It is also argued that products provide advantages for customers through three different dimensions. These are:

Generic dimensions – these are the key benefits of a particular item. For example, shoe polish should, we hope, clean shoes. Freezers should store frozen

FIGURE 3.44 *Product features may be tangible or intangible*

food. Hairdressers should be able to cut and style hair, including that of this author!

Sensual dimensions – these have an impact upon the senses. They might include design, colour, taste, smell and texture. The sensual benefits are frequently highlighted by advertisers. This is clearly the case when advertising food and drinks – 'smooth and creamy', 'the amber nectar' and so on.

Extended dimensions – a wide range of additional benefits are included here. Examples are servicing agreements, credit facilities, guarantees, maintenance contracts and so on.

With any group of products there is a distinct mix of items. They may include:

A *product item* is a specific model, brand or size of a product that an organisation sells, for example, a 2kg box of Uncle Ben's Long Grain Rice.

A *product line* is a group of closely related product items, with similar characteristics and/or applications, for example a line of Uncle Ben's Rice items, including short grain, long grain and pudding rice.

A *product mix* is all of an organisation's product lines, e.g. including rice, flour, sugar, pickles and other lines. Any product mix can be described according to its width, length, depth and consistency.

Width is the number of different product lines on offer. For example, Coca-Cola has 'stuck to the knitting' and produces quite a narrow range of soft drinks including Sprite, Fanta and Coca-Cola. In contrast, a company like Unilever has a wide range of products from Walls ice-cream and Birds Eye frozen foods to many different types of soap powders and cleaning agents. Having a narrow range of products enables you to benefit from economies of large-scale production whereas breadth enables an organisation to benefit from diversification. Broadening a line to create breadth means extending it beyond its current range.

Length is the total number of items on offer. The decision on the number of lines to offer is very important. Too many lines and you may overstretch yourself, and even start to compete

against your own lines. Line stretching involves increasing the product line, either by moving into higher-quality items or moving downmarket.

The process of line filling involves filling in gaps in product lines. For example, confectionery manufacturers regularly develop new chocolate bars to fill perceived gaps in their range of products. Line rationalisation involves cutting out lines that are not central to the organisation's major focus of interest, or those that have lost popularity.

Depth is the number of variants of each brand, for example, the number of different sizes, models or flavours within a product line. Detergent companies like Procter & Gamble or Unilever offer many different sizes of soap powder boxes as well as lots of different kinds of soap powder, all targeted at slightly different groups of customers. It makes sense for a large company to offer a product for all occasions in order to aim for a position of leadership. However, it is important not to cannibalise the sales of your own products. Deepening a product would mean adding more lines within your existing range. Line pruning means cutting the depth of a product line by reducing the number of alternative sizes, models or flavours in the line.

Consistency is the closeness of the relationship between each product line.

Creating the optimum product mix means having the right balance in terms of width, depth, length and consistency. An effective product mix should yield a balanced profit contribution from a number of lines – although there will always be some products that are the highest yielders.

Organisations need to decide whether they have the right mix at any one point in time while having an eye on future changes. Key concerns are: Should we stick to the narrow range of lines in which we are successful? What are our current strengths and weaknesses? What are the opportunities and threats of diversifying? How can we avoid competing with ourselves?

Place

In simple terms, the place element within the marketing mix is probably the most underestimated element. It provides the basic structure for the customer needs to be satisfied.

For example, physical distribution involves getting a product from A to B. Physical distribution management is an important part of the place process. It helps an organisation to meet customer needs profitably and efficiently. In doing so it enables manufacturers and distributors to provide goods for customers at the right time, in the right place and in the condition required. It may also reduce the **lead-time** – from when a

Learning activity

There are many different aspects to physical distribution, most of which should be designed to work together as a whole. For example, if this book were not available on the shelf of your local bookshop, what processes do you think are likely to take place once you place your order?

customer first makes an order until the time when that order is delivered.

Logistics is the process of integrating materials management and physical distribution management, and involves a whole series of activities from moving raw materials through to manufacturing processes and moving finished goods to the final consumer.

Physical distribution must balance the need for customer service against the need to minimise costs. On the one hand to maximise customer service an organisation may need a lot of stock and warehouse space, efficient staff and rapid transport mechanisms, while on the other to minimise costs they need low stock levels, limited storage space, few staff and slower transport. Designing a physical distribution system therefore

CASE STUDY

Research Machines

Founded in 1973 by Mike Fischer and Mike O'Regan, RM plc is the UK's leading provider of commercial education services and a pioneer in the application of technology to education. The Group's first educational microcomputer was launched in 1977, and schools, colleges and universities have become the main market for RM since then. In recent years RM has expanded its range of products and services to include interactive whole-class teaching services, teacher training, ICT-based needs assessment and school management information systems.

According to RM, 'In the 1990s it became clear that the educational community was looking for more from their suppliers than simple technological expertise. RM rose to the challenge. Looking beyond the technology, the Group formed long-term partnerships with both educationalists and other learning technology companies. These partnerships allow us to deliver genuine learning productivity. It is a strategy that has worked as our market leadership shows. RM's passion is education and its aim is to explore and exploit the potential of IT to improve educational standards. Today, RM is expanding its relationships with customers further by providing a diverse range of education services.'

1 What makes RM different to many other IT organisations?
2 In marketing terms describe how RM has developed the products it offers.

involves trading off costs against service, or inputs against outputs.

Inputs involve all of the distribution costs such as freight costs, inventory costs, warehousing costs and other service costs. It is important to know exactly what each of these costs are and control them in order to minimise waste. This may involve a detailed analysis of labour time, transport time, and other factors spent on each product.

Outputs can be primarily measured in terms of the value of services provided for customers. Distribution can provide a clear competitive benefit in meeting customer needs, for example by offering a quick and efficient service. Every business must decide how it is going to use distribution and relate this to their competitive advantage. Weaknesses in distribution would clearly need to be compensated for by strengths in other areas of the marketing mix.

The physical distribution system that an organisation selects will largely depend upon the scale of operations and the size of an organisation's market. A business handling a lot of international mail, for example, might locate near a large airport. Key decisions about physical distribution may include the following:

Inventory – a business that wants to maximise customer service will have the highest inventory costs, because it needs to hold stock to meet all requests. The key inventory decisions are when and how much to order. The danger of keeping too little in stock is that an organisation could lose custom because of dissatisfaction with the quality of service.

Warehousing – a key decision is where to locate warehouses, and how many to have.

Load size – should units be transported in bulk or broken down into smaller units for delivery? Again, an organisation will have to trade-off customer convenience and the cost of distribution.

Communications – it is important to develop an efficient information processing and invoicing system.

Channels are the networks of intermediaries linking the producer to the market. Whereas direct selling methods are *zero-level channels* which do not use an intermediary, indirect selling methods use one or more channels of distribution through which goods are transferred from the producer to the end user. These channels consist of one or more individuals or organisations who help to make the products available for the end user (see Figure 3.45).

Intermediaries such as *wholesalers* stock a range of goods from competing manufacturers to sell on to other organisations such as retailers. Most wholesalers take on the title to the goods and so assume many of the risks associated which include:

Breaking bulk Manufacturers produce goods in bulk for sale but they might not want to store

CASE STUDY

Distribution to Sainsbury's stores

Within the M25 area Sainsbury's has more than 80 branches, each of which requires several deliveries daily. Average traffic speeds in London have fallen to 11 mph over the last decade as traffic densities have increased.

In order to improve their systems of physical distribution Sainsbury's have consolidated their supplies into fewer, larger loads for final delivery. Thirty-eight tonne vehicles enable goods to be delivered in fewer vehicles, reducing delivery costs, carbon dioxide emissions and congestion. As far as possible deliveries are made between 10 p.m. and 6 a.m. to reduce congestion.

'Just-in-time' scheduling reduces time that goods are held in the warehouse. The requirements of branches are relayed via computer, with many product lines on a 24-hour cycle (ordered one day for delivery the following day), while others are ordered once or twice a week for delivery 48 hours later.

1 **What problems might be encountered delivering within the M25 area?**

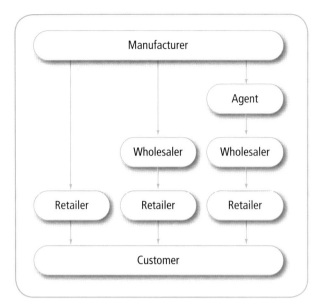

FIGURE 3.45 *Indirect sales channels*

the goods themselves. They want to be paid as quickly as possible. A number of wholesalers buy the stock for them and generally payment is prompt. The wholesaler then stocks these goods, along with others bought from other manufacturers, on the premises, ready for purchase by retailers.

Simplifying the distribution process The chain of distribution without the wholesaler would look something like Figure 3.46. Manufacturer 1 has to carry out four journeys to supply retailers 1, 2, 3 and 4, and has to send out four sets of business documents, and handle four sets of accounts. The same situation applies to each of the manufacturers, so that in total 16 journeys are made and 16 sets of paperwork are required.

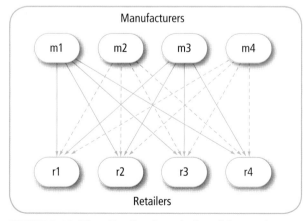

FIGURE 3.46 *The distribution chain without the wholesaler*

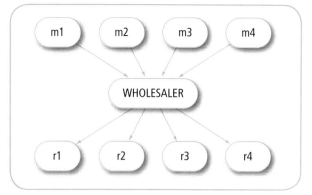

FIGURE 3.47 *The distribution chain with the wholesaler*

This is a simplification because in the real world thousands of different transactions might be involved!

An intermediary can simplify costs and processes of distribution by cutting down on journeys, fuel and other costs as well as cutting down on paperwork such as invoicing and administration.

The chain of distribution with an intermediary such as a wholesaler would look something like Figure 3.47. Clearly everything is simplified.

Storage Most retailers have only a limited amount of storage space. The wholesaler can be looked upon as a cupboard for the retailer. Manufacturers are able to unload finished goods on the wholesaler, which then act as a conduit to the retailers.

Packing and labelling The wholesaler will in some instances finish off the packaging and labelling of goods, perhaps by putting price tags or brand labels on the goods.

Offering advice Being in the middle of a chain of distribution, wholesalers have a lot more information at their fingertips than either the retailer or manufacturer. In particular, wholesalers know which goods are selling well. With this in mind they can advise retailers on what to buy and manufacturers on what to produce.

By contracting out the process of distribution, a company can concentrate on its core functions.

The French word *retailer* means 'to cut again'. We have already seen that the wholesaler breaks down bulk supplies from the manufacturer. The retailer then cuts the bulk again to sell individual items to customers. In the modern retailing environment, *the physical environment* for selling to end-users has become increasingly complex and in tune with customer focus and needs.

Daewoo, for instance, distributed cars in the UK without using a traditional local car dealership network. The use of telephone, modem and the Internet as well as fax are also providing the consumer with new ways to view and purchase products. **Telemarketing** is now being used to sell products such as insurance and pensions, which were previously sold by a one-to-one personal interview. The availability of satellite TV channels, has promoted the introduction of **home shopping**, with the American company QVC launching an English-speaking shopping channel within Europe. Simultaneously, the Internet is increasingly being used for **electronic commerce**, selling goods to consumers. This new channel of distribution is being investigated by many other organisations who are already involved in the distribution chain such as supermarkets. See, for example, the Tesco website through www.heinemann.co.uk/hotlinks (express code 1149P, then go to Unit 3). These imaginative approaches to distribution are being viewed as a major new opportunity to meet customer needs within a rapidly changing physical environment.

This physical environment for retailing largely depends upon:

Ownership Who owns the retail unit? Does a sole trader independently own it? Is it owned by a large multiple with shareholders? Is it a co-operative or a franchised outlet?

Range of merchandise Does the retail outlet specialise in a range of goods or does it have a spread of interests? Examples of specialised outlets include ice-cream parlours, furniture stores and fast-food outlets. Woolworths is an

Learning activity

Use either your own experience or the experiences of people known to you to discuss the advantages and disadvantages of using the Internet for shopping.

Learning activity

Draw a plan of your local shopping area. Make a list of the different types of retailers in the area.

example of a more general outlet. Harrods at one time claimed to sell everything from 'a pin to an elephant'.

Pricing policy Some retail outlets concentrate on the bottom of the price range. They offer discounts and low prices, buying in bulk and selling in large quantities. The early policy of Jack Cohen, founder of Tesco, was 'pile them high, sell them cheap'. In contrast, other retail outlets aim for an upmarket price image. This is true of fashion shops, clothing and jewellery stores.

Location This has become increasingly important in recent years. Low-price stores frequently choose locations where business rates and other site costs are minimised. In contrast, large multiples and department stores need a town-centre location, or a site near a major road. Small 'corner' shops need a healthy volume of custom for their livelihood – their strength is in offering local convenience. The growth of out-of-town centres has provided further opportunities to create a range of retailing opportunities for customers, including multiplex cinemas and restaurants.

Size Many variety stores are now over 50,000 sq. ft. in area, but superstores and hypermarkets have areas from 25,000 to 100,000 sq. ft.

There are many different ways of meeting customer needs through different forms of distribution. These include:

Independent traders According to the Census of Distribution, an independent trader is a retail organisation with fewer than 10 branches. A typical number is one or two branches. The market share for these has been declining, particularly in food.

Multiple chains These are usually owned by large companies, with a high degree of control from a head office. Some multiples are classified as specialist stores concentrating upon a narrow range of items, while others are variety chains such as Marks & Spencer and Littlewoods. Key features of multiples are:

* centralised buying
* concentration on fast-moving lines
* merchandise is widely known
* located in busy shopping areas
* volume sales enable prices to be low
* shops project a strong corporate image
* many key functions are centralised.

Supermarkets A supermarket is defined as a store with at least 2,000 square feet (or about 200 square metres) of selling area, using mainly self-service methods and having at least three check-out points. The layout of the store is designed to speed customer flow, and reduce time spent shopping.

Hypermarkets These are very large supermarkets, usually either out-of-town or on the fringes of towns or cities. They have a massive selling area and offer a wide range of household goods at discount prices. As well as food and clothing, they stock lines as diverse as DIY equipment, motoring accessories, children's toys and hardware.

Department stores The definition of a department store, as used by the Census of Distribution, is a store with a large number of departments and employing more than 25 people. They are to be found upon 'prime sites' in the centre of most towns and cities. The key feature of a department store is that it is divided into separate departments, providing a range of shopping opportunities, within pristine sales areas, so that all shopping can take place under one roof. They have a reputation for selling high-quality branded goods.

Discount stores Today, specialist companies such as Comet and Currys concentrate upon selling large quantities of consumer durables at discount prices. The aim of these stores is to produce a high level of total profit through fast turnover of stock. Many of these stores offer a range of credit services and other facilities to complement their customer offer.

Learning activity

Look at the business information pages in a broadsheet newspaper over a two-week period and collect articles that refer to organisations involved in retailing activity. Discuss how each article or statement describes recent changes in retailing activities.

Co-operative retail societies There are fewer than thirty cooperative retail societies in various parts of the UK. These aim to provide more than business services, to support the community in a variety of ways.

Catalogue shopping Organisations such as Argos and Index publish a catalogue listing all of the goods they sell. Customers visit their high street stores in order to collect their goods. Goods are not generally on display, with the majority of the store's space allocated for stock. Though the physical environment for these types of outlets is not particularly attractive for consumers, the low running costs means that they benefit from low prices.

Home shopping There are three main sectors. Agency mail order catalogues such as Freemans and Great Universal stores bypass intermediaries. Individuals become agents and either buy for themselves receiving a commission or sell goods on to friends and family. Direct mail catalogues such as Next Directory have become increasingly popular methods of ordering goods, usually paying by credit card. Interactive television, the Internet and television shopping channels have massive potential to change our shopping habits in recent years. As consumers become more confident in using them, they have the potential to serve a range of different needs and requirements.

Learning activity

Compare and contrast the physical environment of two retailing organisations. Look, for example, at their size, location, number of branches, pricing structure, market position, range of goods, associated services and support for their customers. Carry out a short shopping survey to find out what type of organisation customers prefer to use for a range of different selected products.

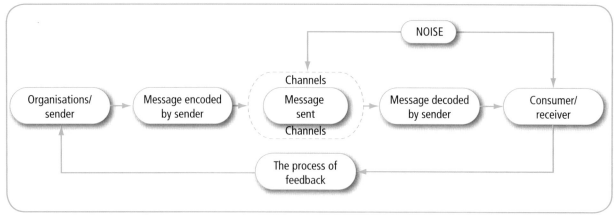

FIGURE 3.48 *The communication process*

Promotion

Promotion includes all of the techniques that an organisation uses to communicate with other individuals and organisations. Organisations are the *senders* in the communication process and *consumers* are the *receivers*. A sender will put information in the form that a receiver can understand. This might involve oral, visual, verbal or written messages to transmit the ideas. This process is called *encoding*. The sender will also choose a particular medium to use to send the message to the receiver (e.g. television, radio, newspapers). If the consumer interprets the message as required, it should have the impact that the seller wished for.

Though the message flows through to the receiver there is no guarantee that the receiver will either receive the full message or understand it. This is because the process may be subject to some form of interference, which affects the flow of information. This is known as *noise* and may lead to the downfall of the message. It will take the form of any barrier which acts as an impediment to the smooth flow of information and may include linguistic and cultural differences between the sender and the receiver. For example, one leaflet put through your door may be lost amongst a sea of direct mail from other organisations.

To increase the chances of a message getting across, an organisation needs to think carefully about the target audience. For example, it is important to channel the message through the most appropriate media. It might also be necessary to repeat the message several times rather than rely on one transmission.

Once the audience has been identified the communicator also needs to think about the sort of response required. If, for example, the final response required through the communication process is purchase, there may be six phases to the buyer-readiness process (see Figure 3.49).

Learning activity

Competition in the market for personal computers is fierce. Imagine that you work for a small organisation selling machines by mail order and you wish to target 'first-time' purchasers of PCs, particularly the over-60s. Explain what you would do to build your communication strategy around the purchasing process.

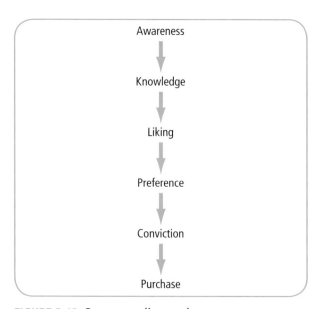

FIGURE 3.49 *Buyer-readiness phases*

Advertising

Advertising is a method of communicating with groups in the marketplace in order to achieve certain objectives. Advertisements are messages sent through the media which are intended to inform or influence the people who receive them (see Figure 3.50).

It can be defined as a **paid-for** type of marketing communication that is **non-personal**, but aimed at a specific **target audience** through a **mass media channel.**

According to the American Marketing Association advertising is 'any paid form of non-personal presentation and promotion of ideas, goods or services by an identifiable sponsor'.

Advertising must be a directed communication at a targeted market, and should draw attention to the characteristics of a product, which will appeal to the buying motives of potential customers. The ultimate purpose of advertising for organisations is to enhance buyers' responses to its products by channelling their desires and preferences to their products ahead of their competitors.

Within this purpose there may be a range of advertising objectives. For example:

* promoting goods and services
* to assist with selling
* to increase sales
* to develop awareness of new products, or developments to existing products
* to provide information that may assist with selling decisions

It is important, therefore, that the promotion mix takes into account each of these stages with different types of promotional activities.

* to encourage a desire to own a product
* to generate enquiries
* developing the image of the organisation
* to provide information to a target audience
* to soften attitudes
* to assist with public relations activities
* to change views
* to provide a better external environment
* to develop support from a community.

Advertising is often classified under one of three headings:

Informative advertising conveys information and raises consumer awareness of the features and benefits of a product. It is often used in the introductory phase of the product life-cycle, or after modification.

Persuasive advertising is concerned with creating a desire for the product and stimulating purchase. It is used with established and more mature products.

Reinforcement advertising is concerned with reminding consumers about the product, and is used to reinforce the knowledge held by potential consumers about the benefits to be gained from purchase.

The starting point for an advertising campaign is to produce an advertising plan. This will involve allocating a budget to a range of activities designed to meet advertising objectives. There are seven steps in an advertising campaign. These are:

Step 1   Identify the target market
Step 2   Define advertising objectives
Step 3   Decide on and create the advertising message

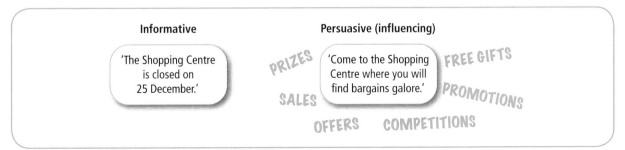

FIGURE 3.50 *The difference between informative and persuasive (influencing) advertising*

Compare and contrast two advertising campaigns, where one is clearly trying to promote goods and services and the other is trying to improve an image by developing public support for its activities. Comment upon how their approaches to advertising are similar, and then where they are different.

Step 4   Allocate the budget
Step 5   Develop the media plan
Step 6   Execute the campaign
Step 7   Evaluate the effectiveness of the campaign

Advertising messages may be sent through a variety of media forms, such as TV, radio, cinema, posters, billboards, flyers, transport advertising and the press. For more information about advertising look at the World Advertising Research Center website through www. heinemann.co.uk/hotlinks (express code 1149P, then go to Unit 3).

At all stages in the advertising process it is important to assess how effectively advertisements have contributed to the communication process. In order to measure objectives DAGMAR have become a fundamental part of good advertising practice. This stands for:

Defining Advertising Goals for Measured Advertising Results

In other words, before any advertising campaign is started, an organisation must define its communication objectives so that achievements can be measured both during and after the campaign.

Printed media make up by far the largest group of media in the UK. The group includes all newspapers and magazines, both local and national, as well as trade press, periodicals and professional journals. There are about 9,000 regular publications in the UK which can be used by the advertiser. They allow the advertiser to send a message to several million people through the press or to target magazines of special interest such as *Business Education Today*, which allows the advertiser to communicate with people in the teaching profession. As a result the media allows for accurate targeting and positioning. Think of all of the hobbies, lifestyles and backgrounds of readers of such magazines. Types of customers are identified by analysing readership profiles.

CASE STUDY
The top six advertisers 2003

ADVERTISING EXPENDITURE

RANK	COMPANY	TOTAL	TV %	RADIO %	PRESS %	OTHER %
1	Unilever UK Ltd	205,249,905	60.1	4.5	15.0	20.4
2	Procter & Gamble Ltd	197,895,564	74.6	6.4	13.8	5.2
3	COI Communications	143,698,612	51.2	16.6	24.4	7.9
4	BT Ltd	96,899,977	53.8	6.0	31.6	8.7
5	L'Oreal Golden Ltd	90,375,244	74.0	0.2	21.9	3.9
6	Ford Motor Company Ltd	79,215,351	48.3	6.3	29.0	16.4

Source: Nielsen Media Research

1 What do the allocations of expenditure tell you about the nature and types of advertising undertaken by each of these advertisers?
2 What forms of advertising might fall into the 'other' bracket?
3 Why do you think the six companies have such a large advertising spend?
4 If you were working for one of these companies, how would you evaluate the effectiveness of such a spend?

The benefit of printed media is that long or complex messages can be sent and, as the message is durable, may be read repeatedly. If an advertisement appears in a prestige magazine it may take on the prestige of that particular publication.

Broadcast media includes commercial television and commercial radio. Television is the most powerful medium – reaching 98% of households and viewing figures for some programmes can exceed 20 million. Television advertisements are, however, high cost and advertising messages are short-lived.

Direct mail

Direct mail is personally addressed advertising that is delivered through the post. By using direct mail an organisation can establish a direct relationship with its customers or prospective customers. Direct mail has been the third largest medium for over 13 years and now represents 14.3 per cent of all advertising expenditure in the UK. 5,418 million direct mail items were mailed in 2004 and £2,468.63 million was spent by advertisers on this medium in the same year. It

Learning activity

Over a weekly period collect all of the direct mail entering your home. Try to explain why your family has been the target of such direct mail.

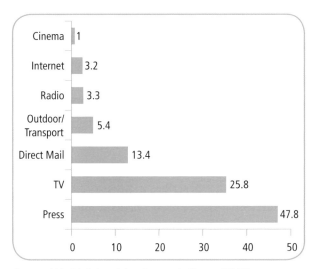

Source: World Advertising Research Center/DMIS

FIGURE 3.51 *Share of Total Advertising Expenditure in 2004*

is estimated that consumer direct mail generates nearly £27 billion worth of business every year.

Public relations

The forces in an organisation's external environment are capable of affecting it in a variety of ways. The forces may be social, economic, political, local or environmental and might be represented by a variety of groups such as customers, shareholders, employees and special interest groups. Reacting positively to such forces and influences is very important.

Public relations is the planned and sustained effort an organisation makes to establish, develop and build relationships with its many publics (see Figure 3.52).

The purpose of public relations (PR) is therefore to provide an external environment for an organisation in which it is popular and can prosper. Building goodwill in such a way requires behaviour by the organisation which takes into account the attitudes of the many people who come across it and its products.

Whereas many of the other promotional methods are *short-term*, public relations is long-term, as it may take a long time for an organisation to improve the way people think more positively about its products and activities. For example, just think about the sort of public relations problems that chemical and oil companies have in a world where consumers have become increasingly environmentally conscious.

The launch of the Millennium Dome in Greenwich in the Year 2000, instantly saw many of the newspapers launch an offensive against some of the activities as they sought to investigate whether the cost of the Dome was money well spent. This was a typical public relations problem for those operating the Dome, who then had to emphasise its positive attributes. In the political arena, talking positively about activities is sometimes known as 'spin'.

According to Frank Jefkins, PR involves a transfer process which helps to convert the negative feelings of an organisation's many publics into positive ones (see Figure 3.53).

There are may different types of public relations activities:

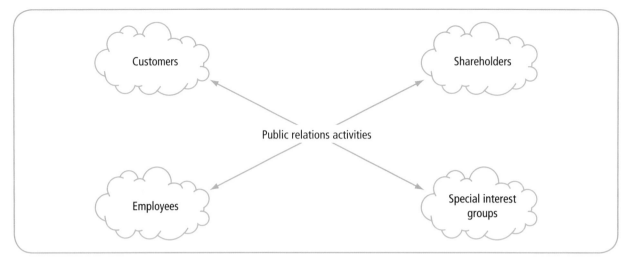

FIGURE 3.52 *Public relations activities*

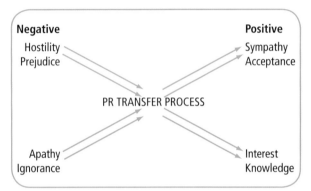

FIGURE 3.53 *The PR transfer process*

Learning activity

Search the press for a PR problem. Having found the problem, discuss how you would attempt to solve this problem and the sort of activities which would help to do so.

Sponsorship of sporting and cultural events is viewed as a useful opportunity to associate an image with a particular type of function. For example, the NatWest Trophy and the Embassy World Snooker Championship.

Lobbying of ministers, officials and important people from outside interest groups, so that an accurate portrayal can be made of a problem or a case, may help to influence their views of the organisation.

Corporate videotapes have become an increasingly popular way of providing interested parties with a 'view' of an organisation's activities.

Minor product changes, such as no testing on animals or environmentally-friendly products may provide considerable PR benefits.

Sales promotions

Sales promotions describes a category of techniques which are used to encourage customers to make a purchase. These activities are effectively short-term and may be used:

✳ to increase sales

✳ to help with personal selling

Charitable donations and community relations are good for an organisation's image, often provide lots of good publicity and also help to promote and provide for a good cause.

Hospitality at top sporting events is a popular method used by organisations to develop their customer relations. For example, there are opportunities to entertain customers at events such as the FA Cup Final, Wimbledon and the Grand National.

Press releases covering events affecting the organisation – such as news stories, export achievements, policy changes, technical developments and anything which enhances the organisation's image.

Visits and open days are a popular method of inviting people to various events to improve their understanding of what the organisation stands for.

* to respond to the actions of competitors
* as an effective alternative to advertising.

The Institute of Sales Promotion defines sales promotion as follows:

Sales promotion is the function of marketing which seeks to achieve given objectives by the adding of intrinsic, tangible value to a product or service.

The essential feature of a sales promotion is that it is a short-term inducement to encourage customers to react quickly, whereas advertising is usually a process that develops the whole product or brand.

As you walk down a town High Street or through a shopping mall, you will see many different examples of sales promotions. Such promotions may serve many different purposes. For example, competitions, vouchers or coupons and trading stamps may be designed to build customer loyalty and perhaps increase the volume purchased by existing customers. Product sampling is a strategy that is often used to introduce new products into the marketplace. Clearance sales of overstocked goods will increase turnover during part of the year in which business might otherwise be slack. Many sales promotions are undertaken in response to the activities of competitors to ensure that an organisation remains competitive. Sales promotions can be divided into two broad areas:

* promotions assisting with the sale of products to the trade
* promotions assisting the trade in selling products to the final consumer.

Selling into the pipeline is an expression used to describe promotions which move products from the manufacturer into the distribution system.

Selling out of the pipeline describes promotions which trigger the end-user to make a purchase (see Figure 3.54).

There are many different types of sales promotion:

Dealer loaders are among the inducements to attract orders from retailers and wholesalers. They may include a 'free case' with so many cases bought. For example, thirteen for the price of twelve is known as a 'baker's dozen'.

Competitions may interest dealers and consumers. For dealers they may be linked to sales with attractive prizes for the most successful dealer. Scratch cards, free draws and bingo cards are popular promotional methods for consumers.

Promotional gifts such as bottles of spirits, clocks, watches or diaries are considered useful bounty for dealers.

Price reductions and *special offers* are usually popular with consumers. They can, however, prove expensive as many consumers would otherwise have been prepared to pay the full price.

Premium offers may offer extra product for the same price. *Coupons* which offer money off or money back may also be attractive incentives for consumers. These may appear in magazines, be distributed door-to-door or appear on the side of a pack.

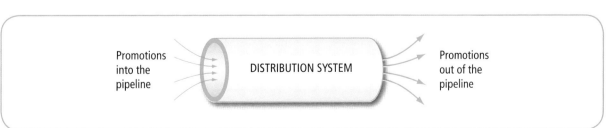

FIGURE 3.54 *Selling into and out of the pipeline*

Charity promotions can be popular with younger consumers, who collect box tops or coupons and send them to a manufacturer, which then makes a donation to charity.

Loyalty incentives are today an increasingly used form of sales promotion. Dealer's loyalty might be rewarded with bigger discounts, competitions and prizes or even have their names published as stockists in advertisements. For consumers, loyalty incentives such as loyalty cards and points may provide 'cash back', free gifts or a variety of other tangible benefits.

Direct selling

Most days of your life you are involved in some form of selling activity. It might be persuading a friend to come with you to the pictures, or asking a relative to buy something for you. What you are doing is using your relationship to sell your ideas to someone else.

Personal or direct selling involves interaction between individuals or groups of individuals.

The objective of personal selling is to make a sale, and it is the culmination of all of the marketing activities that have taken place beforehand. It involves matching a customer's requirements with the goods or services on offer. The better the match, the more lasting the relationship between the seller and the buyer.

The role of personal selling will vary from business to business. It is a two-way process which can be one of the most expensive areas of the promotional mix. This personal communication element can be very important

as the final sale might come only as a result of protracted negotiations.

Personal selling is important in both consumer and organisational markets. However, in consumer goods markets, advertising often helps the process and is often the driving force which *pulls* a product through the distribution network. In organisational markets on the other hand, personal selling may have to work harder to *push* the product through to the market (see Figure 3.55).

The main benefit of personal selling is the ability to communicate with and focus on customers individually and with precision. For example, if you go into a travel agency and ask for details about a holiday, the sales assistant may explain and point out the features of various packages and any discounts or promotions they might offer. All of the other areas of the promotional mix are targeted at groups of people.

Although we have mental stereotypes of the typical salesperson, selling involves special skills. Whereas there is a tendency to downgrade this role in the UK, in many countries (Germany for example), sales staff require a high degree of technical competence and are generally accepted to be part of the corporate elite. Salespeople are key intermediaries who present information to customers and then provide feedback on customer needs.

Sales staff are representing an organisation and so need to reflect a positive image from that organisation. It is important that they do not offend customers by their appearance – the mode of dress should match the nature of the products and the organisation. For example, a sales assistant in a fashion store should wear something up-to-date, whereas an insurance salesperson should wear more formal clothes. It is often said that the way we look determines the ways others look at us!

Similarly, effective speaking will help to create the appropriate image and situation for the sale

FIGURE 3.55 *The push-pull effect*

FIGURE 3.56 *Stages in the selling process*

to take place. Good grammar, vocabulary, diction and voice tone may help to reflect the degree of professionalism required for the sale to take place.

Many organisations spend more on personal selling than on any other area of the promotional mix, and within organisations large numbers of individuals may find that personal selling forms part of their role. Personal selling may involve individuals developing special skills and using them in many different operational situations. To do so, sales staff need to know their products and be well trained in selling techniques (Figure 3.56).

Selling in a highly competitive world means that preparation has never been so important. Though it has been said that salespeople are born and not made, nevertheless skills, knowledge and training can improve performance. Training is designed to build on people's selling skills and to use their personal abilities and understanding to follow the psychological stages of the sales process. Product knowledge is vital, as it allows for feedback from the prospective customer's questions about the product's technical specifications, benefits and functions.

Knowing their customers may help to determine how sales staff communicate with them. For example, some customers may prefer to be addressed with the more formal Mr or Mrs while others like to be called by their first name.

Probing is important in the early stage of a sales presentation, in order to find out the prospect's needs and where his or her priorities might lie. The salesperson can then try to match the product or service with the prospect's requirements. This may involve elaborating on the product's advantages, concentrating on aspects such as savings in costs, design ingredients, performance specifications, after-sales service, etc.

During the presentation, the salesperson must constantly evaluate whether the product is appropriate to the needs of the prospect. It is unethical to sell something that is not needed – although this may often happen! The large and more complex the order, the more complex the negotiations over supply. In many different situations it is important to provide a number of services to help with the process. For example, these might include:

* product demonstrations
* performance specifications
* sales literature
* samples
* a meeting to discuss details
* credit facilities
* sales promotions.

The prospective customer may have a variety of objections to the purchase. These objections may be genuine, or as a result of a misunderstanding. There might be reluctance to make a commitment at this stage. Logical, well-presented arguments and incentives may overcome such objections.

Timing is crucial to the sale. A salesperson must look for *buying signals* which indicate that the prospect is close to a decision, and almost ready to put a signature on an order form and discuss the contractual arrangements.

It is always important to *follow up the sale with post-sale support*. Promises that might have been made during the negotiations will have to be fulfilled. If the salesperson guarantees delivery by a certain date, that date must be held. Servicing arrangements must be efficiently carried out, and

Learning activity

Using an example known to you, show how strong after-sales service may help to promote repeat purchasing patterns.

FIGURE 3.57 *The information link between customers and their suppliers*

any problems dealt with. Contacting customers to see if they are happy with the product will encourage repeat buying and improve the supplier's concern for its customers.

Sales staff may also have a number of other related functions. Communication, for example, is an important role. Sales staff act as an information link between suppliers and their customers. As a result, personal selling involves a boundary role – being at the boundary of a supplying organisation and also in direct and close contact with customers. The role is often not only one of selling but also one of interpreting the activities and policies of each organisation to the other (see Figure 3.57). A considerable amount of administration may also therefore accompany the selling role. For example, reports, schedules and computerised information such as inventory details are a part of daily life for a salesperson.

Comprehensive records on customers should be kept and updated after each visit. Keeping sales records enables the salesperson to respond exactly to each customer's individual needs. Knowledge of competitors and their products enables the seller to respond to queries about the relative merits and demerits of products.

3.4 Other factors influencing the marketing mix

Every organisation involved in marketing activity is faced with a number of constraints that may limit their activity. They then need to work within these constraints.

Costs

Internal constraints relate to the resource capabilities of an organisation such as costs. For example, an organisation might identify potential customers but how capable is it in meeting their needs? It might not have the resources to do so.

For example, in recent years Coca-Cola has developed a global presence. It has been able to do this by ploughing more money into long-term investment. Coca-Cola invests 70 per cent of its profits and achieves a staggering rate of growth.

When a company wants to develop new products or services it needs the resources to finance expansion. The bigger the scale of the development projects, the more resources are required. Sometimes companies finance expansion by selling off existing assets – for example, ICI has moved into higher value-added chemical products, such as components for lip-glosses and eye shadow. To finance this move it sold off a number of its existing heavy chemical plants which had low long-term profit potential.

In addition to financial resources, business organisations need the skills and know-how for a range of marketing activities. Increasingly, companies rely on buying in expertise from outside the organisation.

External constraints involve a series of factors within the business environment in which an organisation operates that limit in one way and another their activities. These will include:

Consumers If an organisation is not market-focused or if consumers are not interested in a product, then it will be difficult to market.
Competitors It may be difficult to market a product for which a competitor already has an advantage.

Becoming millionaires!

Dan and his younger brother Ron are experienced market traders, flitting from one market to another across south-east London. They are self-motivated entrepreneurs whose main aim in life is to become millionaires. As small businessmen, they do not always find life easy!

Dan was recently offered the opportunity to buy some of the latest DVDs, which were claimed to be 'kosher'. These are a big opportunity to expand the business, with an up-to-date consumer product that will bring the punters in. The great benefit is that if customers are interested in the DVDs, Dan knows that he can do a deal with some quick-boiling kettles he bought a few months ago that he has had trouble getting rid of. The kettles look smart but take 15 minutes to boil.

Dan's real problem is that he has not got the 'readies' to buy the DVDs. Ron is always 'skint' and cannot help. He is wondering about whether to sell off the van to provide him with the capital. The problem then would be that they would have to buy an alternative form of transport such as 'company mopeds', but this may have the alternative benefit of allowing them to start some courier work.

Another idea Dan has to expand the business is to use Ron's expertise in information technology to set up training courses. Though Ron was very good with computers, he has not used one for 5 years, and feels that if Dan is going to do this, they need to buy in help from another person.

1 **What internal, and external constraints make life more difficult for Dan and Ron?**
2 **What might be a better business strategy for them?**

Economy In a period of economic recession when consumer have falling incomes, it may be difficult to market a luxury product.

The Law There may be a number of laws constraining the activities of a business and making it difficult for them to do well.

The market-focused company will fully research all of these constraints and try to find solutions that enable it to turn weaknesses into strengths and threats into opportunities.

Political, economic, legal and environmental factors

One of the key influences upon the effectiveness of the marketing mix is the business environment. It is quite possible for an excellent business idea to do badly mainly because of factors outside the control of the entrepreneur. The process of 'knowing the other' is often referred to as 'scanning the environment'.

Examining the business environment helps an organisation to develop appropriate marketing strategies including the marketing mix. Important external forces that influence the marketing strategy might include:

the customer – buying behaviour of customers including why they buy, their buying habits and the size of the market.

the industry – the behaviour of organisations within the industry, e.g. retailers and wholesalers, their motivations and the structure and performance of organisations within the industry.

competitors – their position and behaviour.

the government and regulatory bodies – their influence over marketing and competitive policies.

Selection of an appropriate marketing mix involves creating the best possible match between the external environment and the internal capabilities of the organisation. Though the elements of the marketing mix are largely controllable by marketing managers within an organisation, many of the changes and forces within the business environment are not. The success of the marketing programme therefore depends upon how well an organisation can match its marketing strategies and marketing mix to the external business environment in which that business is operating.

Developing an appropriate marketing strategy involves creating the best possible match between the external environment and the internal capabilities of the organisation.

PEST model

One useful way of analysing an organisation's external environment is by grouping external forces neatly into four areas by using a PEST analysis. PEST stands for **P**olitical, **E**conomic, **S**ocial and **T**echnological influences, all of which are external (see Figure 3.58).

Carrying out a PEST analysis involves identifying the key factors external to an organisation which are in a state of flux and are likely to have an influence on the organisation in the coming months and years.

Whereas identifying these factors is relatively easy, assessing their ongoing impact and effect is more difficult. An effective PEST analysis will be based on detailed research using all of the latest

journals and publications. For example, if certain taxes are likely to be lowered, how much are they likely to be lowered by? What will be the impact on the sales of each product? Figures need to be as accurate as possible – if interest rates are expected to go up, how much will they go up? How long will they be raised for? What will be their impact upon sales and costs?

Political, legal and fiscal factors Business decisions are influenced by political, fiscal (taxation) and legal decisions. For example, although in recent years many people have been encouraged to become self-employed, there has been a feeling by many of these people that they are over-regulated. These influences might include:

* changes in the tax structure
* privatisation
* the influence of unions
* changes in the availability of raw materials
* duties and levies
* regulatory constraints such as labelling, quality, safety.

Economic factors Though the economic environment is influenced by domestic economic policies, it is also dependent upon world economic trends. Rates of economic growth, inflation, consumption patterns, income distribution and many other economic trends determine the nature of products and services required by consumers, as well as how difficult it becomes to supply them! Influences might include:

* inflation
* unemployment
* energy prices
* price volatility.

Social/cultural factors To understand the social and cultural environment involves close analysis of society. Demographic changes such as population growth, movements and age distribution will be important, as will changes in cultural values and social trends such as family size and social behaviour. Factors might include:

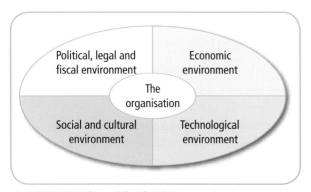

* consumer lifestyles
* environmental issues
* demographic issues
* education
* immigration/emigration
* religion.

Technological factors In marketing goods and services, organisations must become aware of new materials as well as developments in manufacturing and business processes. At the same time organisations have to look at the nature of their products and, in particular, their cost-effectiveness as well as their performance in relation to competition. Factors might include:

* new technological processes
* energy saving techniques
* new materials and substitutes for existing materials
* better equipment
* new product developments.

Learning activity

This activity is best undertaken when working in a small group. The starting point is to identify an organisation which you are going to use as the centrepiece for a PEST analysis. It would be useful if you knew somebody working for the organisation who will be able to provide you with some of the information you require. Meet the person to discuss each of the PEST forces influencing their business. This is the starting point for your analysis. Use the Internet and a reference library to find out more to support the points made through the interview. Present your findings back to the class, and then discuss the impact that all of these external forces have had upon the strategic decisions made by the organisation over recent years.

Forces external to the organisation are rarely stable, and many of these forces can alter quickly and dramatically. It is important to recognise that while some of these forces will be harmful to marketing efforts, others will create new opportunities.

ASSESSMENT EVIDENCE

Having left school/college you have been given a unique opportunity to start a small business with a close relative who, having been left a substantial amount of money by his aunt, wants to put it to good use. This is a really unique opportunity for you. Your relative has a range of practical experience, but has recently left his job because he wants to do something different and work for himself rather than for other people. He has offered you both a salary and a profit share if the business becomes successful, and just wants to do something that is exciting but successful at the same time.

Although you share the enthusiasm of your relative, you are more guarded about the process of setting up the business. The relative has suggested buying an existing business but you would prefer to set something up from scratch, as you feel that you would both then not only feel like owners of the business but also be owners of the ideas.

You want to use your understanding of business organisations to help you start this business, and you're interested in using your experience of marketing not only gained through this module but also through the part-time employment you have had.

Mindstorm your idea for the business. Your idea could be based upon either an existing or new product and business proposition. In doing so identify the aims of the business and discuss your business idea within the context of the industrial context that you will serve.

Describe the customers you intend to serve. In doing this describe the market you intend to work within and the processes of segmentation that you will use.

Undertake market research for your product/service idea. Your market research should include both primary and secondary sources. Discuss how you will use the market research and the conclusions it is enabling you to draw.

Construct a marketing mix for your product/service/business idea. Try to link your marketing mix not just to the segments that you will serve and the needs of your customers but also link the marketing mix to the findings from the research you have undertaken.

Evaluate your actions and proposals so far. This involves you justifying what you have done and making judgments about the potential for your ideas.

In order to score the higher level marks for your coursework you need to provide considerable evidence of the widespread research that you have undertaken. Remember to integrate and use knowledge from your research AND from other areas that you are undertaking on this course. For example, you should show that you have thought about the particular form of business ownership that your business has as well as all of the stakeholders that it serves.

As you work on this:

✳ make sure that you show a good understanding to provide a detailed explanation of the product or service you intend to develop

✳ show that you understand the purpose of marketing aims and objectives and can develop a marketing mix that can successfully enable you to achieve these aims and objectives

✳ carefully construct a picture of your target market and think about how the market you service has been segmented

✳ collect an extensive amount of data from your market research, both primary and secondary

✳ consider how you intend to analyse your market research data in order to draw some meaningful conclusions

✳ try to show how your marketing mix matches the findings from your market research

✳ use the marketing Ps as a framework for your analysis and attempt to show your depth of knowledge when identifying and choosing an appropriate strategy

✳ make sure that you have evaluated your marketing mix successfully. Try to justify and support all of the decisions you have made with relevant data

✳ make comparative decisions of other products or services either direct or indirect to help to justify the decisions you have made.

UNIT 4

Investigating electronic business

This unit contains four parts:

4.1 Understand the purpose of an online presence for business

4.2 Understand the impact that having a website has on a business

4.3 Factors influencing the establishment of an online presence

4.4 Understand the requirements for the planning/establishment of a new website.

Introduction

Most businesses today, with the exception of those that are very small and only serve a very localised market, have developed their own websites. Large and small businesses across the globe are using the Internet to advertise, promote and sell their products and services to the many people who now **surf** the **Internet**. This unit provides you with a range of opportunities to investigate businesses that have developed a web presence. You will need to consider the aims and objectives of setting up an online presence and think carefully about what makes a good website.

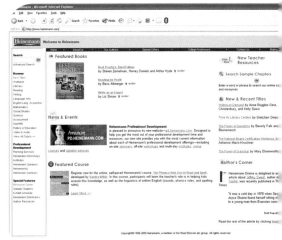

What you will learn in this unit

* The purposes of creating an online presence for business

* The impact that a website has on customers, competitors, suppliers and the business itself

* What should be included on a website

FIGURE 4.1 *The Heinemann website – a high quality website is essential for a book publisher, serving as a modern shop window*

* Factors influencing the establishment of an online presence such as cost, and the opportunities that result

* The requirements for the planning/establishment of a new website.

4.1 Understand the purpose of an online presence for business

Speaking the language of electronic business

Here are some useful definitions to help you get started. There are others in the glossary at the back of the book.

E-business: Commercial activity carried out through networks which link electronic devices (mainly computers). These commercial activities consist of transactions involving the Internet, telephone and fax, electronic banking and payment systems, trade in digitised goods and services, and electronic purchasing and restocking systems.

The Internet: A global collection of networks which connect and share information through a common set of protocols. The Internet allows a variety of forms of communication e.g. voice, data and video transmission.

The World Wide Web (WWW): Links between documents that are communicated over the Internet. Using a web browser, anyone with a computer, modem and Internet account can search and retrieve information from millions of **web servers** around the world.

Web browser: A web viewing program that can access the Internet to search for information. The most popular browser is Microsoft Internet Explorer.

Website: Resource on the Internet containing pages that have been designed and published using HTML.

Business aims and objectives

Businesses must make sure that their activities fit into line with their aims and objectives.

Setting up a company website must therefore fit business aims and objectives. Starting to plan your online presence firstly involves developing an understanding of aims and objectives.

Typical business aims and objectives will include:

* increasing sales

* cost cutting

* maximising profits

* attracting new staff

* improving customer services

* increasing efficiency

* appealing to a global market.

It is easy to see that the creation of a website should help businesses to achieve objectives.

Increasing sales can be achieved through a well-designed website enabling online ordering. For example, a wine retailer can increase sales potential by having an online presence, with a simple and easy to operate ordering and payment system (see Figure 4.2).

An online presence is a good way of cutting business costs. Operating online means that a business such as a retailer can operate from a low cost location, rather than an expensive High Street. A good example of this is Next Direct. As a fashion retailer, Next were first able to slash their costs by moving a large part of their business to catalogue sales. Today Next has an excellent website enabling the company to take orders at very low cost, hence slashing business costs (see Figure 4.3).

✱ DID YOU KNOW?

easyJet, one of the UK's most successful bargain-flight operators, encourages its consumers to book on the Internet and pay by credit card. By having the transaction completed through the Internet, easyJet saves a lot of money, which it shares with its consumers.

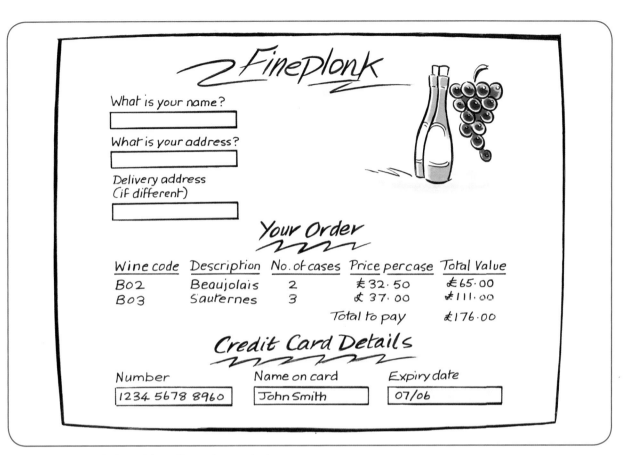

FIGURE 4.2 *A website with online wine ordering*

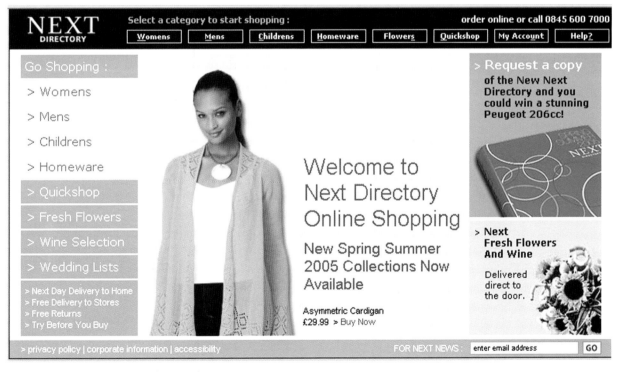

FIGURE 4.3 *Next Direct online website*

CASE STUDY

Creating an online presence

A small specialist bookseller is considering developing an online presence. Currently the bookseller is suffering from cash flow problems. However, the owner thinks that having an online presence will help the business to bring in more cash. The owner has asked an online designer to provide a quote for creating a new site. The price quoted was £10,000. The bookseller has estimated that by using the site his revenues will increase by £1,000 per month, and the variable cost of operating and managing the site will increase his variable costs by £500 a month.

1 How long will it take the bookseller to break-even on business generated from the new website?
2 What advice would you give to the bookseller about whether to go ahead with developing an online presence or not?

CASE STUDY

Selling *The New York Times* to a global audience

FIGURE 4.4 **The New York Times** *as a physical presence*

At present the print edition of *The New York Times* is the driving force for growth in global interest in the paper. However, the online version is becoming increasingly important. On the web, NYTimes.com is the world's leading and most profitable newspaper site – search for it at www.heinemann.co.uk/hotlinks (express code 1149P, then go to Unit 4). Unlike those in this country so far, it makes a great deal of money out of advertising and charging for information. The electronic edition of *The Times*, an exact reproduction of the day's paper, can be downloaded to computers worldwide.

The Americans may be ahead of the game, but there are plenty in this country who believe they have seen the future and know that it works. For example, *The Financial Times* online is growing in popularity. The editor of *The Guardian* believes that 'if I had to be judged by one thing, it would be the Internet and how we have... extended our global reach'.

1 See if you can find a copy of your favourite newspaper online – use today's date.
2 How does the online version differ (if at all) from the paper version?
3 How does the paper appear to be tapping a revenue stream?
4 Why do you think that the paper has opted for an online version?
5 Which newspapers do you think are most likely to dominate the global market for news? Why?

A combination of increasing sales and lowering costs should help the online business to increase profits. Remember that:

Sales revenue – costs = profit

However, it is important to recognise that the start-up cost of creating a new online presence is a fixed cost of a business, and it may be expensive.

Developing an online presence might be a good way for a business to attract new staff. A well-structured website helps people who are interested in a company to find out far more information than is typically available through other sources. The site gives an insight into the company's values and cultures and can provide a wealth of information about company activities, the sort of people it employs, and opportunities within the business.

An online presence also helps to improve customer service. This is particularly true for technical products where customers can use online helplines to find out a lot of product information. Sections such as Frequently Asked Questions (FAQs) help customers to save time in problem-solving. Enabling customers to contact a customer helpline by e-mail is a simple and cost effective way of providing better customer service.

An online presence increases all round business efficiency. Business activities which can be handled in a routine way can be put onto the website. For example, product information can go online freeing up staff time from having to explain product details to customers.

One of the major benefits of an online presence is that it enables a business to market its products to a global audience. This has helped to transform the scale and opportunities faced by many businesses. For example, an artist who might previously have relied on commissions from people who lived nearby, or who had visited an exhibition of the artist's paintings, can now potentially sell their paintings across the globe.

Online business and effective communication

The new Internet-based economy puts a trillion dollars' worth of technology – from network connections, processing power, memory and limitless **databases** – in the hands of anyone with a phone and a PC. This gives tremendous power to consumers.

If consumers don't like what businesses are offering on their websites, they're gone in the click of a mouse. Instead, they'll go to the business where they can get what they want at the price they are willing to pay because the Internet has placed the global market right on their desktop.

Building a good website is therefore essential to modern business, providing companies with the possibility of carrying out global business, 24 hours a day, seven days a week. An online presence allows a business to provide clear visual images of their products including moving images and voice-over explanations. For example, Nike have created a website facility whereby consumers can design and then order their own trainers using simple design tools that are built into their website.

Flexibility of location

One of the major advantages to business of creating an online presence is that if it is successful in winning customers, then the business has far more flexibility about its location. For example, the business no longer has to be physically placed at the centre of its marketplace. Provided the business has a good distribution network it can ship the items it sells directly to customers. This is already having an enormous impact on retailing.

For example, shoppers are able to browse the Internet to order their weekly shopping from Tesco.com and from other retailers. The consumer is able to browse through the various product categories and their price lists, and drop items which they wish to purchase into a shopping basket which can then be paid for when the consumer is happy with the basket contents.

This concept of flexibility gives a business lots of advantages, including:

✱ It can operate from locations where rent, rates and other business costs are cheap

✱ It can locate its online activities in areas where there are skilled IT professionals

✱ It can allow some or all of its employees to work from home for all or part of the week.

FIGURE 4.5 *Shopping for an item online is a simple selection process*

Locational flexibility is particularly suitable for businesses that don't produce a physical product. For example, lots of business activities that were previously carried out in office locations can now be done at home, including:

✳ architectural design

✳ solicitors

✳ book design and editing.

Being user-friendly and responsive

An online presence can be very effective in attracting business if it is user-friendly and responsive. For example, the housebuilder Bryant Homes has created a website that enables potential customers to browse through a range of home designs online. They are able to enjoy a virtual tour of homes they are considering buying. The site is extremely easy to use and saves people the time and effort involved in physically travelling to visit a building site that may be hundreds of miles away.

Research shows that if users find a site boring or difficult to **navigate**, they will surf to another site within seconds. It is essential therefore that websites are simple, appealing and give the browser what he or she wants.

Bricks and clicks

A **'bricks and mortar'** business is one that does not trade online. For example, your local newsagent, or corner shop would have little need to trade online. These businesses operate at a fixed location (made from bricks and mortar). Typically they have high fixed costs in the form of rent and rates.

CASE STUDY

An effective site *Wrangler.com*

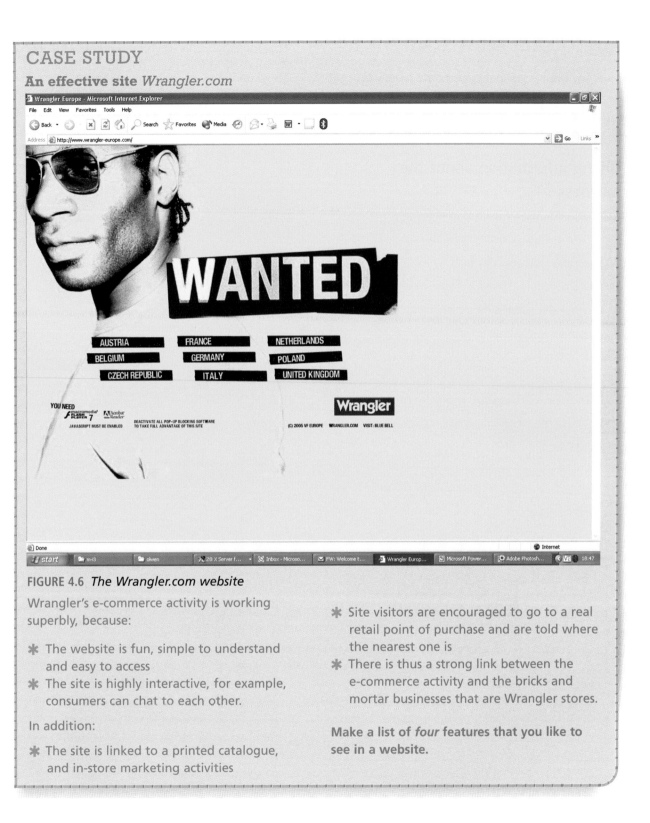

FIGURE 4.6 *The Wrangler.com website*

Wrangler's e-commerce activity is working superbly, because:

* The website is fun, simple to understand and easy to access
* The site is highly interactive, for example, consumers can chat to each other.

In addition:

* The site is linked to a printed catalogue, and in-store marketing activities

* Site visitors are encouraged to go to a real retail point of purchase and are told where the nearest one is
* There is thus a strong link between the e-commerce activity and the bricks and mortar businesses that are Wrangler stores.

Make a list of *four* features that you like to see in a website.

A **'clicks and mortar'** business is one that cuts its costs by using the Internet to carry out trading, as well as having a physical presence. Some, like Wrangler, will have prominent store locations, but others will be located out of town where rates and rents are low, thus reducing fixed costs.

Most modern businesses combine 'bricks and clicks'.

Identify businesses that concentrate mainly on bricks and mortar and others that combine bricks and clicks. What are the advantages of the two modes of operation?

Giving information about the business

A website is a very useful tool for communicating information to:

* potential business partners

* customers

* anyone else interested in the business.

The sort of information that is useful to put on the website includes:

* *The legal format of the business.* Is it a sole trader enterprise, partnership, franchise or company?

This information is often important to business partners including potential suppliers.

* *Type of business.* The great thing about the Internet is that customers do the searching for a business to supply them. It is essential therefore to set out clearly what type of business you are in the first few words of a website. This means that when customers are conducting a search they will find you immediately when using a **search engine** like Google. For example, cinnamonaitch.co.uk set out in the first line of their site that they are a 'greeting cards company'. Find them using www.heinemann.co.uk/hotlinks (express code 1149P, then go to Unit 4).

* *Target market.* In a similar way it is important to clarify who your target market consists of. For example, the video makers TVChoice set out that they provide videos for the educational market. Search for them at www.heinemann.

CASE STUDY

Cinnamon Aitch

Cinnamon Aitch is owned by Sarah Danby and Sarah Burford. It produces high quality greetings cards. In 2003 the business had a turnover of £200,000, and in 2004 was forecast to have a turnover of £250,000. Danby and Burford design three or four collections a year for two main ranges – an upmarket selection where every product is hand stitched and assembled, and a newer printed run that extends the company's commercial reach. Prices range from £2 to £5 and orders passed the 2,000 mark in 2004 from 400 stockists including department stores.

The British send more cards than anyone else – one recent Key Note survey showed that the average person sends 55 each year! This is a market worth £1.2 million and it is growing.

However, Cinnamon Aitch do not show their cards on their website because the card market is so competitive and designs are regularly copied. This is one of the reasons why Danby and Burford regularly have to update their range before new designs can be copied.

1 You should carry out this first task before looking at the Cinammon Aitch website online. If you were designing the Cinammon Aitch website:
  * What details would you put on the first page of the site?
  * How could you go about making sure that the site was friendly and responsive?

2 Examine the Cinammon Aitch site using www.heinemann.co.uk/hotlinks (express code 1149P, then go to Unit 4).
  * Is it as you expected?
  * Compare and contrast the site with that of a charity website that includes the sale of cards such as the NSPCC or UNICEF, using www.heinemann.co.uk/hotlinks (express code 1149P, then go to Unit 4).
  * Compare and contrast the site with that of another private sector card seller (that sells online) such as Hallmark Cards. What improvements would you make to it?

co.uk/hotlinks (express code 1149P, then go to Unit 4).

It is essential that your site attracts the right sorts of customers. What you don't want is:

* the 'wrong' customers to find your site – they will immediately click off.

* the 'right' customers to miss your site because it is poorly signposted.

* *Sector.* It is important that you clarify the particular market sector that you are operating in e.g upmarket or downmarket.

* *Product range.* Finally, it is important that consumers are quickly able to see what your product range consists of. The opening page of the site must introduce them to the extent of the product range, or consumers may think that you have only a narrow range that is not relevant to them.

4.2 Understand the impact that having a website has on a business

A business website will have an impact on a number of major groups, as shown in Figure 4.7.

A business can have a number of attitudes to its website. At one extreme it might regard the website as a necessary tool for providing customer information but little more. Somewhere in the middle of the spectrum it might see the website as being a means to increase sales and to tap into new markets. The other extreme position is that the business bases itself entirely on its website. Many businesses now include their web address on all their advertisements. This symbolises the shift in business model from retailing through stores to retailing through the web.

A website can have an enormous impact on a business:

* *It provides a tool for internal communication within the business.* A company is able to put all of the information that its employees need online e.g. company policies, training manuals, documents (such as travel expenses forms, order forms etc), application forms, details

Learning activity

Analyse the websites of some major companies (such as Iceland, Tesco, Shell or Boots to see the extent to which the website is used by the business – is it simply an informational tool, a marketing tool, or a total business model? Search for the sites at www.heinemann.co.uk/hotlinks (express code 1149P, then go to Unit 4).

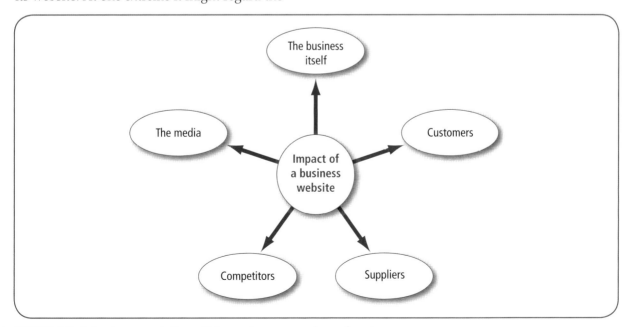

FIGURE 4.7 *A business website will impact on a number of major groups*

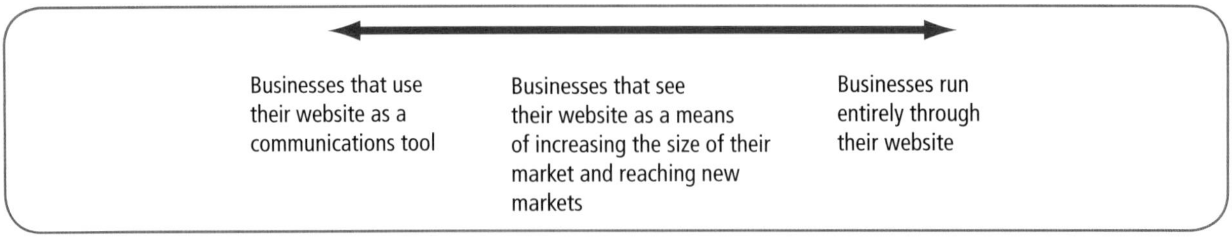

Businesses that use their website as a communications tool

Businesses that see their website as a means of increasing the size of their market and reaching new markets

Businesses run entirely through their website

FIGURE 4.8 *How a business regards its website*

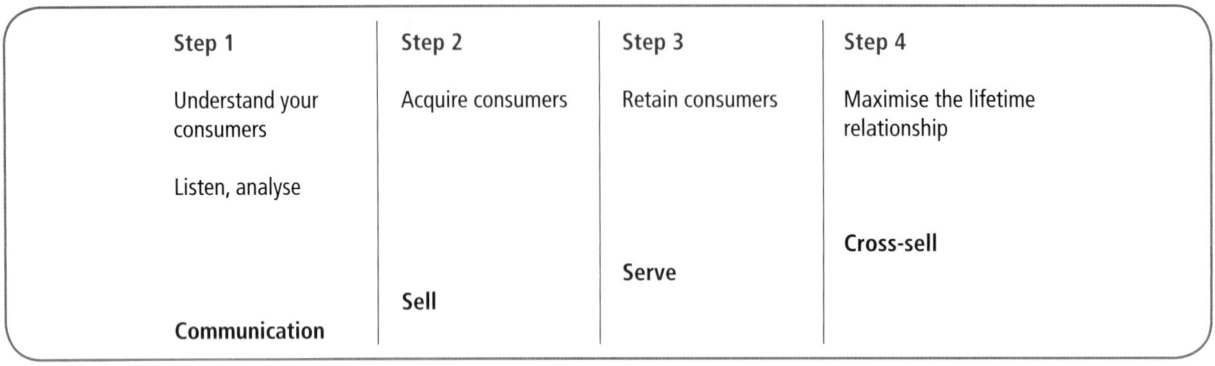

Step 1	Step 2	Step 3	Step 4
Understand your consumers	Acquire consumers	Retain consumers	Maximise the lifetime relationship
Listen, analyse			
			Cross-sell
		Serve	
	Sell		
Communication			

FIGURE 4.9 *Build consumer relationships with a well-organised website*

of payment systems and a thousand and one other things that were previously stored in databases or filing cabinets.

✳ *It provides a tool for external communications with potential customers and anyone else interested in the company.* Product information, technical details, answers to typical after-sales queries, educational materials about the company and so on can be efficiently handled by the website.

✳ *The website helps with a host of internal company functions.* Technical details related to production that were previously stored in detailed manuals, financial details such as company reports and marketing information about customer needs can be provided.

A well-structured website can provide an **information highway** within a company leading users quickly to the information that they require – rapidly speeding up the processes and reducing the time and costs required to run the business.

A website also has an enormous impact upon **customer perceptions** of and attitudes towards a company, product or service. Today, many customers will hear about a company for the first time when they surf the Internet – so the website becomes the first point of contact.

A well-organised website thus becomes a means of marketing to consumers, embracing all of the stages involved in developing enduring relationships with customers.

The site should provide all of the facilities required to build relationships with consumers. For example, building in online market research tools where browsers fill in company questionnaires helps the business to understand its customers. The communications which are placed on the website help the business to acquire customers. Online ordering tools build this process. Advice, support and answers to frequently asked questions, as well as telephone helplines, help the business to serve its customers. A well-organised website also encourages cross-selling. For example, a customer finds a book title that they are interested in on a publisher's website, which also provides links to other works which may interest the customer. Once these connections are shown to be effective, the consumer knows that they have found a site that is helpful and serves their needs, helping to cement an ongoing relationship.

Today, consumers are able to surf the net seeking the best deals.

It is also important to consider the impact of a website on **competitors**. There are a number

CASE STUDY
Seeking the best deal

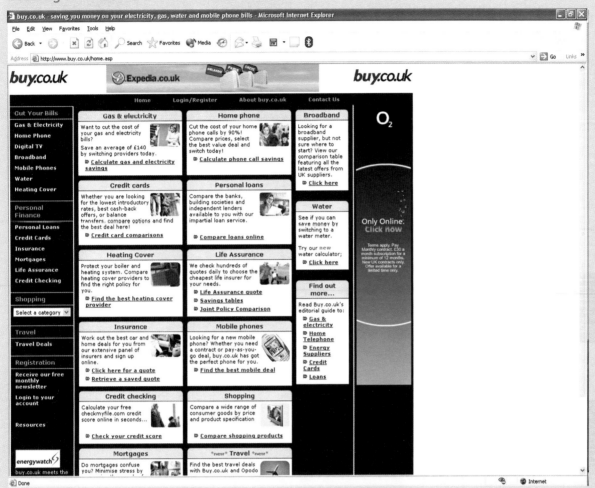

FIGURE 4.10 *A shopping bot*

Modern customers are able to use shopping portals (see Figure 4.10). These may also be referred to as:

* bargain finders
* shopping bots
* comparison engines.

All the potential customer has to do is enter the name of a product or service or other keyword and they are then provided with a list of prices and their availability from a range of retailers. The best bargain finders are the ones that specialise in a particular field, because one of the problems for these services is that it is very difficult to keep information accurate and up to date.

Popular examples are Bestbookbuys.com for books that you can order worldwide, Buy.co.uk for UK utilities e.g. water or electricity and Shopper.com for a range of products including computers.

Search for these sites at www.heinemann. co.uk/hotlinks (express code 1149P, then go to Unit 4), and compare how easy it is to make a purchase.

CASE STUDY

Buying online

Shopping on the Internet can be a speedy process. For example, if you decide to visit Amazon.com to purchase a CD or book, all you need to do is to search the inventory using the form on the screen. Information about Amazon, including how the goods will be distributed (shipping), can be found by clicking on the relevant link.

You might decide to click on the 'music' tab and search for a recording artist that you like, for example Dido. Immediately you will receive a display of entries, and you can choose a title, for example, 'No Angel'. This will appear with a list of all the tracks as well as reviews by customers. You can listen to samples from some of the tracks by downloading a player and clicking on the chosen track.

Like most good commercial websites, Amazon provides the facility for you to make a purchase online. However, to do this you need to have set up an account beforehand. You can then add items to a shopping basket. You are not committed to paying for them at this stage – as in a real supermarket, you pay only for items that remain in the shopping basket when you use the checkout.

When you are ready to pay you then click on 'Proceed to checkout'. If it's your first visit, you will need to sign in by clicking on 'I am a new customer'. For all customers setting up accounts or paying on account, the computer goes into secure mode. The address changes to https:// and a closed lock symbol appears on the bottom of the bar. If your browser does not give you this security, don't shop in this way.

FIGURE 4.11 *Dido*

When you are waiting for your order to arrive you can check where the order has got to. Click onto your account, sign in and examine your 'Order history'. This should give you an idea of where your order is and how long it will take to deliver.

Buying online therefore provides a flexible way of making transactions as well as seeking information about products. The process described for buying through Amazon is similar to that involved in other online shopping. **Visit the website and investigate the purchase of a book or CD.**

---

of ingredients which help to create competitive advantage through having the best website.

Competitive advantages are the plus points that a business has relative to rivals which help to drive sales and customer loyalty.

For example, a web-based bookseller may identify the points in Figure 4.12 as being the main ones providing competitive advantage (each category is marked out of 10).

Learning activity

Use www.heinemann.co.uk/hotlinks (express code 1149P, then go to Unit 4) to search Bestbookbuys.com for three books that you are interested in. Compare prices, and 'hidden' costs such as delivery, and other charges with those of another web-based book seller such as Amazon. com.

CHIEF POINTS LEADING TO COMPETITIVE ADVANTAGE	OUR FIRM	OUR NEAREST RIVAL	OTHERS
Ease of finding the site	10	9	7
Ease of navigating the site	8	9	5
Range of stock advertised on site	10	7	5
Customer focus (friendliness)	8	8	6
Ease of finding relevant information about titles	7	8	7
Ease of payment	7	7	7
Security of payment	10	10	6
Number of consumers using the site	10	9	7
Number of regular customers	8	6	5
Links to other relevant information	7	8	6
Total	85	81	61

FIGURE 4.12 *Main points providing competitive advantage*

Having the best website is an important source of competitive advantage. Important criteria for measuring the effectiveness of a website include:

* the number of hits on the site

* the number of these hits that are converted into buying customers

* the time spent **browsing** the web by customers and other interested parties

* the volume of extra business generated through the site

* the positive effect that the site has on brand imaging

* the increase in customer awareness resulting from website activities.

The nature of the Internet is that it is based on open access. This means that competitors can keep in very close touch with what their rivals are doing in terms of building competitive advantage through e-commerce. The result has been to create intense competition between e-tailers and e-traders in terms of:

* site content and layout

* what is offered on the site

* prices.

A website is also important in building relationships with **suppliers**. In the competitive modern world, suppliers e.g. book publishers seek to build relationships with those businesses that are most likely to give the best exposure to their products. A supplier will want to be able to see that a business that purchases its products for resale is looking after its interests e.g. by presenting the product in the desired way, presenting the product to the appropriate target audience etc. For example, an international magazine supplier would supply a magazine e-tailer that targets their site at an international audience (for example, by dealing with other international titles), and also uses a range of international languages (where appropriate).

Learning activity

Work in pairs or other small groups. Create a set of criteria of your own that you think would be appropriate for comparing the competitive advantages of two competing business websites. You can then personally compare the strengths and weaknesses of the two sites. Alternatively, you can develop a questionnaire to carry out some research among web users to find out which site they prefer using the criteria that you have generated. You can use your findings to suggest ways of improving the site.

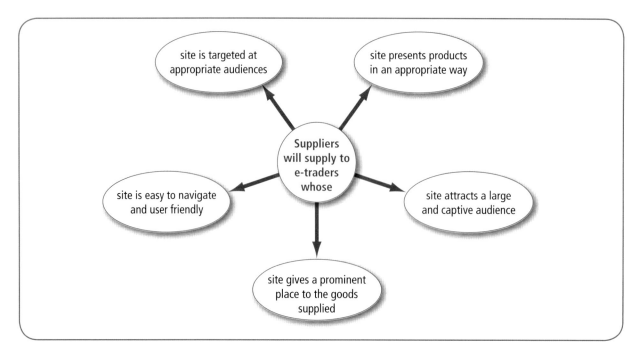

FIGURE 4.13 *Essential features of e-traders' websites*

The immediate effects of the site

Having a good website is an important stepping stone to maximising the benefits of e-commerce. However, it is essential that:

* lots of browsers go to the site

* when they are on the site they stay a long time and access the most important parts of the site

* they make purchases

* they revisit the site

* they recommend the site to other potential customers.

You can see from this list that there are a number of steps that need to be completed before the site can be regarded as a success. This can be seen as a success chain. If any of the links in the chain break, then much valuable time, effort and money can be wasted (see Figure 4.14).

Creating a site should have an effect on both **sales (turnover)** and **costs**. Remember that profit can be calculated by:

Turnover – Costs = Profits

Sales are increased if more and more customers are attracted to buy, both online and through other existing outlets.

However, creating a website can also increase costs:

* There are the costs involved in paying professional designers to create the site

* The costs of maintaining the site so that the information is accurate and up-to-date

* There are also the costs associated with answering online questions and providing distribution channels e.g. mail deliveries to get the goods to customers.

Of course, the creation of a website trading presence can substantially lower costs. For example, a web-based company may reduce costs by:

* operating from a cheaper location

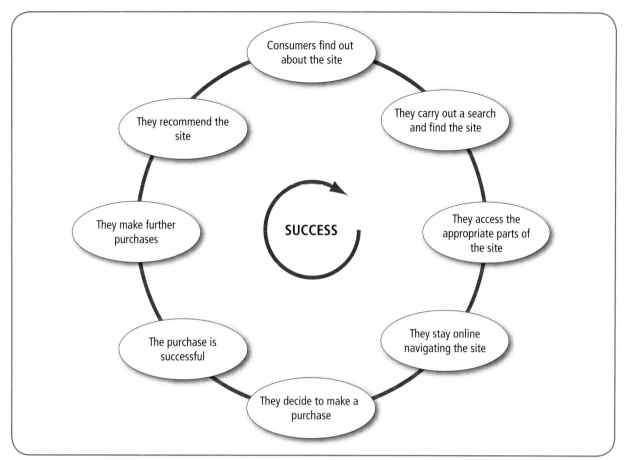

FIGURE 4.14 *Links in the success chain*

CASE STUDY

Boo.com

One of the early casualties of the .com revolution was Boo.com because the owners had not anticipated the high fixed costs in setting up an e-business. The company was set up by two Swedish entrepreneurs who had a brilliant idea – to be the first truly global Internet retailer of fashion sportswear with offices in London, New York, Stockholm, Paris and Munich. They expected to make a profit by selling to young people who were connected to the Internet and who were willing to pay high prices for fashion clothes. They quickly expanded to 300 staff and spent a lot of money on advertising the business which started trading in 1998.

Unfortunately, they were starting from scratch – nobody had previously heard of Boo. They had high fixed costs but they expected to be able to cover these when sales picked up. However, sales did not pick up quickly enough and they soon ran out of money. A great idea but one of e-tailings first major casualties.

1 Do you think that Boo.com was a good idea?
2 Why do you think that it didn't work at the time?
3 Do you think that it could have been made to work with better planning?

* not having to operate from fixed premises

* being able to spread its costs over a 24-hour operation

* having lower staff costs because many employees are willing to accept a lower wage for working at home

* enabling costs to be spread over a larger turnover (i.e. lower cost per unit of sale).

For many web-based companies, a major hurdle is that of retrieving the fixed costs that are involved in starting up the business.

The need to update a site

Most, if not all of us, have been frustrated at one time or another when we have looked something up on the Internet only to find that the pages we seek are no longer there, or that they have not been updated for months or even years.

This sense of frustration should help you to understand the importance of keeping a site up to date. In the modern wired-up world, busy consumers want the latest information, and they want to know about the latest products. For example: you want to buy a new computer. You look at a retailer's site and notice that it has not been updated for six months. The chances are very high that you will not buy from that retailer, because you will suspect that if the site is out of date, the stock will be too.

The best sites therefore are modified and cleaned up on an almost daily basis, some hour-by-hour.

Learning activity

Carry out an Internet search for the following:

* A newspaper story about a current news event

* A state-of-the-art laptop

* A business textbook.

In each case examine a range of sites. Which one needs a regularly updated website?

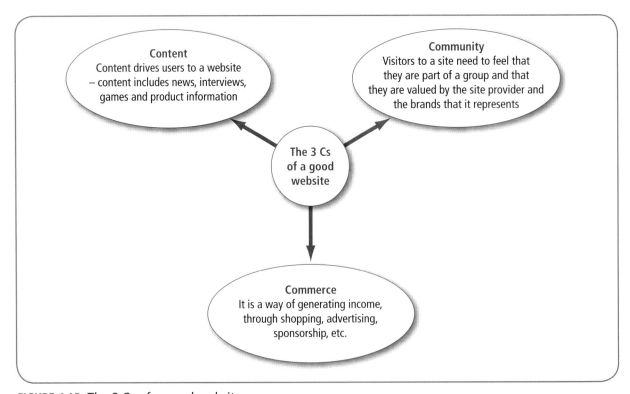

FIGURE 4.15 *The 3 Cs of a good website*

CASE STUDY

Setting up a website for an e-tailing business selling camcorders

Just imagine that you were setting up an online camcorder website for a new business. What sorts of things would you need to include? Here are a few suggestions for an effective site:

1 A clear easy-to-use home page setting out an index of the various pages and sections of the site that the viewer could access. This is your shop window so it should be user-friendly, interesting and inviting.

2 This index could be kept in view on other pages so that the user could quickly navigate their way round the site. This will stop browsers from becoming frustrated and link them to what they want to find.

3 A simple explanation of how to buy online because this is the main purpose of the site. The buying process should be idiot-proof. Of course, you may want to add a telephone number for queries. However, the problem with having a telephone link is that this could lead to people calling from all over the globe 24 hours a day, and would add extra costs of having someone to answer the phone.

4 Clear pictures of items for sale – you must be careful, however, that this does not slow down the ease with which the site can be navigated. Customers are as interested in what a product looks like as they are in other details.

5 Clear sections for each of the manufacturers stocked, or types of camcorders stocked. This helps browsers to home in on sections that interest them. You may want to put in some technical details to support your main pages for real experts and technical wizards.

6 Honest reviews of items stocked so that customers can make fair comparisons.

7 A clear and up-to-date price list so that customers can make comparisons and know how much to pay.

8 An easy-to-use payment system. The site is only successful when customers pay for the goods.

9 A chat line so that customers can ask questions – but restrict this to certain hours of the day.

10 Details of which items are the best sellers. Perhaps the best selling items should be the ones that customers are introduced to first to save time. Customers often need to feel that they have made the right purchase – the fact that others have bought an item helps them to feel more secure.

11 A clear indication of delivery times, methods and cost. You don't want people to complain about late delivery.

12 A full range of supporting accessories, including the cables required to link camcorders to TVs, computers and VCRs. If you don't provide the full service a consumer might be tempted to shop with a competitor.

13 A clear and easy to understand guarantee system.

14 Links to helplines on manufacturers' sites. Manufacturers will have details about how to deal with technical problems etc.

15 A discussion forum for camcorder fans and experts to chat with each other.

16 An online newspaper or magazine, which can be easily printed off and gives up-to-date details of your business and what it offers.

17 Frequently asked questions. Typically customers will have similar types of problems or queries. An FAQ section will save customers and you a lot of time.

Choose *ten* of these features that you consider the most important.

What should be included on a website?

It is important to develop a website that users:

* will want to visit

* will make repeat visits to

* find exciting each time they visit.

A successful site needs to have three main ingredients – the '3 Cs'. These three factors are content, community and commerce (see Figure 4.15).

A product-related website can:

* educate consumers about new or existing products and their use

* provide information, for example about new product developments, different product specifications and what to do if things go wrong with a product

* provide recreational activities such as games, competitions and fun activities

* offer commercial benefits, such as enabling consumers to buy through the medium of the Internet, and sellers to sell their products and services.

> ### ✳ DID YOU KNOW?
>
> The government is seeking to put all of its services online to keep citizens informed of what the government is doing. Let us hope that their efforts prove to be more successful than the Inland Revenue which in 2004, through errors attributed to 'sloppy' procedures, managed to delete the tax records of thousands of people!

Learning activity

Choose a type of business that you are interested in. For example, you may want to examine businesses providing cut price travel such as easyJet or Ryanair, hotels such as Hilton Hotels, or a sports business such as Arsenal men's or women's football club. What should be included in its website and why?

The impact on business of having a website

A website has the ability to transform a business but it should be seen as just one way of creating relationships in a successful business. In addition to the website the business must build relationships with customers through customer-focused telephone links, personal contact e.g. through e-mail links, and many other techniques. To just rely on the website is a recipe for disaster because it takes away the personal relationship which is at the heart of successful marketing. In a well received book *All to One*, Steve Luengo-Jones showed that some misguided people believed that a website on its own was a low cost way of winning customer loyalty. They were wrong because customers want a range of relationships with a company in which they are regarded to be at the centre of the company's attention. What is needed is not One to One relationships with a website, but All to One relationships in which companies use a full range of ways of building relationships with the customer.

Providing businesses bear this in mind, there are enormous benefits to be gained from having a website, including the ability to:

* tap into much wider geographical markets

* increase awareness of brands and products

* increase sales

* lower unit costs

* improve communications

* become more transparent

* share information.

We can look at some of these points in more detail.

Improving communications

A website enables a business to improve both internal and external communications. For example, the website can contain a range of useful information and documents for staff such as policies (e.g. equal opportunities, harassment policies), training programmes, forms (such as expenses claim forms), lists of internal addresses and telephone numbers, access to e-mail facilities, databases of information and many other useful communications. For external customers the website can provide lots of helpful information, for example details of how to install and maintain company products, details of special offers and information about new launches.

Becoming more transparent

Transparency is a buzz word in modern business. It involves people being able to look inside a business to see what it is doing. Transparency is important in a world in which business organisations are increasingly required to be accountable to their stakeholders. The website can therefore provide important information, for example about the company's environmental policy and performance, about corporate social relations, and policies with regards to important issues such as dealing with other companies (e.g. not buying from companies that violate human rights).

Sharing information

A company website is part of an information highway that adds value to products and increases all round efficiency within a company. Today's best companies have well-developed websites providing instant access to information that helps everyone in the company work to maximum efficiency, answering questions such as:

✳ How do I contact a colleague?

✳ Who are the best suppliers to deal with?

✳ How do I fill in this report?

✳ When do I get paid?

✳ How can I find opportunities in the company for personal development?

✳ How do I book a room? flight? projector? and so on.

In an ideal world everyone within a company should be able to ask a question online and be given an appropriate response to their question.

4.3 Factors influencing the establishment of an online presence

There are a number of important factors which influence the use of the Internet by a business (see Figure 4.16).

Relevant legislation and regulations

It is quite easy and not very costly to set up a simple website. However, it is important to realise that you can't just put anything on to your website, because what appears in the public domain on a website is subject to laws (**legislation**) and rules (**regulations**) that govern other aspects of behaviour, for example:

✳ Where the website acts as a trading medium, what appears on the site is governed by a range of consumer protection laws.

✳ Where a website provides information and views, it is governed by laws covering libel – a website owner can be sued for providing untruthful or malicious information.

✳ The website must abide by laws relating to decency.

✳ The website must also not infringe copyright, for example, by publishing information that is the copyright of another author or publisher unless permission has been obtained.

✳ Another minefield for setting up a website is to make sure that your actions do not contravene the Data Protection Act (see page 214).

The **World Wide Web Consortium (W3C)** is an international group made up of representatives from business and academics based at the Massachusetts Institute of Technology (MIT). Members of this group work together to create and develop common standards for the World Wide Web. One of the greatest achievements of this group was establishing Hyper Text Markup Language (HTML), which is the standard for creating **web pages**.

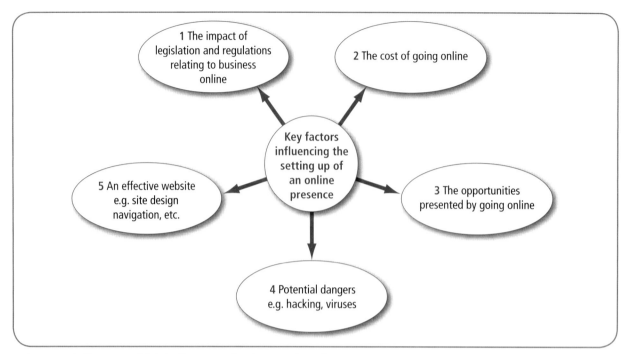

FIGURE 4.16 *Factors which influence a business using the Internet*

A piece of consumer legislation that is particularly important for e-commerce is the **Trade Descriptions Act 1968**. The significance of the Act relates to descriptions of goods and services described for selling. Under the Act the description given of goods forms part of the contract between a buyer and a seller. This Act makes it a criminal act for a trader to describe goods falsely (including on a website).

The two main offences covered by the Act are:

＊ applying false descriptions to goods or supplying goods with such a description

＊ making false statements about the provision of services, accommodation or facilities.

The **Sale of Goods Act 1979** (amended by the **Sale and Supply of Goods Act 1994**) covers most goods and services that are purchased on the Internet, and the consumer has certain rights under these Acts. Goods should be 'as described', 'of satisfactory quality' and 'fit for the purpose'.

Similarly, when consumers buy a service such as banking or insurance using e-commerce, they can expect it to be carried out 'using reasonable care and skill', 'within a reasonable time' and at a 'reasonable charge'.

The **Supply of Goods and Services Act 1982** also relates to the supply of goods and services together, for example when online computer sellers have a maintenance contract to maintain a computer service that they sell online. As part of the contract they will supply goods, parts and labour.

The **Sale and Supply of Goods to Consumers Regulations 2002** gives consumers six months to reject goods which do not conform to expectations at the time when they are sold (for example, when they are purchased through a website). There is a right to have goods repaired or replaced, or have a price reduction, if within that six-month period goods do not conform to the contract of sale. Guarantees made by manufacturers or retailers are legally binding, must be written in plain language, and must provide clear information on how to claim (including the name and address of the guarantor).

The Consumer Protection (Distance Selling) Regulations 2000, known as the Distance Selling Regulations, protect consumers who purchase by such means as digital television and through the Internet. The regulations require that:

＊ the seller provides the buyer with full information, including the name of the seller,

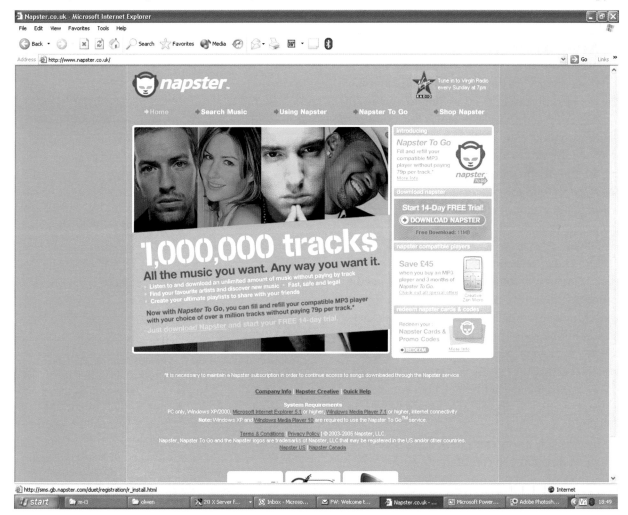
the price, an accurate description of the goods or service, delivery arrangements, payment arrangements – all backed up by written confirmation

✱ the buyer has the right to cancel the agreement:

✱ for goods, seven working days after receipt

✱ for services, seven working days after the agreement to purchase the service (such as a holiday).

There are also important laws and regulations governing the copying of ideas, and products.

The **Copyright, Designs and Patents Act 1988** provides rights to authors not to have their work copied and sold without their agreement. Today it also applies to computer software, as well as all sorts of publications. It is illegal to copy software, or to sell copies of manuals that come with the software, without the permission of the copyright holder. It is also against the law to run software on more than one computer at the same time unless you have purchased a multiple licence.

It is illegal to send software down a telecommunications line in order to create a copy.

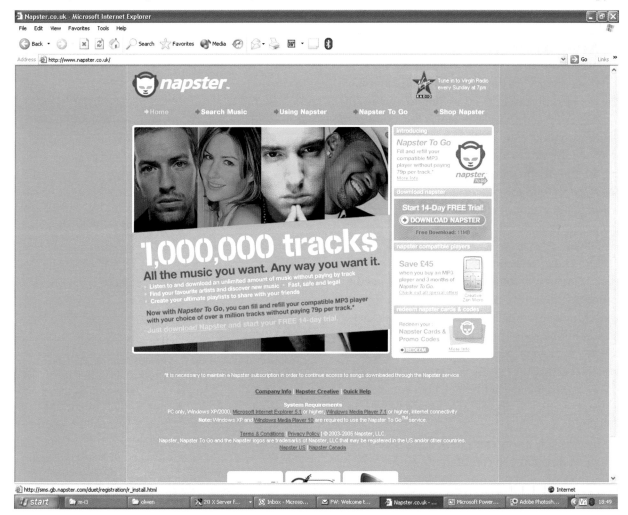

FIGURE 4.17 *The Napster website*

Individuals who download or make available copyright-protected material are breaking the law. In recent years we have seen a large-scale battle against file sharing (Internet users sharing files) and the downloading of music – particularly in the case of Napster. The big music companies took out legal injunctions against the file-sharing application Napster in the US courts.

In a similar way there have been legal battles involving Scour, which made possible a file-sharing network for the exchange of movies. Of course, the record companies realised that it was too difficult to prevent the music to which they owned the copyright from being exchanged illegally on the Internet. Their approach to this problem has been to create systems where Internet users can legally download music for a fee.

Intellectual property rights is the term for all types of protection such as patents, registered designs, registered trade mark and copyright.

A patent is a monopoly giving exclusive rights to an invention. This could be a new product or a process.

Trade marks are the signs which distinguish the goods and services of one trader from another, such as AOL and Google. A registered trade mark ensures that only the company or its licencees may sell the product or service under that trade mark. Initially they last for ten years, but can be renewed indefinitely. You must be careful not to infringe copyright or other forms of intellectual property right, because this can lead to legal penalties.

The **Data Protection Act 1998** has been phased in so that today all organisations need to comply with it. It is very important in protecting individuals' personal data (including both facts and opinions about individuals). The Act relates to both written records about individuals and any stored on computer systems. Users of personal data have to register with the Data Protection Agency (failure to do so can lead to a fine of up to £5,000).

Individuals or organisations that process personal data have to comply with eight principles of good practice. The data must be:

* fairly and lawfully processed
* processed for limited purposes
* adequate, relevant and not excessive
* accurate
* not kept for longer than necessary
* processed in accordance with the rights of the data subject
* secure
* not transferred to other countries that do not have adequate protection.

Individuals are allowed access by law to the information that is held about them, and if appropriate to have this information corrected or deleted. Individuals can make a request to the data holder in writing to obtain a copy of the personal data held about them. The data user may charge a fee of up to £10 for this service.

Individuals can complain to the Data Protection Registrar if they feel that the law has been broken. They can also sue in the courts for compensation if information about them has been used in a way which might damage them.

The role of the Data Protection Registrar is to:

* keep a register of data users
* provide information about the Act and how it works
* encourage individuals and organisations to comply with the eight principles
* encourage development of codes of practice to help users comply with these principles
* handle complaints
* prosecute offenders or serve notice on anyone who contravenes the eight principles.

Learning activity

You want to set up a website selling specialist CDs to a chosen target market. In order to target your customers carefully you plan to set up a database of customers setting out where they live, what type of music they like to listen to, and what items they buy from you. Make a list of the most important legal areas that you will need to be aware of when running your web based business, using the headings shown in Figure 4.18.

LEGAL CONSIDERATIONS
1 Consumer protection
2 Data protection
3 Intellectual property rights

FIGURE 4.18 *Legal considerations in setting up a website*

To find out more about the Data Protection Act, use www.heinemann.co.uk/hotlinks (express code 1149P, then go to Unit 4) to refer to the Information Commissioner's Office and HMSO sites.

The cost implications of an online presence

Online business has helped to transform the way that business is carried out.

Twenty-five years ago the received wisdom was that you had to be large to succeed in business. Large firms were successful because they could benefit from so called economies of scale (advantages of being big which enabled you to produce high outputs at low unit costs).

You can see this in the way that:

* large firms came to dominate mass manufacturing e.g. in confectionery Cadburys, Nestlé and Mars; in oil refining Shell, BP, Texaco etc.

* large firms came to dominate mass retailing e.g. Sainsbury's, Tesco and now Asda Walmart

Learning activity

Examine the website of two of the businesses outlined above. What evidence is given from a study of the website that the companies have used their economies of scale on the web. For example, how extensive is their website? Does it offer a wide range of products? To what extent are they able to advertise an ability to offer low prices for high quality services? What other indications are there about the size of the company – e.g. in the company highlights section does it show the number of employees, and number of markets the company is operating in?

* large firms came to dominate other forms of mass market services e.g. insurance (Norwich Union, Legal and General); banking (NatWest, Halifax) etc.

Then along came the Internet and this has transformed the way that business is conducted. For example, today more than 11 million people bank online and it is expected that, as mobile phone technology develops, people will access banking facilities from their handsets.

The Internet has been around since 1969, but it only really took off as a business tool in the mid-1990s with the development of the first effective web browsers.

The name of the first graphical web browser was mosaic, and the development of this and other web browsers led to a massive escalation in web navigation.

In the year to June 1994, web traffic increased by 25 times. In the same year domain names for commercial organisations (.com) outnumbered educational institutions for the first time (the web had originally been set up to share information between educational institutions).

The World Wide Web consists of web pages that are accessed on the Internet and connected through clickable hypertext links known as **hyperlinks**.

Immediately the Internet generated a great deal of excitement, and this excitement continues today with hundreds of thousands of business ventures trading through the Internet.

The main type of businesses trading through the Internet are:

* B2C (business to consumers) – a business that sells directly to consumers, such as Next Direct (clothes), Iceland (groceries and other items), Manchester United club shop etc.

* B2B (business to business) – a business that sells primarily to other businesses, such as Pittards selling leather to football boot and glove manufacturers and so on.

The Internet therefore provides a powerful medium for large firms to communicate with a large number of customers.

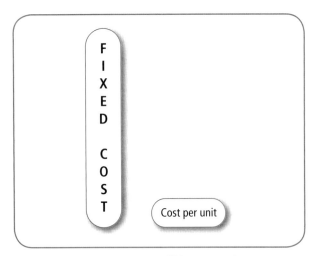

FIGURE 4.19 *Set-up costs will be spread over many sales in the long run*

The cost implications for the large firm are that creating and servicing a website is a very expensive business. A commercial site for a major business has thousands of pages, costs at least £100,000, takes six months to set up, and will then need full-time staff to look after the site. However, once the site is up and running these costs can be spread over a large number of unit sales.

However, it is not only large businesses that can set up websites. A simple dedicated website (e.g. one that concentrates on promoting a business and selling its goods online) can generate substantial revenues for a small business.

An attractive and useful site can generate a lot of sales. Although it is helpful to have an 'all singing, all dancing' website for some purposes e.g. as a communications tool for a global business, a much simpler site will suffice for a small business serving a particular market. Examples of where a simple website could be effective include:

* A site for a coin or stamp seller
* A site for a business service, e.g. an accountancy service
* A site for a ticket agency.

What these small businesses have in common is a product or service that is required by a large number of people who may be physically dispersed, and a product or service that is relatively light and thus easy to distribute.

Web design

One of the most important costs of setting up an online business is web design. This involves a number of ingredients:

1   Setting out the structure/architecture of the site. This involves creating the structure to work the site i.e. the links and connections between pages, the interface with the user, etc.

2   Designing the page layouts. Typically these will be organised in a standard way to create some form of consistency in terms of the look of the site.

3   Building in the content of the web pages. As we have seen these will need to be regularly updated and this is an extra cost.

In choosing a web designer it is important to look at their previous work and to examine the sites that they have created, analysing them in terms of:

* how easy they are to use
* how interesting they are
* whether the structure and operation of the site is similar to one that you would like to create for your own business.

When considering the cost of having a site designed for you it is a mistake to assume that a low-cost solution is automatically a good solution. It is better to think of costs in terms of the revenues they go on to generate – how much revenue will be generated for every pound spent on the site?

There are two main types of site:

1   A *static site* contains information that has been entered on the website that does not alter or change over time.

2   A *database-driven site* is one which can be updated and altered by changing the information entered into a database. Database-

driven sites are more complex and expensive to run. However, businesses that are involved in trading are almost certain to go to the expense of running a database-driven site.

Consultancy

Rather than employ web page designers in-house a firm might buy in the services of IT consultants. The consultants will typically have designed sites for a range of other businesses. Consultants' fees are high but they can save a lot of time and effort, reducing costs in the long term. When hiring consultants it is important to have a clear idea about what you want them to do for you. You therefore need to have a **web project manager** whose job it is to work with the consultants to outline the requirements of the website.

Employing relevant staff

A website needs to be serviced by appropriate staff, including:

* site engineers who will deal with any technical problems involved in setting up and maintaining the site. They will troubleshoot any ongoing problems. Typically these individuals are called **programmers**

* web page inputters who simply input new pages into a site and update existing pages. We use the term web page **designers** for those people who design the pages

* call handlers who are responsible for handling telephone calls related to the site, such as customer orders. Large companies might contract out such work to call centres

* packers and distributors are responsible for handling and posting/delivering customer orders.

Hardware and software

Hardware and software costs are an important consideration for an online business. It makes sense to use the latest computer technology to keep up to date with current trends.

The most important piece of hardware is a **web server** which is used to run the site. A good quality server can be bought for as little as £2,000.

The type and number of servers used depends on the amount of traffic going to the site, i.e. the number of people browsing the pages and making orders/seeking information. Where there is a lot of traffic a company might employ more than one server – each server being dedicated to handling particular types of information.

Training

Training is a cost that is often overlooked. It is all very well creating an expensive website using specialists. However, the reality of most sites is that they need to be operated and run on a day-to-day basis by general users. These users need to be trained to maximise the usefulness of the site. Training will involve showing the general user:

* how to access the site

* how to navigate the site

* how to input data

* how to perform simple operations such as adding up totals, adding new items etc.

* what to do if something goes wrong

* how to explain aspects of the site to third parties such as customers.

Ongoing support

The nature of Information and Communications Technology (ICT) is that most users (if not all) need some support on an ongoing basis. Typical users will want to have someone to turn to when things go wrong – 'a file seems to have been deleted', 'I can't find…', 'how do I?' 'where is the…?' Dedicated user support therefore needs to be built into the running of a website and should be seen as an ongoing cost. If used appropriately it will lead to more than proportionate benefits.

The opportunities created by electronic business

The manutd.com case study (see page 218) highlights the benefits of having an electronic business, both in terms of communicating with your customers and potential customers and being able to increase sales.

CASE STUDY

Manutd.com

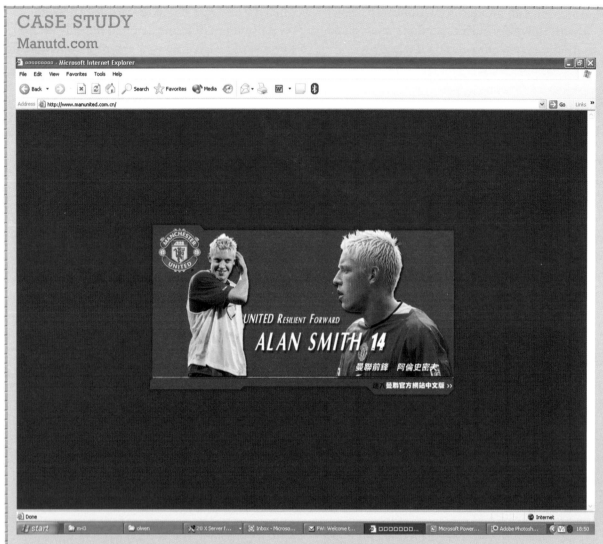

FIGURE 4.20 *The Manchester United Mandarin (Chinese) language website*

Manutd.com is one of the most popular commercial websites appealing to a global audience. One of the main objectives of the site is to deepen the club's knowledge of Manchester United fans worldwide and convert them into customers of MU.tv, MU Mobile and Manchester United club membership. The Mandarin (Chinese) language website manunited.com.cn was launched in October 2002.

Some statistics of interest for this site in 2003 were impressive:

* 40 million average page views per month (about 15 million of these were for manutd.com and 25 million for manunited.com.cn)
* 1 million MU average unique users

* 9 minutes average time online per visit
* 577,000 MU e-members
* 45,000 MU.tv subscribers
* 10,000 MU Mobile subscribers.

You might want to look at the sites to help you answer the following questions. Find them through www.heinemann.co.uk/hotlinks (express code 1149P, then go to Unit 4).

1 How might the sites help the club to find out more about Manchester United fans worldwide?

2 How might the sites help Manchester United convert fans worldwide into consumers?

3 What is the importance of manunited.com.cn?

Increased efficiency for online ordering

Another prime advantage is the increased efficiency for online ordering. For example, take the case of someone wanting to book a cross channel journey with P&O Ferries. Instead of ringing up or writing to the firm you can now book online.

The customer carries out an Internet search or goes directly to the P&O Ferries site and finds a booking form (see Figure 4.21).

The booking form enables the customer to fill in the details of when they want to travel – the day and time. They are also able to see if there are any special offers. Having looked at various options they can book their journey providing there is availability online.

The customer then pays online, and will receive confirmation of their reservation either through e-mail or by post. Now they simply have to turn up at the required time for their ferry, and the customer processing clerk will be able to call up their records online.

From the point of view of P&O Ferries, there are many advantages, including:

1 Fewer booking clerks are needed to administer the booking process, leading to substantial cost reductions.

2 There is much less waste of company time answering queries. Customers can work out the details of their journeys themselves, and when they have come up with the best possible solution, make their own order.

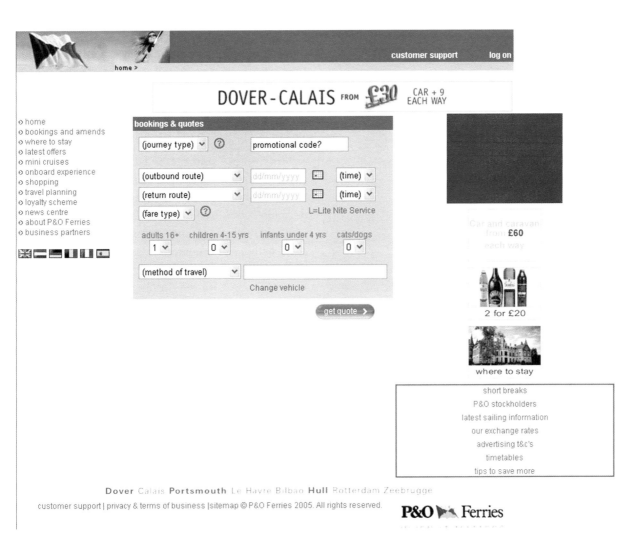

FIGURE 4.21 *Online booking form for P&O Ferries*

3   The expense of training staff in customer relations is cut right back. The new system can be administered from call and processing centres.

4   Online ordering can be simplified to create a system that is easy to administer.

WEBSITE	NUMBER OF UNIQUE VISITORS (000s)
Amazon	5,856
Tesco	2,805
Argos	2,177
Dabs.com	1,163
COMET	1,023
CD WOW	982
Currys	776
John Lewis	717
Dixons	640
Littlewoods	611

FIGURE 4.22 *Top Internet shopping sites in the UK, home and work data, October 2004 (Nielsen //NetRatings)*

Figure 4.22 shows the top ten Internet shopping sites as calculated by Nielsen//NetRatings in October 2004.

Secure payment

The benefits of the site can be further enhanced by developing a system for secure payment. For example, when shopping for books or CDs on Amazon.com customers using the site for the first time are able to create a new account for themselves. They simply have to choose 'I am a new customer' when selecting items to put into their shopping basket. Once the customer moves into the account phase of the transaction the server will move into the 'secure mode'. At this point the address changes to https:// and a closed lock appears on the bottom bar.

Using this sort of facility, an online business is able to transact business online in the same way that when you go to the payment till at your supermarket you are able to buy goods through credit and debit cards. The beauty of online transactions as a business model is that the business of making the payment is done by the customer rather than the checkout till operator.

Personalised marketing

Another important opportunity presented by having an online presence is the ability to engage in personalised marketing. When online shoppers make a 'hit' (visit a site), they provide useful marketing information for the host site. They provide information about their location and the intensity of their interest in a particular subject. For example, a firm that sells new houses on the Internet may find that ten times more customers are interested in certain types of housing than in other types – and that those who browse the Internet tend to develop into firm buyers. Armed with this information the business is able to make decisions about what types of houses to build, and what follow-up marketing to use to attract prospective customers.

A business is able to compare the number of hits to its site with the number of hits to a rival site. By checking on the sites that are getting the most hits and the most follow-up sales, a business can identify ways in which to improve its own product or service. Businesses can also ask customers to fill in on-line questionnaires, providing further useful marketing information.

Direct dialogue with customers worldwide

An online presence makes it possible to increase **'direct dialogue'** with customers. One way of doing this is to use online customer service questionnaires. Customers can be encouraged to state their views and opinions and to put forward ideas for:

* ways of improving a site
* ways of extending the product range offered by a site
* ways of improving delivery and aspects of customer relations.

Another form of interactivity with customers is to encourage online chatlines. Consumers can chat with someone when they have a complaint, or when they need information about installing or maintaining a product. The benefits are that consumers feel that their views and opinions are being listened to, while the company is able to find out valuable information about their market, and customer perceptions of their performance.

It is not only businesses that are able to communicate with customers. The term e-government relates to providing a host of government services and a variety of information online. In 2001, Tony Blair set a target that 100% of government services would be online by 2005. The government has largely been successful in achieving this target. By the end of 2004, one million people had filed tax-credit claims online. In the financial year ending April 2004, about 1.1 million self-assessment tax returns were filed online, as well as 65% of new company

FIGURE 4.23 *Nokia, Finland's best-known company, has been able to tap global markets through online communications and ordering systems*

registrations and three-quarters of first time vehicle registrations.

One of the major advantages of an online presence is that it enables a business to tap into a global market. Take for example, a European manufacturer of state-of-the-art mobile phones like Nokia (based in Finland). People from across the globe know that Nokia is one of the world's leading manufacturers of mobile phones. By browsing the Nokia site a customer in Mauritius, Malaysia, Malmo or Manchester is able to find out about the latest Nokia products and can order them online.

All sorts of organisations are taking advantage of the global links that the Internet provides them with. For example, in the case study outlined on page 218 we saw that Manchester United has developed two websites targeted specifically at

> ## ✱ DID YOU KNOW?
>
> Some people have argued that the government's 100% target became a nightmare. The problem is not getting the first few services online, but mopping up the remaining services when most are online. Another concern is shared government databases such as the proposed national register behind the ID card scheme, which could potentially allow detailed profiling of citizens.

areas of the world where it has its largest fan base, firstly in Europe and North America, then in Asia using the world's most widely-used languages – English and Mandarin (Chinese).

Another important opportunity provided by good website design is that of **projecting the corporate image** of a business. Just as companies benefit from projecting themselves to the public through advertising on the side of bus shelters and buses, on hot air balloons, and in many other ways, a website is a great way to project company image. This is particularly true in the field of modern high-tech products and services which naturally fit with the Internet. Because there is always the danger of adverse publicity about a company finding its way on to the Internet, it is essential to feed the right publicity and the right image onto official company sites, enabling the company to get its own side of the story presented in an attractive and reassuring way.

The dangers of online business

Computer viruses

A major threat to businesses is the danger of computer viruses. A **virus** is a program that infects other program files and can enter via the Internet. Another way of spreading a virus is to insert a floppy disc that contains a virus into a computer that is part of a network. Viruses take many forms and are becoming more and more common. Some can be very difficult to trace. Some can set off a 'time bomb' effect that destroys the content of a computer's hard drive. Companies operating a website are particularly prone to viruses because of the sheer numbers of people logging onto their site.

Competitor access

Another drawback of having a website is that it provides competitors with details of how a business is run, and the products and services offered. Today anyone setting up a business is advised to carry out an Internet search to look at what existing firms are already doing. The implication is that firms that are there first are doing a lot of research work for new firms to copy. Of course, the firms that are already established benefit from 'first mover advantage' – their name becomes established in the market place e.g. Amazon.com for books and Lastminute.com for last minute holidays, theatre tickets and so on. However, the speed at which new firms can catch up with existing e-businesses becomes ever faster.

Poor design

Having a badly designed website is also a good way of putting off potential customers. Potential customers tend to judge a business by the way it presents itself, whether this be through advertising, packaging or website design. In the next section therefore we examine the nature of effective website design.

What makes an effective website?

Good design is an important aspect of web design. A website can be made attractive by an appropriate use of colour, images and text. When using colour a careful balance needs to be struck between the text and background. For example, Google is often regarded to be an icon of web design because it is simple and easy to read.

Simple rules

Simple rules include:

* Do not use very light colours, such as yellow or pale green, for your main text because these will be difficult to read

* Do not use too many colours because there is

a danger of clashes on your pages, as well as slowing down the speed of printing.

Good design involves creating good, 'clean' pages with plenty of space rather than a clutter of images. You can create 'thumbnails' (small picture images that can be enlarged by clicking on them), rather than having graphics that take up a large section of your page.

Avoid too much text on a page. The reader wants you to convey the main messages and ideas in a relatively simple way rather than being bombarded by too much complex material on screen. Use a font which is easy to read on screen, such as Arial or Verdana.

Navigation and timing

When designing your website you need to think about important operating rules for users of the site, particularly related to time spent browsing your site. For example, it is well known that Internet users quickly get impatient with sites that are difficult to **navigate**. The simple rules of '3 clicks' and '7 seconds' remind you of the number of operations and the amount of time that a typical Internet user is prepared to give to a site before expecting to arrive at something of interest. If users have to spend longer or engage in more clicking operations, they will switch to an alternative site. So think about how easy it is to

FIGURE 4.24 *The Google homepage*

navigate on your site, both moving around a page and from one page to another.

Site name

The site needs to be easy to find in the first place. A web address is called a URL (Uniform Resource Locator). Each web page has its own URL. The URL consists of three parts:

1 the protocol e.g. http://

2 the host name (domain) – everything in the address that appears before the first single forward slash.

3 the file path (the first forward slash and everything that appears after it).

The most important aspect of finding a site is the host name.

For example www.ntu.ac.uk would find you The Nottingham Trent University, and www.tesco.com will find you Tesco's site. Typically businesses choose addresses that relate to their name e.g. www.iceland.co.uk for the retailer Iceland. Search for these sites at www.heinemann.co.uk/hotlinks (express code 1149P, then go to Unit 4).

Ease of use

Once the customer is online it is essential that they are able to navigate their way around the site easily. A well-structured site will aim to keep you online until you have found what you want and hopefully have made a purchase from the company in question, or made some form of connection that helps to build your relationship with that company.

A well-designed website will enable a business to find out a lot about their customers e.g. how long they are online, and how much they spend online.

For example, in Manchester United's annual report for 2004, the following information was shown about their website:

* average page views per month 13.0 million
* minutes average time online per view 6.16

Search for the Manchester United website at www.heinemann.co.uk/hotlinks (express code 1149P, then go to Unit 4).

In a world in which most people place great emphasis on not having to waste time, an easy to use site that involves minimum effort is what every browser is looking for. For example, if a student is looking to buy a textbook, they will want to do the following:

* quickly find a site that stocks the book
* find the book
* find some brief details about the book
* find out how much the book costs and when it will be delivered
* order the book.

User satisfaction from a site is based on:

* not having any frustrations when using the site
* finding the site easy to use
* being pleasantly surprised by the site, e.g. finding out new information that broadens their horizon
* wanting to use the site again.

The balance between media-rich and functionally-able

In creating the site it is important to get the balance right between a media-rich site and a functionally-able one.

A media-rich site will be one that involves:

* exciting layout and moving images
* voice and sound options.

However, as you will know from your own experience of media-rich sites, they can be very

Learning activity

Identify a business opportunity that you might be interested in developing and which would require a website. Can the website be based on static information, or would it require the functionality of a database driven website? Explain why you have made your choice.

frustrating to navigate, particularly if bits of them don't work. Often the designers of very sophisticated media-rich sites assume that users have access to the same high-powered computers that they are using themselves – this is rarely the case.

The functionality of a site relates to the functions that it is expected to perform. Businesses that commission a website should consider whether some of the functions they ask for are really necessary because adding more and more functions can be an expensive and time consuming business for site designers. Many e-commerce sites are built around databases that can be updated remotely by multiple users. Small businesses may not require such functionality but if this is an important aspect of the business then it is worth investing in a database-driven website from the outset.

Reaching the target customer

As with any other form of marketing activity, website design needs to consider the extent to which it will reach the targeted customer. For example, if you are producing a website for classical music there is no point in designing it in the same way that you would design a site for fans of techno-rock and vice-versa.

Learning activity

How would you expect websites targeted at three different sectors of the music industry to differ? Research this activity by finding actual sites related to these different sectors. Do this by using keywords, related to particular types of music e.g. hip hop, jazz, classical, Indie, etc. Write down eight points of difference related to the sectors chosen. When you have completed the task check relevant websites to see if your assumptions are accurate.

4.4 Understand the requirements for planning/ establishing a new website

There are a number of important requirements that you will need to consider in planning and creating a website.

The use of appropriate web-authoring tools

There are a number of ways of creating web pages. The simplest way is to create a page using Microsoft Word and then to use the Save as… / HTML Document command. However, the results are difficult to control.

As a result most web page designers use a web-authoring package such as Microsoft FrontPage. Alternatively designers may use **HyperText Markup Language** (**HTML**) to design their work. HyperText Markup Language is the standard form for writing web pages. HTML tags are used to format pages and describe page and text elements. HTML tags tell the web browser how to display the contents of the pages you design. They usually come in pairs – for example, <html> and </html> mean 'html/on' and 'html/ off'.

If you use a package like Microsoft FrontPage you won't have to bother about creating the markup language because it is all done for you behind the scenes.

A commercial site for a major business has thousands of pages, costs at least £100,000, takes six months to set up, and will then need full-time staff to look after the site. The web pages that you are asked to set up as a student are a much simpler matter, but the principles are the same, and everyone has to start from small beginnings and work up.

Starting out

To start out you need to have an idea of what your site should look like, and the content of the site. It is helpful to develop a picture of what the structure of the site will be. When designing a site based on research into a well-known company for a business project, you might decide on the structure shown in Figure 4.25.

Working with FrontPage

First of all you need to have installed Microsoft FrontPage on your computer. Then open FrontPage and Internet Explorer. If you are using Office XP, to open FrontPage you will need to select **Start**, **All Programs**, **Microsoft FrontPage**. Alternatively, if you are using Office 2003, select **Start**, **All Programs**, **Microsoft Office**, **Microsoft**

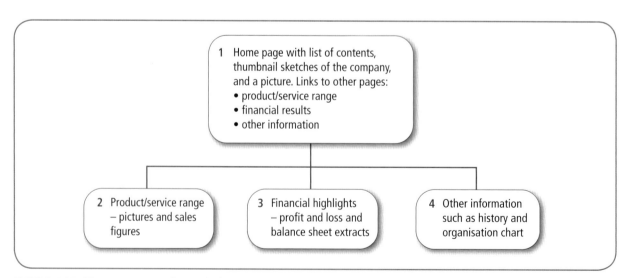

FIGURE 4.25 *The structure of a website*

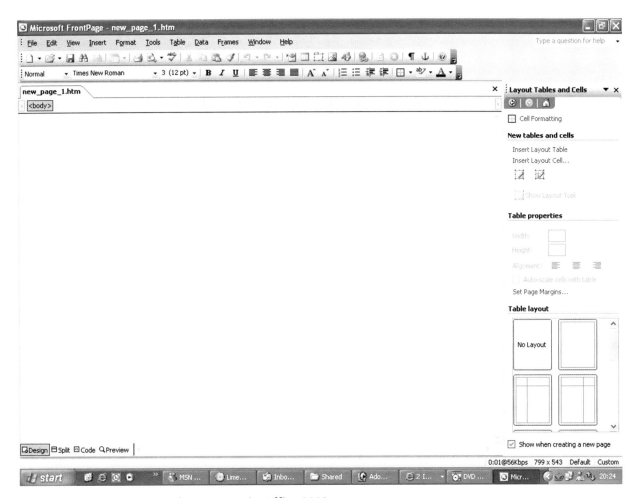

FIGURE 4.26 *FrontPage window as seen in Office 2003*

Office FrontPage 2003. Double-click on the Internet Explorer icon on your computer desktop.

You need to work with FrontPage as your active window so that it is easy to create web pages.

Figure 4.26 shows what this looks like on screen for Office 2003.

Figure 4.27 shows what this looks like on screen for Office XP.

You can now design your web pages onto this background. As with many computing applications, the design features (text, graphics, layout and so on) that you create are what will appear on your web pages.

You can also look behind the scenes by viewing the pages you create in their HTML format, which displays the HTML tags.

Creating a new web page

Before starting out you must create a folder to store all the files that you create which relate to your website. To do this:

✳ Select, **File**, **New** and **Web**.

✳ A menu will appear on the right side of the program.

✳ Under New, select **Empty Web**.

✳ If your computer has a floppy disk drive, name your new web a:/my4web (you need to have a floppy disk in your disk drive). Otherwise, name your new web in another drive.

✳ Now click **OK**.

The program FrontPage will take a short while to set up a web structure for you. Your screen will

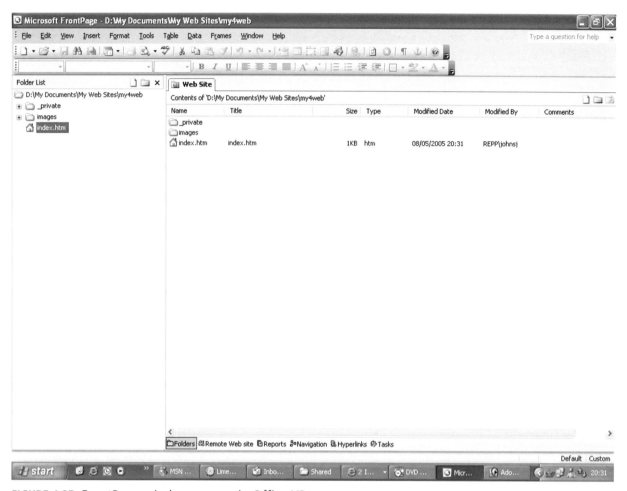

FIGURE 4.27 *FrontPage window as seen in Office XP*

look something like Figure 4.28. You should be familiar with the folder view and folder list that appears on the left side of the screen.

By default you can't see the blank area with the cursor. You need to click **index.htm** in the left-hand web structure menu.

The font that the computer will display is the default font – the one that the computer is already set to. You will probably want to use a more attractive font, as you normally do when you are word-processing. Choose from the menu of fonts that are available on your computer, making sure your choice is suitable to your particular website.

You can now type in the text shown below:

My very first website (press Enter)
The business I am studying is.........
The products/services it produces are......
Its annual turnover last year was........

With FrontPage you are able to make changes to the font style, but choice is relatively limited. You can play around with your text just as you would if you were creating a Word document, for example by:

✱ changing the font

✱ changing part of the text to bold

✱ changing part of the text to italics.

It is also helpful to inform visitors to your site how up to date it is. Just as when you read a newspaper you want to know what date it was published, so on each page of your site you should set out the date when it was last updated (the date on which you created or most recently updated your page).

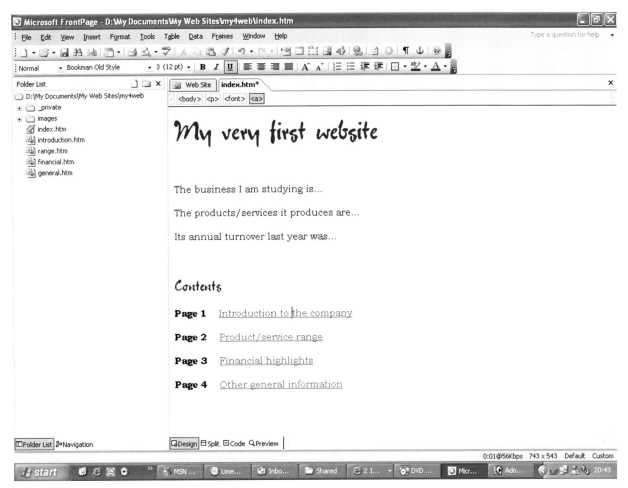

FIGURE 4.28 *The web structure set up by FrontPage is shown in the folder view on the left hand side of the page*

You can now add pages to your site, but remember that it needs to have a clear structure so that it is easy to navigate. Your first page will typically outline what appears on the other pages (setting out a list of contents). It might look like this:

Page 1 Introduction to the company

Page 2 Product/service range

Page 3 Financial highlights

Page 4 Other general information.

Adding extra material simply involves adding a new page, organising the layout of the page, thinking about the content, and saving work as you go along.

In creating your website your objective should be usability – making it accessible to the user. Some of the best information is presented in black and white text, such as newspapers. The same goes for the Internet – a good site tends to have a clean and minimal look. You can read all about creating a usable website on the usableweb.com site and find out what not to do when creating a website by looking at the webpagesthatsuck.com site. Search for these sites at www.heinemann. co.uk/hotlinks (express code 1149P, then go to Unit 4).

You can add a table to your website by choosing the **Table** menu and selecting **Insert Table**. You will need to specify how many rows and columns you want to place in your table,

1 Create a simple four-page website using FrontPage or a suitable alternative package. Save your file regularly while working through it.

2 When you have completed you work switch to Internet Explorer and open the file.

3 Check your pages to see if they work.

for example, by using the dialogue box (the box which appears on your screen asking for commands to construct the table). You might select eight rows and two columns, so that you can create a table showing companies and where their Head Office is located.

Sony	Japan
Microsoft	United States
Virgin	England
Heinz	United States
Ford	United States
Volkswagen	Germany
Manchester United	England
Canal +	France

An important advantage of using an authoring tool like FrontPage is that templates or themes are part of the package (similar to the Design templates supplied with PowerPoint). The designer can choose the theme for the entire web or for individual pages. It is a good idea to have a consistent theme.

Creating the content

We saw earlier that the ingredients of a good website are the '3 Cs' – content, community and commerce (shown in Figure 4.15). The content of a website is the reason that browsers:

1 will visit the site

2 stay on the site

3 make repeat visits to the site.

The content therefore needs to be professionally written and designed to appeal to the targeted audience. The style of writing needs to be

appropriate to that audience. The site should be regularly reviewed to make sure that the content is up to date. Simply copying a brochure onto a website is not sufficient. The web pages need to be exciting and interesting, and wherever possible they should be updated and made fresh.

Adding images

Once you have learned how to create a text-only website, you can go on to add photographs and moving images. You will find a major problem here is that if your graphics are too big they will take too long to load, spoiling the usability and popularity of your site.

There are four ways of adding images to your site:

1 You can create a digital image by using drawing software. At a simple level you can use a paint program, which you will find usually comes with your personal or college computer or which can be ordered through a software guide. If you are lucky you will have access to a high-quality professional product such as Adobe Illustrator (see details on the Adobe website through www.heinemann. co.uk/hotlinks (express code 1149P, then go to Unit 4).

2 Using a scanner you can import an existing drawing, photograph, newspaper page, and so on. The scanner scans in the image as a photocopier does, and will send the image to your hard drive, from where it can be imported to your web page.

3 You can take a picture with a digital camera or digital video camera and import that to your hard drive.

4 You can use freely available clipart from the Internet.

Industry standards with regards to web presence

In creating a website it is important to know what the standards and requirements are which create an overall system for managing electronic communication. For example, the system would be in chaos if there were lots of businesses all trading under the same name with the same web address.

A domain name identifies and locates a host computer or service on the Internet. For e-commerce purposes the name usually relates to a business name. The domain name must be registered.

The domain name is broken down into:

* subdomain
* domain type
* country code.

For example, in a.n.other@ntu.ac.uk:

* The subdomain is ntu (Nottingham Trent University computer services)
* The domain type is ac which shows that it is an academic institution – a university
* The uk part is the country code – United Kingdom.

There are different types of subdomains:

* .co (UK) or .com (US) a profit-making or commercial organisation
* .ac (UK) or .edu (US) an academic organisation
* .gov – a government organisation
* .org – a not-for-profit organisation
* .mil – a military organisation
* .net – an organisation whose activities are related to the Internet.

You can't choose any old domain name because there is a fair chance that someone else is already using that name. You therefore need to register with a domain registry such as Register.com (see this through www.heinemann.co.uk/hotlinks (express code 1149P, then go to Unit 4).

Domain registries will be able to tell you whether a name has already been registered by someone else.

Internet Service Providers (ISPs)

An **Internet Service Provider (ISP)** is an organisation which provides Internet services such as:

* electronic mail – 'e-mail'

* user groups – electronic conferencing for groups of individuals with similar interests
* the World Wide Web.

The company provides the user with a username, password and access phone number allowing connection to the Internet and World Wide Web. Packages provided by ISPs include hosting your website and maintenance, and various security products. Some also offer website building. Some big-name ISPs to choose from include AOL, BT and NTL. You also need to choose between a 'dial up' connection, where you connect to the Internet by making a call through the phone line, or a 'broadband' connection which gives you a faster 'always on' connection.

Internet users find sites in two main ways:

* taking a link from another site
* typing in the site address.

Businesses that want to attract customer can contact other sites to agree to make mutual links between sites.

Wi-Fi is an important new method of connecting to the Internet through 'hotspots' provided by wireless-based ISPs. You can get wireless connections via a Bluetooth cell phone.

> **✱ DID YOU KNOW?**
> The most popular ISPs in the UK today are Wanadoo, AOL, Virgin Net and BT.

Hosting

Having decided to create a website you will need to decide where you will host the site. The host is the place (computer) where your website is based. You can have your site hosted by your Internet Service Provider. Most providers will give free or low cost access, with a package that suits your needs.

Simple security measures

Having created your website it is important to protect it against viruses and other forms of fraud. Nowadays it is standard practice to install **virus checkers** and **firewalls** to protect computer systems.

FIGURE 4.29 *A firewall box*

A firewall is a security system which restricts traffic to a site or computer network. Another important defence for a website is a **secure payment system** to protect customers and thus encourage business to the site. Once a customer to a website moves into the account phase of carrying out a transaction, the server goes into secure mode and the address changes to https:// with a closed lock appearing at the bottom bar to stop fraud taking place.

Appropriate use of design

Some useful points of advice about designing a website are:

* Make sure that graphics involve an appropriate use of colour, fonts and images. The graphics should be easy to download.

* Make it easy to navigate the site. Make sure the user doesn't get lost.

* Keep the home page interesting and clearly set out links to other pages.

* Design the site so it can be viewed on most browsers.

* Make request forms and customer response forms user-friendly.

* Set up auto responders to acknowledge receipt of customer requests.

* Don't design a site that is bigger than customers need.

* Keep modifying your site in line with statistics you get back from customer research.

* Create the right balance between the media you use on your website e.g. advertisements, promotions, sound, videos and graphics.

This last point is very important. When creating a business website for the first time there is a temptation to put too much onto the site, and onto individual pages. The result is that users can quickly become lost or frustrated with the site. For example, if you put pictures onto the site it may take a long time to download pages and if you rely on sound effects these will be lost when the user does not have access to sound. You really need to ask yourself:

* What is the main point of the site?

* What are the best media for achieving this?

For example, if you are creating a music store then you definitely need sound – but this is not the case if you are creating an online pet shop supplies store, or a wine retail site. Selling advertising space online is a good idea. However, you need to get the right balance between advertising and the content of your site. It is a bit like television programming – adverts are important in providing revenues for the TV channel, however, they should not detract from or become more important than the programmes themselves.

The target customer

Earlier we saw that one of the key features of the '3 Cs' of an effective web presence is the community of users.

A good website should be designed and structured with the target customer in mind. In setting up a site (or having it designed for you) the key questions are:

✳ Who are the users and what do they expect?

✳ Why do you want them to use your site?

✳ How often do you expect them to use the site?

✳ Do the customers want to browse products or read about services online?

✳ Do customers simply want to use the site as a company brochure or do they intend to buy from the site?

✳ How often are they likely to buy from the site?

✳ What help might they need when ordering online?

✳ What security measures do consumers want when buying online?

Customer service is an essential ingredient of an effective website. If you have a website it must be designed so that you can respond to requests for information. This requires an e-mail contact address. E-mails must be responded to quickly to maintain the interest of customers. If you fail to respond to your customers you will usually find that your competitors have taken them from you.

Learning activity

Work in pairs or small groups to find a concept for a new business website.

1 Discuss ideas for a new product that would fill a gap in the market. Make it something that interests you and is not currently sold on the web (verify by an Internet search), or something that is currently sold on the Internet but, in your view, not very well.

2 Jot down some ideas on paper about how a website could be constructed. Draw a diagram to show the main structure of the site (see Figure 4.30).

3 Would all the pages be set out using the same layout or would there be a variation according to different sections?

4 How would you present the corporate image/brand of your company?

5 How would the pages be designed? Remember to make them bright and interesting but not too cluttered.

6 What is the overall theme of the site?

7 What exciting features would be included in the site? You may need to research other sites to get some ideas here – look at sites catering for similar markets to your own, as well as some which are quite different.

8 How would you encourage customers to come to your site? Consider ideas such as placing banner adverts on other sites, advertising in relevant media and so on.

Now construct a market research questionnaire to find out what customers expect from the site. Use the outline questions shown above and some of your own to construct the questionnaire.

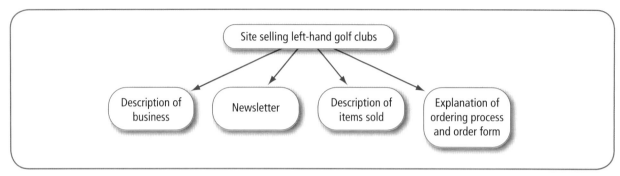

FIGURE 4.30 *The main structure of a website*

Matching the site to its purpose

There are all sorts of purposes for having a website. In creating a website you need to either:

* employ a website designer who has experience of providing the type of site that you want built, or

> **Learning activity**
>
> Review your own school or college website. Who was responsible for designing it? How did they design it? What were the key objectives of the person who designed it? Did they do some market research before designing it? How many other sites did they examine? What sources of advice did they seek? How did they learn to design the site? Is the site up to date?
>
> Carry out an analysis of the main strengths and weaknesses of the site for users. Who are the main groups of users? Students? Teachers? Parents? Other users? Which groups benefit from it most? How could the site be improved? Set out your findings in a brief report which you could deliver as a presentation to those currently responsible for managing the site.

* study types of sites in the category that you want to build.

Typical purposes for sites, and their features are shown in Figure 4.31.

Promoting your business on the Internet

There are a number of ways of promoting your business on the Internet, including:

* Liaising with stakeholders
* Banner advertisements
* Sponsoring trade events.

> **Learning activity**
>
> Use www.heinemann.co.uk/hotlinks (express code 1149P, then go to Unit 4) to study the following sites:
> 1   tt100.biz
> 2   Nike.com
> 3   eBay.com
> Explain what you see as the main purpose of the site:

PURPOSE OF SITE	FEATURES
Educational	Learning materials, activities, quizzes, assignments etc.
Promotional	Clear company branding, special offers, advertisements
Informative	Clear information, facts, tables, pictures
Commercial	Company branding, product and service descriptions, online ordering system, payments systems, advertising and promotions
Recreational	Games, quizzes, puzzles etc.

FIGURE 4.31 *Purposes of websites*

Liaising with stakeholders

Stakeholders are people with an interest in the success of your business, for example, a supplier or an organisation such as a bank that provided finance to set up the business. A business's stakeholders might help promote the business by recommending the site to some of their other customers.

Banner advertisements

Banner advertisements are a good way of promoting the site. A banner appears across the top of each page of a website and these are often used to advertise products or services. You can benefit from banners in two ways:

1 Other sites agree to publicise your site through a banner.

2 An Internet Service Provider offers to publish your website free of charge providing you put some advertising banners for them on each page.

Sponsoring trade events

Another important way of promoting a website is through sponsoring a trade, sporting or other event. For example, at football matches you often see website addresses on the hoardings around the pitch.

FIGURE 4.32 *Websites are often promoted by advertising at sporting events*

The Data Protection Act 1998 and customer confidentiality

We have already examined the Data Protection Act 1998 and customer confidentiality in the previous section (4.3). According to the Information Commissioner for the Data Protection Act, nearly three-quarters of adults in Britain are worried about the amount of their personal details being stored electronically. In setting up your website it is essential to make sure that you comply with the requirements of this Act as the penalties for breaches and non-compliance are severe.

Costs, consultants and ways to create a site

Once you have examined all of the implications of creating a business website and you feel that the benefits outweigh the costs, then you should go about having one designed. It often pays to use a consultant to help you with this process. Although the services of a consultant will be anything from £1,000 to hundreds of thousands of pounds for a large business site, in the end the money is well spent. The consultant will show the business how to design a functional site that is attractive and which brings in lots of customers.

Most professional websites are now built using profession software, such as Macromedia Dreamweaver, which like FrontPage simplifies the task of programming.

As we have seen, basic websites can be built using standard software packages such as Microsoft FrontPage. If you want to put in more effects such as sound, video clips and animation then you will need professional design tools such as Director, Flash and Shockwave. It all depends on how much you are willing to pay to build the site.

UNIT ASSESSMENT

The assessment for this unit consists of four main areas:

1 Examine the websites of two businesses. You may want to look at one small business and one large business or two similar sized businesses. You may want to look at business sites in different sectors e.g. leisure and retailing. Alternatively you may compare the sites of two competing firms in the same sector. In each case you should evaluate whether they fulfil the purpose of an online presence. Which is the better website and why? What are the strengths and weaknesses of each of the sites?

2 Evaluate the website of one of the organisations and make recommendations as to how it can be improved. You may like to create your own matrix for evaluating the sites. The matrix could contain four elements – low and high opportunities plus low and high threats facing the e-business and its site.

3 Analyse the factors which would influence the use of the Internet by a business of your choice. What would be the benefits and drawbacks of engaging in e-commerce?

4 Plan and design a simple website. To score higher marks you will need to construct a website.

Some useful references for the assignment

Websites

Search for these websites at www.heinemann.co.uk/hotlinks (express code 1149P, then go to Unit 4).

amazon.com	Online book and record store.
bbc.co.uk	BBC website.
doubleclick.net	Provides tools for online advertising and marketing.
easyjet.com	easyJet.
google.com	Google search engine.
lastminute.com	Last minute travel/entertainment bookings.
marketing-online.co.uk	Provides Internet marketing training and consultancy.
moonfish.co.uk	Digital communications agency.
msn.com	An Internet Service Provider.
ryanair.com	Ryanair.
tt100.biz	Excellent case studies including those about e-commerce.
webdesign.about.com	Provides advice about website design and software.
webreference.com	Provides advice about website design and software.
websitesthatsuck.com	Provides advice about website design and software.
webtrends.com	Provides advice about website design and software.
unplug.com	Provides advice about website design and software.

Multimedia

Microsoft Word has web page design tutorials.
Macromedia Dreamweaver (specialist web design software).
Microsoft FrontPage (the Microsoft software for web design).

Other reading

Marketing Weekly
Computer Weekly
E-business Review
Net Profit
The Guardian Online Supplement

UNIT 5

Investigating customer service

This unit contains four parts:

5.1 The organisation and its customers

5.2 Effective customer service

5.3 Maintaining and improving customer service and keeping customers

5.4 Customer service legislation

Introduction

Customers are the most important people for any organisation. They are simply the natural resource upon which the success of any organisation depends. When thinking about the importance of customers it is useful to remember the following points:

* Repeat business is the backbone of selling. It helps to provide security and certainty.

* Organisations are dependent upon their customers. If they do not develop customer loyalty and satisfaction, they could lose their customers.

* Without customers organisations would simply not exist.

* The purpose of the organisation is to fulfil the needs of customers.

* The customer makes it possible for the business to achieve everything it aims for.

> *What you will learn in this unit*

* The importance of customers to an organisation

FIGURE 5.1 *Excellent customer service is essential*

* The difference between internal and external customers
* The needs and expectations of different customers
* What is involved in delivering effective customer service
* The skills necessary to deliver effective and efficient customer service
* How to maintain and improve customer service
* The importance of customer service legislation.

5.1 The organisation and its customers

It is easy to forget that just about every moment of a day you are a customer. If you do not sleep well it could be the fault of a bed that had been purchased. The toothpaste, shampoo and soap you use in the morning reflect the purchases made either by you or members of your family. If they do not perform in the way you would like, then you may buy other brands. Similarly your breakfast items have all been purchased, and you may become a customer again if you catch a bus to school or work.

As such a frequent customer you will, therefore, be faced with many different decisions every day and these decisions will be influenced by a number of factors. For example, if the person in the newspaper shop is not friendly in the mornings or is rude and abrupt, you may use a different shop. Similarly, if the bus is not cleaned properly or is always crowded, you may decide to make alternative travel arrangements.

It was management guru Peter Drucker who wrote 'there is only one valid definition of a business purpose – to create a customer'. Having created customers, the next step is to satisfy them: customer satisfaction has become very important to business in the early twenty-first century. A key reason for this change is oversupply. With the globalisation of markets, abundance has become chronic, with everything from motor cars to micro-chips. At the same time, today's customers are active participants in the world of change. They are also more demanding, reflected by the rise in disposable incomes fuelled by economic growth. Rising affluence and education have produced highly active consumers who increasingly want what is available in the marketplace to be tied to what they want.

Customer service has become increasingly important in a rapidly changing marketplace. In marketing terms, it is useful to think of customer service as part of the total product concept (see Figure 5.2). At a very basic level the core product is what a product does. For example, a lawn mower would be expected to cut grass. If that is all mowers did, they would all be nearly identical, but differentiation then begins to take place. In the tangible product, additional factors provide an organisation with competitive advantage such as extra features. At the third layer of the augmented product very special things start to happen. This layer goes beyond the product, offering something which although less tangible is just as important. In this layer there is something that goes beyond simply what the product offers, for example customer service or a brand image. This layer is fundamental in influencing the choices that consumers make, and for many organisations, as we will see, has become the base upon which

Learning activity

On the basis of your own experiences, provide two examples each of good customer service and poor customer service. In each instance, explain how these affected your repeat purchasing patterns.

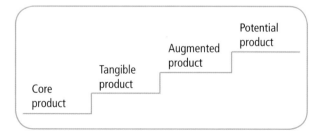

FIGURE 5.2 *The product concept*

CASE STUDY

Competing on the basis of customer service

It was in 1988 that Travis & Arnold and Sandell Perkins, two building merchant public companies, merged to create Travis Perkins. Sandell Perkins had origins stretching back to 1797. The business originally traded as joiners and carpenters but then moved to selling and trading in hardwoods before becoming a public company in 1986. Travis & Arnold was founded in 1899 by Ernest Travis in London. It then moved to Northampton where it sold timber and other wood products before diversifying into other building materials.

Today the Travis Perkins Group is one of the largest buildings materials distribution businesses. Throughout the Group, the business objective has not simply been to provide a high level of service and constantly strive to exceed customer expectations, but to use customer service to build a strong business that is able to provide a base for increasing the number of branches from its present level of 740 to 1,200 during the next six years. Travis Perkins uses customer service at the centre of its staff development programme to develop a culture that provides a foundation for growth. It shows how Travis Perkins has managed to balance the strategic objectives of the organisation with the service needs of its customers (see Figure 5.6).

At the heart of Travis Perkins' culture is the belief that the quality of service is more important than price. It is possible to get a feel for the culture of an organisation simply by looking around and talking to people working for it. In an industry dependent upon project planning and timings, people who buy materials from Travis Perkins want to pick up the right materials quickly so that they can get on with their projects. The Travis Perkins vision is to 'deliver a professional, high quality service that keeps us ahead of our competitors in our customers' eyes'. To achieve this vision and to turn this commitment towards customer service into practical actions, Travis Perkins have invested heavily in a process of training, development and performance monitoring.

It was not so long ago that the UK government published what become known as the Competitiveness White Paper, 'Our Competitive Future: Building the Knowledge Driven Economy'. The paper emphasised that in a modern and changing world, employees are the assets of the future that help organisations to develop 'a culture in the workplace that allows knowledge, creativity and commitment of the workforce to be fully exploited'. For Travis Perkins, the products and the locations do not in themselves meet customer needs, it is their employees and their understanding of how to help customers solve problems and deal with issues that makes the organisation distinct and provides a base of care so important for their continued competitiveness (see Figure 5.3).

1 From the dialogue above, what seem to be the business objectives of Travis Perkins?
2 How might an organisation in the buildings materials industry exceed customer expectations?
3 Explain how customer service would help Travis Perkins to compete more effectively than other organisations within their industry. Provide examples to support your answer.

FIGURE 5.3 *The contributions of employees are essential to meet the needs of customers*

they compete. Finally, the potential product covers aspects that may become part of the product offer for the future.

In a modern marketplace it is, therefore, clear that organisations cannot afford to compete simply on the basis of price or minor product modifications. Service differentiation helps organisations to achieve their business strategies better than many of their competitors. According to author Sarah Cook, 'Surveys suggest that service-driven companies can charge up to 9 per cent more for the products and services they provide. They grow twice as fast as the average company and have the potential to gain up to 6 per cent market share.'

Organisations are finding it more and more difficult to demonstrate product superiority or

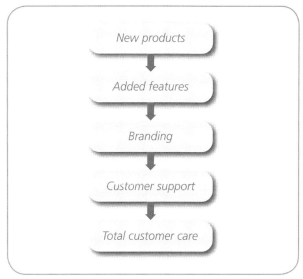

FIGURE 5.4 *The movement towards customer care*

CASE STUDY

How not to provide customer care!

This particular episode is based on the experience of a customer who was disappointed with the customer service provided by a major UK hardware chainstore.

'I had already selected my items and needed batteries. I went to the counter that sells batteries and waited for the staff member to finish a phone call before serving me. However, putting down the phone, he came out from behind the counter completely ignoring me and simply started chatting to another staff member and began to walk away!

'I then called after him asking him if I was invisible. He told me that he had been dealing with a customer. I told him that he had finished his phone call and that he had walked past me around the counter. He then told me that the counter wasn't open for sales service.

'I replied that he could have told me that, as I wanted batteries and that was the only place they were stocked in the store. Besides, the counter had a sales till as well.

'He then had the cheek to say that he didn't know that I had wanted to be served. I informed him that I was standing by the counter with credit card in my hand and

an arm full of products. Being a sales staff member he should have had enough hints. I then proceeded to place my items down (worth around £40 in total) and told him not to bother serving me as he obviously had ignored me in the beginning and was coming up with various lies as to why he hadn't served me.

'He then had the audacity to tell me that I was out of order and was angry for nothing. I replied that I was angry because I was waiting to be served and that he, as a staff member, had quite blatantly ignored me. I then asked him to call the manager as I wanted to make a formal complaint and – can you believe this? – he refused to call the manager and continued arguing with me until I walked out of the doors and only then got onto the phone!'

1 Why was the customer service poor in this instance?
2 How should the assistant have dealt with the problem?
3 Discuss how this might influence the customer's actions when shopping for hardware goods again.

even product differentiation over competitors (though they are constantly trying and often succeed). Customer service is an area that offers almost endless opportunities for developing product superiority.

The ideal relationship is one where the customer feels that he or she is receiving the desired quality and good customer care.

Consumers know what they mean by desired quality and the marketer needs to find this out and translate the concept into required goods and services. Desired quality does not necessarily mean the most expensive – it means a solution that best meets a customer's need. For example, in Japan a chain of 'capsule hotels' has been set up for business people in major cities. Each room is only just large enough for a person to lie down and watch TV. However, they are popular because they are 'fit for purpose' in that they meet the needs of busy business people. In contrast, other people (including the author!) prefer to hire spacious penthouse suites in large hotels. The job of marketing is to identify how different market segments perceive quality and then to deliver a marketing mix that provides it.

It can be argued that consumers become aware of products rather than service in the early days. The product itself is at that time 'king'. However, as competition arrives, companies have to differentiate to maintain their market position through added features and branding. As markets develop, products become technically much more similar. As this happens, customer service becomes more important. Initially this involves keeping the product working or providing customers with support, but eventually it moves into customer care, the aim of which is to make sure that the benefits the customer receives are delivered reliably from the time the customer approaches the supplier.

The impact of new and old customers on the organisation

It has been estimated that it costs five times as much to attract a new customer as it does to retain an old one. Common sense dictates, therefore, that an organisation will gain more value from working to retain existing customers than looking for new customers.

Customers are simply the natural resource upon which the success of any organisation depends. When thinking about the importance of customers it is useful to remember the following points:

* Repeat business is at the backbone of selling. It helps to provide security and certainty.

* Organisations are dependent upon their customers. If they do not develop customer loyalty and satisfaction they could lose their customers.

* Without customers the organisation would simply not exist.

* The purpose of the organisation is to fulfil the needs of customers.

* The customer makes it possible for the business to achieve everything it aims for.

According to Sarah Cook in her book *Customer Care*, customer relationships can be depicted in terms of a loyalty ladder (see Figure 5.5). The willingness of individual customers to ascend the loyalty ladder will depend upon how they are treated when doing business with the organisation. Well-targeted sales methods and efficient personal service will help to convert one-off purchasers to occasional users, then to regular customers and advocates. Advocates will be very important as these will be the people

Learning activity

To what products or services are you loyal? Explain why you are loyal to those products and services.

* DID YOU KNOW?

According to the insurance industry, customer service is a significant differentiating factor in the service-orientated marketplace. Research within the industry has indicated that firms that provide first-class customer service are more successful at retaining and attracting loyal, profitable customers.

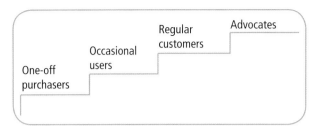

FIGURE 5.5 *The loyalty ladder*

who recommend goods and services from one organisation to all of their friends and colleagues.

In developing a relationship with its customers, an organisation must concentrate on both the selling process and how the relationship between the buyer and seller is managed. This is part of what is widely known as relationship marketing, where an organisation has to develop all of its activities in ways that take into account how they may affect its relationships with customers. Examples are order times, reputation, the changing of goods or providing of refunds, dealing with faults, correctly addressing letters and the overall efficiency of operations.

When developing suitable ways of meeting the needs of their customers, organisations have to balance their own objectives against the needs of customers (see Figure 5.6). To be able to do this, they need to understand how customers view

FIGURE 5.6 *Balancing the organisation's objectives with the needs of customers*

their organisation as well as what their customers want from their organisation.

The starting point in providing customers with appropriate customer service is to identify potential customers and their expectations by listening to their views. The organisation can then develop suitable service procedures to satisfy their needs. For example, they need to find out:

＊ what customers want

＊ how important this is for them

＊ why they need to have it

＊ how to provide it in the best possible way.

Roderick M. McNealy, in his book *Making Satisfaction Happen*, refers to the 'Making Customer Satisfaction Happen' model (Figure 5.7). This, he claims, is a continuous circular process that provides an equation for satisfying customer needs that can then be used as part of an organisation's strategic approach to business.

Customer service is thus associated with developing bonds with customers in order to create long-term relationships that lead to advantages for all groups.

Avis, the car-hire company, have a customer care balance sheet that takes into account business they may be losing from both customers who complain and from those who are dissatisfied but who do not bother to complain (see Figure 5.8). This emphasises the need to listen to customers and shows the annual sales lost from customers whose needs have not been met.

So, what do customers want and how can their expectations be satisfied by the different services and selling methods provided by an organisation? Customers may require the following:

＊ *Quick and easy purchasing procedures.* For example, it is important customers understand purchasing procedures. At the same time customers may wish to sample products, see how they function or ask for specialist help.

＊ *Clear and accurate information.* This may refer to products or purchasing procedures, and may influence the final decision. In particular, consumers may wish for advice that helps them weigh up a range of alternatives.

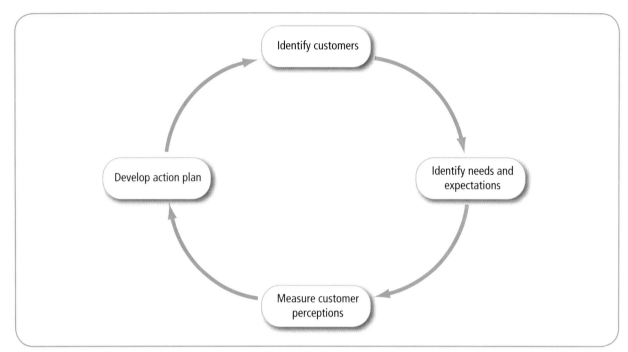

FIGURE 5.7 *The Making Customer Satisfaction Happen model*

FIGURE 5.8 *Customer care balance sheet*

✳ *Clear refund procedure.* Consumers are much happier to commit themselves to a purchase when they know that, if the product does not match up to expectations, is damaged or does not perform to its advertised functions, they can bring it back easily for a refund. Many supermarkets have a refund desk at their entrance, and some large organisations, such as Marks & Spencer, have a good reputation for dealing with returns.

✳ *Easy exchange of goods.* Similarly, exchanging goods if they are not suitable helps to provide a service that closely meets the needs of customers.

✳ *Complaints procedure.* There is nothing worse than customers having their complaints passed around from person to person and department to department. This creates a bad impression of the organisation, wastes time and may cause a lot of personal anguish. An efficient customer complaints procedure may help to retain business that might otherwise be lost if the complaint is handled inefficiently.

✳ *Special services to meet special needs.* Different groups of customers may have different needs. For example, how many stores can cope with wheelchair access or parents with

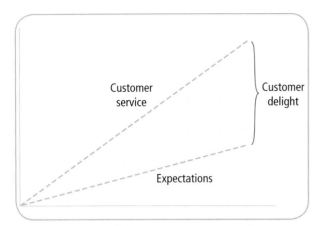

FIGURE 5.9 *Exceeding customer expectations*

Learning activity

Working in groups, decide what procedures a large retailer of computers should put into place to ensure customers are happy with the service provided.

young children in buggies? Similarly, will organisations provide specialist help or a wide range of services for their customers? Does free delivery extend outside the boundaries of a local town? What credit facilities will an organisation provide? Do the opening hours meet the needs of all customers? Does the product range provide enough specialist products for all types of consumers? Is there a customer helpline and do customers know about it? Is the organisation willing to order products on behalf of customers?

Building a one-to-one relationship with customers is always ideal. Organisations selling products that must be mass-produced tend to use two main techniques to help build relationships with specific groups of customers:

1 Market segmentation, as we see later, involves producing and presenting different products to suit different groups of customers. For example, a multiplex cinema shows a wide range of films for many different customer groups or segments, such as those for younger children, teenagers, families, twenty-somethings, and older people, all of them comprising different groups of customers – although some may enjoy more than one type of film.

2 The second technique used by organisations aiming to achieve a one-to-one relationship with customers is through the provision of customer service. In one sense, customer service is the overall objective of all that a company does, but the term can be used more precisely to describe a personal relationship between the customer and the organisation and more particularly between the customer and the people who represent the organisation. For example, it would include how the customer is treated by sales staff on the telephone and in the shop, the way in which complaints and queries are handled, and the use of ICT to communicate.

In her influential 1992 book *The Popcorn Report*, the American guru Faith Popcorn charts the rise of consumer bonding or relationship marketing. The principles that she identifies are encapsulated in the following sentence:

'We do need to build relationships with our consumers, to create a dialogue, expose them to our corporate values, establish a bond based on something more deep-seated than product quality, brand image, or even simply meeting consumer needs.'

The American writers Don Peppers and Martha Rogers urge organisations to form impregnable relationships with individual customers, and they provide a range of examples of ways in which even mass marketers can strike up relationships. This involves gathering as much information as possible about individual customers and then developing the organisation to meet individual needs. They refer to this as customer segmentation.

Peppers and Rogers give the following example of gift order catalogues to illustrate their point:

* The customer may order gifts for friends and relatives many months in advance

✳ The supplier then schedules the delivery of gifts on the right days

✳ The customer would be charged for each gift two days before delivery

✳ The customer would receive a reminder postcard ten days before each gift is sent

✳ When the annual catalogue is sent to the customer, they would receive a reminder form of last year's gifts and addresses.

Although the authors acknowledge that the product must remain important, they identify the change in focus from high-quality products towards high-quality relationships.

Internal and external customers

All organisations have both internal and external customers (see Figure 5.10). The belief is that the quality of customer service provided outside the organisation is dependent upon how well employees within the organisation treat each other. For example, if an employee makes an enquiry to personnel or requests some stationery, he or she should expect to be treated with the same respect as a customer outside the organisation. This approach helps to encourage teamwork and customer care, which leads towards total quality management.

Internal customers within an organisation would include all colleagues, ranging from support roles such as delivering post within the organisation, to jobs at the top of the organisation. For example, if a senior manager is dictatorial and treats his subordinates badly, creating a stressful situation for them, they may well pass on this stress to other colleagues. The internal customer would include everybody, irrespective of the department they worked for and may also include contracted staff such as electricians.

External customers may include individuals from different organisations working in business-to-business markets (B2B) as well as individual customers. B2B customers may include overseas clients whose culture and background need to be respected. For example, they may have a particular way in which they expect to do business, so it is important that their cultural differences are taken into account as well as linguistic differences and different types of legal systems. Customers in international markets may reflect different purchasing habits and trade according to different rules and procedures which may be difficult to understand.

It is also important to understand individual external customers. For example, a customer's age might reflect the sort of services they associate with the product. It is also important to respect a customer's different culture and all of the other factors that might affect or influence their behaviour, so that it is possible to match the products or services on offer with their individual

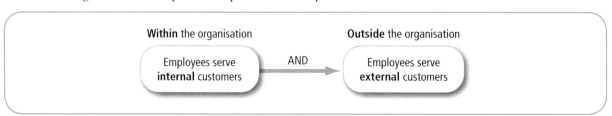

FIGURE 5.10 *Internal and external customers*

motivations. In Unit 3, we looked at consumer behaviour and this understanding of such behaviour helps individuals within a company respond in an appropriate way to their external customers.

Many UK companies try to explain the concept of the internal and external customer by referring to the link which starts with the needs of external customers and then includes all of the people involved in bringing together resources to satisfy such needs. Everyone has a role in satisfying customers. This process helps to emphasise that all employees within an organisation are part of a quality chain which is improved with better teamwork, training, employee care and communications procedures.

Though the concept of the internal and external customer is widely used, it has been criticised for focusing an organisation's efforts internally upon itself instead of spending more time and attention using resources to satisfy the needs and expectations of external customers.

The needs of different customers

A key element in meeting the needs of different customers is to make some attempt to understand their behaviour. It is important to provide customer service that helps consumers satisfy their needs both today and in the future. This may depend both upon where and how they live, as well as their own personal circumstances. For example:

❋ *Routine response behaviour.* This describes what happens when customers frequently buy items of low value that require little thought. For example, consumers might go into the newsagent to buy a newspaper, where it is important the product offered in the shop and the service provided meets the needs of the customer.

❋ *Limited decision-making.* Some thought might be necessary if an unfamiliar brand comes to the market. For example, if a new chocolate brand is launched in competition with a well-known brand, the consumer might try to find out more information before making a purchase.

Customer service would involve providing the appropriate information.

❋ *Extensive decision-making.* Some products are durables purchased less frequently. The buyer will need to think about the benefits of different products, will require further information and may need extensive help and support before coming to a decision.

One important factor in understanding buyers' needs so that appropriate customer service can be provided are demographic characteristics. These may include features such as class or status, occupation, age, gender, race, education, culture, nationality, religion and family size. Demographic factors may influence purchasing decisions or form the basis for marketers to target specific groups of consumers with a range of benefits, many of which may involve elements of customer service. The study of demography also involves examining the characteristics of people who live in certain areas.

As people move through their lives their needs change, so their buying behaviour and lifestyle changes as well. Many models have been put forward to describe these changes, but each recognises a familiar pattern.

For example:

❋ Young people, up to the age where they settle down with a partner, now have significantly more spending power than ever before and, since they have no commitments other than to please themselves, they spend money freely on such things as holidays, entertainment and eating out.

❋ Those in their twenties and thirties are setting up home, buying cars and having children, so this is the period when they borrow the most money.

❋ Middle-aged people repay the debts incurred in previous years and start to put money aside for retirement.

❋ Older people draw on their savings or pensions and spend.

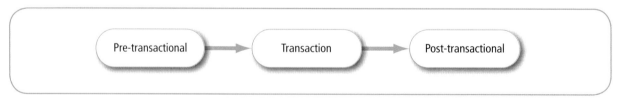

Describe two elements of customer service that you would include in each of the following instances:

* Selling an upmarket car to an aspiring couple in their thirties.

* Offering adventure holidays for 16–24-year-olds.

* Providing financial services to individuals from different ethnic cultures.

Organisations looking to provide good customer service need to understand lifestyle changes and will seek to understand the needs and aspirations of their customers so that appropriate customer services can be matched to their expectations.

Pre-transactional, transactional and post-transactional stages

Customer service is something that does not just happen. It is a process that has to be built and developed across the relationships that an organisation has with the customer. It means creating expectations before the transaction takes place, building customer service into the transaction process and then dealing with post-transactional support.

It is therefore a process that involves pre-transaction, transaction and post-transaction considerations. Emphasis upon customer service will change from one product to another. For example, when planning customer service before a transaction it is important to understand the motives of customers so that it is possible to respond to their precise needs. Knowledge of competitors and their products enables an organisation to create expectations that help to show how their products are differentiated from those of their competitors.

During the transaction it is important that customer service helps to relate the product or service to the needs of the customer. There may be many queries during the transaction that will need to be dealt with. It is also important to use this time as an opportunity to deal with any misunderstandings, making sure that the product or service relates to customer expectations. It is always important to use customer service to follow up a sale. Promises that might have been made during the transaction need to be met. If the product or service involves a guarantee by a certain date, then the date must be held. It is also important to contact individuals to check that they are happy with the product and service, and then use this feedback for future customer service transactions.

An organisation might choose to include post-sale surveys in its customer care programme as a means of identifying the levels of customer satisfaction experienced by customers who have recently purchased items. These may be sent home to purchasers shortly after purchase, although some retailers might hand them out before a customer leaves a store. Others may conduct a telephone survey.

A typical post-transaction survey might cover the following:

1 How did the sales staff deal with the customer as he or she made the buying decisions? This might include:

* where the product or service was bought

* whether the literature was suitable and informative

* staff telephone manner

* whether the customer was offered a demonstration of the product

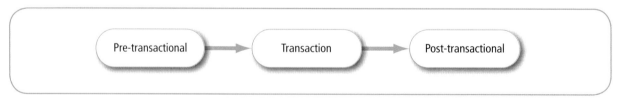

FIGURE 5.11 *Customer service has to be built into all aspects of an organisation's relationship with the customer*

CASE STUDY

United Airlines

Customer service is increasingly important within a changing marketplace, and particularly important for airlines for whom service is at the heart of the choice made by customers, as well as a key base upon which airlines compete. It is not something that just happens. It involves pre-transaction considerations, the processes designed to satisfy customer needs, as well as post-transaction considerations so that as customers finish their journey they become advocates. United Airlines have:

* Developed a route structure spanning five continents and offering the most non-stop flights from the Pacific Rim to the US.
* Set standards for comfort and safety of its fleet, and with an average age of just eight years have one of the youngest fleets of aircraft in the industry.
* Developed the Star Alliance Network bringing together 14 carriers who offer services to over 700 airports in more than 120 countries.
* Further developed and invested in its airport lounges.
* Created the Red Carpet Club providing members with access to over 40 facilities worldwide.
* Offered First and Business customers the use of an arrivals suite with the opportunity to shower, enjoy a continental breakfast and make use of business services.

In a technologically-based industry, actively using technology to move forward is fundamental in countering adverse environmental forces. For example, United's E-Ticket service has simplified check-in procedures. Changes in computer hardware have enabled United to provide large-screen electronic display systems as well as gate readers and baggage scanners to improve the tracking of luggage. United recently received the highest ranking among airlines for their effective use of the Internet and behind the scenes there are flight information systems and other software systems designed to provide up-to-date information for customers.

At the heart of United's operations in this difficult business environment is market orientation. United Airlines' Chief Executive believes that even when times are difficult and the leasing of aeroplanes and manpower may be reduced, marketing activities should not be cut. For United Airlines this means that marketing helps to sustain, maintain and, in the medium- to longer-term, develop customers' perceptions and thoughts about the business by developing a series of brand values that keep the brand of United Airlines moving forward.

1 **How important is it for United Airlines to be market-focused?**
2 **Discuss how their procedures influence transactions with First and Business customers.**

---

* the appearance of staff
* the quality and clarity of the explanations given by sales staff
* how well the sales staff understood the customer's requirements.

2 Delivery details might include:

* was the product available from stock or was there a delay before delivery?
* was the customer informed of any guarantees?

* was the customer told how to access after-sales service?
* was the product in good condition when received?
* was delivery on time and as agreed?
* was the delivery time acceptable to the customer?

3 The retail outlet, which might include:

FIGURE 5.12 *Customer surveys are part of customer care*

* whether the location of the outlet was convenient
* the quality of the parking facilities
* the convenience of the opening hours
* the appearance of the outlet – tidiness and cleanliness.

4 The customer's overall level of satisfaction, probably rated on a scale.

5 Recommendations – whether the customer would be prepared to recommend the product or company to friends.

6 Suggestions opportunities – an opportunity for the customer to make suggestions as to how the buying process could have been improved.

Of course, post-transaction there is no guarantee that customers will complete a questionnaire, but it is possible to improve the completion rate by making it straightforward to use.

In manufacturing industries for goods such as bread or shampoo, customer service may involve developing strong customer relationships with many of the large retailers. In a pure service industry, such as hairdressing or insurance, there are no tangible goods, and so final customers will view nearly all the benefits they get on the basis of the service they receive.

Customer expectations

According to Sally Dibb et al (1994), 'Customer satisfaction with a purchase depends on the product's performance relative to a buyer's expectations.' This emphasises that, depending upon the product or service being offered, customer satisfaction will vary, with the product either meeting and exceeding expectations providing them with 'delight', or falling short of expectations and providing dissatisfaction and disappointment.

Customer expectations are complex interpretations of what is offered within a marketplace. Sometimes they are based upon past experiences or the recommendations of a friend. For example, if you have been really happy with a meal from a restaurant, when you go back there again, you expect the same level of cuisine or service. Contented and happy customers will also be prepared to pay more when they are happy with a product.

Customer expecations will influence the degree of customer service that will be provided. The Lexus case study illustrates that when customers

CASE STUDY

Customer comments

Some pubs and restaurants ask customers to fill in a questionnaire like the one below:

Welcome to Ploughman Pubs

Please take a few minutes to answer the following questions. Your views are important to us, and we will take note of your comments.

1. How often do you eat out?

☐ Once a week or more   ☐ Once a fortnight

☐ Once a month   ☐ Once every 2–3 months   ☐ Less often

2. Have you eaten here before?

☐ Once   ☐ Every week   ☐ Every 1–2 months

☐ Once or twice a year   ☐ Less often   ☐ Never

3. Would you come here again?

☐ Yes   ☐ No

If not why not?

4. Using the scale of 1 to 10, where 10 is excellent and 1 is poor, please rate the following by circling the appropriate number

Quality of the food	1 2 3 4 5 6 7 8 9 10
Value for money	1 2 3 4 5 6 7 8 9 10
Service	1 2 3 4 5 6 7 8 9 10
Surroundings	1 2 3 4 5 6 7 8 9 10
Toilets	1 2 3 4 5 6 7 8 9 10
Overall experience	1 2 3 4 5 6 7 8 9 10

5. Please add any other comments or suggestions that you would like to make:

FIGURE 5.13 *Ploughman Pubs questionnaire*

1 What is the purpose of a questionnaire such as this one?
2 How might this information be used?

FIGURE 5.14 *Customer dissatisfaction and customer delight*

make high-value purchases of complex or expensive products, customer service is part of the product itself and is an essential accompaniment to the whole process. On the other hand, when buying a low-price product such as potatoes or a bar of soap, the customer service is not necessarily from the manufacturer but from the retailer instead. The customer might opt for a low-price budget retailer with fewer customer services such as Aldi or Netto or alternatively decide that customer service is more important than price and buy from somewhere like Waitrose.

> **✱ DID YOU KNOW?**
>
> Mercedes offer customers the opportunity to collect their new car from their factory in Germany for a low and subsidised price.

CASE STUDY

A new customer experience

For the motor industry, Lexus is a relatively young company designed to provide upmarket motor cars from a Toyota background. The following dialogue is taken from the Lexus website:

At Lexus we believe what makes owning a Lexus special, unique even, is the way we treat our customers, which is why, from the company's US launch in 1989, we have put customers at the very centre of our thinking.

For the first ever model, the LS400, the engineering challenge was for it to drive as well at 80,000 miles as it did at new, recognising the demand for greater quality and reliability. It also offered complete specification, from leather interior to climate control and hi-fi quality audio, making extras obsolete and great value standard.

We also realised that customer satisfaction was about having the right people as well as the right cars. Since 1998 we have been building a totally new network of Lexus Centres across the country, run by teams committed to improving and redefining the luxury car experience. Our growing network of showrooms has been designed from the customers' viewpoint – in look and feel,

convenience and ease of access. The result is a contemporary luxury environment that encourages customers to feel at home, to relax, browse and enjoy themselves.

For the third year in a row Lexus's pre-eminent position as Britain's best-respected car manufacturer has been reinforced with the ultimate prize in the 2004 Top Gear Survey. Its success in being named the highest ranking manufacturer is all the more notable as this survey is the largest yet to have been conducted in the UK. It attracted more than 52,000 responses from readers of Top Gear Magazine and its associated website, and viewers of the BBC's Top Gear TV programme.

The Lexus IS200 scored 93.1 out of 100 and was ranked third out of the 142 listed models in the survey.

(Lexus 2004)

1 How important was it for Lexus to establish an upmarket image?
2 To what extent does customer service become a product itself when providing high-value motor cars?
3 In what way does the provision of customer service provide Lexus with a strategic opportunity to position itself within the motor marketplace?

5.2 Effective customer service

At the heart of developing good customer service is the process of communication. It is very difficult for service to happen at all without any form of communication and it is this process of communication that provides the basis for people to evaluate what an organisation and its people represents.

For example, the visual elements come into play the moment a customer looks at anything associated with an organisation. At a very basic level it might simply include how the building that the organisation operates from looks, but may include the appearance of staff, advertisements, any printed materials or anything that might influence how the customer perceives the organisation.

Verbal elements of customer service are also important. It is vital that staff have good interpersonal skills and know how to deal with customers in an appropriate way. Training is clearly important in helping to equip staff to deal with customers. The verbal element may also include meetings or any form of discussion with either internal or external customers.

There are many different forms of written communication. Letters and e-mails are an important communication medium for providing good customer service, as are newsletters or customer-focused magazines. Again, they help to form an appopriate impression of the organisation, based upon how they are presented.

It is easy to forget that behaviour is an important and vital part of the customer service process. It has been said that training is an essential part of any customer service provision. Although the degree of training may depend upon the priorities of a business organisation, it is generally accepted that training in service quality is not just about developing a customer care philosophy but about providing employees with the specific skills and attitude to deal with customer service issues.

It must be remembered that any form of training aids an employee's personal and professional development as part of his or her career. Once training has taken place, an organisation needs to record each employee's training achievements and use this as a basis for ongoing training and development.

Staff

Front line staff are often the people who have the greatest exposure to external customers. From the moment a customer enters the building, they will have expectations about how they should be dealt with and their thoughts will be influenced by the standard of service that they receive.

The appearance of staff is particularly important in creating the right first impressions of an organisation. If staff are scruffily dressed or are neither tidy nor clean, it will communicate such values about the organisation itself. Clearly the appearance of staff will depend upon the sort of organisation that the customer enters. Many people associate appearance with the values that an organisation represents. They might associate smart appearance with efficiency and professionalism. For example:

✳ Most schools expect their male teachers to wear ties. In some schools, particularly those concerned about their image, male staff are

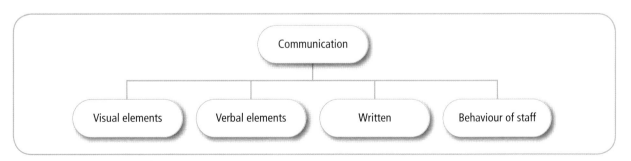

FIGURE 5.15 *Processes of communication*

The following is a quote from a website discussing the school uniform at Gordon Boys' School:

> For Sunday parades, church and other special occasions all boys, whatever their age, dressed in the traditional Gordon Boys' School uniform. This consisted of a Glengarry cap with the Gordon brass cap badge, a dark blue tunic with gold braid epaulettes and brass Gordon School buttons, the tartan trews and army style hobnailed boots.

> Whenever we left the school grounds, for example on Saturdays to spend our pocket money at the local shops, or when travelling home at the end of term, we had to wear this Gordon's School formal uniform. Needless to say, our boots were expected to be highly polished, trews neatly creased and brass cap badge and buttons gleaming. It was a smart uniform and we often drew admiring glances from young girls – as well as matronly women!

Discuss whether you are influenced by the uniforms worn by others. What does the wearing of a uniform signify?

Working in groups, discuss the appearance of staff you have encountered during the last few days. How has the appearance of such staff influenced you as a customer? Were there instances when their smart appearance hid an inefficient service?

asked to wear suits and female staff are not allowed to wear trousers.

* In most banks staff are usually smartly dressed in dark uniforms.

* In a butchery department of a large supermarket, it would be expected that staff not only need to wear suitable white coats, but that clothing also be regularly cleaned and meet health and hygiene regulations.

* At a railway station, staff are expected to wear uniforms which help them to be recognised so they can provide suitable customer service for passengers.

On the other hand it could be argued that smart appearance is rather superficial and that associating staff dress with efficiency is not an appropriate thing to do.

Prompt service and helpfulness is also important when dealing with customers. We can probably all think of situations where we had to wait in queues when we have returned goods to shops, or had been angered by employees who

have ignored or not listened to customers. The author was in a pub of a national chain recently. After he had waited nearly ten minutes to be served, and exasperated by the wait and the delay, the member of bar staff closest to him suddenly stopped serving despite the queue and went out of the bar. The author has not been into a pub in that chain since!

When dealing with customers, staff should not:

* turn away from the customer

* leave the customer without any form of explanation

* be rude to the customer

* talk to other staff and ignore the customer

* imply that the customer is wrong or stupid

* criticise the customer or attempt to argue with them

* treat the customer dismissively

* fail to believe the customer or treat them seriously

* make the customer feel guilty

* shout at the customer

* tell the customer that they are wasting their time

* leave the customer dissatisfied.

These points may sound a bit like stating the obvious, but they are very important. Providing customer service is not easy, and it does require the right approach based upon meeting customer expectations. It is imperative that those involved in customer service have the right personal qualities.

So, what should staff do and how should staff treat customers? It is important that they:

Working in pairs, develop a scenario between a dissatisfied customer and an employee. The customer has bought a watch which does not work. He or she has also noticed that it is damaged. The packaging had been opened beforehand and he or she is convinced that you have sold a product that had been returned from a previous customer. Try to show within your scenario how important it is for those providing customer service to have the right personal qualities.

* are well trained in customer care procedures and know how to deal with customers and the issues that arise from dealing with customers

* have a range of good interpersonal skills that enable them to handle people and situations

* understand the organisation they are working for as well as its procedures and policies

* also have a good understanding of the products and services on offer from their organisation

* are experienced in dealing with customer complaints

* know how to manage what might be potentially stressful situations

* are able to make decisions and contact the right people in response to complaints from customers

* are able to diffuse stressful situations and deal with difficult customers

* do not get stressed themselves

* are able to provide customers with appropriate and informed feedback

* are able to make apologies to customers where required.

One important element of customer service is accurate and reliable information. There could be

FIGURE 5.16 *Accurate information is essential*

A number of 'reality' TV programmes such as *Airport* show how difficult it is for staff to provide good customer service. Discuss the well-used cliché 'the customer is always right'.

Discuss how members of a customer service team might learn from each other.

nothing more frustrating, for example, than to be told that a train will leave the station at 11.35 am and then to arrive to find out that there is no 11.35 am train – or that it left at 11.30 am! Similarly, if you are told that as part of a service you are going to receive something, then it would be frustrating to find out that you are not entitled to it.

Accurate and reliable information informs customer expectations and creates a certainty that gives customers confidence in what they receive. It is part of the service they expect. On the other hand, inaccurate information confuses their expectations, and makes the customer less certain or confident in the organisation.

Many organisations now work within flatter structures so that they can respond more closely to changing customer service requirements. For many of these organisations the operation of teams has become an important customer service tool. In a customer service environment a team is a group of people who work together and who have clear, agreed and shared objectives, coupled with an effective communication system. Where teams are successful they may contribute to improved customer service and higher levels of customer satisfaction.

It was Meredith Belbin, a leading expert in the field of team building, who identified a number of characteristics that different individuals can contribute to teams. He felt that although individuals contribute in a number of areas, their particular strengths lie in specific areas. The contribution that individuals make to teams relate to leadership, providing ideas, resolving conflicts, gathering and analysing information, developing relationships and carrying out procedural work. In the area of customer service this might lead to:

* innovative and creative ideas for meeting customer service requirements

* drawing out the contributions from quieter members of the team who may be intelligent thinkers

* making sure that the fine details of customer service are carried out.

Premises

It is easy for customers to make value judgements based upon how premises look or how they are arranged. A key objective for an organisation is to use its physical resources in a way that helps to meet the overall business objectives of the organisation.

Layout of resources is particularly important. In order to provide and improve customer service many organisations have changed their methods of dealing with customers in recent years to make their premises more focused upon meeting customer needs. For example, banks aim to increase throughput of customers via the various methods they use for automating transactions. Some banks have dedicated assistants for particular types of services such as foreign exchange, mortgage advice and so on. Their premises have been adapted to focus upon meeting the needs of customers more efficiently.

Working in groups, imagine that you are the manager of a main Post Office in a large town. You have ten full-time staff and fifteen counter positions. At peak periods, particularly lunchtimes, queue times invariably exceed 20 minutes, and you are not meeting your customer service objectives. Think about how you might change the layout of the post office in order to meet your customer service objectives.

FIGURE 5.17 *Customer service in a post office*

Tidiness is another factor that may influence the quality of customer service being provided. From the moment the customer enters the premises they will be making judgements about the organisation. If the premises are badly decorated and look untidy, they may question whether this is the sort of organisation with which they wish to do business. We can probably all think of examples of untidy or scruffy organisations, and it is probable that we might link our perceptions of their premises with their levels of efficiency.

Premises must also be accessible. If it is difficult to locate the premises or they are located in an area that may be inconvenient for a customer to visit, then this may influence the choices that customers make. There are clearly different criteria about locating each type of business organisation and there are some significant criteria. For example, to provide good customer service a sandwich bar would have to be located in a city centre, whereas an envelope manufacturer would be located in the suburbs where accessibility to good transport links would be paramount.

Demographic data will help to provide information about the best location for customer-focused organisations. Some business organisations undertake a pedestrian or traffic count in order to choose a good location. Visibility and signage may also create appropriate impressions of an organisation and may be important so that customers know that the business is there. Another factor associated with premises and their accessibility is access to parking and other facilities for customers.

It is very irritating for an organisation to offer various resources within its catalogues and then for the customer to turn up to find that it does not have such items in stock. Stocks are a resource that flow into and out of a business organisation. It is the stock inventory system and how it is managed that ensures that balances of goods are kept in order to meet customer requirements over a period of time.

FIGURE 5.18 *Modern communications have transformed offices*

Using customer service to provide a competitive edge

Within an increasing number of industries, the provision of customer service is there to provide organisations with a competitive edge. In other words, the quality of service provides the base upon which they compete. In the past, many of these organisations would have competed on the basis of different product features or price, but as competition has developed customer service has become the key differentiator. So what has using customer service as a base for competitive activity provided for the customer?

In order to compete on the basis of customer service, organisations have had to provide high-quality products and services. The customer care element associated with these products and services is, as we have seen, an important part of the product itself as it not only adds value to the product but also adds value in a way that makes the product more competitive. A product and its accompanying services can provide a higher level of satisfaction designed to make the customer more of an advocate in the future.

Methods of written communication

Written communications serve to provide an image of an organisation. In many instances written communications are the main methods for communicating and keeping in contact with both internal and external customers. For example, a mail order business would keep in touch with their customers through the catalogues they supply, and all of the follow up documentation they provide.

Internal communication is communication that takes place within an organisation, while external communication takes place between the organisation and the outside world. Both internal and external communications change from time to time, particularly in recent years where digitisation and developments in information and communications technology have transformed the ways in which groups of employees (internal customers) and external customers communicate.

Internal written communications

Examples of internal written communications might include:

* Memoranda – the increasing use of e-mail makes the sending of memos almost obsolete. When used they are usually an informal way of communicating, frequently in conversational English.

* Reports – written reports are a key feature of organisational life. They may have a title page (subject matter, name and position of writer, date, etc.), contents page, terms of reference (explaining the reason for the report), procedure (how the task was completed), findings and conclusions or recommendations.

* Notice boards – a useful way of communicating to groups of staff.

* House magazines – a form of internal publicity or public relations, providing positive perceptions about what is happening within the organisations.

* Telephone message pads – provide useful information for colleagues and make sure that all calls are directed and receive a response.

* E-mail – faster than all other forms of mail, e-mails can reduce paper usage.

* Intranet – internal web-sites within an organisation, providing employees with access to a wealth of information and associated electronic services. These are increasingly the first area that employees use to access information and support.

* Other house literature such as magazines and brochures.

External written communications

Examples of external written communications might include:

* Letters – a well-written business letter conveys a message and goodwill. It also provides a permanent record of the message to which both parties can refer. The style and layout will vary from organisation to organisation and it

Look at each of the rules for using e-mail below and prioritise them in terms of importance, labelling the most important rule as number 1 and the least important as number 14.

* answer e-mails quickly

* do not attach unnecessary files

* do not be too personal

* use proper spelling and punctuation

* add disclaimers to the e-mails

* do not label them as 'urgent' unless they really are

* read the e-mail before sending it

* do not recall a message

* do not send confidential e-mails

* avoid long sentences

* do not forward viruses or chain letters

* use a sensible structure and layout

* do not write in capitals

* do not copy and attach information without permission

is important that the letter helps to provide positive values about the organisation and its customer service.

* E-mails

* Logos, signage and branded literature – each of these helps to provide some form of impression of an organisation. They are particularly important in helping customers to position the organisation in their minds.

* Brochures – many individuals receive brochures through the post and order goods by mail order. Brochures are often the main point of contact with customers and so are important in setting out their expectations.

* Faxes – a good way of communicating and responding with detailed information.

* Websites – increasingly websites have become a much more important way of communicating with external customers.

* Corporate videos and DVDs – many organisations supply customers with information videos and DVDs.

* Tickets – straightforward though these sound, they do help to communicate a series of values.

* Timetables – for a range of companies and organisations these are an invaluable guide to services on offer.

It is important that a high standard of care is taken with all forms of written communication as it is a very important form of customer service. For example, a customer may be impressed by the staff they meet from an organisation, but they may change their mind if they feel that the written communications are poor and convey a bad image.

Face-to-face communications

When dealing with customers face-to-face, employees will use a combination of both verbal and non-verbal communications.

Verbal communications require speaking in a way that is acceptable to customers. Although many people have regional accents, these are not generally considered to be a strong barrier to communication as long as the person speaks clearly and is aware that elements of their accent might be difficult to understand. The voice is a powerful medium and there may be a range of circumstances in which the tone of the voice as well as the emphasis and expression help to communicate information.

Comment upon your reaction to each of the following situations:

* A receptionist using bad language in front of customers.

* A shop assistant refuses to listen to you and simply wants to sell you a particular item.

* A customer service assistant at an airport fails to give you vital information about your flight.

Face-to-face communication skills accompany a variety of other very personal qualities that are necessary for customer service activities. For example, how an employee looks and their personal hygiene will reflect both the organisation as well as their general attitude and behaviour in a situation when they have to deal with customers.

It is important that:

* information is delivered clearly and with precision
* the use of slang or very technical terms, or jargon, is avoided
* the customer is listened to. Listening skills in a face-to-face context are just as important as verbal skills
* appropriate body language is used to accompany the verbal skills
* customers are not ignored while conversation takes place with other employees
* employees have a good understanding of procedures and practices.

Non-verbal communications involve communications based upon body language. Body language is a visual form of communication that may convey a host of information about you and may be interpreted in a variety of different ways by customers. It is important that when working in a customer service environment individuals are careful about how they represent themselves through their body language. A range of studies have shown that only 7% of a message is verbally transmitted, whilst 93% of the message comes from non-verbal cues, which makes body language an extremely important part of customer service.

Body language is said to be the oldest language of all. For example, if we said to someone 'have a nice day' and then sneered at them or made some very negative signs, the 'nice day' message would have been cancelled out. Body language involves facial and bodily expressions and the way we use our bodies to send messages to somebody else.

It is thought that body language helps individuals to develop effective powers of persuasion and make better presentations. Using body language in conversation enables individuals to reduce conflict and increase understanding.

Body language can be divided into open body language and closed body language. Open body language is welcoming and outgoing, showing the customer that the employee is interested in what they have to say and is positive about the relationship. On the other hand, closed body language implies that the customer service assistant is negative and disinterested.

CASE STUDY

Spreading fear through body posture

According to Dr Gelder from Harvard Medical School:

'A menacing body posture can be as threatening as a frightening facial expression, according to new research. In the past, scientists have said that human emotions are communicated mainly by facial expressions. But a new study suggests that body posture may be as important as the face in communicating emotions such as fear. The discovery suggests that the immediate response to other people's fear may be more automatic than previously thought. The study shows that images of fear affect the emotional part of the brain. Since the link between the emotional brain and action is stronger than the link between the visual brain and action, viewing fearful body expressions may automatically prepare the observer to respond to fear.'

1 Describe situations in which you have been influenced by negative body language.
2 To what extent could the understanding of menacing body posture and closed body language influence staff training?

FIGURE 5.19 *Open and closed body language*

Open body language would include:

* smiling and looking welcoming
* good eye contact with the customer
* looking comfortable and relaxed
* using gestures to support dialogue
* showing interest and concern
* chin level to floor.

Closed body language would include:

* looking unhappy and scowling or slouching
* chin or head looking upwards or at the floor
* avoiding eye contact with customers
* fiddling with clothes or hair or doodling
* showing no feeling or concern for customer issues
* fidgeting, crossing legs and moving from foot to foot
* looking uncomfortable
* looking unwelcoming.

Product knowledge

In a customer-focused environment, customers want to deal with individuals who know what they are doing and can be trusted to provide reliable and accurate information. At the heart of all customer service training is the provision of product knowledge in order to provide staff with the ability to deal with any queries or issues that arise. The type of information that customers may want will largely depend upon the sort of environment in which staff work. However, in providing information it is important that it is:

* Accurate – a key source of irritation may occur if the customer is told one thing and then finds out that what they have been told is wrong or inaccurate. This could be a source of a later complaint or difficulty with a particular customer.

* Provided promptly – although in some circumstances it may not be easy to provide answers to a query straight away, customer issues should be dealt with promptly. It may be necessary to refer a query to another member of staff or somebody with a particular expertise.

* Impersonal – providing the customer with the member of staff's own tastes, preferences and interests is usually not appropriate. It is important to be impartial and try to analyse what the needs of the customer are in order to satisfy them.

* Objective – information should be unbiased and should include everything that a customer needs to know. This is not easy, but it can mean not hiding any information and helping them make impartial comparisons with the products on offer from different manufacturers.

Customer needs v organisation needs

Any customer-focused situation should involve matching the needs of the customer with the needs of the organisation and in doing so reaching an equitable balance.

An organisation has a responsibility to its many different stakeholders and, through its actions, it will attempt to balance its responsibilities in a variety of different ways. For example, on the one hand it has to take into consideration the needs of its managers and shareholders but on the other it has to take into account the needs of its customers, members of the wider community and employees.

It could be argued that an organisation might go the other way and become too customer-focused at the expense of the needs of the organisation. It is possible to offer customers too much and this could affect the profitability of the business. Hoover's famous sales promotion in which they offered customers free flights to the USA certainly helped to move products, but at the same time it caused the company a lot of financial problems.

Total Quality Management (TQM) is a philosophy that shapes relationships between suppliers and customers. Three principles guide the relationship:

1 **Customer-focus**. The customer is an important stakeholder in a business – quality should be judged by the customer, and all products and

FIGURE 5.20 *Three principles of Total Quality Management (TQM)*

services contribute value to the customer and lead to customer satisfaction.

2 **Win-win**. The most productive relationships are the ones where all parties benefit from an activity – there are no winners or losers, but rather everybody wins.

3 **Trust**. The underpinning basis of any relationship is trust.

Within the context of sales this means that a salesperson must be constantly gathering information on customer needs, which informs management of their requirements and

Learning activity

Working in pairs, create a scenario in which you would deal with the following:

'Waiter, I have a fly in my soup.'

'The jacket I bought does not fit.'

'My flight time is 11.00 am. Nobody told me I had to turn up 1 hour beforehand.'

'I have just waited 35 minutes to be served and you are telling me that I am at the wrong counter.'

'But when I phoned up you said that you had the item I wanted in stock and were going to hold one back for me.'

contributes to the design of the company's products and the services that support the sale of the product. Within the wider marketing context, total quality marketing involves energising and engaging everybody within an organisation with the needs of the customer so that they can each appreciate the value of the contribution they make towards customer satisfaction.

Mission statements

For the quality of service and customer care to be considered at the heart of the activities of an organisation, it is important for senior management to try to establish a way of orientating the business around the notion of service quality. One way in which this can be done is to create a 'mission statement' or 'vision' as a long term overview emphasising the direction in which the business is orientated. Some organisations talk about mission statements while others emphasise their vision.

A mission sets out the long-term purpose of an organisation and helps to emphasise why the organisation is there. Some examples of mission statements include:

'To provide our customers with a range of finest quality ready meals, through commitment to innovation, service and value, in a mutually profitable relationship.'

'Our main goal is to provide a professional yet personal service to our clients with service and customer care as our primary objective.'

'Our mission is to enjoy exceeding our clients' expectations.'

'To deliver quality IT solutions on time and to budget whilst ensuring the highest level of customer satisfaction and service is delivered by our staff.'

'We will provide quality logistic and support services that meet the real needs of all our customers.'

One of the purposes of a mission statement is to coordinate the needs and expectations of all stakeholders. Some stakeholders, for example, shareholders, may have a limited objective, such as profits. This might be in direct contrast to final

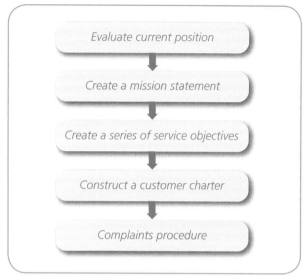

FIGURE 5.21 *Creating a mission for an organisation*

customers who may want value, or employees who may want promotion and professional opportunities. As a result there are several sides with the potential for conflict. One of the purposes of having a mission statement is to try to bring the different stakeholders together and unify them within the context of a mission or vision. For example, the company could emphasise how important it is to provide good quality customer service on one hand, but to do so profitably so that it can afford to invest more in producing higher value services and goods.

Having developed a mission statement an organisation may then try to take this broad statement and translate it into a form that has an active influence in the workplace. After evaluating their current position and creating the statement, they will develop a series of quality or service objectives and then incorporate these objectives into a customer or service charter. The customer charter will underpin the commitment of the organisation to its customers. For example, the charter might set out response times for dealing with customer complaints or for replying to e-mails or faxes.

A key element within the process of customer service is to create customer lifetime value by adopting processes and practices that enable the organisation to care for the customers it has got and helps to ensure that the customer remains

The Football Association customer charter

The Football Association (FA) has its customer charter which focuses upon the following areas:

* Staff conduct and response time
* Stakeholder consultation on customer issues
* Ticketing
* Loyalty and membership schemes
* Merchandising.

According to the FA:

'Every professional club in the country now has a "customer charter", as do the FA Premier League and Football League.

A hierarchy of complaint handling has been established to ensure that complaints about customer issues are handled initially at the correct level. The Football Association handles only complaints that have been referred to us from the relevant league. The Independent Football Commission is the final stage in the complaints hierarchy.'

1 **Identify some of the issues that might arise under each of the headings within the FA's customer charter.**
2 **What is the FA telling customers through its customer charter?**
3 **How should the FA deal with clubs that do not adhere to the charter?**

loyal. Although some customers may only use the organisation once, others will stay loyal over a long period of time and use its services on a regular basis.

Effective and ineffective customer service

A key function of customer service is to resolve problems and deal with customer-related issues. Even if a customer is not happy with a service or a product on one or two occasions, if the complaint is handled well it is possible to sustain a positive relationship with the customer. An important reason for sustaining customer relationships is that existing relationships create new business opportunities, and as it is more expensive to create new relationships than sustain old ones, existing customers have to be treated well.

To deal with complaints an organisation should have some form of complaints procedure.

Handling complaints is not always easy and can be stressful, particularly when there are aggressive customers. When handling complaints it is important for the person involved in customer service:

* Not to be upset by the complainant
* Not to take any comments made personally
* To try and deal with the customer in a constructive way
* To provide the customer with accurate information
* To ask the customer how they would like the situation to be rectified
* To follow through the complaint and use the procedures within the organisation to try and rectify the problem.

It is important to keep customer records and to monitor complaints and customer compliments. Feedback from customers helps to provide an important form of market research data and enables the organisation to monitor customer service levels.

The monitoring of complaints can be a little misleading as usually only a few customers complain formally. However, it may be possible to take feedback from staff who deal with customers every day and are able to provide a more accurate picture of customer feedback.

Look at the Customer Complaint Procedure for an insurance company. (Note that the Financial Services Authority mentioned in the case was set up in 2000 to regulate firms providing financial services in this country. It is financed by the financial services industry but is accountable to the government and parliament.)

Customer complaint procedure

It is the policy of our business to make sure that any complaint made by a customer is dealt with quickly and in a professional way. Complaints, whether received in writing, by telephone or e-mail will be acknowledged within 14 days. In cases where this is not possible, an acknowledgement will be issued as soon as possible.

The acknowledgement will give the name and contact details of the person dealing with the complaint and the time scale for a more detailed reply. The complaint will be investigated thoroughly and a detailed response will be provided. While the investigation is being carried out, a regular written update will be provided at intervals no greater than one month.

We will write to the complainant within 7 days of the completion of the investigation setting out the outcome of the investigation and where appropriate, explain the terms of any offer of settlement.

If a client is still dissatisfied with the outcome, or if the complaint has not been resolved within three months, the client is entitled to refer the complaint to the Financial Services Authority (the official body that deals with complaints).

Dealing with the complaint

1. The complaint (by e-mail, phone or letter) is recorded and details are set out in the customer's file within one working day.

2. An acknowledgement letter is issued to the complainant within 14 days of receipt of the complaint.

3. The complaint is investigated immediately. If there is a delay with the investigation, the Complaint Officer will keep the complainant informed of the progress of the investigation at intervals of not more than 1 month.

4. When the complaint has been finalised, the complainant will be informed in writing of the outcome within 7 days of the completion of the investigation. Where applicable, terms of any offer of settlement will be issued to the complainant.

5. The customer (complainant) file is updated and kept in an orderly fashion.

6. Should the complainant be dissatisfied with the outcome of the investigation, the complainant will be advised that they are entitled to refer their complaint to the Financial Services Authority.

7. All correspondence concerning the complaint will be kept on file for a period of 5 years from the date of the last correspondence.

8. The firm will provide all information with regard to a complaint to the Financial Services Authority, if so requested.

The purpose of monitoring customer complaints is to ensure that issues have been dealt with fairly and resolved in an appropriate way. By monitoring customer feedback, it may be possible to take corrective action that deals with causes of customer dissatisfaction.

Describe some of the customer service situations that you have been faced with. Discuss how organisations could improve service or products if they listened to your views.

FIGURE 5.22 *Keeping calm is the best way to handle complaints properly*

5.3 Maintaining and improving customer service and keeping customers

In a business environment that has become increasingly competitive, the quality of service often differentiates organisations from one another. Increasingly organisations today have realised that if they want to achieve their marketing objectives and meet the needs of their shareholders, they first have to meet the needs and requirements of their customers.

As we have seen, having a focus upon service quality should start from the top of the organisation with managers developing a mission designed to guide the whole of the organisation. A useful starting point for creating a mission statement is to find out from customers what they want. The mission needs to be communicated to employees in a meaningful way via discussions, training and through meetings as well as within organisational literature. Once the mission is in place, the organisation can then put together the processes and practices necessary for dealing with customer service issues.

Internal procedures

Staff will often try to hide complaints and deal with them before the manager discovers what has happened because they are afraid of the consequences. Why are they afraid? Almost certainly because the manager has given them no indication that they will be dealt with respectfully and constructively, and so they assume that the manager will react badly to problems or mistakes. The result is that problems get 'swept under the carpet'. The long-term implications for the management of such a firm are worrying.

Internal customers could include colleagues, management and supervisors, staff teams and other employees. It is important that managers try to establish effective customer service to internal customers in order to establish positive working relationships.

If a manager does not hear of complaints, he or she will assume that everything is going well and will not see any need for change. Since one of management's main functions is to make decisions, this will lead to decisions being based on inadequate information, resulting in poor decision-making. It is vital, therefore, that staff be encouraged to report and record complaints, so that managers obtain a true picture and can identify corrective actions where necessary.

A manager must prove by his or her actions that staff will not automatically be criticised for problems. Staff must learn through experience that the manager is willing to accept mistakes as long as staff learn from them and that they will not be dealt with harshly for one mistake if the majority of their work is of a good standard. If complaints are logged, they can provide valuable information helping to identify areas for improvement.

A service culture will be of little value to an organisation if it does not take into account the views, interests and feelings of the internal customer within the organisation. For example, a manager within an organisation will receive little respect if they keep emphasising the role of customer service and the need to listen to customers but, at the same time, fail to listen to the views of staff when they have complaints or issues that they wish to discuss. Within the workplace, and in order to provide good service to other employees, senior managers should:

✳ Encourage dialogue and communication

✳ Be good listeners

✳ Foster trust and confidence

✳ Solve problems and welcome feedback

✳ Look for new ideas

✳ Be prepared to delegate responsibility

✳ Be honest with staff.

To ensure that internal procedures take on processes of quality, managers might set up some form of internal complaints procedure which,

FIGURE 5.23 *Managers should listen to staff concerns*

like an external complaints procedure, provides individuals with a series of guarantees that problems and issues are dealt with in a responsive and responsible way.

Customer service charters/codes of practice

A service charter or code of practice emphasises the commitment of an organisation to its customers and will attempt to show how

Learning activity

Produce what you think would be a useful code of practice for your college or school that could be followed and acted upon by both lecturers and students. Identify a range of commitments that your school and your tutors could give to you as a school customer. How might the code of practice influence the quality of service you receive?

CASE STUDY

Vodafone Ireland

Look at Vodafone's Code of Practice below.

Our aim is to resolve your enquiry on initial contact with Vodafone. Where we cannot resolve your enquiry we will let you know, within three hours of your initial contact, the estimated time of resolution. We will keep you informed of progress and notify you of the resolution.

We commit to providing a high level of service under the following enquiry categories with the maximum time to resolve the enquiry where the solution is within our control. All your enquiries will be uniquely recorded so that we will always know the status of any particular enquiry. In extreme circumstance and where it is beyond our control e.g. if a third party is involved, or if we lack complete information, or in the case of adverse weather conditions, we will keep you informed of progress and respond to your enquiry as soon as possible. In the instance of a billing error, Vodafone will reimburse the affected account as soon as we become aware of the discrepancy. We will notify you by text message once your rebate has been applied.

In exceptional cases where we are unable to respond or acknowledge your query within the times specified below, Vodafone have established a Customer Guarantee Scheme to compensate for that delay. Where it is brought to our attention that, in relation to your query, we have failed to meet the response time outlined in the table below, we will apply a credit to your account*.

* A credit offered for this purpose is given as a gesture of goodwill only and does not imply an acceptance of liability, breach of contract or otherwise on the part of Vodafone.

Enquiries by letter

Enquiries sent to Vodafone by letter or fax will be responded to by letter within three working days. Where we cannot resolve your query in this timeframe, we will send an acknowledgement of your query by letter and follow up with a telephone call in line with our Code of Practice.

Enquiries by e-mail

For enquiries sent to us by e-mail, we will automatically confirm on receipt and aim to respond with a resolution within 24 hours. Where we cannot resolve your enquiry in this time, we will resolve it in line with our Code of Practice.

1 **What is the purpose of this code of practice?**
2 **How would it influence the actions of employees within Vodafone Ireland?**

any elements of dissatisfaction or issues can be resolved. Such statements reinforce an organisation's commitment to customer service in a way that can be communicated to customers, and also emphasise to employees the importance of good customer service. It is important, however, that if an organisation makes such a commitment and publishes this in a charter or code of practice, that promises are kept.

Monitoring customer service and complaints

Very few organisations encourage complaints even though they provide valuable information for planning. It takes brave managers to implement a system that encourages negative feedback, but it can help to provide an accurate picture of an organisation's activities.

The proportion of people feeling disgruntled is usually only small, and so complaints usually only represent a small number of people. Making it easier to complain can provide more accurate analysis of how an organisation is faring. This may be undertaken by:

✳ Providing forms for customers to complete and post back (using a Freepost address) – sometimes customers may be prepared to write down their feelings, even if they lack the courage to complain directly face-to-face

✳ Providing telephone numbers where customer care assistants will assist with complaints

✳ Providing an e-mail address to which customers could forward their concerns

✳ Randomly writing to customers to obtain their views

✳ Making customer follow-up calls – telephoning buyers of large items a few days after purchase to check their satisfaction with what they have bought. Car retailers often adopt this practice. Sales assistants will ring recent purchasers within a month to check satisfaction levels and follow up with any problems that have been identified.

If complaints are collected they can then be monitored and analysed, and this will provide a rich source of data about the organisation and its activities. By looking at such data, consistent problems can then be addressed. Complaints are a good source of data about customers and provide an opportunity to benchmark the quality of service provided by one organisation against those of competitors. For example, it may be possible to buy goods from competitors and see how their service features compare to a company's own goods or services.

Assessing customer care should be constantly undertaken to examine the current situation of an organisation. Careful and regular monitoring of the process will reveal where additional effort and training is required.

A scheme run by British Telecom (BT) involved telephoning customers who had either called directory enquiries or used BT repair or installation services. After a number of years they realised that this system prevented them from talking to a large section of their customers who did not fall into either of these categories. They have since employed a system of contacting a random sample of customers and using a wider variety of interviewing techniques.

This example indicates a problem in the way many customer care programmes are designed – they are event-driven, often measuring what the organisation thinks the customer wants, rather than the customer's actual needs (see Figure 5.24).

It is now commonly accepted that the best starting point for such programmes is to engage in qualitative research aimed at ascertaining exactly what the customer wants from the organisation.

The Post Office ran a customer care scheme monitoring how quickly letters travelled from the collection box to await delivery after sorting. The scheme indicated that customers should be happy as targets were being met, but what it failed to recognise was that customers judged the standard of service on the time from collection box to delivery. The Post Office had failed to check exactly what their customers were looking for. This should always be the first step in monitoring customer feedback.

FIGURE 5.24 *Is speed what the customer actually wants?*

CASE STUDY

Telewest wins Broadband award at Call Centre Association's Excellence Awards

For many people broadband is changing the way they live. There are many decisions to be made about which broadband supplier to use and customer service has become a key differentiator in what is now a crowded market. Telewest recently won the Best in Sector (IT, telecoms and utilities) gong at the Call Centre Association (CCA) Excellence Awards.

Anne Marie Forsyth, chief executive officer of the CCA, said: 'We would like to congratulate Telewest Broadband on their success. Their achievement highlights our members' dedication to providing better standards of service, as well as their support of the CCA.

'We were overwhelmed by the quality and quantity of entries for these awards, which are a reflection of commitment to high standards of professionalism. Both the judges and myself were impressed with the exceptional standard of entries and every single submission was of a commendable quality.

'Telewest has undertaken several major initiatives used to develop their customer care initiatives. These include a focus on resolving customers' issues at first point of contact, a service excellence development programme for employees, customer feedback channels and online guides to topical issues.'

1 Why would customer service be important in the market for broadband services?
2 Discuss and comment upon the initiatives undertaken by Telewest.

Recommending changes to customer service procedures

Customer care programmes are designed to improve the experience for customers and to encourage them to become advocates and repeat-purchasers. The findings from such programmes should help an organisation to build changes into their procedures that enable them to meet customer needs more effectively.

In changing to meet customer needs in a focused way, an organisation will have to make decisions that will be influenced by:

* Their flexibility and speed in adapting to new customer service requirements

* Requirements for accuracy and precision

* The quantity and quality of products or service required by customers.

In order to make changes to customer service procedures, organisations are usually faced with two problems. These are company inertia and customers' perceptions of the level of quality provided.

Company inertia. One of the problems with implementing change in any organisation is people's reluctance to alter what they are doing, and their inability to see any need to change. Implementing customer service and customer care programmes invariably requires a shift in attitude, and this can be hard to achieve. 'We don't get many complaints' is a common cry, but that may simply be because the customers who are prepared to put up with unsatisfactory service outnumber those who speak up. Convincing staff that real change may be necessary can be difficult. Paying lip-service to change will never be sufficient – it requires a true turnaround in attitudes to improve things.

Customer perceptions. The general public will have an overall impression of the level of service they expect an organisation to provide, and this will take some changing if it is wrong. People's preconceptions affect the way they interpret what happens, so if a customer expects poor service he or she will interpret everything that happens in a negative way in order to reinforce that opinion. But, if customers approach expecting high-quality service, an organisation will have to perform very badly in order to change that opinion. Changing customer perceptions of existing organisations may take time and long-held opinions are difficult to dislodge. It took Tesco many years to shake off their original image as a low-cost, low-quality supermarket, but it is now the most profitable UK supermarket with a reputation for high quality and good customer service.

In order to make changes based upon feedback from customers, organisations need to take a broad view of everything they do and not simply confine their approach to service within a single aspect of the business.

Within the organisation, many customer services issues may affect internal customers. Issues may arise from human resource management, the use of computer systems, communication procedures, teamwork problems, marketing issues and so on. Improving customer services procedures within the organisation involves a total focus upon how the organisation and its people operate.

Outside the organisation, issues might not just focus upon customer contact with the organisation. For example, areas that might involve changes could include sales and promotions, the value customers receive from doing business with the organisation, customer support procedures, the image of the organisation and customer and supplier relationships.

In order to change procedures and become more customer-focused organisations have to be flexible, and often this flexibility will include a level of teamwork. Some organisations will even restructure in order to be more flexible and so more responsive to change based upon the evolving needs of their customers. By cutting layers of management, they often feel that they are then in a position to make frequent changes to fine-tune their activities in a way that creates a better customer response.

Customer service training

In the light of changes to customer service procedures, processes of training provide the basis for any form of change. The first step in assessing the training requirements for customer service is to look at how well employees are already trained in customer service, and then look at what they need to meet the new customer service strategy.

A training needs analysis may be carried out by the personnel department or by someone from outside the organisation. This may take place after a discussion and after interviewing a few members of staff. The needs analysis should identify the dimensions required for a new customer service strategy. It will create a picture of current skills and attitudes towards customer service and identify areas that need to be developed in the future.

Any training in customer service will prioritise the areas that require training and development most and then determine the methods required to meet these needs. There are a number of different training methods, some of which are shown in Figure 5.25. In developing the most appropriate method, it is important to recognise that different employees will have different learning styles. Clearly, developing skills and understanding involves high levels of employee involvement, while telling and showing will require little participation from employees.

It is argued that most training in customer service is simply common sense. The training may help those who have developed bad habits to get back on track and also improve the attitudes of staff. A typical programme will be unique to a particular organisation and relate to its specific

needs in the area of customer service. Training may also occur at a range of levels, to include:

* senior managers
* line managers
* supervisors
* other employees.

A typical workshop for employees might include the following:

1 An explanation of why an organisation is undertaking a customer service strategy.

2 A definition of service quality and customer care, with clear examples.

3 An assessment of current performance.

4 The setting of customer service standards.

5 A customer service action plan to meet such standards.

6 A description of how the process of customer service will continue.

Learning activity

Working in a team of five or six people, develop a customer service strategy for your school or college, using the guidelines contained within the workshop outline above.

METHOD	TECHNIQUES
Developing skills and understanding	Role playing Case studies Simulation Mentoring Work experience Workplace exercises
Discussion	Training exercises Meetings Workshops
Knowledge	Programmed learning Training manuals Group instruction
Telling and showing	Formal lectures Reading and booklists Demonstrations

FIGURE 5.25 *Employee training methods*

Fostering customer loyalty

An organisation that can develop repeat and frequent business with its customers will have a more established market position. Some customers may only use an organisation's products once, while others will make multiple and repeat purchases. The ways in which customers will be treated will determine whether or not they decide to continue to do business with a particular organisation. By providing efficient and high value services customers are much more likely to remain loyal and to become advocates.

The notion of adding value to products and services in order to foster customer loyalty is an important one. Adding value is simply the taking of something of lower value and constantly increasing its attractiveness for customers. A manufacturer of clothes, for example, might take raw materials which in themselves are not expensive, and produce an item of clothing that has more value to the customer, therefore commanding a higher price than the original cloth. Developing a brand image also helps to add value to products in a way that makes customers more loyal as long as that brand image exudes positive values. Anything that further adds value to the finished item is clearly beneficial to the organisation, because of the loyalty it fosters.

The customer care and marketing processes can identify opportunities for adding value. For example, they might be aimed at identifying how customer services could be improved. It might even provide evidence of how much more customers would be willing to pay for additional features. It would not be unreasonable to set targets for the amount of new or repeat business that the programme should attract.

Schemes that would add value and encourage customer loyalty could include:

* Loyalty cards – these use some form of points system to foster repeat purchase. As with the Boots Advantage Card or the Tesco Clubcard (see Figure 5.26), the points create cash opportunities that can be reclaimed using the card.

FIGURE 5.26 *Tesco Clubcard*

* Discounts – these are a good way of retaining regular customers by providing them with tangible advantages. It is possible to provide some form of 'club' identity which enables members to get special discounts, in the same way that members of Co-operative societies were granted special privileges. For example, members of an air-softing club, which is a slightly more sophisticated form of paint balling, might get special privileges and treatment both from the air-softing venue, and also from retailers who have an arrangement that provides discounts for club members.

* Mailshots, leaflets and other publicity materials – these may be used to inform regular customers about events and special deals. For example, Nottinghamshire Cricket Club regularly inform Notts members about events within the club as well as about offers within the club shop.

Collection of data – sources and methods

A number of different methods of collecting information about customer satisfaction should be included in the monitoring carried out by an organisation.

Consider the last major purchase you made. Design a series of questions that could be included in a post-sale survey for that purchase. Swap questions with a fellow student and examine each other's questions critically. How easy are they to answer and analyse? Will they reveal the quality of information required?

Methods of data collection

An organisation may choose to include post-sale surveys in its customer care programme as a means of identifying the levels of satisfaction experienced by customers who have recently made a purchase. These may be sent to the homes of purchasers shortly after purchase, although some organisations hand them out before a customer leaves a store while others might choose the telephone survey method.

A typical post-sale survey might cover the following issues:

1 How staff dealt with the customer and the level of care they received as he or she made the buying decision. This might include:

   * where the product or service was bought
   * whether product literature was suitable and informative
   * staff telephone manner
   * whether the customer was offered a demonstration of the product
   * the appearance of the staff
   * the quality and clarity of the explanations given by sales staff
   * how well the sales staff understood the customer's requirements.

2 Whether the product/service met the expections of the customer. This might include:

   * was the product available from stock or was there a delay before delivery?
   * was the customer informed of guarantees?
   * were they happy with the product or service?

   * details about the product/service that they provided feedback about
   * was the customer told how to access after-sales service?
   * was the product in good condition when received?
   * was delivery on time and as agreed?
   * was the delivery time suitable for the customer?

3 The customer's overall level of satisfaction. This could be rated on a Likert Scale.

Another way of collecting customer feedback might be through providing a suggestions box so that customers can provide their thoughts and ideas about a particular good or service. For example, recently a supermarket in Nottingham installed ticket machines for customers in the car parks, requiring customers to pay £1 for a ticket which could be reclaimed from purchases. So many customers complained using the in-store suggestions box that shortly after the introduction of the scheme it was withdrawn.

There are a number of other different ways in which data can be collected. Mystery shoppers are a useful way of adding to customer feedback. Although employees see mystery shoppers as spies, it is a useful way of finding out about customer service from the perspective of the customer.

Setting up a freephone enquiry line is a popular way of gaining feedback from customers. This is a good way of encouraging customers to provide useful data, adding to an organisation's understanding of 'customer perspectives'.

On a suggestions slip, produce a series of comments indicating how the quality of service could be improved within your school/college environment.

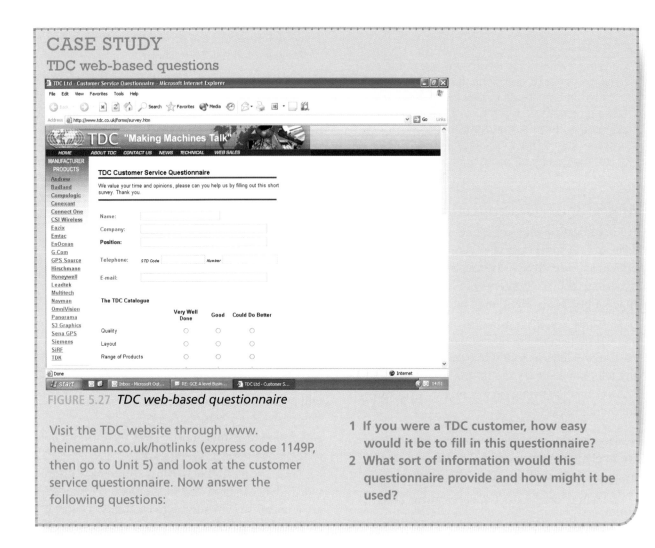

CASE STUDY
TDC web-based questions

FIGURE 5.27 **TDC web-based questionnaire**

Visit the TDC website through www.
heinemann.co.uk/hotlinks (express code 1149P,
then go to Unit 5) and look at the customer
service questionnaire. Now answer the
following questions:

1 If you were a TDC customer, how easy
   would it be to fill in this questionnaire?
2 What sort of information would this
   questionnaire provide and how might it be
   used?

Another way of collecting data could be through consumer panels, focus groups or through any other form of consumer group. This is a powerful technique that encourages direct consumer feedback. Customers will meet in small groups, perhaps of between eight and ten, to discuss a series of issues and questions related to an organisation's products and services. For example, they could discuss their views on particular products and any issues such as areas of improvement and ideas for new products and services (see Figure 5.28).

It may also be possible to get an agency to undertake some third party surveys where they monitor customer satisfaction not only of the business paying for the survey but also of all of the competitors.

It is also important to remember the views of the internal customers. Internal customer surveys are important for monitoring how well the organisation is geared to meeting the expectations of external customers. Service quality programmes are important to show how changing practices are influencing the expectations of employees as customers.

Another way of collecting information within an organisation could be through the use of quality circles. These provide a valuable opportunity for employees to meet together and think of ways to improve how they work and how they meet both internal and external customer needs. They are, in essence, a form of internal consulation.

Sources of information

Sources of information for surveys come from both within and outside an organisation. Outside

FIGURE 5.28 *A consumer panel (focus group)*

the organisation, in nearly all cases, sources are likely to be customers. However, in some instances it might be useful to obtain information from local residents or from other organisations within the community. For example, if a fast-food chain operates within a community, the survey might identify the extent to which it deals with issues such as litter.

Within an organisation there are various sources of information. Staff teams would be an invaluable source of information as well as individuals at different levels and with different responsibilities, including senior and junior managers.

Reliability

Although listening to customers is a vital element of customer care, both within and outside the organisation, it is important to think about the reliability of data that is collected. Organisations have to make decisions about where and when to capture data, and clearly the reliability of data will depend upon the methods of collection and the particular group that the data is collected from.

5.4 Customer service legislation

We would all ideally want to work in an environment where organisations always have consumers at the heart of their focus, with harmonious relationships based upon good customer service, charters and codes of practice. In reality, relationships between organisations and their customers are not always good and in some circumstances, there needs to be some form of framework around which organisations can deliver their own customer service. This framework is provided by legislation both within the UK and the European Union.

The European Union

As part of its strategy of improving the quality of life of EU citizens, consumer policy within the EU is designed to create legislation that helps to complement the consumer policy and legislation of member countries in order to promote the interests and health and safety of EU citizens across the community.

The stated aim of EU consumer policy is:

'to safeguard the health, safety and economic interests of European consumers, allowing them to make informed choices, to make the most of the internal market and e-commerce and to enjoy safe, nutritious and good quality food. Consumer interests are also addressed in a wide range of other EU policies from the internal market to environment, transport, financial services, agriculture, competition and external trade.'

Surveys by the EU showed that EU consumers are less confident about shopping in countries other than their own. As a result of this the EU developed a consumer policy strategy in 2002. Under this strategy all food, safety, public health and consumer issues are dealt with under the responsibility of a European Commissioner for Health and Consumer Protection. The aim of this role is to provide a co-ordinated approach to consumer interests with three key objectives:

1   To provide a high common level of consumer protection – this means bringing together and harmonising not just the safety of goods and services but also economic and legal elements that enable consumers to shop with confidence anywhere in the EU.

2   To create effective enforcement of consumer protection rules – rules are not particularly good if they are not enforced. This provides for procedures that enable consumers to be protected with co-operation across states providing the opportunity for consumer concerns to be redressed.

3   To provide the basis for the involvement of consumer organisations in EU policies – consumer organisations are now able to participate actively in EU policy making.

Current legislation already in force within the EU covers: price indications, misleading advertising, distance selling, consumer credit, unfair terms in consumer contracts, package tours and timeshares, and product safety standards.

Recent European legislation has included:

✱   An amendment to the consumer credit directive so that consumers are now protected across the European Union when they carry out cross-border transactions.

✱   A directive concerning unfair business to consumer practices within the internal market

✱   An action plan aimed at bringing together and harmonising the law of contract across the European Union.

European legislation also affects consumers and customer relationships across agriculture, product labelling, air and water quality, transport and food safety.

> ✱ **DID YOU KNOW?**
>
> The European Food Safety Authority (EFSA) is the keystone of European Union (EU) risk assessment regarding food and feed safety. In close collaboration with national authorities and in open consultation with its stakeholders, EFSA provides independent scientific advice and clear communication on existing and emerging risks.

UK legislation

Ofcom

In the UK, the regulation of television is undertaken by the Ofcom. Previously, this duty rested with the Independent Television Commission (ITC), but Ofcom was created in 2003 with wide-ranging responsibilities across the UK's communications markets.

Ofcom licenses and regulates commercial television and undertakes to protect viewers' interests by setting and maintaining standards for programmes and advertising. Ofcom's powers are derived from the Broadcasting Acts of 1990 and 1996.

Ofcom issues licences that allow commercial television companies to broadcast in and from the UK. It then regulates these services by monitoring broadcasters' performance against the requirements of published codes and guidelines on programming content, advertising, sponsorship and technical performance, and has the power to issue a range of penalties for failure to comply.

Learning activity

It is unfair to restrict the advertising of specific products, such as cigarettes, on television. Discuss.

The ITC/Ofcom Code of Advertising Standards and Practice has four general principles to which advertisers are expected to adhere. These are that:

* Television advertising should be legal, decent, honest and truthful.

* Advertisements should comply in every respect with the law, common or statute, and licensees must make it a condition of acceptance that advertisements do so.

* The detailed rules set out are intended to be applied in the spirit as well as the letter.

* The standards in this code apply to any item of publicity inserted in breaks in or between programmes, whether in return for payment or not.

FIGURE 5.29 *Does advertising affect behaviour?*

Monitor advertisements you watch on television over a two-day period. Do these advertisements meet the guidelines of the ITC/Ofcom code of practice?

The Sale of Goods Act 1979

The purpose of The Sale of Goods Act is to ensure that sellers provide goods that are of 'merchantable quality' – that is, they must not be damaged or broken. Goods sold must also be fit for the purpose intended. If you bought a pair of shoes and they fell apart at the seams within a week, they would not have been fit for the purposes for which they were sold – serving as footwear. Under this law you can ask for replacements if goods do not meet the requirements you specified to the seller.

The Trade Descriptions Act 1968

The Trade Descriptions Act attempts to ensure that the description given of the goods forms part of the contract the buyer makes with the seller. This Act makes it a criminal offence for a trader to describe goods falsely. One type of case frequently prosecuted under this Act is the turning back of odometers on used cars to make them appear as if they have covered fewer miles than they really have. The main objective of the Trade Descriptions Act is quite straightforward – descriptions of goods and services must be really accurate. Articles described as 'waterproof' or 'shrinkproof' must be exactly that (see Figure 5.30).

The Weights and Measures Act 1963

The Weights and Measures Act ensures that consumers receive the actual quantity of a product they believe they are buying. For example, pre-packed items must have a declaration of the quantity contained within the pack. It is an offence to give 'short measure'.

The Food and Drugs Act 1985

The Food and Drugs Act is concerned with the contents of foodstuffs and medicines. The

FIGURE 5.30 *Descriptions of items offered for sale must be accurate*

government needs to control this area of trading so that the public is not led into buying harmful substances. Some items have to carry warnings – packets of dried kidney beans, for example, must carry clear instructions that they need to be boiled for a certain length of time before they can be eaten. The contents of medicines are strictly controlled by this Act. Certain substances such as mercury are not allowed at all!

There are numerous sources of help and advice for consumers, providing opportunities for people to follow up complaints and grievances. For the consumer it is important to consider carefully the circumstances of each grievance before deciding on the most appropriate way forward.

Government regulatory bodies

The government protects consumers through a number of official bodies.

The Office of Fair Trading (OFT), a government body, was set up to look after the interests of consumers and traders. It publishes a wide variety of information and encourages businesses to issue codes of practice to raise the standards of their service. Traders who persist in breaking the law must provide an assurance they will 'mend their ways'. The OFT also keeps an eye on anti-competitive practices, monopolies and mergers and might suggest changes in the law. Find the OFT website through www.heinemann.co.uk/hotlinks (express code 1149P, then go to Unit 5).

The Competition Act 1998 replaced the Monopolies and Mergers Commission (MMC) on 1 April 1999 with the Competition Commission. The Competition Commission has two functions. It has taken on the role of the former MMC, investigating and reporting on matters referred to it by the Director General of Fair Trading, such as monopolies, mergers and regulatory disputes. It now also hears appeals against decisions made under the new Competition Act. Find the MMC website through www.heinemann.co.uk/hotlinks (express code 1149P, then go to Unit 5).

The base of British health and safety law is the Health and Safety at Work Act 1974. The Act sets out a series of general duties which employers have towards their employees as well as the duties they have to members of the public, many of whom may be customers, and also the duties that employees have to themselves and to each other. The law emphasises the importance of good management and the need for employers to take sensible precautions to avoid risks.

Local authorities and trading standards departments investigate a range of issues such as misleading offers or prices, inaccurate weights and measures, and consumer credit.

Environmental health departments enforce legislation covering health aspects of food – for example, unfit food or unhygienic storage, and the preparation and serving of food.

Industry-based constraints

The Advertising Standards Authority (ASA) was set up in 1962. This is an independent body that exercises control over all advertising. This control includes the following:

* Press – national and regional magazines and newspapers.
* Radio and television – local and national.
* Outdoor advertising – posters, transport and aerial announcements.
* Direct marketing – including direct mail, leaflets, brochures, catalogues, circulars, inserts and facsimiles.
* Screen promotions – including cinema commercials and advertisements in electronic media, such as computer games, video, CD-ROM and the Internet.
* Sales promotions – such as on-pack promotions, front-page promotions, reader offers, competitions and prize draws.

The authority draws up its own codes which it uses to ensure advertisements are 'legal, decent, honest and truthful'. Advertisements should be prepared with a sense of responsibility to both consumers and society, and conform to the principles of fair competition. The ASA has no statutory powers to force companies to comply with its rulings but replies on consensus, persuasion and an effective network of sanctions which stems from its own authorship of the codes.

The ASA identifies a number of advantages of self-regulation over a legislative process. The ASA process is accessible – with complainants needing only to write a letter to initiate action – and fast, with no complex legal procedures to undergo. This means the ASA can secure the withdrawal of misleading or offensive advertisements within a very short time. The process is free, with complaints investigated at no cost to complainants and incurring no legal fees.

It is argued that, in many instances, the ASA's codes go further than the law requires and, while the ASA does not enforce the law, it will refer complaints that fall directly under legislation to the appropriate law enforcement body. Should an advertiser refuse to remove an advertisement, the ASA could use a number of sanctions to enforce its decisions, such as:

* Adverse publicity generated by monthly reports of adjudications.

* Refusal of media space.

* Withdrawal of privileges, such as discounts and incentives resulting from membership of advertising bodies.

* Legal proceedings against persistent offenders.

Advertisers, agencies and the media whose representatives make up the Code of Advertising Practice Committee support the British Code of Advertising Practice. This code sets out rules which those in the advertising industry agree to follow. It also indicates to those outside advertising that there are regulations designed to ensure advertisements can be trusted.

The Chartered Institute of Marketing has its own code of practice to which members are required to adhere. The code refers to professional standards of behaviour in securing and developing business, and demands honesty and integrity of conduct.

Voluntary subscriptions and government grants finance the British Standards Institution (BSI). Its primary concern is with setting up standards that are acceptable to both manufacturers and consumers. Goods of a certain standard are allowed to bear the BSI Kitemark, showing consumers the product has passed the appropriate tests.

FIGURE 5.31 *Voluntary controls for advertising work well*

Over the period of a month, look at various types of advertisements by surveying magazines and periodicals. Make a list of advertisements (if any) you feel are not altogether 'legal, decent, honest and truthful'. Explain why in each instance.

Do consumers simply want low prices and high-quality goods? Is consumerism dead or has the process just begun?

Professional and trade associations promote the interests of their members as well as the development of a particular product or service area. In order to protect consumers, their members will often set up funds to safeguard consumers' money. For example, the Association of British Travel Agents (ABTA) will refund money to holiday-makers should a member company fail to do so.

Another area of concern relates to business practices, where restrictive practices and poor treatment of employees have been highlighted in the media, and businesses have faced criticism from the public. The trading policies of companies who buy cheap imports from overseas organisations involved in 'sweat-shop labour', or who trade with businesses employing young children in unacceptable conditions, have also faced critical scrutiny from both the media and the public.

In recent years environmental issues have been highlighted by accidents at chemical plants or at sea with oil tankers. Such accidents can not only damage wildlife and the environment but also the image of the organisation concerned.

With many companies' environmental performance becoming central to their competitiveness and survival, a range of new tools for environmental management have been developed. These include environmental impact assessments, which assess the likely impact of major projects, and environmental audits or eco-audits, which involve carrying out an audit of current activities to measure their environmental impact. Alternatively, by looking at the environmental impact of a product through its life cycle, from the sourcing of raw materials to the final disposal of waste products, a product life cycle analysis can be established.

Organisations face many potential dangers with regard to ethics and public opinion, and no organisation is capable of satisfying all

CASE STUDY

Eating GM convenience foods

Green pressure groups have dubbed genetically modified products 'Franken foods', arguing they are unsafe and that their development is ecologically unsound. During their early introduction into the UK, genetically modified foods faced little resistance. However, increasing knowledge about such foods has resulted in offensives being mounted by some consumer and green pressure groups against companies such as Unilever, who became one of the first manufacturers to put their weight behind genetically modified foods when they launched their Beanfeast brand.

With the European Union about to rule upon whether these products should be specially labelled, Unilever accepted consumer concerns. Their food labels inform customers about the presence of genetically modified foods. They have also undertaken a campaign to tell customers more about genetic modification.

1 What are the arguments for informing customers about specific details of the products they are consuming?
2 Is it possible to change negative perceptions of GM foods into positive ones?
3 Can you think of another instance where food labelling should be changed?

stakeholders but, by becoming good corporate citizens and being socially responsible, they can generate considerable goodwill. This strategy can be developed as a marketing advantage.

The idea of organisations working in and for the community is not new. Companies like Boots and Marks & Spencer have long advocated and contributed to community programmes, with involvement in areas as diverse as health care projects, education and training, arts and sport.

This movement towards responsible marketing is an acceptance by most organisations that they have a responsibility to serve their stakeholders.

There is no doubt that, in a world of increasingly articulate consumers, we shall see more social marketing, linking the actions of organisations to the interests of consumers in social, ethical and environmental issues. If consumers are unhappy with the actions of certain organisations, they can either set up or join pressure groups.

Protection pressure groups may be set up to fight a specific issue, such as the closure of a plant or the increased traffic on a road as a result of a local business. Promotional pressure groups are usually more formal and would be set up to create highly organised campaigns across a range of issues. They often have clearly defined long-term objectives related to a particular concern. Political pressure might come from political parties unhappy with the actions of an organisation. Support for politicians and their actions would come from the electorate.

There are also a number of independent consumer groups. For example, The Consumers' Association examines goods and services offered to the public and publishes the results of its research in *Which?* This magazine was founded in 1957 and has developed a circulation of more than half a million. It has become an invaluable source of information for consumers.

The National Federation of Consumer Groups is a co-ordinating body for voluntary and local consumer groups. Local groups survey local goods and services, publish reports and campaign for changes.

There is no doubt that, when consumers' rights are abused or when dangerous goods are brought

Learning activity

Set up your own consumer group to monitor the standards of products and services you regularly use. For example, you might set up a consumer group that monitors whether the cost of visiting your local football Premiership side is worth the money. You might set one up to look at the social facilities for young people in your district or perhaps a group that provides feedback to your course leader on the quality of your course.

into the marketplace, feelings run high. The media – newspapers, television and radio – increasingly become involved in campaigns.

The implications of not complying with legislation

In the sort of competitive environment in which UK businesses exist, failing to comply with EU and UK legislation should not be an option. Although it is sometimes difficult to work within a regulated environment, organisations that do not are likely to have their name tarnished if they contravene any of the consumer and customer-

CASE STUDY
Summer Sun Holidays

A number of customers of Summer Sun Holidays were recently moved from their chosen holiday accommodation to other studio apartments. Some customers were disappointed with the accommodation they were allocated which was dark and dismal. Summer Sun apologised for the suffering caused and provided refunds in some instances. Recently Summer Sun went into liquidation.

1 Is it possible for a business to be successful if it treats customers badly?
2 Look at each of the different forms of consumer legislation. To what extent do they provide genuine protection for consumers in this example?

focused legislation identified within this section. Consumers increasingly want to have confidence in the organisations supplying them with goods and services, and if organisations abuse the law this will influence their perceptions, as well as the decisions and choices they make about the products or services they buy.

By failing to comply with regulations, not only do organisations put themselves in a situation where litigious customers could take action against them, they are also in a position where such actions and subsequent publicity could seriously harm their competitive advantage.

Safe and secure working environment

In any situation in which customers come into an organisation, safety and security are important. For example, if someone visits a factory showroom they would not expect to be exposed to any serious mechanical hazards. Some organisations might provide special health and safety codes of practice or requirements for visitors. For example, an organisation providing cave visits would have to ensure that visitors were supervised, kept to particular routes and wore hard hats and so on. Organisations may have a code of practice or procedures that covered any of the following influences upon customers:

* safety and valuables

* fire

* control of hazardous substances

* behaviour of customers/guests

* security

* bomb threats.

In order to ensure that the working environment is safe for customers, staff have to be trained to ensure that they can carry out procedures to deal with such issues.

COURSEWORK ACTIVITY

The purpose of this activity is to investigate the customer service of two different organisations and examine how those organisations undertake the function of customer service. You may choose any sort of organisation, but to make sure that they are contrasting so that you can bring out many different details, look for two very different types of organisations. For example, the following organisations would have very contrasting customer service requirements:

* your school or college and Boots

* a local SME and B&Q

* your local hospital and WHSmith

* the army and Whitbread.

Of course, your choice should really be based upon some preliminary research so that you can easily find out about the customer service of the organisations. When undertaking this contrasting research think about:

* the need for customer service in each organisation. Think about the internal and external customers, their needs and expectations and discuss how far the customer service meets those expectations

* how the customer service is delivered. Remember to evaluate the quality of customer service and in doing so make judgements, draw conclusions and make recommendations

* the strengths and weaknesses of customer service in each organisation. As you do this try to provide a detailed review and analysis of customer service in each organisation and discuss methods that they use to maintain their quality of customer service

✳ the impacts of legislation upon the customer service offered by one of the two organisations, referring to the specific requirements in that context. Try to provide examples in which the organisations are influenced by the legislation, describing how it influences their specific actions.

Remember as you do this to show how you have undertaken the research and analysis and how this research meets the expectations of customers.

UNIT 6

Investigating promotion

This unit contains four parts:

6.1   Promotional tools and how they are used to affect buyer behaviour

6.2   Investigating promotional media

6.3   Constraints on promotion

6.4   Assessing a promotional campaign

Introduction

Promotion is one of the key elements of the marketing mix. Its purpose is to create an awareness and positive image of an organisation and its products. Promotion involves channelling money and effort into successfully managing what people think and feel, consciously and subconsciously about a company or product.

If the consumer is not aware of a brand it will not be on the shopping list. Promotion covers a range of activities that combine to form the promotional mix: the combination of **communication** strategies used to convey benefits to customers and influence them to buy. There are many different promotional tools that include:

* advertising
* sales promotion
* public relations
* direct marketing
* sponsorship.

FIGURE 6.1 *Promotion of services and goods is obvious here but there are many less obvious aspects of promotion*

✳ To understand how each of the promotional tools can be used to influence buyer behaviour

✳ The difference between each of the different types of media used for promotion

✳ How to evaluate and compare different types of media

✳ The internal constraints affecting promotional decisions

✳ External constraints upon promotional activities

✳ How to plan, organise and co-ordinate promotional activities

✳ The criteria used to assess and evaluate promotional campaigns.

6.1 Promotional tools and how they are used to affect buyer behaviour

The purpose of promotional tools is to influence buyer behaviour in one way or another. In order to do so, such tools are used to communicate a product's values and ways of operating to customers. It is easy to take such tools for granted. However, in an increasingly competitive marketplace crowded with products and services providing us, as consumers, with multiples of choices, it is often the way in which organisations promote and communicate with us that influences both what we buy and how we make our buying decisions.

No organisation should ever take the choices of promotion for granted. To promote products well, decision-makers within organisations not only need to understand the motivations of their customers but also how they will respond to various promotional activities. Any process of understanding people involves consumer psychology and, therefore, many theories have developed from psychologists.

Promotion is a form of communication. So, the starting point for understanding promotion is to consider its value as a form of communication. Wilbur Schramm (1955) defined communication as 'the process of establishing a commonness or oneness of thought between a sender and a receiver'. Today, the exchange of information takes place though sophisticated media such as networks of computers, fax machines, telephones, etc. An effective network of communications is essential for promotional activity; it enables an organisation not only to communicate with its customers but also to build up an image in the world at large. Such an image helps people to form a judgement about what the organisation stands for and will influence their dealings with it.

For marketing purposes, communication about products and services contributes to the persuasion process that encourages consumers to buy what is on offer. As all promotion activities involve an element of communication, an understanding of communication theory helps an organisation to make the most of its investments. There are a number of different models of communication.

Organisations are the *senders* in the communication process and consumers are the *receivers*. A sender will put information in the form that a receiver can understand. This might involve oral, visual, verbal or written messages to transmit the ideas. This process is called *encoding*. The sender will also choose a particular medium to send the message to the receiver (e.g. television, radio, newspapers). If the consumer interprets the

Learning activity

Think about how one organisation attempts to communicate with you. This could be through advertising or by enticing you to buy things through sales promotions. It could be the values associated with a particular brand. Describe how they do this and how the promotion, either positively or negatively, appeals to you.

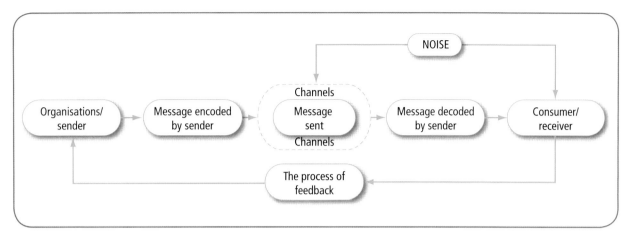

FIGURE 6.2 *The communication process*

message as required, it should have the impact that the seller wished for.

Though the message flows through to the receiver there is no guarantee that the receiver will either receive the full message or understand it. This is because the process may be subject to some form of interference, which affects the flow of information. This is known as *noise* and may lead to the downfall of the message. It will take the form of any barrier which acts as an impediment to the smooth flow of information and may include linguistic and cultural differences between the sender and the receiver. Another example is that a leaflet put through a door may be lost amongst a sea of direct mail from other organisations.

To increase the chances of a message getting across, an organisation needs to think carefully about the target audience. For example, it is important to channel the message through the most appropriate media. It might also be necessary to repeat the message several times rather than rely on one transmission.

Once the audience has been identified the communicator also needs to think about the sort of response required. If, for example, the final response required through the communication process is purchase, there may be six phases to the buyer-readiness process (see Figure 6.3).

It is important, therefore, that the promotion mix takes into account each of these stages with different types of promotional activities.

Another way of thinking about effective communications is a model based upon the

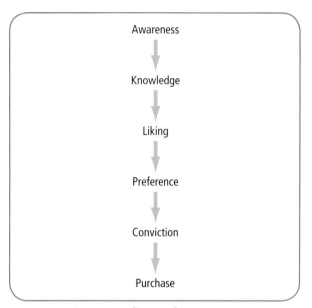

FIGURE 6.3 *Buyer-readiness phases*

Learning activity

Competition in the market for personal computers is fierce. Imagine that you work for a small organisation selling machines by mail order and you wish to target 'first-time' purchasers of PCs. Explain what you would do to build your communication strategy around the purchasing process.

6 Ms. In creating effective communications it is necessary to have a clear *mission*, i.e. an understanding of goals and objectives. What are you trying to achieve? If a brand is being introduced, the first objective is to establish brand awareness. The next is to create a positive

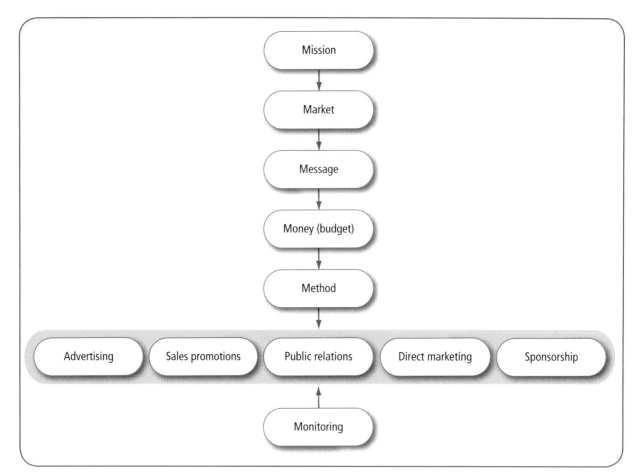

FIGURE 6.4 *The 6 Ms of effective communication*

attitude towards the brand. A third objective is to encourage trial of the product, and a fourth is to induce existing users to repeat their purchases so as to create brand loyalty.

You must be clear about the *market* at which you are targeting your communications and the best way of reaching this audience. The *message* is what you want to get across to the audience, and it will be concerned with developing awareness of the product and a positive image of the company or brand.

It is vital to decide upon how much *money* to spend on communications, i.e. there will be budget constraints. Money must be spent in the way that achieves the best possible results. The *method* employed will depend on the money available, the target market and the message that the advertiser wants to get across. The characteristics of various media will involve creative areas such as sound, vision and scripts, and the success of an advertising campaign will depend upon using creative skills effectively within the correct choice of media.

Monitoring is an essential part of the process and the one that completes the model. Detailed evaluation will identify possible improvements and check on the effectiveness of existing approaches.

Marketers are famous for acronyms that describe a process or exist as a checklist for some form of communication. SOSTT + 4 Ms is another strategic tool with a purpose of providing a checklist for strategic and tactical communications. The acronym refers to the following:

Situation – This is the current position of the organisation and its relationship to markets. This involves an analysis of the product range and the organisation's resources.

Objectives – These relate to the future. An organisation needs to think about what it hopes to achieve, both in the short and long term.

Strategy – This is usually long term and envelops the whole organisation. Strategies have to fit objectives.

Tactics – These are shorter term and are devised in order to match strategies.

Targets – Wherever there are objectives it is important to identify what they are. Targets are specific quantitatively-based aims that fit the objectives.

Men – People are important in the marketing process. The marketing strategy will influence people and it is necessary to identify people for different tasks.

Money – In order to meet promotional objectives, there has to be a budget and this must be used effectively.

Minutes – All promotional strategies must have a timescale as well as a series of deadlines. Planning and booking space in the media is important.

Measurement – Monitoring and evaluating the results helps to provide a base for understanding the effectiveness of a promotional campaign. It also provides useful feedback for future campaigns.

Another acronym that helps to decide how an organisation meets its objectives is AIDA. With this method:

A = attention – a customer's *attention* is captured and they are made aware of the product

I = interest – an impact stimulates their *interest*

D = desire – they are persuaded that they are deprived because they do not have the product, and this helps to stimulate a *desire* or *demand* for it

A = action – *action* involves the purchase of the product.

Learning activity

Using an example of a form of promotion known to you, describe how the AIDA acronym is used to prompt the consumer to make a decision. If, as AIDA suggests, consumers are persuaded that they are deprived of goods or services, to what extent could it be argued that some promotional activities are unfair to consumers?

Promotional tools

The promotional mix comprises all of the marketing and promotional communication methods used to achieve the objectives of the marketing mix. These methods can be broken down into two distinct areas:

Non-controllable methods are marketing messages communicated by word of mouth, personal recommendations and a consumer's overall perception of a particular product or service.

Consumer opinions are influenced by a number of factors such as whether their family has regularly used the product. A brand's history, character, colour and image will also have helped to create brand loyalty and influenced regular purchasing patterns. Perhaps the most famous brand heritage is that of Rolls Royce. The term 'a Rolls Royce company' is applied to organisations that build a strong reputation for their goods and services.

On the other hand, public displeasure with a particular organisation may influence purchases, for example if there is criticism of an organisation's employment practices, this could influence consumer perceptions.

Controllable methods are marketing methods that are carefully directed to achieve the objectives of an organisation. They include a number of areas:

1 *Advertisements* are paid, ongoing, nonpersonal communications from a commercial source such as a manufacturer or retailer.

2 *Sales promotions* are of two main types. Consumer promotions are short-term inducements of value to consumers to

CASE STUDY

Re-energising a brand character

Frosties is one of Kellogg's core products. With Frosties comes Tony the Tiger.

In 1999 Kellogg's undertook a huge process of strategic market research. The company hoped that the research would provide valuable information about the brand, its icon Tony the Tiger and the current position of Frosties within its product life cycle. The research focused on children under the age of 12 years, who are the main target market for Frosties. The data collected was both qualitative and quantitative.

The Frosties qualitative research showed that Tony, while 'cool', was losing relevance for some kids, which resulted in Frosties not having the 'playground credibility' like some other kids' brands, e.g. Dairylea and Tango.

Quantitative research about Frosties produced some key data. The research showed that the Frosties brand was nearing the end of the growth phase in its life cycle and was moving towards maturity as more competition entered the market. One effect of newer products from competitors was that children no longer considered Tony to be as 'cool' as other cereal characters.

Market research showed that although Tony the Tiger's new role should rely heavily upon the image and activities associated with Tony's past, his role should be updated and linked with current and futuristic activities.

An advertising agency came back with TV scripts, and showed how these scripts could be used within the whole promotional mix, particularly in special promotions, merchandising and public relations. The animated script needed to be tested with consumers so that it would be possible to predict accurately whether an investment made in modernising Tony would increase the sales volume and value of Frosties to an extent sufficient to justify the financial outlay.

A key decision in redeveloping the animation for Tony was whether to go for a flat TV cartoon animation, as used with Tom and Jerry, or for 3D animation as used in *Toy Story* and *Toy Story 2*. After much discussion, it was decided to create a 3D Tony and to use him not only in standard advertising media but also in new media such as the Internet.

Tony is a particularly valuable brand character, and Frosties remains a key brand for Kellogg's. In the highly competitive market for cereals, the sales performance of Frosties relates directly to the positive images projected by Tony. Giving Tony a new injection of life was seen as a vital contribution towards improving the competitiveness of the brand and prolonging its useful life.

1 Identify two brand characters and briefly discuss their qualities.
2 Explain why an advertising campaign needs to be evaluated.
3 Imagine that you are a brand manager for a consumer product of your choice.
   a Explain the criteria by which you would monitor the product's performance.
   b What research methods would you use to determine whether or not your advertising of the product needed to be reshaped?

FIGURE 6.5 *Cereal is a popular choice for breakfast*

encourage them to buy a product or service, e.g. money-off coupons, free samples and competitions. Trade promotions and promotions to retailers may also be used to encourage them to stock a particular brand.

3   *Public relations* (PR) can be defined as the development and maintenance of positive relationships between an organisation and its publics, achieved through activities designed to create understanding and goodwill.

4   *Personal selling* is face-to-face communication between sales representatives and customers, and is designed to influence the customer to buy the company's products or services.

5   *Direct marketing* involves using a first-hand way such as direct mail or telephone marketing to reach consumers and promote products or services to them.

6   *Sponsorship* involves creating opportunities for organisations to connect with a range of activities, and providing such activities with opportunities to function and bring in other revenue streams. They are commonly associated with the arts and theatre, music festivals, sporting leagues and competitions.

7   *Packaging* plays an important part in the promotional mix, although its importance is often neglected under the assumption that it is merely a production cost. In recent years packaging has accounted for an increasing proportion of the total cost of convenience goods.

It is possible to divide promotional strategies into two clear areas, one of which involves a 'push' strategy, while the other creates a 'pull' strategy. A push strategy focuses upon the channel of distribution. This might involve wholesalers or retailers. The aim is to push products into markets through the distribution channel. Sales promotions and various offers may be issued to distributors in the hope that they will equally promote products to eventual customers. This method involves pushing products into markets and this creates a heavy emphasis upon personal selling.

A pull strategy focuses upon the consumer. By promoting to the end user, advertisers are creating a demand for the product amongst consumers, who will ask for and demand products from retailers. Whereas push strategies are focused upon distribution and involve personal selling, pull strategies focus upon consumers. Most campaigns will contain both push and pull elements.

Advertisements

Advertising can be defined as a paid-for type of marketing communication that is non-personal, but aimed at a specific **target audience** through a mass media channel (See Unit 3).

If promotional activities do not meet these criteria, they are likely to fit another part of the promotional mix such as sales promotion, personal selling, direct marketing or public relations, and should not be referred to as advertising.

The multitude of opportunities for advertising through the media include the media channels outlined below – and each medium provides the potential to access different types of target audience:

✱ television

✱ radio

✱ newspapers, magazines and journals

✱ cinema

✱ posters, billboards and flyers

✱ transport advertising.

The types of advertising an organisation may undertake can be divided into three broad categories based on the targeted groups they are attempting to influence, and the purpose of the message. These three types of advertising are trade advertising, consumer advertising and corporate advertising.

In many markets, especially in consumer goods, advertising constitutes the largest spending area for marketing communications. This is because of the advantages of advertising as a communications medium over alternative promotional activities. The major advantages of

FIGURE 6.6 *There are many different ways to advertise*

advertising as a promotional tool are that it has a potentially low cost per target audience reached if the appropriate medium is used, and allows continued repetition of the message.

The potential disadvantages associated with advertising as a promotional medium are that while it can have a low cost per customer reached if appropriately targeted, the costs of advertising in absolute terms are very high. Also, its lack of flexibility in adjusting its message to the audience may mean its persuasiveness is less effective than more personal promotional tools, such as personal selling. The lack of feedback obtained also means its effectiveness is often difficult to establish. Throughout the advertising process it is important to assess how effectively advertisements contribute to the communication process. In order to measure the link between advertising and the achievement of objectives, an organisation must closely define the goals of its communication policy.

The target audience is made aware of the product, of which it previously had no knowledge, then its interest in the product is stimulated to the point where it desires the product. The purchase of the product is referred to as the action.

Advertising must be a purposive communication to a target market, and should draw attention to the characteristics of a product, which will appeal to the buying motives of potential customers. It can create awareness, persuade, inform and reinforce awareness of characteristics of a product, and it should differentiate it from other products and highlight characteristics that give it an increased value for the target audience. If a product does not have a distinguishing characteristic – referred to as a **unique selling proposition (USP)** – uniqueness can be promoted by brand image.

The ultimate purpose of advertising for organisations is to enhance potential buyers' responses to its products by channelling desires and by supplying reasons for consumers to prefer its products over those of its competitors. Advertising is often classed under one of three headings:

* *Informative advertising* conveys information and raises consumer awareness of the features and benefits of a product. It is often used in the introductory stage of a product, or after modification.

* *Persuasive advertising* is concerned with creating a desire for the product and stimulating purchase. It is used with established and more mature products.

* *Reinforcement advertising* is concerned with reminding consumers about the product, and is used to reinforce the knowledge held by potential consumers about the benefits to be gained from purchase.

In the absence of product differentiation, that is the identification and promotion of differences between similar products, all advertising would be generic – that is, it would benefit all producers equally. Hence it is vital for an individual firm to differentiate its brand from competitors if spending on advertising is to be worthwhile.

Sales promotions

Sales promotions can be defined as any short-term incentive designed to encourage sales of a product or service (see Unit 3). These promotions can be aimed at three groups: consumers, the sales force, and trade or other intermediaries.

Sales promotional techniques are used extensively by some industries, and when successfully implemented there is a direct link between the promotion and short-term sales. Such promotions can be highly successful in encouraging trials by consumers and are often used as a brand switching strategy in highly competitive markets.

Ultimately, the objective of sales promotions is to increase sales revenue by encouraging the consumer to purchase more. They can be undertaken in an attempt to clear old stock or to encourage the purchase of slow moving items. In some cases sales promotions may also be implemented to counter the promotional activities of competitors, or even simply to motivate the sales force.

Promotional activities can be implemented through the mass media, through product packaging or by merchandising.

Consumer promotions

Consumer promotions can take various forms including:

* prize promotions and competitions

* free gifts with a purchase

* redeemable coupon offers

* money-off labels

* combination pack promotions (e.g. two for the price of one)

* loyalty cards.

£M	1998	1999	2000	2001	2002	2003
Press	4,134	4,338	4,687	4,458	4,285	4,224
TV	4,029	4,321	4,646	4,147	4,332	4,374
Outdoor & transport	613	649	810	788	816	901
Cinema	97	123	128	164	180	180
Radio	460	516	595	541	545	582
Direct mail	1,666	1,876	2,049	2,228	2,378	2,431
Internet	19	51	155	166	233	376
Total	11,018	11,873	13,071	12,491	12,768	13,068

Source: The Marketing Pocket Book 2005, World Advertising Research Center

FIGURE 6.7 *Sales promotions*

Promotional activities that may be targeted towards the retailer or salesforce can include such benefits as extended credit facilities or even prizes or financial bonuses for volume of sales achieved.

Whatever the promotion is, it is important that organisations remember that sales promotions are short-term sales measures and should be aimed at increasing immediate sales in the hope that at least a small proportion of that increase in sales will remain after the promotion has concluded.

An organisation undertaking a sales promotion campaign should not be tempted to sacrifice long-term objectives such as the development of a corporate image for the sake of short-term sales increases. Such tactics can seriously affect the positioning and image of a company or its products in the eyes of the consumer, and may eventually be to the detriment of that organisation.

Despite this danger, sales promotional activities can be a very effective tool. The specific techniques available are outlined below.

Prize promotions

Prize promotions may include free draws, games of chance or contests of skill. With all such promotions it is vital that the rules and conditions of the competition are clearly stated, including the closing date, and that the prizes are appropriate to the product being promoted.

Free gifts

In some cases free gifts may be given with a purchase, but this technique is only likely to be successful if the consumer values the free gift. In many cases the use of a collector's range of gifts is made in an attempt to increase loyalty to the brand.

Redeemable coupons

Redeemable coupons can be distributed via direct mail, as part of a press advertisement, or handed out as flyers at given geographical locations. One advantage of redeemable coupons is that special product labels do not need to be printed, and this makes them easier to distribute when large stocks of pre-labelled products have already been produced.

Next purchase coupons

This is a form of coupon which the consumer receives after purchasing the product at its regular price. This coupon is then redeemable on a later purchase. Coupons can be placed on-pack, but it is considered better to put the coupon inside the pack if possible to prevent dishonesty.

One major problem with this technique is that while coupons are intended to be redeemed only against a specified product, some retailers will redeem coupons for their face value without purchase of the relevant product.

Money-back offers

In a money-back offer, the consumer buys the product at the normal price and then reclaims some or all of the money from the manufacturer. Such offers enable the consumer to have more experience of the product than a free sample allows, but they put the buyer to some inconvenience. They are usually limited to one per household to prevent abuse of the offer.

FIGURE 6.8 *Supermarket loyalty coupons*

Tesco Clubcard

Tesco launched its Clubcard in February 1995. This is a customer loyalty scheme that rewards shoppers with a 1 per cent discount on purchases. Within nine months of the launch, 6 million shoppers held the card and Tesco was rewarded with a 16 per cent increase in interim profits and the fastest sales growth in the grocery sector.

Loyalty cards have several aims. The first is to increase the number of shoppers, the second, to encourage each shopper to spend more and the third is the hope that the cards will tie consumers to a particular retailer.

However, a further aim of the scheme is to provide businesses with detailed information about its customers. Details on how much they spend – and on what items – can be used to segment the market and then target consumers.

Using direct marketing techniques, consumers with very young children, for example, can be targeted with information or offers on baby food and nappies. The ultimate aim of this promotional technique is to use information technology to mimic the relationships established in the old corner shop, where the owners knew each customer's tastes and needs.

1 With so many retailers now offering loyalty cards, what do you feel may be the consequences of this competition?
2 Do you feel there is a problem with the long-term principle behind such loyalty cards, or Is there more to this promotional technique than simply offering discounts to consumers?

Combination pack promotions

In some cases it is appropriate for a manufacturer to offer the incentive of a related product included with the standard product – an example being a sample of a conditioner attached to a shampoo. The objective of this type of promotion is that it can help to develop loyalties to a range of complementary products.

Loyalty cards

Store cards are used to encourage long-term relationships with consumers, but despite the fact that the principle is long term rather than short term, such techniques are still considered to be part of a sales promotion category.

Public relations

Public relations can be defined as the development and maintenance of positive relationships between an organisation and its publics, achieved through activities designed to create understanding and goodwill.

Whereas many of the other promotional methods are short term, public relations is long term, as it may take a long time for an organisation to improve the way people think more positively about its products and activities. For example, just think about the sort of public relations problems that chemical and oil companies have in a world where consumers have become increasingly environmentally conscious.

Despite their differences, press publicity and public relations are often planned together. Frequently companies use the services of a specialist publicity and PR agency, which can offer a flexible, professional and proactive approach to this often under-utilised part of the promotional mix.

The major advantages of press and public relations as a promotional tool are that they are potentially very low in cost, and the publicity generated is often perceived by consumers as less biased than some other forms of promotion.

Some disadvantages are that it is difficult to control media reactions to press relations and PR, which at times may be negative rather than positive. In addition the timing is hard to predict, and hence it is difficult to assess the real impact in terms of marketing objectives.

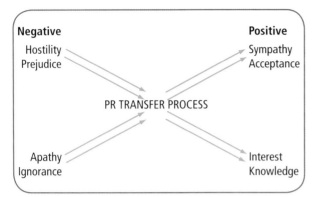

Negative	Positive
Hostility	Sympathy
Prejudice	Acceptance

PR TRANSFER PROCESS

| Apathy | Interest |
| Ignorance | Knowledge |

FIGURE 6.9 *The PR transfer process*

Despite these difficulties, with the increasing pressure on advertising space, time and costs, the importance that organisations place on press and public relations is undeniably increasing.

According to Frank Jefkins (1974), PR involves a transfer process which helps to convert the negative feelings of an organisation's many publics into positive ones (see Figure 6.9).

When an organisation is attempting to develop a public relations approach, a number of factors must be established. First, the objectives of the public relations exercise must be clearly identified. Second, it is necessary to identify the publics that the organisation has to deal with and is attempting to influence. Third, the organisation must establish the target public's current view of the product or company and fourth, the PR plan has to be developed with respect to the public relations tools available to the organisation.

A wide range of tools are available, none of which is exclusive to public relations, and any of them could be used in other areas of the promotional mix. The list can include, exhibitions, competitions, school visits, open days and sponsorship, or more press-directed activities including press releases, information packs and press conferences.

Whilst it may not be appropriate to use them all in one campaign, they should all be considered on their various merits with regard to the objectives identified by the organisation.

Personal selling

Most days of your life you are involved in some form of selling activity. It might be persuading a friend to come with you to the cinema, or asking

Learning activity

Think about a recent situation in which somebody has been involved in trying to personally sell something to you. It could be somebody selling over the phone, somebody calling at the door, an individual trying to sell you tickets for a concert or play or even your teacher encouraging you to attend a session or go on a school trip. Describe and then evaluate the success of the various techniques they used.

a relative to buy something for you. What you are doing is using your relationship to sell your ideas to someone else.

Personal or direct selling involves interaction between individuals or groups of individuals.

The objective of personal selling is to make a sale, and it is the culmination of all of the marketing activities that have taken place beforehand. It involves matching a customer's requirements with the goods or services on offer. The better the match, the more lasting the relationship between the seller and the buyer.

The role of personal selling will vary from business to business. It is a two-way process which can be one of the most expensive areas of the promotional mix. This personal communication element can be very important as the final sale might come only as a result of protracted negotiations.

The main benefit of personal selling is the ability to communicate with and focus on customers individually and with precision. For example, if you go into a travel agency and ask for details about a holiday, the sales assistant may explain and point out the features of various packages and any discounts or promotions they might offer. All the other areas of the promotional mix are targeted at groups of people.

Although we have mental stereotypes of the typical salesperson, selling involves special skills. Whereas there is a tendency to downgrade this role in the UK, in many countries (Germany for example), sales staff require a high degree of technical competence and are generally accepted to be part of the corporate elite. Salespeople are key intermediaries who present information to customers and then provide feedback on customer needs.

FIGURE 6.10 *Personal selling*

Sales staff are representing an organisation and so need to reflect a positive image from that organisation. It is important that they do not offend customers by their appearance – the mode of dress should match the nature of the products and the organisation. For example, a sales assistant in a fashion store should wear something up to date, whereas an insurance salesperson should wear more formal clothes. It is often said that the way we look determines the way others look at us!

Similarly, effective speaking will help to create the appropriate image and situation for the sale to take place. Good grammar, vocabulary, diction and voice tone may help to reflect the degree of professionalism required for the sale to take place.

Many organisations spend more on personal selling than on any other area of the promotional mix, and within organisations large number of individuals may find that personal selling forms part of their role. Personal selling may involve individuals developing special skills and using

them in many different operational situations. To do so, sales staff need to know their products and be well trained in selling techniques.

Selling in a highly competitive world means that preparation has never been so important. Though it has been said that salespeople are born and not made, nevertheless skills, knowledge and training can improve performance. Training is designed to build on people's selling skills and teach them how to use their personal abilities and understanding to follow the psychological stages of the sales process. Product knowledge is vital, as it allows for feedback from the prospective customer's questions about the product's technical specifications, benefits and functions.

Knowing their customers may help to determine how sales staff communicate with them. For example, some customers may prefer to be addressed with the more formal Mr or Mrs while others like to be called by their first name.

Probing is important in the early stage of a sales presentation, in order to find out the prospect's needs and where his or her priorities might lie. The salesperson can then try to match the product or service with the prospect's requirements. This may involve elaborating on the product's advantages, concentrating on aspects such as savings in costs, design ingredients, performance specifications, after-sales service, etc.

During the presentation, the salesperson must constantly evaluate whether the product is appropriate to the needs of the prospect. It is unethical to sell something that is not needed – although this may often happen! The large and more complex the order, the more complex the negotiations over supply. In many different situations it is important to provide a number of services to help with the process. For example, these might include:

* product demonstrations
* performance specifications
* sales literature
* samples
* a meeting to discuss details
* credit facilities
* sales promotions.

The prospective customer may have a variety of reservations about the purchase. These reservations may be genuine, or the result of a misunderstanding. There might be reluctance to make a commitment at this stage. Logical, well-presented arguments and incentives may overcome such reservations.

Timing is crucial to the sale. A salesperson must look for *buying signals* which indicate that the prospect is close to a decision, and almost ready to put a signature on an order form and discuss the contractual arrangements.

It is always important to *follow up the sale with post-sale support*. Promises that might have been made during the negotiations will have to be fulfilled. If the salesperson guarantees delivery by a certain date, that date must be held. Servicing arrangements must be efficiently carried out, and any problems dealt with. Contacting customers to see if they are happy with the product will encourage repeat buying and improve the supplier's concern for its customers.

Sales staff may also have a number of other related functions. Communication, for example, is an important role. Sales staff act as an information link between suppliers and their customers. As a result, personal selling involves a boundary role – being at the boundary of a supplying organisation and also in direct and close contact with customers. The role is often not only one of selling but also one of interpreting the activities and policies of each organisation to the other. A considerable amount of administration may also therefore accompany the selling role. For example, reports, schedules and computerised information such as inventory details are a part of daily life for a salesperson.

Comprehensive records on customers should be kept and updated after each visit. Keeping sales records enables the salesperson to respond exactly to each customer's individual needs. Knowledge of competitors and their products enables the seller to respond to queries about the relative merits and drawbacks of products.

Direct marketing

In its most common forms, direct marketing includes direct mail and telephone marketing (or telemarketing). However, leaflet-dropping and even handing out flyers in the street all fit this category of promotion, which allows an organisation to approach the consumer without going through the process of mass-media advertising.

Direct marketing can be used in much the same way as advertising, and the objectives of such a campaign can range from promoting special offers to offering the opportunity to try new products. However, in comparison with conventional advertising, which can reach a much wider audience, the cost of direct marketing can be high and it may not be suitable for developing an awareness campaign for products which have a potential mass-market appeal.

Like telemarketing, direct mail has a much narrower reach than traditional advertising and hence is generally more closely targeted. As a result, it is not always appropriate unless a more niche market exists.

FIGURE 6.11 *Direct mail might be junk mail*

Many direct mailings are of no interest to the recipient and are dismissed as junk mail, usually because they are inappropriately targeted or poorly produced. If direct mail is to succeed, companies must target their markets more selectively and they must stimulate interest with better designed and more interesting letters and inserts.

The success of direct marketing is highly dependent on a well-researched and properly constructed mailing list, targeted appropriately.

Enquiries and orders contained in internal company records can be used to compile what is commonly referred to as a first-party list. These are based on existing customers or potential customers who have shown a genuine interest in the company or its products, so they are likely to be superior to lists acquired from other sources, which are referred to as third-party lists.

Lists can be developed by organisations in a number of ways, including swapping lists with other companies who are not in direct competition but have a similar customer profile. Renting a list from a bureau is also common practice and in some cases it may be possible for an organisation to buy a list from a competitor that is leaving the market. It is possible for a company to do the research work itself by using direct response advertising to generate further contacts, and it is not unknown for a company to take over another company in order to get its list.

Once a list has been developed it must be kept up to date, and duplication must be avoided where a number of lists have been purchased or rented. In addition, as part of a review of the mailing list, the addresses of letters returned because the addressee has moved should be removed from the list. It should also be noted if the rate of such returns is high, since this indicates a poorly compiled or out-of-date list.

Some organisations may choose to undertake mailing in-house, but it is possible to use a bureau, or a lettershop, to undertake the enveloping and addressing. A full-service bureau will not only develop the mailing list, but will print and distribute the direct mailing.

Some companies offer an omnibus mailing, where a number of organisations' promotional literature is sent out together. However, such mailings often lack impact, and solus (single) mailings are generally considered a better option.

Similar to omnibus mailings is the process of piggy-backing, which allows businesses to get cheap mailing by inserting information into another company's mailing. Once again it is vital that the target audiences of both companies are appropriately matched, and while it is not as diluted as an omnibus mailing it can still lack impact.

Personalisation of literature can strongly influence the likelihood of recipients reading what is sent to them. With improved information technology and computer-driven printing, personalisation can be applied to a range of areas within direct mailing, from simple adjustment of the salutation at the beginning of the letter, to more complex procedures where details are adjusted within the body of the text.

In order to assess the impact of a direct mailing campaign, the organisation should undertake a review by comparing the number of letters sent out with the number of positive responses. This helps to establish the appropriateness of the **targeting**.

As well as using lists to approach potential customers through direct mailing or telemarketing, it is possible to use mass-media promotions in order to generate inbound enquiries, and so limit the amount of wasted mail or telephone calls. Mass-media advertising of the direct-response type can be used to generate sales or new leads. The main form is off-the-page print media campaigns, which are used to stimulate initial interest and enquiry. Potential consumers pre-select themselves by making use of a reply coupon or a phone number.

TV and radio advertisements can also be used, but the difficulty with using broadcast media is the time required to allow viewers or listeners to take down an address or phone number. For this reason, print media are often preferred.

Direct-response advertisements are fairly straightforward to monitor since advertisements can be coded and sales or leads can be credited directly to codes in order to measure success rates.

Telemarketing is direct marketing by telephone. The outbound form of direct marketing (business to customer calls) is often used to generate leads which are passed on to specialist sales staff who pursue the prospects further.

Suffering from the same failings as direct mailings, many telemarketing calls have become junk calls because of poorly targeted lists and poorly produced scripts. In order to operate effectively, telemarketing needs the same attention to detail as would be undertaken with direct mail and perhaps requires even more highly trained staff as telephonists.

The inbound system (where the customer contacts the business) is where a free call service is offered to customers in a media campaign. This form of direct marketing requires appropriate customer care and helps save customers time and expense, allowing them to compare a range of companies.

Such campaigns can, however, suffer as a result of their success. Inability on the part of the advertiser to cope with large numbers of calls in a short period of time, generated by a successful

FIGURE 6.12 *Call centres often handle incoming and outbound calls*

campaign, can negatively affect the image of the company.

Telemarketing is a complex task and requires a highly-trained task force if it is to be successful. The selling aspect involves more than simply reading from a script, and requires sophisticated selling techniques in order to sell other products within the range offered or sell more of the same product. Good telemarketing requires staff with excellent interpersonal skills, a sound knowledge of products and services, and good administrative capabilities to deal with such matters as processing orders and estimates.

Letterbox leafleting, which also comes under the title of direct mailing, involves dropping non-personalised flyers through letterboxes. Typical users of this approach are fast-food outlets, where there is no need for complex targeting procedures and geographical segmentation is sufficient to reach the target audience. Like all direct marketing, this process can lose impact when a number of leaflets are dropped at the same time.

Flyers may also be handed out on the street or placed under the windscreen wipers of parked cars. This can be an effective means of contacting potential customers but once again the most important aspect is the establishment of appropriate targeting systems.

Beyond the more traditional forms of direct marketing, the emergence of interactive television has now extended the concept of direct mail advertising into full-scale television channels devoted to home shopping.

Improvements in technology have resulted in the proliferation of satellite and cable channels and the widespread availability of home-shopping channels such as QVC (Quality, Value, Convenience) which allows consumers to view and purchase goods in the comfort of their own home.

At present, the response mechanism is the telephone system, but with the advance of interactive technologies, consumers may soon be able to buy what they see on screen using remote controls. The interactive nature of this technology is likely to be developed further with viewers able to determine the type of advertisements they wish to view at the flick of a button.

Organisations are always looking for alternative ways of meeting their business objectives. The Internet provides a useful and different source not just for secondary and sometimes primary market research, but also different ways of reaching groups of clients and customers.

Having said this, many companies invested quickly in Internet technology, expecting that

CASE STUDY
Ofcom guidelines
According to Ofcom, the UK's regulator for the digitial communications industry,

'Interactivity is a functionality rather than a specific type of service, and it can be applied in a wide variety of contexts. Its distinguishing characteristic is the ability of viewers to interact with TV programmes by one of two methods:

✳ by changing the content which appears on the screen, for example to access background information, to change camera angles, to view more than one picture at a time, or to view associated text at the same time as a main picture

✳ by providing information to the broadcaster through a return path, usually a telephone line, for example to order a product, to exercise votes on options provided by a programme or to participate in an on-screen quiz show.

These services are available only to members of the public with digital equipment, whether satellite, cable or digital terrestrial.'

1 What are the purposes of interactive technologies such as interactive television?
2 Why might such activities need regulation?
3 As a form of direct marketing, how could they be used to develop relationships with consumers?

CASE STUDY

Selling Discount Books

Richard Strang had owned and managed a business, but also felt that he was a budding entrepreneur. He just wanted to be his own boss. His hobby was collecting old books and so Richard decided to sell books that were not vital to his collection on eBay, the on-line auction site and marketplace. He also bought books and posted them for sale on eBay, setting up his business, Richard's Discount Books (http://stores. ebay.com/Richards-Discount-Books-And-Stuff).

Richard now sells more than 90 per cent of his books on eBay and the rest at flea markets. The great benefit is that he does not need a shop, just a warehouse to store his books.

Richard is just one of many who have started eBay-based businesses. About 430,000 people around the world earn money by regularly selling on eBay. The eBay site currently carries an average of more than 29 million items, with more than 3.5 million new ones added daily. eBay is sometimes referred to as the world's biggest garage sale, and provides a useful opportunity for small businesses to develop electronic sales beyond their existing customer base.

1 What is eBay?
2 How has it helped Richard to identify business opportunities?
3 What are the advantages of developing a business over the Internet compared with traditional ways of developing a small business?

FIGURE 6.13 *eBay*

alongside the huge growth in the number of users, business opportunities would abound, only to have their fingers burnt with many users wary about buying online. However, there have been some big success stories, and Amazon and eBay are today well-known e-business operators, both of whom operate in widely different ways.

As we have seen, marketers are famous for their acronyms, and the Internet has provided many opportunities to develop new ones including: AJ – Ask Jeeves, AOL – America Online, ASP – Application Service Provider, AV – AltaVista, CPA – Cost Per Action, CPC – Cost Per Click, CPS – Cost Per Sale, CTR – Click-Through Rate and DH – Direct Hit.

The evolution of the Internet has:

* provided many organisations with opportunities to reach different markets, and in many cases export overseas

* enabled organisations to build better relationships with customers through relationship marketing

* become a valuable opportunity to undertake secondary market research. It has also enabled organisations to use online questionnaires with customers and potential customers

* provided links with offline tools such as direct mail

* created a steep but evolving learning curve that now has become significantly more scientific as a marketing tool.

Sponsorship

Sponsorship is a form of PR activity which has particularly taken off in recent years, becoming increasingly common in connection with the arts and theatre, music festivals, sporting leagues and competitions (see Unit 3). Sponsorship is cost-effective and tends to be viewed by the public less cynically than other forms of PR activity. A weakness of sponsorship is that the company name becomes associated with an event or performance, rather than with the product itself.

Sponsorship is a good way of increasing brand awareness which, in turn, helps to generate preference and foster brand loyalty. Sponsorship is the material support of an event, activity or organisation by an unrelated donor. It reinforces awareness through an appropriate event whose

Learning activity

Using an example, identify the advantages of sponsorship for the sponsoring organisation.

CASE STUDY

Sponsoring *Friends*

Nescafé had a long-term sponsorship deal with the popular US comedy *Friends*.

The *Friends* series carried a lot of youth appeal with a lot of 20-something friends frequently sharing fun experiences with beverages. It appealed specifically to 16–24-year-olds within an upbeat social environment. *Friends* shares many of the core values of Nescafé which made a partnership so logical.

Within a short period of time 75% of all 16–24-year-olds were aware of the sponsorship and research showed that the sponsorship had successfully reached Nescafé's core market.

Those who associated Nescafé with *Friends* felt that Nescafé was good for drinking with friends, was modern and contemporary and had now developed an association for being youthful and lighthearted.

1 **Why would Nescafé want to sponsor *Friends*?**

2 **What links the brand values of Nescafé with *Friends*?**

3 **How might Nescafé gain through such sponsorship?**

target market and appeal are similar to that of the sponsoring company.

Sponsorship involves an arrangement between a sponsor and a sponsee where the sponsor provides support, either by supplying a product or service or through financial support, to an event or activity of which the sponsee is at the centre. Sponsorship is not an act of charity as far as the sponsor is concerned, and it must show some form of return. Since sponsorship is a business arrangement, standard evaluative criteria should be used to establish the suitability of a proposed event in relation to the image of the sponsor and its products.

Sponsorship can offer a wide range of benefits for the sponsor. For example, it can be used to raise the image of the organisation as a whole, to promote the virtues of a specific range of products, or even as part of a sales promotion campaign. It can be used as an exercise in corporate hospitality or even, at a local level, can simply be seen as a good community relations initiative.

Before sponsoring an activity, the sponsor must be sure that the event will be successful. It is clearly much easier to sponsor an event with a proven track record. Sports sponsorship is the most common form of sponsorship, and can range in scale from international and national down to regional and local events.

Packaging

The basic function of any pack is to protect its contents in transit, in storage and in use, and this plays a major part in determining its shape, size and the materials used. However, consumers increasingly see attractive packaging as adding value to products.

The packaging of consumer goods was originally carried out by retailers. Today, manufacturers play the major part in packaging, enabling them to control the image and presentation of the product. Packaging performs the following functions:

✳ It identifies and promotes a brand – e.g. the distinctive Coca-Cola bottle and can design.

✳ When distinctive, it catches the eye of the consumer.

FIGURE 6.14 *Nescafé and Coca-Cola packaging promotes the brands*

✳ It identifies a line of related products.

✳ It communicates information on ingredients, quantity and product uses.

✳ It helps with the preservation, storage and safety of products.

Influence upon buyer behaviour

Businesses use consumer models in order to help understand consumer behaviour, in terms of how and why purchasing decisions are made. It is also important to understand how consumers behave and try to assess how promotions influence consumer behaviour in a way that enables organisations to meet their company objectives.

Achieving business objectives

There may be a number of organisational objectives such as:

✳ *Increasing sales*. This may be in terms of volume and value of products sold, leading to changes in market share.

* *Changing market positioning*. Promotions are particularly effective in influencing how consumers think about products in relation to those of competitors.

* *Improving the competitiveness* of an organisation, particularly where there are constantly changing market conditions, with organisations constantly having to review and amend their strategies.

* *Providing information for customers*. Before making decisions customers may want information, particularly if that information might influence the purchase.

* *Changing the image of the organisation or the values represented by the brand*. As part of the positioning process, promotion is a valuable tool that influences how people think about organisations.

* *Appearing to be creative and modern*. Promoting an organisation involves a range of creative skills associated with products and brands. When memorable, promotions have a positive impact upon an organisation.

* *Raising awareness* involves simply communicating key features about products and brands in order to dispel myths and rumours and to communicate truths.

* *Develop a means of communicating effectively with customers*. Promotion, as we have seen, is a form of communication. It may be possible to use promotion to develop meaningful relationships with customers, particularly through direct methods, and develop various form of relationship marketing.

In order to achieve such objectives, promotions are used to influence buyer behaviour as shown in Figure 6.15.

Customer behaviour involves a wide range of personal and situational variables including attitudes, motivations, learning processes, perceptions and social and cultural influences, and through the development of a model, the marketer attempts to translate relationships into systems. Once developed these models can help the marketer by providing a frame of reference and suggesting variables that might not be

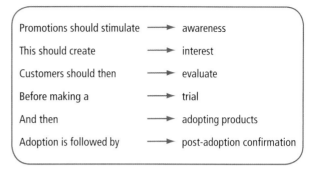

FIGURE 6.15 *How promotions influence consumer behaviour*

immediately apparent when trying to understand the reasons behind consumers' actions.

There are many potential influences on consumer behaviour. One major influence is risk, which is involved in all purchasing decisions. The extent to which an individual considers a purchase risky is highly personal, and relates to the consumer's individual perception of what is risky and his or her circumstances.

The risks a consumer faces in making a purchase can be classified under certain headings:

* Functional risk – will the product do what I want it to do?

* Physical risk – will I be injured or hurt by the purchase?

* Financial risk – is it worth the money or would I be better buying an alternative?

* Social risk – will people think I'm stupid to purchase this product ?

* Psychological risk – will it affect my self-image, and am I going to feel unhappy with myself?

* Time risk – am I wasting my time, and would I be better doing something else?

One particular aim for promotion is to influence the attitudes of potential customers. Attitudes can be defined as a learned orientation or disposition, towards an object or situation, which provides a tendency to respond favourably or unfavourably to the object or situation. Marketers are concerned with understanding how attitudes are formed because part of the role of marketers is to modify consumer attitudes and develop positive ones towards the products they are attempting to sell.

Joining a health club

Holmes Place in Nottingham is a health and fitness club, using a grade two listed building next to Nottingham Station. Health clubs like Holmes Place offer an extensive mix of activities and facilities that do not just include swimming and health and fitness studios, but also personal trainers, as well as aerobics, street dance, yoga and pilates.

Charlie lives in Nottingham and is going through a mid-life crisis. Since he turned 40 he has put on a lot of weight, got divorced and changed jobs. Unhappy with the way things have been going over the past six months, he has thought seriously about joining a health club so that he can work out in the gym, but he never seems to get around to it. He has not been active in terms of sport since he left college at 18.

1 How would a health club like Holmes Place attempt to promote itself to somebody with Charlie's profile?
2 If Charlie came to your health club, what would you say to help him overcome his perception of the risks that have been preventing him from joining?

FIGURE 6.16 *The Holmes Place logo*

An attitude is formed from a combination of mental processes and expressed by actions. Most psychologists agree that at some level, attitudes contain three components:

* A cognitive component – the knowledge and perceptions about an object, for instance, its colour or price.

* An affective component – what a person subjectively feels about the object, i.e. whether he or she is favourably disposed towards it.

* A behavioural component – how a person responds to the object, i.e. does he or she purchase it.

An individual's attitudes can cover a wide range of tangible and intangible factors, and may be strongly or weakly held. Many attitudes may be entrenched in an individual's psychological make-up and may be strongly resistant to change. However, the fact that attitudes are based on a continuous evaluation and are learned through conditioning and social modelling leaves the door open for marketers to influence them and therefore the actions of consumers.

Marketers are not interested simply in being able to develop positive attitudes in consumers. They want individuals not only to have a positive attitude towards the product, but also to buy it.

All communications undertaken by businesses to potential consumers are an attempt to convince the target audience that their needs are best met by the products offered by the advertiser, rather than those of its competitors. The principle behind all promotional activities involves meeting a need, and Maslow categorised human needs in five groups which he arranged into a hierarchy of importance (see Unit 1). Maslow's hierarchy has proved useful in applying a behaviour-orientated structure to the market.

From a needs perspective, each product or service addresses a needs category. Most products only address the basic physiological and safety needs of consumers, but from a communications perspective it is possible to position products so that they appeal to the full range of needs categories by adjusting the promotional message to encompass elements of self-esteem, social or belonging needs and even self-fulfilment. For example, while the purchase of bread may seem to satisfy only the core physiological needs of the consumer, through effective advertising and image creation the higher needs of the individual may be met through intangible attributes such as image.

6.2 Investigating promotional media

The term 'media owners' refers to the publishers of the media and their supplying contractors, including press, cinema, TV and radio broadcasting as well as the owners of advertising hoardings and billboards.

The advertisers are those individuals or businesses with a product or service they wish to publicise, who depend on the availability of methods of advertising offered by media owners. The requirements of reciprocal trading could be met with the media owners acting as suppliers to meet the demand of the advertisers, and for many small businesses this is how supply and demand for advertising is undertaken in trading terms. However, many advertisers lack either the skills or resources required to undertake an advertising campaign efficiently, and as a result they turn to an advertising agency to help in the promotion of their services or products.

Advertising agencies range in both size and in the services they offer to potential advertisers. They specialise in promotional activities and may offer either a full range of services starting with the creation and planning of a campaign, including the execution of it, or they may specialise in one or more specific areas within a range of services required by advertisers.

Agencies that offer the full service will be heavily involved from the outset in planning the promotional strategy in consultation with the client. This planning process would involve them in such areas as the development of marketing research projects to establish consumer profiles, and will necessitate the establishment of clear and specific objectives. In addition, both parties will be involved in the determination of specific consumer target groups, and the strategy to be undertaken for the promotion.

In addition to the planning aspects of the campaign, a full service agency also offers the development of the creative elements. At this stage of the campaign it is the responsibility of the creative department to design and write the advertisement's images and slogans related to the selling propositions that fit the profile of the products or services being offered.

The third and final stage of the advertising campaign involves the media department, whose role it is to research, plan and purchase the media time or space in order to reach the target market in the most cost-effective manner.

Not all agencies offer the full service and many organisations such as media independents offer businesses only a media buying service without the additional creative services. Creative independents and designers offer only creative services, without the media buying options.

Even where organisations do offer a full range of services including supporting services such as press and public relations and sales promotion development, it is not necessary for an advertiser to contract for all these services with the same provider. Advertisers should examine the services offered by an agency and select those that they feel are most appropriate to their requirements – choosing to use a number of agencies if necessary.

Both the size and the position of advertising in the print media are of vital importance to the marketer. Too small an advert won't be seen, and if placed in the wrong part of the page or publication an advert is easily skipped over by the potential target audience.

Newspapers and magazines offer standard sizes for display advertisements, ranging from quarter-page, half-page and full-page to double and even three- or four-page spreads in the case of magazines, which have the option of fold-out pages. In practice, it is possible to negotiate an advertisement of any size and shape.

Advertisements may be positioned at different places throughout most publications. Standard specifications include outside back cover (OBC), inside front cover (IFC) and inside

Coca-Cola

Coca-Cola's US advertising agency, McCann-Erickson, stipulates clearly within its briefs to publishers where Coke ads can and cannot be placed. Coca-Cola itself stipulates that all insertions are placed adjacent to editorial. That is consistent with the brand's marketing strategy – in general Coca-Cola aims to be associated with positive and upbeat editorial, in an attempt to communicate the positivism it feels should be associated with its brand.

Included in the subject areas that Coca-Cola considers inappropriate as adjacent facing matter are articles relating to or discussing hard news, sex-related issues, drugs (prescription or illegal), politics or religion. In addition, health-related issues such as cancer, diabetes, Aids, and mental or physical medical conditions are considered inappropriate. Negative diet information such as discussions of weight loss issues or articles about bulimia and anorexia are definitely out, as are articles containing vulgar language. Coke takes its

positioning as seriously as its brand image, and if an appropriate positioning option is not available it reserves the right to omit adverts from the issue in question. Coca-Cola also requires a minimum of six pages of separation between its advertising and competitive advertising, which covers any non-alcoholic beverage including coffee, fruit juice and mineral waters.

1 Do you agree that, as the leading soft drinks product in the world, Coke gets a lot right?
2 To what extent do you think this strict approach to advertising positioning is necessary?
3 Do you feel that other companies should adopt such an approach to the positioning of adverts?
4 What problems can you foresee for publishers if all advertisers took this approach?

back cover (IBC). Some magazines will even permit advertising on the outside front cover (OFC). In some cases, however, the editor places the advertisement anywhere it will fit, which is referred to as run-of-paper (ROP).

In addition to page selection, a further specification that can be made for an advertisement its facing matter (FM). This means that the advertisement will be placed opposite some editorial feature and not opposite other advertisements, which gives it a better chance of being read than others. Once again this costs more but can be worth the money, especially in magazines that contain a lot of advertising.

Apart from selecting the correct size and location for an advertisement, an organisation must select the appropriate message to convey to the intended audience.

In general terms messages can be categorised into seven types of content:

1 *Informative*
   This straightforward approach is often used for new products, and for products of a technical nature if it is perceived that the audience is unlikely to be influenced by more creative approaches.

2 *Humour*
   This technique is often used on television, but is hard to deliver in print. Humour can backfire if it is offensive to minority groups, or if it is simply not funny.

3 *Fear*
   This tactic is used by many companies that market cosmetics, deodorants, washing powders and many other products. It is rare that a fear is directly addressed – an advert is unlikely to say 'use this deodorant or you will smell and nobody will talk to you', or 'if you're in your fifties you should buy life insurance because you might die in the next few years'. It is more usual to suggest what should be

feared in a number of subtle ways. Consider how many adverts suggest that some form of social or physical inadequacy can be corrected by using a certain product. The morality involved in doing this is questionable but it is a widespread technique.

4 *Creative*

Some advertising is simply obscure or off-the-wall in its content. Certain cigarette and alcohol advertisements are like this. Some adverts to young markets also tend to have a bizarre element to them.

5 *Lifestyle enhancing*

This technique is similar to the use of fear but suggests that a product or service will suddenly bring the purchaser a completely new and better lifestyle. It may include exotic locations, a successful love life and more friends.

6 *Sex*

Sex sells, particularly in leisure and entertainment. The suggestion that a product will make the opposite sex fall at your feet is a very powerful tool – once again this is usually implied rather than explicit.

7 *Cute*

Often used to advertise children's products or mother and baby items, this method can be used for a range of items that relate to softness or caring.

There is no sure way of guaranteeing that any advertising campaign will be a success. In simple terms we can say there are four types of adverts:

* good ideas well produced
* good ideas badly produced
* bad ideas well produced
* bad ideas badly produced.

It is not just the idea that needs to be good – it is essential that the production of the advertisement is of a suitable standard to reflect the quality of the organisation and its products.

All individuals have specific needs that can be fitted into a particular needs category. The role of the successful marketer is to associate those needs with the qualities of a specific product, by promoting products using a message that appeals to the needs of the consumer. In many cases the

FIGURE 6.17 *Advertising messages are powerful*

needs of the individual may seem to be limited to lower level, physiological needs, but other needs may be addressed by attributes such as style or perceived value, which can be promoted by specific messages aimed at satisfying those needs.

Nobody needs to eat caviar at £100 per ounce to satisfy a basic physiological need, so it must be a higher order need that encourages the consumer to pay such a high price for a food product. This is likely to have been established through promoting the product with a message appealing to the self-esteem needs of those consumers.

In order to understand how the design of an advertisement develops, we need to look at the elements that make up an advertisement and establish the terminology used in this aspect of the advertising process.

At a basic level an advertisement includes text and the display or visual elements. The text elements include the headline or strapline (also sometimes referred to as the display copy), whose purpose it is to tell the main story and to grasp the attention of the reader with only a few words. In addition to the headline, the advert may include a solid block of explanatory text, known as the body copy, and there may be some subheadings, which are used to break up the body copy and often provide reference points for the reader. Further text elements that may be used include captions, which are explanatory text used in conjunction with illustrations or diagrams, and slogans, which are designed to be memorable and aid recall.

A range of typefaces may be used. There are many distinctive styles available which have different 'personalities', such as masculine or feminine, traditional or modern, and thus have different psychological effects on the reader.

The choice of typeface may be influenced not only by the creative elements of the advert or the character of the product being advertised, but also by the method of reproduction – some typefaces do not reproduce well on poorer quality paper, such as newsprint. Selecting the right typeface is vital, since it reinforces the basic message of the advertisement.

Once the text content has been established the next stage in design is **copy fitting**. This involves fitting the words required to the space available within the advertising frame. The role of the typographer is to calculate the number of characters that will fit in a given frame or to take a piece of copy and calculate how much space it will take up. Adjustments to both the point size of the type and the number of characters used may be required. All text elements, which may be in different typefaces as well as different point sizes, have to be fitted around the visuals to produce an aesthetic and balanced effect.

There are likely to be a number of visual elements in the design, which in the cases of most branded products will include logos and trade marks. These are elements that a company uses to distinguish itself and its products. They are the property of the company and are protected in law. Advertisement designers must never attempt to adjust or alter either of these elements without consultation with a client, and they should ascertain whether inclusion of the trademark is mandatory in the production of an advert.

The options to use photographs or drawings may be influenced by the method of reproduction. If the advert is for a newspaper, which is likely to be of lower production quality than a magazine, there is the danger that a photograph, particularly a small one, may not reproduce well. In that case a drawing may be more appropriate. The mood of an advertisement may also effect the choice, with humour being more easily conveyed by cartoon figures, and photographs being more appropriate for emphasising credibility.

Other design factors that should be taken into consideration at a creative level are margins, white space, rules and bleeds, each of which are discussed briefly below.

Margins may be left around the advertisement to provide a visual break from surrounding matter. Even if margins are not used, it is essential that the body copy is not set too close to the edge since once the publication is printed and trimmed, ends of lines could be lost. Letting matter run to the edge of the page is a process termed bleeding.

Apart from using margins, effective use of white space can enhance the impact of an advert. White space is any area of the advertisement that has no text or visual matter. It is used to help emphasise the most vital information, and counters the temptation to try to cram too much information into the advertisement. In addition to white space, rules or lines can be used to frame copy or break it up into visual blocks of type by underlining, overlining or boxing a block of copy.

The text may be justified, where the space between characters and words is adjusted so that all of the lines are of equal length, or it may be centred, where the text is placed in the middle and the space at the end of each line is redistributed between the left and right margin. Text may also be aligned to the left-hand margin with the right ends of the lines uneven. This is called ranged left or ragged right. Less commonly, text may be aligned to the right-hand margin so that the left ends of the lines are uneven. This is described as ranged right or ragged left.

All of these elements take time and effort to get right and the production of an aesthetically pleasing advert is not simply a matter of luck but involves calculation and a continual readjustment of both the text and the visual elements.

The choice of whether to produce an advert in black and white (mono) or in colour will in many cases be dictated by the medium used. Many smaller newspapers are still limited to mono reproduction. Whilst many advertisers feel that full colour is preferable to mono, such decisions may depend on the quality of the design, and a one-colour advert can be very effective if well-designed.

Where use of colour printing is available, as in the case of poster design, a number of options are available to the designer as to the number of colours used. In one-colour printing only one ink is used, hence the printing costs are much lower, but screens will allow for variations in shade and a non-white paper can also be used to provide a second colour.

A slightly more expensive process is a two-colour printing, which enables the colours to

Learning activity

Using two adverts from magazines selected by you, describe the structure of the adverts using *all* the terminology explained above.

be mixed to produce a third colour, with the fourth colour being the paper itself. Once again variations in shade and density are possible through the use of screens.

Three-colour printing is not commonly used since it does not always look much better than two colours, and for a little extra expense a superior four-colour process can be used. This allows for a full-colour illustration.

A four-colour printing process uses the four process colours: black, blue, red and yellow. The colours in a photograph or artwork are separated by computer into the four basic colour values; this is referred to as colour separation. The combinations of these four colours allow for the production of all the colours needed for commercial printing.

Before the creation of an advert or an advertising campaign, a creative brief must be developed. The brief should state clearly the purpose of the advert or campaign, what is to be undertaken by whom and by what methods, and the time-scale and budget involved.

Usually a number of briefs are developed, with one main brief or draft brief providing the broad picture and several derivative briefs covering narrower fields of operation such as media purchasing or creative design.

The draft brief is developed through discussion between the advertising agency and the client, and identifies the general purpose of the campaign. Following discussions, an account executive will present the preliminary ideas in the draft brief to the media and creative departments of the agency in an attempt to develop further ideas.

These departments will develop the creative brief and the media brief, while the media

FIGURE 6.18 *Adverts and campaigns need teamwork*

planners will develop proposals for the choice of media and present these to the account executive. The account executive's role is to act critically on the client's behalf. When all departments are satisfied that their proposals can be presented to the client, the account executive makes a presentation and discusses the project with the client.

Client approval is required before any further work is undertaken, and a poor pitch at this stage can sink a campaign. However, it is not necessary to present only one brief – often two or more sets of advertising proposals may be considered and presented to a client, offering the opportunity to select from a range of options.

If successful at this point the brief will be signed off, which confirms the brief has been agreed by all parties. The final document will probably have three key sections:

1   The background to the creative and media briefs.

2   The creative brief.

3   The media brief.

All briefs relating to the same account will have some information in common. Once the brief has been agreed the creatives can begin work. They usually work in pairs, the copywriter working on the copy or text while the art director develops the visual elements – using the copywriter's ideas but taking responsibility for the overall appearance of the advert.

The background brief should include information about the key characteristics of the brand, details of its previous performance, information on the competition and an account of previous advertising and promotional support. It should also describe any legal or other restrictions as to how the product might be advertised.

The creative brief will include details of the target audience, the desired brand image (including reference to any unique selling proposition) and the objectives of the campaign. It will also outline the type of campaign that the client wants – for example, a sustained television campaign or a one-off newspaper advert – and will identify any mandatory inclusions such as

the client's logos or trademarks. Finally, the brief must include a creative budget to cover design and production costs, and outline the time-scale of the campaign.

In addition to all those factors, the media brief will also include an outline of the media selected by the client, and will detail a media budget to be used to purchase media time and/or space.

Advertising agencies specialise in creating, planning and executing a client's advertising strategy. Such agencies are normally divided into three main departments.

* *Planning.* Under consultation with the client, the planning department determines the type of consumer at which to target the advertising, and the strategy for undertaking promotion.

* *Creative.* The creative department designs and writes the advertisements, developing slogans and images related to selling propositions.

* *Media.* The media department plans and buys the media time or space in order to reach the target market in the most cost-effective manner.

As discussed above, it is during the development of the brief that we come into contact with the account executive or account manager, whose job it is to oversee the entire process of negotiation and liaison in the development of the brief. Account executives do not work alone but form part of an account team, which will include specialists from the marketing, purchasing, media and creative departments within the agency.

The role of the account handler is to liaise with the client and take responsibility for the day-to-day management of the account, acting as a link between the client and the agency staff. In addition, the account handler is responsible for financial elements of the project and will oversee the project.

The role of the account planner is linked with that of the account executive, and also includes undertaking responsibility for commissioning research, analysing and interpreting market data and developing the creative brief in line with the campaign objectives.

If a business decides to produce its own advertising the process is referred to as in-house. If it appoints an agency, it is said to be contracting out-of-house. The choice is made on the basis of whether an organisation believes it is better to use its own marketing team or to enter into a contract to use the skills of outside agencies.

Lack of internal resources may mean that a company has no choice but to use an external agency in order to establish a professional and effective campaign. However, some businesses may feel they have the specialist skills and the time to undertake their own advertising and promotions.

It is not necessarily the case that all the advertising work of an organisation has to be done in-house or all of it put out to a single agency. An organisation may choose from the following options:

* Doing all the work in-house.

* Giving all the work out to one agency.

* Splitting the work between itself and one agency.

* Splitting all the work between a number of agencies.

* Keeping part of the work in-house and dividing the remainder between a number of agencies.

The choice will depend on the resources and skills available to an organisation. However, even when an organisation contracts out all of its work to an agency it is vital that it still employs sufficient people in-house to liaise with the agency successfully.

In-house or out-of-house work

The criteria to be used when deciding between in-house and out-of-house work and selecting specific agencies include the following.

Where activities can be standardised, comparisons of costs such as the purchase of advertising space are simple to make. However, in other areas such as creative work, the costs are not standard. Estimates of costs may need to be based on subjective analysis.

A business working on an innovative product may need to limit the number of people aware

of its development, and since contracting an agency would involve external parties this may not be acceptable. However, this concern over confidentiality can be overcome by working with agencies with whom the company has had previous dealings, and who will ensure confidentiality.

Companies will undoubtedly gain more objectivity from using an outside agency rather than internal staff, who may either be too close to the project or unwilling to take a more critical approach, and may be unimaginative in their approach to new projects.

It is rare that an agency has only one client, and as a result simultaneous demands are likely to be made on its resources from other clients. This may persuade an organisation to undertake the work in-house, where the commitment of staff may be more assured, or to consider only agencies that have a limited number of clients. This approach may be based on misconceptions, however – in-house staff may be working for several departments at the same time, causing problems of divided loyalties.

A major advantage of using in-house facilities is ease of access. However, with multi-site companies, a public relations department based at a different site may be just as inaccessible to a particular department as an external agency.

An agency may have a reputation for particular skills, which are not available in-house and/or are considered to be greater than their rivals. If the skills gap identified is one that the organisation is likely to meet often in the future, it may consider appointing or training staff in relevant areas.

Results. An organisation is unlikely to know how successful a campaign is until well after it has been implemented, so it is difficult to use campaign success as a criteria for agency selection. Organisations can and should, however, look to the reputation of agencies as an indication of success.

Speed of delivery. Most campaigns can be planned in advance, but there are situations which require an organisation to respond quickly to unforeseen circumstances. In such cases, some agencies might offer the capacity and resources to mount a quicker response than an in-house department or other agencies.

An organisation is likely to get a greater opportunity to sample original ideas by using agencies rather than keeping the work in-house. Once again, however, an organisation may have to rely on reputation and the demonstration of creative ability in previous campaigns.

One advantage of appointing an outside agency is that, in case of difficulty, it is easier to change agencies than it is to sack an entire in-house department, although this is obviously subject to the contracts that have been agreed.

Financial arrangements

Financial arrangements should be clearly stated in the contract, since several remuneration options are available to an agency. These alternatives are outlined below.

With commission-based remuneration, agencies buy advertising space and sell it to advertisers at the full rate as shown on published rate-cards. The media, however, charge agencies less than the rate-card price. The agencies make a profit or commission on the difference between the rate at which they buy from the media and the price at which they sell to the advertiser.

An agency may work on a project for a fixed period, performing work for the client for the contract period only. In this case problems are likely to arise towards the end of the period, when an agency may feel that promotional activities already undertaken have been appropriate for the fee paid but the client disagrees. In some cases clients may be persuaded to top up the fee but in others the agency may carry out further activities, despite cutting into its own profits. The opposite scenario may also occur, where the agency may be requested to do very little during the contract period and the client may feel its fee is unjustified.

Ad hoc fees are charged when an agency contracts to carry out one specific task for a specific fee. Problems may arise with respect to establishing absolute costs, and it is not a good idea to use ad hoc systems until the whole campaign is fully costed, or once again there are likely to be problems with regard to outcomes and final expenditure.

Hourly rates are used by some public relations agencies, particularly on small accounts where creative or production costs might be low and the major input into the account is time.

It is surprising that any agency will contemplate a 'payment by results' system, when the success of its efforts is often outside its direct control and in some cases can be extremely difficult to measure. Situations where payments by results may be appropriate include campaigns where responses can be measured objectively, for example a campaign to raise name awareness where market research is carried out after the campaign. Even with these types of campaigns, however, payment by results has its problems.

FIGURE 6.19 *Promotions use a range of media to convey the same brand and message*

FIGURE 6.20 *A promotion from the web*

A reversal of this payment system is the practice of penalties for non-results, where the agency is penalised when satisfactory results are not achieved through a campaign. Obviously this method too has its problems, especially over fair assessment of results.

In some cases a company may pay an agency a small annual fee as a retainer in case that agency should be required. The fee is kept by the agency even if its services are not called upon.

Planning the campaign

There are seven stages to planning a promotional campaign, which take the following sequence:

1   outline objectives of the campaign

2   identify the target audience

3   specify the promotional message (the creative strategy)

4   establish a promotional budget

5   select the media of communication (the promotional mix strategy and tactics)

6   schedule the promotion

7   evaluate the effectiveness of the promotion.

The objectives of the campaign must be clearly established, quantifiable and set out in a given time frame. An objective stating that a company wishes to increase awareness cannot be assessed or evaluated in terms of outcomes unless a clear statement of the extent of awareness (such as 95 per cent recall) and a clear time frame (say, within three months) are established.

The second stage in planning marketing communications is to identify who the target audience is. In some cases it may be customers, in others it may be intermediaries or shareholders, etc. Factors that can be used in identifying the target audience may be defined in terms of segmentation variables such as demographics, socio-demographics, psychographics and lifestyle.

The essence of specifying the promotional message is identifying the function of the campaign, which could range from stimulating interest or providing information, to offering reassurance or altering perceptions. The type of message selected may also affect the medium considered most suitable.

Having identified the intended message, at this point the organisation should establish the finances available before it moves on to the stage of selecting the promotional mix to be used. Obviously, a limited budget may restrict the options available.

The marketer must plan, implement and control each of the individual elements of the promotional mix in order to maximise the benefits of each of the tools available. In other words, if all four elements are being used, the marketer must plan advertising, personal selling, sales promotion, publicity and PR, in relation to each other and their interrelated benefits.

Having determined the budget available, the organisation must now establish the allocation of this budget between the different elements of the promotional mix. Among the factors affecting the choice of promotional mix are all the elements that have been previously identified, i.e. the target market, the intended message and the budget available. Now the organisation must also establish the availability of promotional tools and must compare the characteristics and cost-effectiveness of each promotional tool in achieving the communication objective.

A communications campaign should not be restricted to one short period, but should be considered as an ongoing process which, despite changes in message, runs throughout the product's life cycle.

In the short term, what may be referred to as bursts of promotional activity may be undertaken, as opposed to a constant drip of promotional activity over a more sustained period. But for a product or service to be promoted effectively, a long-term and strategic view must be taken if the product life cycle is to be extended.

In the long term, messages must be repeated continually because many of the target audiences will miss a message the first time it appears. It is also likely that the use of a number of promotional tools and several media, rather than just one, will increase the effectiveness of a campaign, as long as each tool and medium used is appropriate to the target audience.

A campaign can be termed successful only if it achieves the objectives originally stated prior to its implementation.

In many cases this assessment may be based on the sales or profit it generates for the company. However, it is almost impossible to measure the effect on sales and profits directly. Promotional activities cannot be isolated, since the organisation does not act alone in the market and other factors, such as competitors' actions, changing attitudes and relative price changes can affect the outcome of all promotional activities.

It may be more appropriate to observe changes early on in the buying process, on the assumption that favourable changes in awareness and attitude will eventually result in higher sales and thereby increase profits. There are a number of ways in which the marketer can obtain feedback from customers regarding the effectiveness of marketing communications apart from sales, and these can include recognition tests, aided recall tests, and unaided recall tests.

Printed media

The **printed media** make up by far the largest group of media in the UK. The group includes all newspapers and magazines, both local and national, as well as the trade press, periodicals and professional journals. There are about 9,000 regular publications in the UK that can be used by advertisers. They allow the advertiser to send a message to several million people through the press or to target magazines of special interest, such as *The Times Educational Supplement*, which

FIGURE 6.21 *There is a vast range of printed media*

allows the advertiser to communicate with people in the teaching profession.

As a result, the media allow for accurate targeting and positioning. The benefit of the printed media is that long or complex messages can be sent and, as the message is durable, may be read repeatedly. If an advertisement appears in a prestige magazine it may take on the prestige of that particular publication.

The major advantage of national newspaper advertising is that it offers national coverage and is relatively cheap compared to television. A further advantage is that in-depth information and details about products can be provided more easily, and the reader has the opportunity to refer back to it at leisure.

Obvious disadvantages include no movement or sound, and advertising may sometimes be limited to black-and-white. A major drawback is that individual adverts can be lost among large quantities of other advertisements, and most newspapers have a shelf life of only one day before they are thrown away.

The advantages of advertising in regional newspapers are similar in many respects to national newspapers, but they can be especially useful for regional campaigns and test marketing. A drawback is that cost per reader is often higher than national newspapers, and in the lower

quality papers reproduction and layout may be poor.

The major advantage of magazines over newspapers is that quality is improved, and the opportunity to use colour is more likely. Targeting is more specific with specialist magazines, and often advertising can be linked to editorial features. In addition, the shelf life of magazines is longer – adverts may be referred to a month or more after publication. The disadvantages of magazine advertising are similar to those of newspapers – there is no movement or sound and in specialist magazines it is likely that competitors' products are also being advertised, thereby saturating the target market.

Audio/moving image

Audio and moving image largely refer to the broadcast media which include commercial television and commercial radio. Television is the most powerful medium – reaching 98% of households, and viewing figures for some programmes can exceed 20 million. Television advertisements are expensive, however, and advertising messages are short-lived.

Creative TV advertisements can attract attention and have a great impact, and they have the advantage that they can demonstrate the product in use and can reach a potentially huge audience on both a national and global level. There is also now increased opportunity for targeting specific audiences, through the

FIGURE 6.22 *How effective is radio advertising?*

proliferation of specialist cable and satellite channels. A further advantage is that the advertising message can be regularly reinforced by continuous repeats.

Disadvantages associated with television advertising are that there is a relatively high initial cost in terms of producing adverts, and a 30-second message is short lived. This problem has been compounded with the introduction of remote controls and the main advantage of radio over paper media is that it is able to make use of sound. It can cover most consumer groups but also gives the opportunity to target specific groups through the proliferation of independent radio stations and programmes of minority appeal. In addition, it can be produced relatively cheaply. Disadvantages obviously include the lack of visual impact or the opportunity for the consumer to refer back to the advert.

The question of impact is open to debate – can a radio advert really capture the audience's attention? See Figure 6.22.

Ambient

Ambient media are effectively media designed to be mobile or meet consumers in their own territory. As forms of media their most important element is their location. Ambient promotion involves using a range of different media designed to reach customers in a variety of different ways. The various types of ambient media is almost endless, but can be best understood with examples:

* Messages placed upon petrol pump nozzles.
* Beer mats.
* Recipe cards on the back of product packets.
* Advertising on buses and bus tickets.
* Poster sites.
* Business cards.
* Sponsorship of T signs on golf courses.
* The sides of articulated lorries.

FIGURE 6.23 *Piccadilly Circus*

* Linked promotions with other products, with adverts or messages placed upon other products.

* Free samples.

* Product placement (this may include images of products within films, such as the Ford logo within Thunderbirds), or may include merchandising, determining where products and promotions are placed within a supermarket.

* Direct mail.

The most expensive section of neon lighting in Piccadilly Circus was recently promoting Fosters lager. It covers a wall space of 1,525 sq ft and is situated immediately across the road from the statue of Eros and Piccadilly Circus tube station.

With over 1,000,000 pedestrian visitors, 450,000 vehicles including buses carrying nearly 2,000,000 passengers, and the tube catering for around 600,000 shoppers in an average week, the site is highly sought after – costing just less than £1 million per year (See Figure 6.23).

New media

With the pace of the introduction of new technology continually increasing, new marketing opportunities are opening up a range of markets. Modems, fax machines, etc. have accelerated communication from business to business, while satellite links and use of the Internet have shrunk the communications world. The improved quality of audio-visual messages through the use of digital technology and computer graphics mean businesses can communicate visual effects previously beyond their capabilities. Much of the new media is, therefore, web-based, and may include pop-ups or banner advertising from the web.

Two-way communications to consumers through fibre-optics have revolutionised information and advice provision, as well as transactions. A number of on-line systems such as Mintel and Euromonitor can provide detailed assessments of the marketplace and media within minutes, as compared to the days it used to take to source such information.

Whatever your opinion on the advance of new technology or its consequences for the workforce and the consumer, it is undeniable that the future holds considerable change, and over time sophisticated computer systems should eradicate the need for the broad, blanket communication common in today's direct marketing programmes. One thing that will remain constant, however, is that advertisers will still want to know how to reach the maximum number of potential consumers at the lowest possible cost.

Costs

The resources available to any organisation are limited – not only money but time – and people's skills should be allocated carefully if the business is to be both efficient and effective.

The term 'promotional budget' is used to refer to the amount of money allocated for promotional purposes over a specific period of time or to a given project. A wide range of budget formulation strategies can be used to determine the budget allocated to promotional activities, but these can generally be categorised under one of three alternatives:

1   *The percentage of sales/profit approach.*
    With this method, the promotional budget is linked to sales or profit. The budget is determined as a percentage of either sales or profit from the last period, or a percentage of projected sales or profit for the next period.
    The problem with using sales revenue

CASE STUDY

Technology and advertising

With more and more advertising messages competing for consumers' attention, many companies are turning to high-tech point-of-purchase solutions, such as videowalls and interactive kiosks, to make their brand stand out from the crowd.

Many marketers believe that at the point-of-purchase, the use of moving images is becoming more critical in an increasingly sophisticated selling environment. The same advocates are becoming increasingly negative about the use of static displays, which they argue are like wallpaper, in that no one actually sees or takes notice of them.

When Sky began selling the decoders for its digital satellite television service in October 1998, movement was considered a prerequisite for the satellite broadcaster's point-of-sale promotion, and it turned to the use of in-store TV monitors on which Sky broadcasts a dedicated retailer channel previewing its digital offerings.

This may appear an obvious move for Sky, but a less obvious use of this system is demonstrated in the Dr Martens store in Covent Garden. The shop boasts a 48-screen, cylindrical video tower which plays music videos, ads and Dr Martens TV broadcasts, as well as pages from the Dr Martens website and Sony PlayStation images.

The display works on two levels. First, it has the ability to draw people into the store who might otherwise have passed it by, and second, when customers get closer to it they can be enticed to make purchases as a result of informative and promotional messages displayed on-screen. As a result of these benefits, many companies – particularly those targeting a youth audience – use in-house TV screens and videowalls to put their message across.

Not all target groups are so easily converted through this medium, and while TV and videowall displays are a useful tool for firing sales and promotional messages at customers, interactive kiosks go a step further by encouraging two-way communication. These interactive systems achieve one-to-one marketing, and give customers the chance to address any query they may have about the product or the brand. If a retailer is cramped for space, having a touch-screen system allows it to extend the range of goods it can provide for customers without having to display them in the store. This system can also encourage customers to try new lines, and can offer advice with regard to the options available. It can be an enjoyable experience for some, offering change and variety in the purchasing experience.

While all these high-tech point-of-sale solutions can undoubtedly work, they represent a serious investment, and should form part of a brand-marketing strategy rather than be a one-off gimmick used to push up sales temporarily. A further problem is that while younger buyers might use an interactive kiosk, the likelihood of an older generation using such tools remains open to question.

1 Discuss in a group whether these high-tech point-of-sale promotions are just gimmicks or really serve a marketing purpose.
2 Which kinds of products do you feel would be suitable for the use of
   a videowalls?
   b interactive kiosks?
3 State your reasons for each.
4 Discuss in your group whether such high-tech promotional techniques are likely to remain solely in the domain of youth markets.

to create the budget is that poorly selling products receive smaller budgets, when in fact an increased promotional spend may be required to increase sales. A further problem related to this method is that products that sell well receive large promotional budgets – perhaps far larger than what is required to maintain their current level of sales. This would be a waste of a company's valuable resources.

2 *The competitive parity approach.*
This approach involves an organisation setting its budget in relation to the budget allocated by competitors. The amount allocated can be based on the same percentage of sales/profit as used by competitors, or the same total budget in real money terms. The reason many organisations select this method is the fear that if they fail to keep up with their competitors in promotional terms, they are likely to fall behind in terms of sales or market share. However, this methodology does not take into account the true buying power of money in different organisations. Also, the success of promotional activities is not solely dependent on expenditure but also on the quality and appropriateness of the campaign.

3 *The objective task approach.*
The third approach, which is arguably the most marketing-orientated, is based on executive judgements clearly identifying the promotional objectives of the campaign.

The first stage in this approach is to determine and clearly state the objectives of the campaign, without taking into consideration the costs involved. The organisation should then list the tasks required to meet those objectives, and the cost of undertaking each of the tasks. The total cost for the tasks will give a clear measure of the promotional budget required to meet the original objectives.

The problem with this method is that it is sometimes difficult to determine the cost of individual tasks, especially where the objectives are outlined in such terms as increased loyalty or improved customer perceptions. A further difficulty is that once the total promotional cost is calculated, it may be far in excess of the financial capabilities of the company. If this is the case, the organisation must go back and review its initial objectives.

In developing any budget, promotional costs can be broken down into three areas:

* The cost of design.
* The cost of production.
* The cost of exposure in the media.

The cost of design

Good design takes imagination, skill and time, and the use of a good designer (or 'creative' as they are often termed) can make the difference between the success and failure of a promotional campaign. The cost of employing designers varies from agency to agency, and is often based on reputation and the success of previous campaigns. Such historical evidence can act as an important indicator of the skills of designers, but this is not to say that less expensive designers will necessarily produce inferior creative concepts. Selecting a good designer involves the development of good relationships between the advertiser and the creatives, which often takes time.

The cost of production

Production costs, like design costs, can vary enormously from project to project and company to company. The production cost of a 30-second television advert can vary from a few thousand pounds for a poorly produced advert, to a few million pounds for a highly sophisticated one incorporating computer-generated graphics or celebrity endorsement. Similarly, posters can vary from poor quality photocopies at two pence a copy to full colour, gloss, fire-retardant posters costing in excess of £20 a print.

With respect to production of print, costs can vary depending on the quality of paper used, the number produced and the number of colours used in the print process. In order to establish costs for a particular print, an organisation should specify a range of production factors and seek quotations from various printers. A simple adjustment in

FIGURE 6.24 *Low-cost material might not be adequate!*

one criterion may significantly affect the price of production.

When considering costs it is important that the advertiser also considers the impact of the quality of the advert on the target audience – a poor quality advert may reflect badly on the products or services offered.

The cost of media exposure

All reputable media owners offering advertising space will provide potential advertisers with what is known as a media pack. This pack outlines the profile of readership or listenership in terms of demographic factors such as gender, age, geographical location, social class, etc., as well as giving more detailed information such as psychographic profiles.

In addition to this audience profile, which allows potential advertisers to determine if the readership/listenership corresponds to target audiences, the media pack includes a rate card which details the charges for adverts in relation to size and location.

General lists of media and details of their basic rates can be found in the *BRAD (British Rate and Data)* publication which is available at most good libraries and should be in all business libraries. The *BRAD* journal should be the first point of reference when considering advertising in national or local media.

Where a range of media publications all potentially reach the same target audiences, it is possible to compare like for like in terms of costs. This area is discussed in more detail in the last section of this Unit. One point to remember when purchasing advertising space is that you can and should always negotiate on the stated rates.

It is often impractical to compare the costs of various promotional techniques because of the complexity of space, readership, location and production differences.

Promotional techniques have different characteristics, strengths and weaknesses and to try and compare them in terms of cost would be like trying to compare the cost of the ingredients used in baking a cake. If the cost of flour per pound in weight is lower than that for eggs, it does not follow that with a restricted budget you should add more flour and leave out the eggs. Similarly, because leafleting in the street is cheaper per head than television advertising, it does not mean that an organisation should concentrate all of its efforts on handing out flyers.

Promotional activities cannot be compared on cost alone but must be assessed in terms of the objectives of the campaign and the quality of the activity undertaken.

6.3 Constraints on promotion

We have already seen that the organisation and structure of the industry strongly influences the access to advertising available to potential advertisers. In addition, the costs advertisers are required to pay for media space (given the monopolistic or oligopolistic tendencies of the market) could be prejudicial to fair trade. It has also become apparent to successive governments and consumer bodies that there is a need for regulation to protect the consumer from false or misleading promotional activities.

Legislation

Detailed over the next few pages are the most significant legislative and regulatory measures intended to protect the rights of the consumer.

Sale of Goods Act 1979

One Act that directly impacts upon promotion is the Sale of Goods Act 1979. The Act ensures that sellers do not mislead buyers and that goods or services provided are of merchantable quality and fit for the purpose intended. We do not live in a perfect world, and this Act places responsibility on sellers to make sure that goods perform to contract and promotional activities do not mislead buyers. Within the context of this Act:

* goods must conform to contract and be as described and fit for purpose as well as of satisfactory quality. It is particularly important that promotions describe goods appropriately and that goods or services fit the purpose of each description.

* goods must be of satisfactory quality reaching the standard that a reasonable person would regard as satisfactory. Goods must be satisfactory, particularly in relation to the description given to them in any form of promotion.

* aspects of quality that must match the description in the promotion include fitness for purpose, freedom from minor defects as well as appearance and finish.

* it is the seller, not the manufacturer, who is responsible if goods do not conform to contract.

* if goods do not conform to contract at the time of sale, purchasers can request their money back 'within a reasonable time'.

The principle of fitness for purpose does not apply if:

* the buyer does not rely on the skill and judgement of the seller; or

* if it was unreasonable for him or her to rely on this.

FIGURE 6.25 *An exaggerated and unrealistic promotion could contravene legislation*

Section 15 includes a term that if the goods are sold by sample, the bulk matches the sample. If goods are sold by sample three conditions are implied:

1 The bulk must correspond with the sample.

2 The buyer must have a reasonable opportunity of comparing the bulk with the sample.

3 The bulk must be free from hidden defects, which would render the goods unmerchantable, if these defects would not be discovered on a reasonable examination of the sample.

The Sale of Goods Act covers the purchase of goods, while the Trade Descriptions Act of 1968 plays an important role in the legislative protection of consumers.

Trade Descriptions Act 1968

The purpose of the Trade Descriptions Act is to impose **criminal liability** on traders who falsely describe their goods or services.

The Act states:

'Any person who, in the course of a trade or business – i) applies a false trade description to any

goods; or ii) supplies or offers to supply any goods to which a false trade description is applied; shall, subject to the provisions of this Act, be guilty of an offence.'

In establishing the requirements of the Act it is important to define the terms used. The first term that needs defining is *in the course of trade or business*, which sets the criteria for who can be prosecuted under the Act. The Act is intended to penalise only dishonest businesses, so a private seller cannot commit an offence under the Act.

The second term to which we should refer is the concept of applying a *false description*. A business can be deemed to have applied a false trade description through a range of activities such as advertising, placing marks on the goods or their packaging, or the use of shelving or containers in which the goods are placed. In addition, oral statements can constitute the application of a false trade description, as can the supply of goods which were requested under a description if they do not correspond with that description.

The Act defines a trade description as including such matters as quantity, size or gauge; method, place or date of manufacture, production, processing or reconditioning; composition; fitness for purpose, strength, performance, behaviour or accuracy; testing; approval by any person or conformity with a type; person by whom manufactured, produced, processed or reconditioned.

Consumer Credit Act 1974

The control and regulation of credit and hire transactions is undertaken through a framework of rules outlined in the Consumer Credit Act 1974. This Act exercises control in two ways:

1 General regulations, which apply to all creditors.

2 Regulation of individual credit agreements.

General regulations

The Director General of Fair Trading controls the credit industry through a system of supervision and licensing.

Almost all providers of credit are legally required to hold a licence, the provision of which is the responsibility of the Director General. Those companies who have a record of inappropriate trading may be denied the provision of such a licence. In addition to licensing, the advertising of credit is also strictly controlled by regulations issued by the Secretary of State.

One of the most important requirements in this area is that all advertisements clearly show the relevant Annual Percentage Rate (APR). This is so that any debtor or potential debtor can establish an honest and clear rate of interest, which is calculated according to a standard formula to ensure parity amongst providers.

It is prohibited for an individual to be canvassed to take credit except at the lender's place of business, which means it is not possible for lenders to approach individuals without their previous consent, outside of the business environment.

Regulation of individual credit agreements

The Consumer Credit Act implies very important rules in regulated credit agreements. An agreement will be regulated if two conditions are satisfied:

1 The debtor is not a company, and

2 The credit supplied is less than £15,000.

It is important to note that it is the credit which must be less than £15,000. The credit does not include interest or any part of the price paid in cash.

Two types of agreements that are not regulated include:

✳ Mortgages if provided by non profit-making organisations such as charities, building societies or local authorities – however, if the mortgage is provided by a bank, the agreement will be a regulated one if the credit is less than £15,000.

✳ Low-interest agreements where the APR is either below 13 per cent or lower than 1 per cent below the existing base rate.

Areas of protection under a regulated agreement

There are often three parties involved in a credit transaction – it is not uncommon for a dealer in goods to arrange a triangular transaction involving a finance company. In order to ensure adequate consumer protection, the Act establishes that if the supplier of the goods made any claims before the contract then these claims were made as an agent for the creditor who finances the transaction. The creditor therefore remains responsible for the terms and representations of that contract.

Before the Consumer Credit Act, in this type of transaction it could be argued that the customer had made two separate contracts with the supplier of the goods and the credit company, and he or she would have to establish that a **collateral contract** existed in order to challenge the integrity of both parties in the case of a sale where the creditor may be responsible for the dealer's misrepresentations.

With respect to breaches of contract, the Act protects a customer who uses credit supplied by a third party – the creditor remains liable for any misrepresentation or breach of contract made by the dealer subject to the following conditions:

1 The contract must relate to the supply of a single item with a price of between £100 and £30,000, and to a commercial transaction.

2 The credit must have been given either under a credit card or under an agreement between the dealer and the creditor.

This is particularly useful when the supplier has become insolvent before the contract has been performed, as in the case of liquidation of travel agents or airlines.

This does not apply where a customer arranges his or her own credit in advance, as in the case of a bank loan.

Other protections in the Act include the provision of a cooling-off period, where a debtor who signs a regulated agreement in any place other than in the creditor's place of business is given a short period for reflection during which the debtor can cancel the agreement if he or she so wishes. This cooling-off period lasts for five days after the customer has received the second copy

FIGURE 6.26 *The Consumer Credit Act 1974 provides a 'cooling-off' period*

of the credit agreement, which must be delivered to the customer within seven days of making the original agreement.

Early settlement is also covered in the Act. This entitles the debtor to require the creditor to express the full amount required to be paid in order to clear the debt, and entitles the debtor to clear the debt at any time.

Another part of the Act covers cases where exceptionally high rates of interest are charged by a creditor. In such cases the court retains the authority to rewrite credit agreements and alter the rate of interest charged if it is considered that the existing rate is extortionate.

As with all conditional sales and hire-purchase agreements, ownership remains with the seller until the final instalment has been paid, and if the debtor breaks the contract, the seller may repossess the goods. In order to undertake this the seller must apply for a court order if the purchaser has paid at least one-third of the total purchase price of the goods.

Data Protection Act 1984

The majority of businesses increasingly develop and store a huge range of data in their computer systems. **The Data Protection Act** attempts to regulate the storage of information through a registration process to protect individual consumers and businesses. This is particularly important within the context of promotion where an organisation may collect a considerable amount of information about its customers which it then keeps within some form of database.

Under the Act it is a criminal offence to hold personal data without registering, and registered data users commit an offence if they knowingly or recklessly fail to keep their register entries complete and up to date.

Personal data is information about particular and specific individuals held in electronic form or in a physical database of some sort. A person's name and address in a marketing database is personal data.

The Data Protection Act prohibits the use of personal data, particularly that used for direct marketing unless certain conditions are met and the mailer has obtained the consent of the

Learning activity

Why might somebody feel that their rights are being abused when they receive junk mail or unsolicited and promotional telephone calls?

recipient. Before an organisation uses personal data for direct marketing they have to formally notify the Information Commissioner (the person responsible for administering the Act). Individuals, therefore, have the right to request that somebody does not use their personal data for direct marketing by post or by telephoning or faxing them. For example, to avoid telephone promotions it is possible to phone and register with the Telephone Preference Service.

When applying for registration with the Data Protection Registrar, data users are required to describe the compilation and use of the data and the purpose for which it is held, as well as where the information was obtained and to whom the data user may disclose the information.

There are eight data protection principles, the first seven of which apply to all data users. The eighth principle applies only to computer bureaux. The eight principles are:

1 The information to be contained in personal data shall be obtained, and personal data shall be processed, fairly and lawfully.

2 Personal data shall be held only for one or more specified and lawful purposes.

3 Personal data held for any purpose or purposes shall not be used or disclosed in any manner incompatible with that purpose or those purposes.

4 Personal data held for any purpose or purposes shall be adequate, relevant and not excessive in relation to that purpose or those purposes.

5 Personal data shall be accurate and, where necessary, kept up to date.

6 Personal data held for any purpose or purposes shall not be kept for longer than is necessary for that purpose or those purposes.

7   An individual shall be entitled at reasonable intervals and without undue delay or expense to be informed by any data user whether he or she holds personal data of which that individual is the subject; and to access any such data held by a data user, and where appropriate, to have such data corrected or erased.

8   Appropriate security measures shall be taken against unauthorised access to, or alterations, disclosure or destruction of, personal data and against accidental loss or destruction of personal data.

The rights of the individual

Individuals have a number of rights in respect of personal data held about them, which include:

* The right of access to the data held.
* A right to take action for compensation.
* A right to have incorrect personal data corrected or erased.

The right to access gives individuals the right to be told whether the data user holds personal data and allows them to access the information subject to a written request and payment of a small fee, which cannot exceed £10.

An individual who identifies incorrect data held on a computer system can, under the Act, apply for a court order requiring that data to be erased or corrected. Only factual details are covered by the Data Protection Act, and where opinions are concerned the court can order correction only if they are based on inaccurate facts.

An individual who suffers either a financial loss or a physical injury as a result of a data user holding incorrect information about him or her may bring a court action in the civil courts in order to recover damages. Although the Information Commissioner cannot award compensation where there has been a breach of the Data Protection Act, they can help individuals to enforce their rights.

Race Relations Act (1976) and the Sex Discrimination Act (1975)

These Acts have a number of similarities and, because of this, they are often interpreted in the same way by industrial tribunals. Both Acts protect employees irrespective of age or status and attempt to deal with:

1   Direct discrimination – this occurs when one employee or candidate is treated better or more favourably than another because of his or her race or sex.

2   Indirect discrimination – this takes place when all employees seem to be treated the same on the surface, but when closely looked at, members of a particular racial group or gender are found to be discriminated against.

3   Victimisation – this occurs when an employee is singled out for unfair treatment because he or she has attempted to exercise his or her rights.

Clearly there are a number of circumstances within the context of promotion where these Acts would be relevant, particularly if it was felt that promotions were in some way discriminatory, or such promotions were being used for the purpose of victimisation or a group of people.

Disability Discrimination Act 1995

This protects employees categorised as disabled. Anyone with a physical or mental impairment that has long-term effects upon his or her ability to carry out everyday activities is termed disabled. This makes it unlawful for an employer to discriminate against a disabled person in relation to areas such as the recruitment process, promotional opportunities and dismissal.

For example, an organisation that constructs a promotion that treats a disabled person less favourably because they are disabled has been unlawful since December 1996. In the same way, service providers now have to make adjustments to the way in which they reach and deal with disabled customers, including physical adjustments to their premises.

Ofcom

The regulator for the UK communications industries is Ofcom, which has responsibilities across television, radio, telecommunications and wireless communications services.

Although Ofcom has a key role in communications industries, from 1 November 2004 complaints about advertising on television and radio are now dealt with by the Advertising Standards Authority rather than Ofcom.

Voluntary codes

Advertising Standards Authority (ASA)

Officially set up in 1962, the ASA was established with the objective of protecting the public by ensuring that the rules in the British Codes of Advertising and Sales Promotion, written by the industry, are followed by all parties who either produce or publish advertisements. Independent of both the advertising industry and government and working through a system of self regulation, the ASA is funded by a small levy on display advertising and direct mail expenditure which is collected by a separate body, the Advertising Standards Board of Finance.

The ASA is responsible for all advertisements and promotions in broadcast and non-broadcast media, which include the following:

* Radio and television broadcasting
* Press – national and regional magazines and newspapers.
* Outdoor advertising – posters, transport and aerial announcements.
* Direct marketing – including direct mail, leaflets, brochures, catalogues, circulars, inserts and facsimiles.
* Screen promotions – including cinema commercials and advertisements in electronic media such as computer games, video, CD-ROM and the Internet.
* Sales promotions – such as on-pack promotions, front-page promotions, reader offers, competitions and prize draws.

As well as the content of such material, the use of mailing lists for targeting consumers is also covered by the ASA.

The ASA will investigate complaints and carry out research for advertisements and promotions in all the media listed. The ASA protects the consumer by helping advertisers, agencies and the media to produce advertisements which will not mislead or offend consumers.

The basic principles are that advertisements should be:

* legal, decent, honest and truthful
* prepared with a sense of responsibility to consumers and to society
* in line with the principles of fair competition generally accepted in business.

The ASA has no statutory powers to force companies to comply with its rulings but relies on consensus, persuasion and an effective network of sanctions which stems from its own authorship of the codes. Its rules are both practical and actively supported by practitioners, and where rules are broken, peer pressure can be brought to bear on the offender.

The ASA identifies a number of advantages of self-regulation over a legislative process. The ASA process is accessible – with complainants needing only to write a letter to initiate action – and fast, with no complex legal procedures to undergo. This means the ASA can secure the withdrawal of misleading or offensive advertisements within a very short time. The process is free, with complaints investigated at no cost to complainants and incurring no legal fees.

A further benefit highlighted by the ASA is that the onus is always on advertisers to back up any factual claims they choose to make. Unlike the legal system, burden of proof is placed on the advertiser. The ASA can also update its rules easily to accommodate new issues or concerns and new forms of advertising – it is flexible and quick to respond to changes in advertising.

Despite the fact that the ASA has no statutory powers, the system of advertising control operates within a legal framework which has over 100 statutes directly affecting advertising. In many instances the ASA's codes go further than the law requires, and while the ASA does not enforce the law it will refer complaints which fall directly under legislation to the appropriate law enforcement body.

The ASA can ask for an advertisement to be withdrawn immediately, but this is rarely requested and advertisers are usually given a limited time in which to put their case. If, following consultation, an advertisement is deemed to breach the codes, advertisers will be told to change or remove it. Should an advertiser refuse to remove or adjust the advertisement, the ASA has no statutory powers but is able to use a number of sanctions to enforce its decisions, which include the following.

* Adverse publicity is generated by the ASA's monthly reports of its adjudications. Negative publicity is often underestimated by businesses as a sanction, but it can seriously tarnish an organisation's corporate image, which can be costly to repair.

* Refusal of media space can result if media are advised not to publish specific advertisements. Since the majority of publishers support the ASA and include its rules in their terms of business, they are likely to respond favourably to an ASA request and not carry advertisements that breach the codes.

* Withdrawal of trading privileges such as financial discounts and incentives resulting from membership of some advertising bodies can be effected by the ASA.

* Legal proceedings can result in the case of persistent or deliberate offenders, who may be referred to the Office of Fair Trading for an injunction.

The importance of consumerism

Consumerism can be defined as *'a social movement seeking to augment the rights and power of buyers in*

CASE STUDY

Protecting UK consumers from European organisations

Recently the UK Office of Fair Trading (OFT) won a cross-border case in the commercial court in Brussels against a Belgian marketing company that sent 'misleading' mailings to UK consumers. This is the first case brought under the Injunctions Directive of 1998, allowing a consumer body from one EU country to sue in the courts of another to enforce consumer protection.

The OFT took the action against Belgian company D Duchesne SA, which trades as TV Direct Distribution and Just 4 You, in order to stop the mail order company sending misleading mailings to UK consumers, contrary to the 1984 Misleading Advertising Directive. This Directive provides protection against misleading and unacceptable comparative advertisements and states that an advertisement is misleading if it 'in any way, including its presentation, deceives or is likely to deceive the persons to whom it

is addressed or whom it reaches and which, by reason of its deceptive nature, is likely to affect their economic behaviour or which, for those reasons, injures or is likely to injure a competitor'.

D Duchesne SA had been sending unsolicited mail order catalogues to UK residents notifying them of a large prize win, typically £10,000. According to the OFT, many consumers were led to believe that they had to make a purchase from the catalogue in order to secure their alleged win. However, prize winners were pre-selected and the vast majority of recipients were unlikely to receive the cash prize they thought they had won. The OFT claimed that D Duchesne SA's prize notifications were misleading.

1 To what extent were the prize notifications from D Duchesne SA misleading?
2 How important is cross-border legislation in the control of misleading promotions?

relation to sellers'. Advocates of consumerism argue that consumers have four main rights:

1 The right to safety.
2 The right to be informed.
3 The right to choose.
4 The right to be heard.

Ethics

Ethics are moral principles or rules of conduct generally accepted by most members of a society. Most organisations today believe it is necessary to take up a stance that shows the public they operate in an ethical manner.

Emphasis on the interests of the consumer is a key aspect of most successful organisations, with the objective of meeting and, where possible, exceeding customer expectations. By looking at stakeholder satisfaction, organisations make sure that their strategic policies take into consideration consumer ethics and opinions. Organisations must strike a balance between different stakeholder aspirations, and recognise the role that consumer opinion plays as a constraint on their activities.

Some ethics are reinforced in our legal system and thus provide a mandatory constraint on business activities, while others are a result of social pressure to conform to a particular standard. Pressure can be brought to bear by special interest groups who set out to force individuals or organisations to operate in an acceptable way. Businesses may accept the need for a change in ethical standards as a result of media coverage, which is often used to publicise moral issues underlying business decisions.

Potential areas of concern for organisations include product ethics, for example in the food industry, where issues such as genetically modified foodstuffs, salmonella in eggs and BSE-infected meat seriously affect short-term consumer demand. Criticism of the marketing of various baby milk products in developing countries resulted in widespread criticism and boycotts of powdered milk manufacturers.

FIGURE 6.27 *Companies must recognise public opinions*

European Union

Before the development of satellite television, the regulation of broadcasting was a matter for individual governments. Since then, EU directives applying to all the member states have been developed. The EU is committed to deregulation of broadcasting with state owned media and independent media subject to regulation.

The EU directive on programming allows material to be broadcast by satellite to all member states providing the material is acceptable to just one member state.

The Maastricht Treaty gives the EU powers to bring the Union's 'common cultural heritage to the fore'. In the smaller nations of Europe in particular there is concern over the protection of national cultural values and the degree to which these have been watered down by media from other parts of the world. The EU Transfrontier Broadcasting Directive requires broadcasters to devote the majority of airtime to programmes originating within the EU.

6.4 Assessing a promotional campaign

Objectives

The first stage in developing a promotional campaign is to establish where the organisation presently stands, before attempting to determine where it wants to go and how it is to get there.

From the outset it is important for realistic objectives to be set for the promotional campaign. These could involve:

* increased product awareness
* increased market share
* changes in market positioning or to brand values
* increased sales
* providing product information.

This **situation analysis** requires a study of the broad trends in the external factors which affect the business, such as the economy, and a detailed analysis of markets, consumers and competitors.

In addition, the organisation needs to look at internal matters such as its own resources, facilities, reputation, staff and expertise to judge how it is functioning with regard to its own capabilities, strengths and weaknesses.

Market research and external databases can be used to provide information on the external environment, while an audit of the organisation's activities provides information on the internal environment. The information obtained can help the organisation develop a SWOT analysis which helps to identify the internal strengths and weaknesses of the company and the external opportunities and threats the organisation may face.

The SWOT process provides a method of organising information to identify the strategic direction the company could or should take. Effective compilation of a SWOT analysis matrix should incorporate some evaluation of the relative importance of the various factors to the organisation, in terms of its existing or potential market performance.

The promotional tools that are available to the marketer within the marketing mix, such as advertising, sales promotion, public/press relations and personal selling have all been discussed in isolation, but it is important to remember that organisations should use a combination of these promotion methods and that ultimately the most suitable communications mix will depend on the nature of the product, the market and the consumer. Through combining promotional techniques the opportunity for success is expanded beyond the sum of the separate elements, since each promotional tool can offer different benefits.

Targeting

A key element in setting promotional objectives is targeting, and it is important for the organisation to match targeting with the profile of individuals within a particular market as well as the numbers that an organisation hopes to reach. For example, *The Sun* in 2004 had a daily circulation of 3.489

million, reaching 8.824 million readers. Of its readers, 56% were men and 44% women, and of these 32% were aged 15–34, 35% 35–54 and 34% 55+.

All methods of promotion can act as effective marketing communications with specific target markets, and analysing the profile is the first step in making decisions about the nature and type of media to use.

While advertising can be used to reach a huge market of potential customers, its message is generally much weaker. Advertising attempts to influence the attitudes of the target audience and develop positive attitudes towards the product advertised.

Promotion can remind existing customers how good a product is, and help reassure them about their original purchase. Promotion and other corporate activities can also be used to position a company and its products in relation to its competitors, thereby removing some companies from the evaluation process undertaken by customers and reducing the level of competition the organisation has to face.

Each of the communication elements complement each other and work towards a more effective marketing mix. Advertising and sales promotions raise awareness of a company's products as well as providing leads for the sales force. Public relations initiatives establish credibility for a company, and third-party endorsement and sales promotions offer the final incentive for customers to purchase.

Barriers to integration

It is clearly advantageous for an organisation to integrate the full range of promotional activities available to it across the full range of products and services it provides, but this is an extremely difficult task.

With increasing specialisation within most large companies, we often find conflicts of objectives between departments, each closely guarding its budgets and position within the organisation. Where the philosophy of marketing orientation has not permeated an organisation, we are likely to find departments challenging each other for limited resources, which in turn can result in a lack of integration in terms of both activities and objectives.

Where sales departments, advertising departments and public relations departments are separate, we may find sales teams complaining about the budget spent in the two other areas, and arguing that an increase in the number of sales staff would greatly benefit sales volume. At the same time, the advertising department is likely to argue in favour of additional advertising expenditure and the public relations department likewise will favour more spending on PR.

The specificity of the roles of each department means that none can see the benefits gained by the activities undertaken by other departments. This is caused in part by the lack of knowledge each party has about the roles of the other parties in supporting each other. This problem can be further magnified when the organisation's promotional activities are undertaken by an agency, or even worse a number of agencies.

There is only one method of overcoming these barriers to integration and improving the levels of integration throughout an organisation, and that is the development of effective communication channels through which the activities of all departments are clearly explained to all parties.

A true marketing philosophy that places customer satisfaction at the centre of all activities of the firm will ultimately break down these departmental barriers and lead to a greater understanding of the role all departments play in the development of a successful business.

FIGURE 6.28 *Good communications help everyone to understand that teamwork is required for effective marketing*

FIGURE 6.29 *Some high-profile agencies are large and therefore more costly*

Agency v in-house

Advertising agencies vary considerably in size and type, the smallest of which might involve just a handful of people whereas others may employ hundreds. There are many different ways to advertise and many different media, which means that advertising has increasingly become a specialised job.

Although small organisations may wish to conduct their promotional activities from in-house, large organisations, particularly if they compete in a difficult business environment, will need the expertise that agencies can provide.

The agency is particularly good at finding out what the message is that the advertiser wants to give the audience and then turns this message into a form that is both attractive and acceptable to the audience in order to meet the client objectives.

Cost

Cost-effectiveness in relation to target audienes should be calculated prior to placing an advert, since it will help to identify the most appropriate media to use. An example is shown below.

Cost of reaching the target audience

❋ Publication A charges £6,000 for a full-page advert and has 60,000 readers. Therefore publication A provides advertising at a cost of £0.10 per reader.

❋ Publication B also charges £6,000 for a full-page advert, but only has 20,000 readers. It therefore provides advertising at a cost of £0.30 per reader.

At face value Publication A appears to provide the best value for money. However, Publication A gives us a media pack showing a breakdown of its readership. Ten per cent of its readers are within the defined target market for our product. Publication B provides a similar breakdown which shows that 40 per cent of its readership is within our target market. Calculations now show that:

❋ Publication A reaches the target market at a cost of £1.00 per person.

❋ Publication B reaches the target market at a cost of £0.75 per person.

In cases where media publicity is generated by press releases and public relations campaigns, the organisation will not be able to choose the publication in which the story is published, so the above technique is of no use in trying to quantify effectiveness in financial terms. However, a number of other campaign effectiveness measures are suitable, and these will now be described.

Measuring campaign effectiveness

Whenever campaigns are undertaken, it is vital that evaluation is carried out with a view to the original objectives. It is easy for organisations to forget that the original objectives do not always concentrate on immediate sales increases, but are part of a long-term strategy.

An easy way to remind oneself that not all promotional campaigns are aimed at creating an immediate impact on sales is to remember the AIDA acronym, which describes the different points in the purchasing process. You will recall that AIDA stands for Awareness, Interest, Desire or Demand, and Action. Since the rules for measuring effectiveness must be clearly established in terms of original objectives, the organisation should consider its activities in terms of one or more of these stages in purchasing.

Having established the principle guideline in measuring effectiveness, the business should then consider the tools available to measure or quantify the success of specific promotional activities in terms of results.

Generally speaking there are two kinds of results, qualitative and quantitative. Qualitative results are not measured statistically but are based on experience. Quantitative results show statistically measured evidence, such as a measured increase in awareness or the number of column-centimetres of newspaper space dedicated to a company or product.

Qualitative, self-evident results

In the case of self-evident results no expenditure need be undertaken to obtain evidence of the results of a promotional campaign since its effectiveness can be identified without the need for research.

For example, if the objective of a promotional campaign was to improve trade relations with retailers and distributors, and following the campaign the sales staff report better sales and improved responses and attitudes, then the campaign has worked. Of course, the monetary value of additional business can be assessed quantitatively if required.

Quantitative results

Quantitative methods of measuring campaign effectiveness involve collecting statistical data on audience numbers and ratings.

Press, radio and television coverage can be assessed in volume, using column-centimetres or time, but a more appropriate and effective measure of exposure is likely to take into account factors such as readership figures and audience ratings.

In the case of assessing print advertising, the simplest assessment of audience reach can be undertaken by calculating the circulation figures of the newspaper, magazine or journal involved. This has inherent weaknesses since in the case of some free newspapers, the circulation may be high

FIGURE 6.30 *Opportunity to see or hear does not necessarily mean actual viewing or listening!*

but the number actually read can be significantly lower, with many being treated like junk mail and thrown away immediately.

In the case of many quality magazines, however, while only a small number are printed and sold, the readership can be considerably higher, with more than one individual reading each copy.

'Opportunity to see' (OTS) figures can be calculated, which measure the coverage the media can offer through identifying the number of people who have an opportunity to view an advertisement once. In some cases this figure can be multiplied by the frequency with which the advert is displayed, with each individual being given, for example, an OTS score of six. The term 'opportunity to hear' is used to describe the radio equivalent of written media.

The number of people who have an opportunity to see or hear should not be confused with the number of people who do see or hear an advertisement – this is where such a method of assessing promotional activity falls down. A radio station with a listenership of 300,000 offers an 'opportunity to hear' of 300,000, but this does not mean that 300,000 listeners will have heard the advert.

Research can be undertaken to establish how many people have in fact seen or heard a promotion. This can be established by using market research questionnaires, which identify customer recall of an advert. Frequency distribution measures not just how many individuals recall the advertisement, but how many times they had seen it.

These methodologies can be useful in assessing the overall reach and awareness of a campaign, but for such measurements to be of any use to the organisation, all calculations should be undertaken in relation to the target market identified in the objectives of the campaign, rather than the population as a whole. Appropriate calculations can be made through readership figures that allow the use of demographic profiles.

COURSEWORK ACTIVITY

This unit is to be tested through an external assessment. In order to prepare for this test, have a look at information on the following useful websites. Use www.heinemann.co.uk/hotlinks (express code 1149P, then go to Unit 6) to access these websites.

The Advertising Standards Authority (ASA)
The information centre of the Advertising Association
DDB Worldwide Communication Group (agency)
American Association of Advertising Agencies
Adbrands.net (information on advertisers and agencies)
The Brand Counsel (agency)
Saatchi & Saatchi (agency)

To help you with your revision, use both your reading and your understanding of promotional activities to think about how promotions of various types through various media are used to influence target audiences. In order to develop the skills necessary to pass your external assessment:

✳ work in groups to conduct your own promotional campaign for a product or service of your choice

✳ assume the role of an advertising agency, finding out about media rates

✳ comment upon how you would assess the effectiveness of your campaign.

To see the specimen assessment material for this unit, look at the Edexcel site through www.heinemann. co.uk/hotlinks (express code 1149P, then go to Unit 6).

UNIT 7

Investigating enterprise

This unit contains four parts:

7.1 Launching a company and enterprise

7.2 Company officers, roles and responsibilities

7.3 Monitoring the performance of a company

7.4 Winding up your company

Introduction

Almost 70 per cent of sixth formers and half of undergraduates would consider setting up their own business when they finish full-time education, according to the 2004 NatWest Money Matters Survey. What's more, nearly a quarter of sixth formers are studying with the specific aim of becoming entrepreneurs. More independence (71 per cent), desire to be their own boss (53 per cent), and earning more money (45 per cent) were the main reasons given for considering going it alone.

This unit offers you the opportunity to investigate and experience the role of enterprise and innovation in the business world. It encourages you to think about the skills necessary to be successful, together with giving you the opportunity to investigate factors which lead to the success/failure of a business.

Working as part of a group you should participate in the launching, running and monitoring of a company and new enterprise and will, therefore,

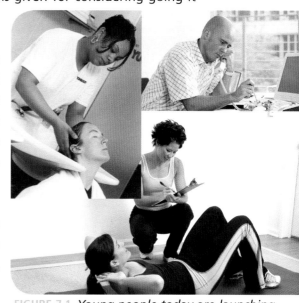

FIGURE 7.1 *Young people today are launching all sorts of exciting new enterprises – as hairdressers, web designers, fitness trainers and many other types of businesses*

gain first-hand practical experience of business. You will have the opportunity to reflect on and assess your own individual and team performances. You will also participate in the 'winding up' of the company.

What you will learn in this unit

As a result of studying this unit you will:

* be able to set up and run a business for a period of time
* understand the importance of and be able to complete key documents involved in setting up a company and have a good understanding of legal requirements
* be able to choose an appropriate name for a company and relevant products and services to produce or trade
* know the skills and abilities required by various key people in an organisation
* choose key people to run an enterprise
* organise the market research, acquisition of funds and other resources to run an enterprise
* monitor the ongoing performance of a business, making appropriate decisions to control the business
* evaluate the performance of the business
* wind up the business after an appropriate period of trading.

This unit therefore enables you to investigate enterprise by being involved in the creation and running of a business so that you are best placed to identify the trials and tribulations of a range of marketing, financial, production and other business activities.

Carrying out the learning tasks in this unit should be seen as an ongoing sequence of activities which are part and parcel of running a successful enterprise. Key tasks therefore include:

* Choosing a name for your business
* Deciding what line of business to get involved in
* Creating the forms and documents of the business
* Carrying out market research
* Choosing key people to run the enterprise
* Acquiring resources
* Monitoring business performance
* Winding up the enterprise.

7.1 Launching a company and enterprise

Have you got what it takes?

Setting up and running a business is something that only energetic, enthusiastic people should tackle – people who like hard work, who enjoy challenges, who can adapt to change, and who are not put off by failure. Perhaps *you* are one of these people!

Starting up an enterprise is a big step. It is always vital to carry out a lot of research and think things through carefully before rushing into it.

People start their own businesses for a variety of reasons. Some have a bright idea that they think will make them rich. Others find themselves unemployed and start their own business to survive. Some can only be themselves when they are their own boss. Others want to give something to their community and can see no other way of doing it except by creating an enterprise.

Of course, an important starting point for a business is the business idea. Most people at some time or another have said things like: 'If only someone sold x here they could make a fortune…' or 'I have a great idea for a new product.'

There are many ways of coming up with a bright idea. The table below shows a few examples. Try to add two suggestions of your own for each example given:

To launch a company it is necessary to understand the structure and relevant legal formalities and requirements. Planning and research for the product/service to be provided by the company will also be necessary. When setting up a company, you will need to consider a number of things (see Figure 7.3).

> **✱ DID YOU KNOW?**
>
> Chrissie Rucker started the White Company in 1993. She had found she could not buy for a friend's new flat white china and linen that was high quality but inexpensive. In her frustration, the company, which turns over nearly £40m a year, was born. The company was set up with £20,000 of savings and a grant from the local council.

> **Learning activity**
>
> Think of ideas under each of the headings listed in the table in Figure 7.2. Discard ideas that are not feasible for a small enterprise that you can set up with class mates (for example it would be absurd for you to set up a company to manufacture mobile phones because the technology and the cost would be out of your reach. However, it would be feasible to set up a company making Christmas cards, candles or Christmas bags).

SOURCE OF IDEA	EXAMPLES	HOW REALISTIC IS IT FOR YOU AND YOUR FRIENDS TO SET UP AN ENTERPRISE DOING THIS?
Developing a hobby	Making wooden toys	
Using your skills	Plastering/painting	
A chance idea	A musical tooth brush	
Spotting a **gap in the market**	A home hairdresser	
Improving a product or service	A better restaurant/website design service	
Combining two existing ideas	Coffee shop/bookshop	
Solving problems for people	Financial/IT adviser	
Listening to people	Teenagers want a mobile disco	

FIGURE 7.2 *Finding ideas for a business*

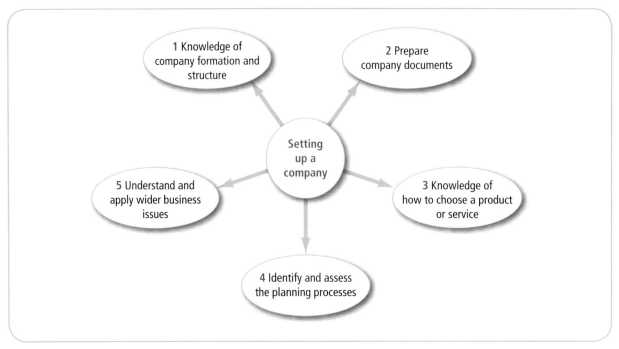

FIGURE 7.3 *Setting up a company*

CASE STUDY

Record numbers of women setting up their own enterprises

Record numbers of women are setting up their own enterprises inspired by role models such as the Body Shop founder Anita Roddick and Internet entrepreneur Martha Lane Fox.

Around 130,000 women decided to set up their own firms in 2003, generating £130bn for the UK's economy. Fourteen per cent of small firms are owned by women, a figure which is expected to rise to 20% within two years.

1 Why do you think increasing numbers of women are setting up their own enterprises?
2 Why might you expect this figure to rise?

FIGURE 7.4 *Internet entrepreneur Martha Lane Fox*

FIGURE 7.5 *Some enterprises are named after their founders*

Knowledge of company formation and structure

Choosing the right name for a company is a very important decision. During the 20th century many companies took on the names of their founders, for example:

✳ Ford Motors – after Henry Ford

✳ Marks & Spencer – after Michael Marks and Tom Spencer

✳ Ann Summers – after Ann Summers.

The law sets out clear requirements as to the naming of companies so that some names are allowed and others are prohibited.

The name of a public company must end with the words 'public limited company'. A private company must typically have 'limited' after its name.

Companies are not allowed to choose the 'same' name as one already registered. A company is likely to be asked to change its name if it is in breach of this requirement. Companies may also not be allowed to use a name which is 'too similar' to an existing name. For example, if a company wanted to use the name 'Pizza Huts' or 'Virgins Records' simply by adding an 's' to an existing name, they would be likely to be stopped.

Some names are also considered offensive and wouldn't be allowed – you can imagine what these might be!

If a company feels that another company is using the same name or a 'too similar' name they can take action through the civil courts. Companies can change their name by a special resolution at an Annual General Meeting of shareholders.

Types of company

A company needs to be registered with the **Registrar of Companies** in Cardiff. As an incorporated body it then becomes a legal entity

Learning activity

Working in a group, come up with a list of 20 ideas for a new business that could be set up by your group. At this stage you don't have to justify the reasons for your choice of business idea – simply use the first ideas that come into your head. When you have come up with a list of twenty ideas try to refine the list to those likely to work by using a set of criteria such as:

	Yes	No
Do we have the skills to make the idea a working reality?		
Is it feasible to turn the idea into a business in the time available?		
Is there a market for the product/service suggested?		
Would we be able to raise the finance to make the idea work?		
Would legal implications such as Food Safety and Health and Safety laws enable us to develop the idea?		

FIGURE 7.6 *Refining ideas for a business*

Once you have decided that it is feasible to set up a company you can start to ask and answer other questions, as shown in Figure 7.7.

	Yes	No
Are enough of us committed to the idea?		
Is it possible to research the idea or get sufficient advice from an expert to make the idea a working reality?		
Would we be able to have access to the appropriate buildings, equipment and materials to make the product/service?		
Are we excited enough about the idea?		

FIGURE 7.7 *Assessing whether a business idea is feasible*

You should choose the three ideas which best meet the criteria outlined (and others that you would like to add to them). Having chosen three ideas, you should research them further (see Resources at the end of the book).

You can also develop some possible business names that are appropriate to who you are and the ideas that you have chosen. You should all go away and think about suitable names and then bring them back for voting on at a meeting when all of the members of your group are present, remembering that there are certain names which are not suitable including:

* ones that have a rude connotation
* ones that copy existing names.

in the eyes of the law. Any debts that arise become the debts of the company. The main types of company are:

1 *Public limited companies (PLCs)* with shares traded on the London Stock Exchange

2 *Private companies* whose shares are traded privately with the permission of the Board of Directors.

The quickest route to becoming incorporated is to buy a 'ready made' company from a registration agent or Companies House. The company name can then be changed. All the paperwork involved with setting up the company has already been done when you buy a 'ready made' company.

For this Unit, we will assume that you are setting up a private limited company. You will not register it at Companies House, but we expect you to go through all the procedures required to set up your company.

Number of shares in the company

When a company is set up, it is authorised to raise a certain amount of capital known as the nominal capital. Let us assume that this is £1,000. Shareholders are the people who put money into buying shares in the company.

For example, a company with a nominal capital of £1,000 may have raised this share capital through 1,000 ordinary shares at £1 each.

Of course some individuals may hold several £1 shares. In setting up your company you must decide how much capital you want to raise by issuing shares. Figure 7.8 shows a share certificate that may help you in setting up your business.

In issuing the shares you will need to decide:

 * The total number and value of shares to be issued

 * How much individual shares will cost

 * The minimum/maximum that can be owned by a particular individual

Share Certificate in _____.

_____ is the owner of _____

shares in _____Company.

A dividend will be issued to shareholders

_____

Signed _____

Company Secretary

FIGURE 7.8 *Share certificate*

 * When the dividends will be issued, and the basis for paying out dividends.

The **dividend** is the share of the profits received by shareholders. For example, if you have issued 100 £1 shares, and in a six month period you have made a profit of £50, then you might want to issue a dividend of 50p per shareholder. Alternatively you may want to keep part of the £50 to reinvest in the business, and pay a smaller dividend to shareholders.

Shareholders have a right to vote at company annual general meetings. Usually the amount of votes they can have depends on the number of shares they hold. An individual shareholder is able to control company decision-making if they have 75% or more of the shares.

Directors

Shareholders appoint directors to represent their interests. The Board of Directors has an overall responsibility for overseeing the running of a company. The duties of directors are concerned with making sure that businesses are run in a responsible way.

What directors can do is set out in two legal documents – the **Memorandum of Association** and **Articles of Association** of a company. At all times the directors must act with honesty and in the company's best interests.

In the annual report of a financial company you will find a statement which says:

The directors are required by company law to prepare financial statements for each financial year that give a true and fair view of the state of affairs of the Company and of the profit of the Company for that period.

There are two main types of directors in a company:

1 *Executive Directors* are ones with a responsibility for carrying out day-to-day direction of the company. For example, the Managing Director will have overall responsibility for steering business decision-making. Executive Directors are likely to be paid a lot more than non-executives.

FIGURE 7.9 *Manchester United FC is a large business enterprise as well as a sports venue*

2   *Non-executive Directors* bring their expertise to Board meetings and help the company to make important contacts with other firms. Often non-executives sit on the Board of several companies. They will usually have expertise in a particular area such as accounts or the law.

As well as looking after the interests of shareholders, directors are also responsible for looking after the interests of employees.

The directors must make sure that the company produces accurate accounts, pays taxes and national insurance, and abides by laws

covering subjects such as Health and Safety and various Employment Acts.

The right to vote

Company documents will set out when the company will have meetings and the various rights of shareholders to vote at such meetings. The rights of shareholders depend on the types of shares that they hold. Ordinary shareholders will typically be able to vote depending on the number of shares they hold. They will vote:

✱ DID YOU KNOW?

For the year ending 31 July 2004, the salaries and bonuses of directors in Manchester United Football Club were as follows.

	Salaries/ Fees £000	Cash Bonuses £000	Share Bonuses £000
Executive directors			
Andy Anson	92	55	14
David Gill (managing director)	435	270	185
Nick Humby (finance director)	222	135	94
Peter Kenyon	44	–	14
Non-executive directors			
Sir Roy Gardener	100		
Ian Much	25		
Maurice Watkins	25		
Philip Yea	25		

Source: Manchester United Football Club Annual Report 2004

FIGURE 7.10 *Manchester United directors' remuneration for the year ending 31 July 2004*

- Whether to accept the annual company report
- On a number of major issues which the company is required to present to the Board of Directors
- Whether to approve payments to the directors.

Preparation of company documents

To register as a company it is necessary to send documents to the Registrar of Companies. These are the Memorandum and Articles of Association. This is being reformed so that in future there will only be a single document.

Learning activity

Copy the document shown in Figure 7.11 and fill it in as it relates to your company. The document should be posted on the wall of the room where your company meets.

In addition, the following will need to be sent with these documents:

- Form 10 – setting out the names of the first directors and secretary and the location of the Registered Office. Also send in details of any director's business occupation and nationality.

Registration documents for ______________________

Details historically kept in the Memorandum of Association:

Name of the Company ______________________

Location of Registered Office ______________________

The objects (purposes) of the company ______________________

Details historically kept in the Articles of Association:

Rules about the internal management of the company.

Rules about when company meetings will be held.

Rules about the voting rights of shareholders.

Rules about the appointment and removal of directors.

Rules about the payment of dividends to shareholders.

Signed: ______________________

Company Secretary

FIGURE 7.11 *Company registration documents*

* A registration fee made payable to 'Companies House'.

Once these documents have been accepted by Companies House, a business will receive a Certificate of Incorporation.

The Certificate of Incorporation and the registration date must be displayed in a public place.

Company stationery must show:

* the registered name of the company
* the place or registration
* the registration number
* the registered office address.

Choice of product/service

How do you choose a good or service to supply?

The three key questions to ask are shown in Figure 7.12.

In ordinary conversation, we make a clear distinction between goods and services. A 'good' is something tangible, like a car; a 'service' is something intangible, like babysitting.

In practice, a company will know that its expertise and experience lie within a certain category of products, and that there is a wide range of different people who are potential customers for different products in that category.

It is the matching of a particular product with a particular customer segment that creates a good business.

For instance, a car manufacturer might have built up a very strong business selling saloon cars to middle-aged people, but want to extend its business into the younger end of the market by manufacturing sports cars. It cannot properly answer the question 'Who are we selling to?' until it has decided that 'what they want' is something it can make i.e. sports cars.

FIGURE 7.12 *Key questions in choosing a product or service to supply*

You need to identify your **target market**. Your target market is the group of people you think will be interested in your product or service. Until you have decided what your market is, and found out all you can about it, you cannot design a product with maximum sales appeal, nor can you promote it effectively.

For instance, if you know that your target market is the 15–20 age group in your town, you can reach it by advertising at the local cinema. If you don't know who you're selling to, you could waste a lot of money by advertising in the wrong place and/or in the wrong way.

Researching on the Internet can be a useful way of finding out about buying behaviour, particularly if your school or college subscribes to an online marketing research provider of information such as Mintel. This publication gives details of spending patterns on particular items.

Businesses have to specialise – they can offer only a comparatively limited range of products. You should find out as carefully as you can which

Learning activity

The Managing Director should delegate work to the members of your company to research the questions outlined in Figure 7.13. Small groups of company members should be given the brief to research each of the questions and to report back (using a PowerPoint presentation and supporting notes). This research information will be invaluable in helping you to decide what products/services to produce and whether some ideas should be eliminated.

of the possible products that you can supply will have the most appeal to most people. You should also work out which is the most attractive design, the best packaging and the most tempting price.

You must be able to deliver products at the right time. People like to buy their bread when it suits them – in the morning – not when it suits the baker – in the afternoon. If you are starting up a home delivery service for morning newspapers,

KNOWLEDGE OF:	QUESTIONS TO ANSWER:
Costs	What are the main costs involved in supplying the product or service? Approximately how much are these costs: **i overhead costs**　　　**ii direct unit costs**
Timescales	How long will it take to prepare for the first production of the product or service? How long will it take to produce each item?
Materials	What are the main materials that will be required to produce the product or service? Where can they be acquired? How much will they cost?
Resources	What other resources will the business require? For example, machinery and equipment, buildings, labour, financial resources, information technology resources, marketing resources.
Demand	What is the expected level of demand for the product? How will this demand alter with the price charged? What is/are the best prices to charge e.g. per hour/per service/per unit etc? Will we be able to meet the expected demand? Are there different segments to the market? If so, which segments should we be seeking to satisfy?
Market research	How much market research do we need to carry out? What questions should we ask? When should the market research be carried out?
Prototypes	Do we need to produce prototypes of the product or service? If so, how should we test them and when?
Environmental issues	What are the most likely environmental impacts resulting from the creation of our good or service? How can we minimise the negative impacts on the environment?

FIGURE 7.13 *Factors in choosing a product or service to supply*

then they must arrive before people leave home for work. If you are a designer and promise to produce artwork by a certain date, then you must keep to that date.

Figure 7.13 sets out a number of questions that you will need to answer in deciding on a good or service to supply.

Market research

A business carries out market research to find out information about its target market, and the attitude of the market to the products provided or proposed (to review work on market research refer to part 3.2 of Unit 3).

Professional market research is expensive, but usable results can be obtained by beginners and amateurs.

Market research information is either primary or secondary. Primary information is information you gather yourself; secondary information is information that someone else has already gathered and published.

In setting up a small local enterprise, primary research will be particularly important to find out details of the local market.

Primary information is usually obtained by interviewing a sample of the target market. The questions should be clear and simple and wherever possible should be pre-tested in a pilot survey – which can be tried out on a few people. It is often easier to analyse the results of a questionnaire if you give the interviewees alternative answers to the questions. These are called closed questions, for example:

How often do you shop here?

a   every day

b   once a week

c   once a fortnight

d   hardly ever.

The questions can be asked either in person (often the best way), or through the post (this can be slow and produce only a poor response), or by telephone (which is quick and easy, but perhaps not so reliable – people sometimes don't take a telephone questioner seriously as they do someone they actually meet).

Sampling might be 'random', which in effect means that you simply ask the first people you see, or 'structured', which means that you only interview people who are representative of your target market. For instance, if you are interested in selling to male teenagers, you don't ask old ladies to answer your questions.

Data must then be sorted out and organised into an easily understood form. In this way you can identify patterns of buying behaviour. For instance, if you are selling high-quality chocolates, you might learn that your target market only buys products like yours on Fridays and Saturdays. If you repeat the survey several times over a period, you might be able to identify trends – perhaps you will learn that people are gradually starting to buy expensive chocolates on Thursdays too.

This information can be represented in graphs, pie charts, bar charts and pictures. When the information has been studied and digested, the business then will be able to initiate a plan of action, or adapt an existing one.

Identify and assess the planning process

Effective planning lies at the heart of running a successful business enterprise.

A business plan is a plan for the whole organisation and covers such questions as:

* What is the purpose of our organisation – the mission statement?

* Have we taken the required health and safety precautions?

* How are we going to raise the capital?

* Have we created a financial plan?

* Have we a plan to make a profit?

> **✱ DID YOU KNOW?**
>
> That there is a well-known saying in business – 'To fail to plan is to plan to fail'. A third of businesses do not make it to a third year. This highlights the need for businesses to plan far more carefully when first setting up.

Business planning

A commonly asked question is 'How long should a business plan be?' There is no easy answer to that question – but remember, typically the plan will need to be read by external people who may lend the business money or invest capital in the business. Therefore, the business plan should:

* not be so short (two or three pages) that there is not enough detail.

* not be so long (over 15 pages) that it takes too long to read.

As a general rule, therefore, the business plan should take up about ten pages.

Here is some useful guidance about the structure and content of the plan.

Part 1 – Introduction and overview (about 2 pages)

This should include a brief description of your company, including its history, and how the idea was developed. Give a brief account of the experience of senior managers/directors. Give a summary of the major plans of the organisation, market opportunities, requirements for funds and resources by the organisation, and projected financial performance for the coming period of trading e.g. coming year.

Part 2 – The business (1–2 pages)

This section provides a more detailed overview of the business. Start out by explaining why the business is being formed – i.e. the purpose of the business. Describe the key markets that it will be operating in and the products and services it will be developing to supply to these markets. Describe these products and services in detail, outlining the key factors that are likely to lead to the success of the product/service mix.

Part 3 – Market overview (2–3 pages)

Describe the markets you will be operating in. Give an approximation of the total market size in terms of numbers of consumers, or the value of the market in pounds. Then state what percentage of the total market you expect to capture and hence how much this market will be worth. Use bar and pie charts to illustrate your work. State who your chief competitors are in the markets you will be operating in and how you expect to compete with your rivals.

Part 4 – The main plan/strategy (2 pages)

A strategy is a plan for the whole of the organisation, and it involves long-term planning with serious quantities and values of resources. Start by outlining the key objectives of the business and the steps that will be taken to achieve these objectives. This could be set out in a table as shown in Figure 7.14.

You may also want to add additional columns setting out the timescale to achieve the objective, and the individuals responsible for achieving these objectives (see Figure 7.15).

Part 5 – Organisational structure (1–2 pages)

Provide a brief introduction to the organisation's structure, followed by an organisational chart

OBJECTIVES	MEANS TO ACHIEVE OBJECTIVES
Objective 1	
Objective 2	
Objective 3	
Objective 4	
Objective 5	

FIGURE 7.14 *Key objectives for the business*

OBJECTIVE	MEANS	TIMESCALE	WHO RESPONSIBLE

FIGURE 7.15 *Objective with timescale and responsibility*

setting out who does what in the business (i.e. the key personnel).

Part 6 – Financial information (2–3 pages)

You will need to provide a projected cash flow statement for the business for the next twelve months (or period for which your business will be trading). In addition, you need to provide a projected profit and loss (P&L) account (setting out what you expect your P&L account to look like in six months' time and in one year, or other relevant time period). You need to explain the assumptions you are making about the figures you will achieve e.g. the sales and price figures that underpin figures for turnover, etc.

Appendices

Some of the information may be better placed in the appendices e.g. a summary of the market research information, summary of financial projections, a curriculum vitae of senior personnel, etc.

Mission statement

You may want to include a brief mission statement setting out the purpose of your organisation in the introductory overview in your plan. Work in a group to create your mission.

The mission should give a clear picture to all those who come into contact with the organisation, about what the organisation is seeking to achieve.

For example, the mission of a leading hotel chain might include the following statements:

* To be the best hotel chain in the world.
* To provide unrivalled customer service.
* Committed and loyal staff.
* Happy customers.
* To provide long-term growth for shareholders.
* Delighted customers.

The mission statement that gains the highest number of marks should be used as the basis for creating a mission for your company.

Health and safety

In setting up any business, the health and safety of employees, customers and the general public is always of paramount importance. One of the first steps you must take before setting up your enterprise is to carry out a risk assessment of all the potential risks associated with your business. You have to have a system with procedures and responsible people in place to manage health and safety. All businesses that employ more than five

CRITERIA	MARKS 1–5 (5 HIGHEST)				
	1	2	3	4	5
Inspiring					
Realistic					
Achievable					
Identifies key stakeholders					
Easy to communicate					
Other criteria					

FIGURE 7.16 *Evaluating a mission statement*

people must have a written health and safety policy.

* You have to identify the main hazards.
* You have to record the results of your risk assessment.
* You have to make sure that risk control measures are in place.
* You have to provide training and back-up emergency procedures to deal with any potential problems.
* You need to publish your plans for dealing with health and safety issues.

An essential step will be to acquire all the information available from the Health and Safety Executive. It is strongly suggested that your teacher arranges for a Health and Safety expert to talk to your group about health and safety issues, and to advise about risk assessment and the creation of health and safety documents. One member of your group should be given responsibility for health and safety and risk assessment issues.

Capital of the business

You business will require:

* Start up capital
* Injections of capital for expansion if required.

A major source of capital will be your share capital. You may decide in your start up documents to authorise the issue of a certain amount of shares but to hold back some of the capital to a later date.

For example, you may have authorised capital of £200 but only raise £100 in the first instance. A shareholder with a £1 share may therefore only be expected to pay 50p for the share. At a later date you may want to call up the other 50p if needed for expansion.

Additionally you can raise finance for your business in other ways, for example:

* *A bank loan* for a given sum which you will need to pay back in instalments with interest charges.
* *An overdraft* where you set up a bank account but have permission to draw out more from your bank than you have placed in the account. Again, you will pay interest on the sum overdrawn on a daily basis.
* *Trade credit* involves buying in stock to resell on credit and then paying for the stock at the end of a given period, e.g. 30, 60 or 90 days.

Financial planning

Important financial plans will include the cash flow forecast and the profit and loss account (see Unit 2).

Many small businesses collapse because they do not pay enough attention to the prices they need to charge to make a profit. Before setting up in business, you must estimate your cash flow for several months ahead. If you calculate that your costs will consistently exceed takings, there is no point in setting up.

A simplified cash flow is shown in Figure 7.17. The business starts off with an overdraft of £200 (negative balances are shown in brackets). In January, the business expects to sell £200 worth of goods and to make purchases of £100. As a result, at the end of January, the business overdraft will reduce to £100. This 'minus' figure is then carried forward to the beginning of February and the cash flow rolls on.

The cash flow forecast must include all the expenditure and receipts of the business. When the business has actually started, you can refer

	JAN	FEB	MARCH	APRIL
Starting balance	(200)	(100)	0	100
Receipts	200	200	200	
Outgoing	(100)	(100)	(100)	
Closing balance	(100)	0	100	

FIGURE 7.17 *A cash flow estimate*

back to the forecast to check that everything is going according to plan.

In addition, you should set out a projected profit and loss account for your business. Profit provides a business with a 'surplus' or 'cushion' which supports their activities in future periods. For example, it may be sensible in future periods to use profits to finance business expansion rather than having to rely on loan capital. In simple terms, 'gross profit' can be calculated by subtracting the variable costs involved in making sales from the income from these sales.

In calculating expected gross profit you will therefore need to do the following calculation:

Expected sales (units) × price charged = Expected sales revenue

Expected sales (units) × variable cost per unit = Expected sales costs

Expected sales revenue − expected sales costs = Gross profit

In order to arrive at the figure for net profit you will then need to take away your overhead expenses (i.e. expenses which can't be directly associated with a particular unit of output).

You should set out a forecast profit and loss account for your business as shown in Figure 7.18.

Learning activity

Produce a cash flow forecast for your business for an appropriate future period. Also produce a budgeted profit and loss account showing what you expect profits to be at the end of given periods. You should write down the assumptions on which you are creating your budgeted figures (for example, how can you predict your turnover, costs, expenses etc).

Understanding and applying wider business issues

Setting up your own enterprise gives you the opportunity to learn about wider business issues which are relevant to the setting up and running of an enterprise.

Types of businesses

The business that you set up is likely to fit most closely the pattern of a private limited company. It will have shareholders but its shares will not be traded on the Stock Exchange. It will have a Board of Directors and managers appointed by these directors. It will have meetings of shareholders, and will pay a dividend to these shareholders.

Running your enterprise will help you to think about the strengths and weaknesses of this type of business when compared with other formats.

SALES FORECAST: number of units (Q)   = _____

                    price per unit (P)   = _____

Gross Turnover (Q × P)   = _____
                                                   _____

Minus: variable costs (of making forecast sales) = _____

Gives GROSS PROFIT   = _____
                                                   _____

Less overheads   = _____

Gives NET PROFIT/LOSS   = _____
                                                   _____

FIGURE 7.18 *A forecast profit and loss account*

For example, you will note that the advantages of being a company are that:

* You can raise money from shareholders who leave executive directors and managers to run the business.

* A private company is relatively easy to set up.

* Shareholders are prepared to provide capital, because the risk they take is limited to the sum they have invested in the business.

* The company is able to benefit from appointing specialist managers.

Opportunities and risks

Businesses will often flourish when they take advantage of an available opportunity. For example, many new businesses have set up because of the opportunities provided by the Internet for e-commerce. However, at the same time businesses are continually faced by risks and threats – for example, the threat of competition, or the threat of changes in social trends (perhaps people buying by e-commerce may be a fad which is later replaced by other patterns of buying).

A useful tool when considering the ability of a business to cope with opportunities and risks is to set out a SWOT analysis for the business as shown in Figure 7.19.

A SWOT analysis consists of two main parts:

1   An **internal analysis** of the **strengths and weaknesses** (SW) of the business. The strengths relate mainly to the resources available to the organisation, including its capital, skills and people. Weaknesses relate to a lack of these.

2   An **external analysis** of **opportunities and threats** (OT). Opportunities usually relate to the market in which a business will operate and the development of new technologies. Threats typically relate to competition and changing social trends.

Innovation, creativity and entrepreneurship

Everything we use at home, at school or college has its origins in simple, perhaps ingenious ideas. However, it takes more than creative thinking

S	W
Internal strengths Resources People Skills Capital Products and services	**Internal weaknesses** Lack of resources and skills
O	T
External opportunities New markets New technologies Other	**External threats** Competition Other

FIGURE 7.19 *SWOT analysis*

Set out a chart like the one in Figure 7.19. Working in a group, identify the main strengths and weaknesses of your business. Then work out the opportunities and threats which it faces.

Then outline:

1 Ways to build on your existing strengths.

2 Ways to eliminate your weaknesses.

3 Ways to take advantage of opportunities.

4 Ways to deal with threats.

to make a good idea work. Good ideas have to be turned into realistic, affordable solutions that people want. This process is known as innovation.

It is not hard to think of innovative ideas such as:

* Post-it notes

* Cat's eyes in our roads

* The development of e-commerce

* The development of the mouse pad.

What else can you add to the list?

Innovation involves original thinking 'out of the box', such as:

* The designer who was lying on his bed one day looking at the bed springs, who thought the spring shape would make a wonderful new design for an egg cup

* James Dyson, who was looking at an industrial size air cyclone and realised that it would make a brilliant design for a vacuum cleaner.

FIGURE 7.20 *Turning a creative idea into a business plan*

Creativity and good business ideas therefore go hand in hand. However, the creative idea needs to be shaped into a business idea if it is to work.

An **entrepreneur** is a person who has an idea for a business or enterprise and is prepared to take a risk without the certainty that a profit will result. The entrepreneur then needs to have the business skills to make the business work, prosper and grow.

Factors and limitations on growth

Businesses are able to grow:

* through acquiring more capital for expansion

* by ploughing back profit into growth

* by acquiring other businesses

* by developing new products or services.

When you have set up your business you will probably find that your ability to expand is limited by the factors outlined above. Without fresh capital and profit sources the size of your business may be limited. In the world of business, it is often necessary to borrow and to bring investment partners into your business if you want to seize opportunities that are available. However, the problem of bringing others into the business is that they will want to share in the profit of the business, and will also want to have a say in how the business is run and managed.

What opportunities are there to expand your business as you go along? What extra resources do you require to expand the business? How can these be acquired? What are the dangers of expanding the business too quickly?

✱ DID YOU KNOW?

One of the major factors leading to the collapse of new small businesses is overtrading. Encouraged by early successes, they borrow too much money in order to expand their trading. Often the profits that they expect are slow in coming in. In the meantime they are faced by rising costs and interest payments, leading to cash flow problems.

The impact of market forces

The fortunes of small businesses are determined by the twin market forces of demand and supply. Demand consists of the level and intensity of purchases of your good or service. Supply is typically constrained by the costs of producing goods and services.

The ability to expand a business is determined by the growth of demand in the market place. The skill is in charging the right price and in providing a good that consumers want to purchase in order to maximise sales.

At the same time it is important to control costs and to guarantee a steady supply to the market in order to be able to offer your customers the best possible deal.

7.2 Company officers, roles and responsibilities

As a company is a legal entity and not a person, it needs officers to run it. It is necessary to understand the roles and responsibilities of company officials. When setting up your company you will want to make sure that you have the right officials in the right posts, so it is helpful to consider the different skills that different officers will need.

Figure 7.21 sets out the roles and responsibilities of key people in the company.

In choosing members of your group to take up the various roles and responsibilities within your company, you will need to consider the skills required before selecting appropriate individuals to take up these posts.

One approach might be to first appoint a Board of Directors. The Board can then choose the other officials to take up responsibilities within the company. Figure 7.22 sets out the skills required by each of the key officials in a company.

Learning activity

a How do the posts and responsibilities outlined in the table (Figure 7.21) relate to your school or college management hierarchy?

b Carry out some Internet research into companies including Marks & Spencer, Manchester United, Tesco and another company of your choice. Identify the Managing Director, another senior director and the auditors of the business.

Directors	To look after the interests of shareholders, to take responsibility for legal affairs of the company.
Chair	To take charge of Board meetings and responsibility for shareholders meetings. To act as a figurehead for the company.
Managing Director	To make key executive decisions for the company. To lead the company and to motivate others.
Marketing Director	To organise market research, to find out what customers want and to analyse the results produced.
Financial Director	To keep financial records, and to take responsibility for costing out activities and making calculations which form the basis for pricing decisions.
Human Resources Director	To organise the management of people within the organisation. To organise payment and to make sure that people are motivated.
Company Secretary	To take responsibility for official paperwork of the company such as the creation and display of Memorandum and Articles of Association. To inform shareholders of meetings etc.
Auditors	To check that financial statements provide a true and fair record of financial activities within a company in a given period.

FIGURE 7.21 *Roles and responsibilities*

DIRECTORS

Need to be responsible individuals who will look after the interests of shareholders. He or she will therefore need to have the following characteristics:

* Responsible attitudes
* Good research skills
* Confidence to make contacts on behalf of the company e.g. to find out about Health and Safety requirements.

CHAIR OF THE BOARD

The Chair will take overall responsibility for company meetings. The skills he or she needs to possess are:

* Commitment – they need to regularly attend meetings
* Good communication skills
* Ability to manage a meeting
* Skill of encouraging others to voice their opinions
* Decisiveness
* Willingness to speak in public to a range of audiences
* Ability to form good relationships with adults met for the first time.

MANAGING DIRECTOR (MD)

In overall charge of management decision-making in the organisation. Needs to continually oversee the running of the business. The managing director will arrange when the company will meet, and the objectives and targets for each meeting. The MD will steer the activities of others and will make sure that the company makes the right decisions and that plans are carried out. The MD has overall responsibility for the creation of the business plan and will delegate key tasks to others. You can clearly see that if you have a weak or uncommitted MD your company will fail. One of the main tasks of your group therefore is to choose the right MD.

Skills required by the MD include:

* Commitment
* Decisiveness
* Willingness to make unpopular decisions
* Ability to plan and organise
* Ability to delegate powers to others
* Willingness to censure individuals who are not showing commitment to the organisation
* Ability to understand and keep in touch with all important decision-making processes in the organisation.

FIGURE 7.22 *Skills required for the company roles*

MARKETING DIRECTOR

The marketing director is responsible for organising the company's market research and producing marketing reports for discussion by the Board of Directors. The skills he or she will require include:

* Ability to make decisions
* Ability to create questionnaires and other research documents
* Ability to analyse information
* Ability to organise a small team of researchers
* Good IT skills.

FINANCIAL DIRECTOR

The Financial Director keeps the accounts of the business and is responsible for costing and pricing decisions. This person will need:

* To have good knowledge of accounts and accounting procedures
* Ability to pay attention to detail, e.g. the recording of transactions, payments and receipts of a business
* To be trustworthy as he or she will have to look after company money
* Ability to create cash flow forecasts and profit and loss accounts.

HUMAN RESOURCES DIRECTOR

Needs to organise people in the workplace. For example, will take responsibility for ensuring the right people, in the right numbers, are available to complete the work of the organisation. Represents both managers and employees so acts as an intermediary between both groups. Pays wages for the company. Looks after personal problems and issues. Skills include:

* Ability to get on with people
* Well-organised and disciplined
* Friendly and approachable without being 'a soft touch'.

COMPANY SECRETARY

Handles paperwork of the organisation. Keeps records such as a register of shareholders, and details of Memorandum and Articles. Calls shareholder meetings. Skills required:

* Highly organised
* Good IT skills
* Very good at organising paperwork
* Very disciplined.

AUDITORS

External individual who looks at the accounts to verify they are true and fair. Needs a person with a good knowledge of accounts and ability to work independently.

FIGURE 7.22 *Skills required for the company roles – Continued*

CASE STUDY

Choosing the key people for the company

Read the following descriptions of the characteristics and skills of five different people. State what role in a company they would be most suited to.

1 Pritesh is a tidy and well-organised individual who keeps his study folders tidy and can always find the notes that he has kept on various topics that he is studying. He has organised an index folder, and colour codes the different subjects and topics that he is studying at college. He has good writing skills and gained grade As in English Language, English Literature, Mathematics and 7 other GCSE subjects.

2 Paul is a very sociable individual. He has lots of friends and he is a loyal and hard working person. He can always be relied on in an emergency. One of his greatest assets is listening to others. Some people don't take much notice of what others say because they are more interested in talking about themselves. In contrast, Paul is very thoughtful and sympathetic as well as being intelligent and hard-working. Paul has 7 grade Bs at GCSE.

3 Jason is a very dynamic individual. He is good at persuading others to do what he wants to do. However, he is quite erratic and may suddenly change his mind, or lose interest in what he is doing. If he enjoys something he will take an interest in it, but sometimes he loses interest and then drops something completely. Although he could have achieved good results in his exams he only ended up getting a B in Physical Education and a C in art. He achieved Ds and Es in all his other subjects.

4 Jaymini is a popular student who did well in her GCSEs achieving 4 grade As and 5 grade Bs. She is a born leader, but is also very interested in the views of others. She has a dynamic personality and has lots of friends. She is a very determined, but also hard working student who can always be relied on to be the first to start a task and see it through right to the end. She has excellent communication skills and is a great problem solver.

5 Martin is a first-class mathematician who achieved grade A stars in Maths and Business Studies at GCSE and four other grade As as well as three Bs. He is now studying Business and Maths A levels. He likes to work on the computer, and is forever drawing up spreadsheets and other applications for calculating sets of figures. He works well with others but prefers to play a backseat role rather than being the centre of attention.

Learning activity

Having examined the various skills required for different business roles in Figure 7.22, answer the following questions.

1 Which role do you think you are best suited to?

2 Appoint members of your group to fill the various roles outlined.

Remember when appointing members to choose the ones that best fit the skill requirements. If you simply choose your friends you may be picking the worst people for the roles required.

The importance of teamworking and communication skills

One of the reasons that many businesses fail is because people fail to get on with each other. They lack teamwork skills. In setting up your enterprise it is essential that you work well with the others in your team, and you communicate well with them if the business is to flourish.

Communication skills are essential in making an important contribution to a team and include:

✳ *Clear articulation.* To speak clearly and with confidence you need to feel sure that your ideas are worth sharing. Focus on the key message that you want to get across, and avoid getting sidetracked into irrelevant issues. Avoid long pauses and 'ers' and 'ums' that break up the flow of your message. For example, the various directors of your company will need to provide others with good clear reports, and argue fluently and convincingly at meetings.

* *Effective self-presentation.* A good upright body posture is helpful in enabling you to put yourself across in a confident way. Avoid crossing your arms into a defensive position. You also need to look the part, so follow the dress code for the team you are part of.

* *Ability to envision consequences.* You need to think about the impact of given actions, and the implications for your team, yourself and your work organisation. For example, the Financial Director needs to envisage the likely impact of certain decisions on future cash flows and profit figures.

* *Charisma.* Personality is helpful in winning the support and confidence of others. Everyone can help to build the morale and confidence of the team they are part of by encouraging and supporting others. Key roles like the Managing Director and Chair will need to have charisma.

* *Awareness of the need for consultation.* You can't just make decisions and go ahead with them without consulting other members of the team who are involved. If you do so you risk alienating team members. If Directors are to make good decisions they need to have important inputs from others with knowledge of what is going on in the organisation.

* *Ability to ask appropriate questions.* You should help to clarify issues in a team and show you are aware of areas that need clearing up. If you don't ask questions you are more likely to make mistakes.

* *Awareness of appropriate timing.* This is important when making interventions in team activities. For example, you need to know when not to interrupt others and when it is appropriate for you to carry out actions or to get involved in discussion. For example, the

Managing Director needs to know when to step in to push through actions. The Chair needs to know when to open up an issue for discussion and when to put an end to discussion to move a meeting forward.

* *Willingness to be held accountable and to take responsibility.* This is particularly important for the smooth functioning of a team. Some of the members need to be prepared to take the responsibility of having an executive role e.g. Managing Director and other executive directors.

* *Ability to resolve conflict.* This is important in reducing tension in a team and raising team morale.

* *Are you an organised type of person?* If you want to be a good member of a team then you will probably need to be well organised. Areas to work on include the following:

  * *Being effectively prepared for meetings.* Make sure you arrive on time and have done the appropriate background work. For example, if the meeting is to discuss an action plan, you need to make sure that you have completed all the actions required from the last meeting.
  * *Organising information well.* Make sure that information is collected and stored in a systematic way, and then organised in such a way that it can be communicated clearly.
  * *Effective diary/calendaring skills.* Record the dates of future meetings and important events and then keep the diary safe and refer to it regularly.
  * *Reliability.* Do what is expected of you, and what you say you are going to do. Do it in an appropriate manner, at the right time.
  * *Decisiveness.* Make a decision and stick to it (where appropriate) rather than constantly changing your mind.
  * *Time management.* Allocate time in a well-organised way. By focusing on one activity at a time it is possible to maximise attention on that activity, before moving onto another prioritised area.

Good team members should be approachable

by others. You therefore need to possess the following skills:

* *Effective listening.* When others are talking to you or making contributions in a team discussion, do you listen to their views, or do you cut them off to put in your own ideas? Do you understand what they are trying to say? If you are not sure, ask them to clarify. Try listening more actively – you may be surprised at what good sense others are making and what you can learn from their ideas.

* *Sincerity.* Are you sincere in your interactions with others, or are you 'two faced'? If you are insincere you will quickly be found out and will lose the respect of others. If you want people to be sincere with you, be sincere with them.

* *Genuine concern for personal welfare of team members.* Genuine concern involves finding out about them and what interests them, and a little about their family and friends if they want to talk about this. But don't be nosy!

* *Observance of appropriate boundaries.* Team members need to know where to draw the line – for example not to be too familiar with the team leader or try to become too close to individuals who don't welcome your attentions.

* *Discretion.* Not gossiping about others' problems or revealing confidential information is a basic requirement.

* *Fairness in dealings with others.* Avoid favouritism or discriminating unfairly between individuals.

* *Ability to accept criticism.* Understand that acceptable criticism relates to fair judgements about your abilities and performance, based on objective criteria. In these circumstances critics are seeking to help you and to help the team to improve its performance. You can learn a lot from constructive criticism.

Evaluating individual roles of company officials

If the organisation is to work smoothly it will be helpful to evaluate the roles of the various company officials to see if they are being performed well.

It is useful to establish a set of criteria for the various key roles in an organisation, as follows:

The role of managing director requires the following characteristics:

1 Decisiveness

2 Clear communication skills

3 Ability to motivate

4 Ability to make difficult decisions

5 Hard work

6 Good organisation skills

7 Problem solving skills.

Evaluation of Jane Smith's role as Managing Director

(rank performance from 1–5. 5 excellent, 4 very good, 3 good, 2 satisfactory, 1 poor)

	1	2	3	4	5
Decisiveness			*		
Communication		*			
Motivation		*			
Decision making			*		
Hard working					*
Organised		*			
Problem solving				*	

FIGURE 7.23 *Evaluation of performance*

You might then want to evaluate the performance of the person who has been chosen as your Managing Director to give them some constructive feedback about how they are performing in their role. An example is shown in Figure 7.23.

Each role could then be evaluated and the people carrying out the evaluation could additionally be asked to provide:

1 Examples to illustrate good performance by the individual in role.

2 Examples to illustrate bad performance by the individual in role.

3 Suggestions as to how they could improve performance.

Interrelationships between roles

The various roles that officials take within an organisation should not be seen in isolation. The purpose of a management team is to work together to solve shared problems and to share information.

The Managing Director plays a key role in seeking to integrate the various roles and to get people working together as a harmonious team for the benefit of the enterprise as a whole.

A useful way of getting this across is to organise a session early on when individuals are beginning to develop an understanding of their roles. The facilitator of the session can set out a diagram like the one shown in Figure 7.24.

FIGURE 7.24 *Teamworking*

Learning activity

Ask each individual at the meeting to:

1 Identify one way they have already worked interdependently with others in different roles.

2 Suggest ways in which they could work together with those playing other roles in the future.

7.3 Monitoring the performance of a company

Once the company is incorporated, monitoring the daily performance of your company and its functional areas is essential.

You will need to take account of:

* creating an effective team

* running efficient meetings

* holding regular reviews of individual and company performance

* making sure that production totals are on track and that quality is maintained

* assessing the financial performance of the company

* purchasing from appropriate sources and at value for money prices

* achieving **sales forecasts** and targets.

Teamworking – creating an effective team

When people work together in a team, they adopt particular roles. For example, one person may have the role of monitoring progress, checking the time-keeping or acting as the leader. There is a tendency for at least one member to take on the task functions and for others to adopt the maintenance role.

Task functions are those which help the group to get tasks done as effectively and efficiently as possible, including:

* proposing objectives, clarifying goals
* seeking information and opinions
* keeping the group on track
* summarizing ideas
* suggesting ways forward
* evaluating contributions.

Team members who take on the **maintenance role** offer support and encouragement to the group. This involves:

* supporting other group members
* ensuring all members of the group are included
* reconciling disagreements and reducing tensions
* making suggestions for compromise
* monitoring the group.

Learning activity

To find out the typical role – task or maintenance – that you play in a group, tick the eight statements from Figure 7.25 which most typically illustrate the way that you like to work in a group or team.

I LIKE TO...	TICK 8 OF THE STATEMENTS
1 Concentrate on completing a task	
2 Find out what the objectives are	
3 Help others to join in	
4 Move the team forward rather than wasting time	
5 Build up good group relations	
6 Try to reduce conflicts	
7 Keep an eye on the clock to cut out time wasting	
8 Concentrate on ideas and information	
9 Find ways to compromise	
10 Build friendships with other team members	
11 Bring people into line who are not on track	
12 Support others in the team	
13 Help to bring in people who are left out of team activities	
14 Get the task finished	
15 Identify priorities for the team	
16 Listen to other people's ideas	

FIGURE 7.25 *Characteristics of task and maintenance roles*

If you predominantly ticked numbers 1, 2, 4, 7, 8, 11, 14 and 15 then you are someone who likes to concentrate on task functions of the team. In contrast, if you chose 3, 5, 6, 9, 10, 12, 13 and 16 you tend to concentrate on maintenance roles in the team.

The effectiveness of a team will, to some extent, depend on the mix of roles which team members take on. Successful teams tend to have a range of appropriate personalities and qualities.

Meetings

You will need to hold meetings for the efficient and regular sharing of information.

Some meetings are called to generate ideas. Individuals have different backgrounds and the number of ideas put forward tends to increase with team size. One popular problem-solving technique is brainstorming, which was originally used in the advertising industry to come up with new ideas. In a brainstorming session, the problem is stated and participants to the meeting are encouraged to produce as many ideas as they can, out of which the best is selected.

Meetings can be called to give people information or spread knowledge. These are particularly important if a lot of people need to be informed or if the information is confidential. Meetings allow parties from both sides of an issue to negotiate an agreement.

Often meetings are used to get collective decisions from members by democratic means. If an individual does not have the authority to make a decision, he or she might call a meeting so that others can agree to some proposals. Sometimes when a decision is made by a senior member of staff, it then needs ratification (confirmation) by others in a meeting.

Finally, meetings can be called to investigate something that has happened – for example an accident or a series of thefts.

Meetings range from informal discussions or unstructured gatherings between a few people to formal, heavily structured meetings controlled by rigid rules and procedures.

Informal meetings involve the gathering together of individuals, often at short notice and without any set procedures. Informal meetings are flexible, can be called to respond to any issue, or can be used to share responsibility for a decision.

On the other hand, the rules and procedures for a formal meeting may be contained in the Memorandum and Articles of a company.

The features of a formal meeting are:

* The meeting is called by a notice or agenda
* Conduct in the meeting depends on the formal rules of the organisation
* Decisions are reached by voting
* Formal meeting terms are used
* The proceedings are recorded in the minutes.

Formal meetings must be conducted according to legal requirements or a written constitution. It is usual to give notice of the meeting to every person entitled to attend according to the rules and regulations (see Figure 7.26). The notice should be signed by the issuer and should specify the date, time and place of the meeting.

A notice of meeting will be accompanied by or followed by an agenda, which is a list of topics to be discussed at the meeting. It will normally be sent to all those entitled to attend the meeting so that they can consider the topics in advance of the meeting (see Figure 7.27).

The **chairperson** has certain duties and powers in a meeting. He or she makes sure that the meeting is properly constituted, preserves order, works through the agenda preventing irrelevant discussion, and seeks the views of the meeting by putting **motions** and amendments to those attending.

Often a chairperson will have a special copy of the agenda known as the chairperson's agenda. On this, further information is provided for the chairperson's guidance and space is provided on the right hand side for notes to be made.

NOTICE OF MEETING

BOARD OF DIRECTORS – AMITY LTD

The monthly Board meeting will take place in the Blue Room at the Angel Hotel on Wednesday 8th December 2004 at 7.45 pm. Please find enclosed a list of Agenda items for the meeting.

Narinder Singh

Company Secretary

FIGURE 7.26 *A notice of a meeting*

Agenda

Board of Directors Meeting

To be held on 8 December 2004 at 7.45 pm in the Blue Room of the Angel Hotel.

1 Apologies for absence

2 Minutes of the last meeting

3 Matters arising from the minutes

4 Chairman's report

5 Managing Director's report

6 Proposal to raise more capital

7 Proposal to introduce new product lines

8 Any other business

9 Date of next meeting.

Narinder Singh

Company Secretary

FIGURE 7.27 *An agenda for a meeting*

Learning activity

The Company Secretary of your company should produce and distribute notices of meetings and agendas for the meetings which you hold of your company. These meetings should take place at regular times, and a schedule of meetings should be distributed to all company members.

Shortly before the time a meeting is designated to start the chairperson makes sure that there is a **quorum** – this is the minimum number of people required for the meeting to go ahead according to the rules. He or she will also ensure that everybody has an agenda and that all new members are introduced.

The secretary then states whether any apologies have been received for absence and reads through the official record – the minutes of the last meeting. If the minutes have already been circulated, it will be assumed that they have been read! Members are asked to approve them as a correct record of the last meeting and, if necessary, the secretary will amend them before they are signed by the chairperson.

At this stage any **matters arising** from the minutes will be discussed. For example, if the last meeting suggested that certain individuals undertake certain actions, these may be mentioned.

The chairperson then works through the business of the meeting according to the agenda. If reports are to be read (again, circulated reports are assumed to have been read) the writers may be asked to speak briefly about theirs. If a motion is proposed, the chairperson will ask for a proposer and a seconder, allow for discussion of the motion making sure that all sides are heard, and then call for a vote. The chairperson usually has a casting vote if the voting is tied.

Personal and business reviews

Personal and business reviews are an important way of monitoring the ongoing performance of a business and of the people that work for it.

A performance appraisal works on the basis:

Desired performance minus **Actual performance** equals **Need for action**

Many businesses use a performance cycle approach in measuring the performance of teams and individuals.

Performance management

Performance Management is the process involved in getting the best performance from:

* Individuals

* Teams

* The organisation as a whole.

Effective performance management involves sharing with team members an understanding of what needs to be achieved and then managing and developing people in a way that enables these shared objectives to be attained.

Individual team members are involved in **individual performance reviews**. A team leader and team member sit down and:

* agree on meaningful task objectives for the employee and for the teams within which he or she operates

* identify individual needs and aspirations.

Performance can then be measured against agreed standards. Salaries and bonus payments can reflect the success of each individual's performance against a rating system.

The process of performance review also makes it possible to identify individual team members (or teams) who are performing below the expected targets. Extra support and training can be given to individuals or teams to help them improve performance.

At an organisation-wide level it is also important to carry out periodic performance reviews. The starting point for the review is to examine the business plan and the objectives and targets set in the plan. Targets can be set for achievement by particular dates – e.g. for production, sales and profit levels. The review meeting will involve a range of people in the business identifying progress to meeting present objectives, and the establishment of new targets and objectives where appropriate.

A further purpose of a review meeting is to check on action plans. An action plan is simply made up of a list of actions that need to be carried out to meet particular objectives, by a particular time, which individuals are responsible for. For example, see Figure 7.29.

Learning activity

In your company, organise regular performance reviews for individuals and for the organisation as a whole. At performance reviews, create action plans for the period ahead. Monitor the performance of these action plans to make sure that designated officers in the company meet their obligations.

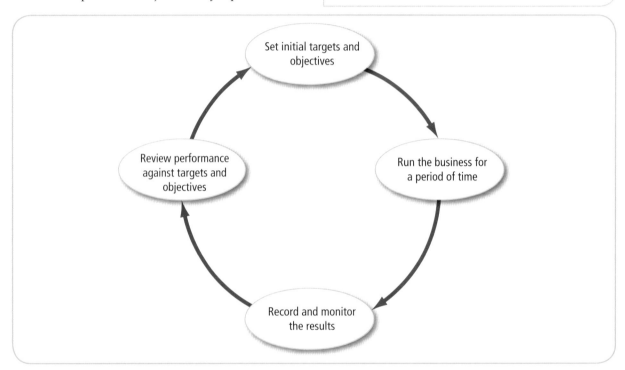

FIGURE 7.28 *Reviewing performance*

OBJECTIVE: TO LAUNCH PRODUCT ON THE MARKET			
ACTION	BY WHO	BY WHEN	ACTION COMPLETED
Market research	Marketing Director	Jan 31	Yes
Creation of prototypes	Production Director	Feb 24	Still in progress
Costing of products	Finance Director	Feb 24	Yes
Preparation of sales literature	Sales Director	Feb 24	Yes

FIGURE 7.29 *An action review*

Production totals and quality control

Most business organisations that you are likely to set up will be concerned with providing a product or service to a market.

You will find that sometimes there is a tension between providing high quantities in a given time period, and maintaining the quality of your output. (See Figure 7.30)

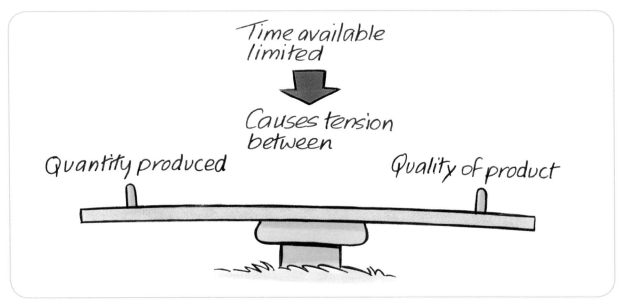

FIGURE 7.30 *Quantity versus quality*

FIGURE 7.31 *Seasonal production for Christmas*

Production

In ongoing planning for your business you will need to create a production budget. The production budget sets out the total number of products that you plan to produce in given time periods. Where demand for your product is highly seasonal you will need to start building up stockpiles in advance of peak sales periods. For example, if you are producing Christmas gifts such as a calendar, Christmas cards, Christmas bags or wrapping paper then you will need to plan future sales and make sure that production keeps up with the requirements (Figure 7.31).

You can then monitor your budget on an ongoing basis to see how you are performing against budgeted production figures. If some areas start to fall behind it may be necessary to switch resources into those lines.

You can see in Figure 7.32 that when managers monitored their production budget at the end of June they were able to see that production totals were falling behind for Christmas logs whereas production was being exceeded in bags. It would therefore make sense to switch time and resources from bags into logs to get back on budget.

Quality

You will want to make sure that your products are of a high quality – i.e. they meet the requirements of your customers. Total Quality Management is the name given to a process of structured good management practices which result in measurable continuous quality improvement. It is this ongoing process of quality improvement which contributes to changes in production.

The process as we have seen, requires clear identification of customers and their needs, and development of products and services that conform with the customers' requirements and are 'fit for the purpose'. 'Fit for the purpose' is the key: a Rolls-Royce is a quality vehicle for use at a wedding, a Land-Rover is a quality vehicle for rough terrain and a Mini is a very suitable shopping car. They are very different, but all meet their respective customers' needs.

Total Quality Management (TQM) is a series of processes that focuses on customer requirements and responds with products which are defect-free for a particular use.

This involves three stages:

Learning activity

The production manager of your company should set out a production budget. It will then be possible to discuss achievement or non-achievement of production targets on an ongoing basis.

PRODUCTION BUDGET									
	CARDS		LOGS		BAGS		CALENDARS		
	Budget	Actual	Budget	Actual	Budget	Actual	Budget	Actual	
April	50	50	30	10	50	50	0	0	
May	50	50	30	10	50	60	0	0	
June	50	50	30	10	50	70	100	100	
July	50		30		50		100		
Aug	50		30		50		100		
Sep	50		30		50		100		
Oct	50		30		50		100		
Nov	50		30		50		100		
Dec	50		30		50		100		

FIGURE 7.32 *Production budget*

FIGURE 7.33 *Quality means fitness for the intended purpose*

Discuss how you will be able to achieve processes to ensure Total Quality Management in your enterprise.

* Stage 1 – *Quality Planning.* This is a process of identifying customers, defining their needs or requirements and designing products and services to meet them.

* Stage 2 – *Quality Control.* This is the process of measuring, comparing and correcting to make sure that products and services are designed and made to meet requirements.

* Stage 3 – *Quality Improvement.* This is a continuous effort to cut out wasteful practices and improve quality.

Failure to conform to requirements costs money, because customers do not want products and services to contain faults. There are plenty of rival products for customer to turn to if they are not satisfied.

Promotion strategies

Sales promotion is all about convincing the people who form your target market that your product is the one they should buy – convincing them in such a way that they remember your product name and qualities even when competitors start trying to promote their product.

You should time your promotion campaign to 'break' when customers are most likely to buy and you are ready to supply. Posters, press advertisements, radio commercials, even TV

FIGURE 7.34 *Simon Cowell*

commercials are all-important media. They can be expensive.

Producing simple leaflets and handing them out yourself or putting them through letter boxes are cheaper and still effective methods (don't forget to put your name, address, e-mail address and phone number on the leaflet).

You could try persuading the local media to give you editorial coverage for nothing. This might involve inviting journalists to see you work or inspect your premises. Sometimes newspapers are keen to publicise the result of local market research.

The best publicity is 'word of mouth' – personal recommendation. 'Word of mouth' publicity is free in one sense, but it has to be earned. You must look upon every customer as a potential sales representative. This keeps you on your toes. A satisfied customer can bring you in many more customers. A dissatisfied customer can do you a great deal of damage.

✱ DID YOU KNOW?

Simon Cowell – the brains behind shows like 'The X-factor' – has developed the perfect tool for promoting new acts. Millions of fans switch on to the shows in which he showcases new talent acting as the perfect promotion to launch their careers.

Financial performance

Cash flow is vital to any business. Cash flow is
the passage of money into and out of a company's
current account. Even if a company's long-
term prospects are good, it can suffer cash flow
problems when it needs to pay out more money
over a short term than it receives during the same
period.

In each column of the cash flow you should list
your target figure for cash received in the month.
The items that you include in your cash flow will
depend on the type of business your are in. Here
are some examples of the types of payments most
businesses make:

* **Capital** includes any finance raised from
  financial sources, partners or shareholders and
  used as working capital

* **Finance repayments** includes hire purchase
  and other finance agreements

* **Rent/property payments**

* **Fixed asset purchases**

* **Net cash flow** shows the difference between
  your targets for total receipts and total
  payments of cash

* **Cumulative cash flow** adds all receipts and
  payments for the period under consideration
  and includes the opening book balance. If
  you do this for each month, then you obtain
  a forecast of the closing credit balance (or
  overdraft) for each month.

You will find below (Figure 7.35) an outline cash
flow chart which you can adapt for your own
business by using appropriate headings.

	January	February	March	April
Receipts				
Sales				
Other receipts				
Total receipts				
Payments				
Purchases				
Wages				
Rent				
Light/heat				
Insurance				
Interest payments				
Other expenses				
Total payments				
Net cash flow				
Opening bank balance				
Balance brought forward				
Closing bank balance				

FIGURE 7.35 *Actual cash flow*

One of the very first things that you should do in your company meetings is to create a break-even analysis for your business (See Unit 2 for break-even analysis), and for the individual products that you expect to make.

There is little point in running an enterprise (except a charity or not-for profit organisation) unless you are able to achieve results which go well beyond the break-even point. A company breaks even when all its outgoings over a specific period are equalled by income.

A business needs to cover two types of costs:

✳ Fixed costs which are fixed in amount whether the firm produces and sells no output or 100,000 or even a million units of output.

✳ Variable costs are the cost of producing each unit of a product.

A firm receives revenues when it sells products.

It is very easy to calculate the break-even point for a product or a business as a whole.

To do this for an individual product:

1 Write down the budgeted (expected) price of the product.

2 Write down the budgeted unit cost of making the product.

3 Write down the amount of fixed costs.

4 Now calculate the contribution of each unit of output/sales. This is worked out by:

Contribution = Sales price per unit – Cost of making a unit

5 You can now calculate the break-even point.

$$\text{Break-even} = \frac{\text{Fixed cost}}{\text{Contribution}}$$

When keeping bank accounts you should use the statements to keep a regular check on your

bank position. In addition, you may want to keep a separate record of petty cash and other payments to double-check the accuracy of your bank records.

Purchasing

It is helpful to keep a record of the purchases made by a business. This information should be recorded by the Financial Director and stored in a safe place. This is typically done in a purchases day book which you can get from any good quality stationer. The book should provide basic information about the date of invoice, invoice number, supplier, type of goods or services, costs of goods, VAT and total amounts (Figure 7.37). You may also want to record a reference to an

```
Balance sheet of ........................as at ...............................
                                              £                         £

Fixed assets
Buildings
Furniture
Other

Current assets
Stocks
Debtors
Bank

Cash

Less current liabilities
Bank overdraft
Other

Net current assets

Less long-term liabilities
Bank loan

Financed by
Share capital
```

FIGURE 7.36 *Balance sheet*

DATE	SUPPLIER	INVOICE NO	TOTAL	VAT

FIGURE 7.37 *Purchases day book*

DATE	CUSTOMER	INVOICE NO	TOTAL	VAT	SALES TYPE

FIGURE 7.38 *Sales day book*

order number, which will help in checking back to other records. Purchases should be recorded in date order.

Sales forecasts and targets

You may also want to keep a sales day book to record sales made (see Figure 7.38).

In a similar way to that which you create production budgets, you will want to generate sales forecasts and targets. Sales forecasts are based on previous sales achievements. For example if we sold 1,000 items last June and there has been a 10% increase in demand we might forecast that we can sell 1,100 items this June.

It is important to produce accurate sales forecasts so that we can provide information to production on how much to produce.

The sales forecast is therefore what we expect to happen. In addition, we will want to create targets for individual sales people and for the sales function as a whole. By setting targets we

FIGURE 7.39 *Sales forecasting*

Learning activity

Create monthly sales forecasts for your company. Set these out on a spreadsheet so that you can compare the forecasted and the actual figures. Also create sales targets for your sales force. Perhaps you might want to create a bonus scheme for achieving sales targets. This work is the responsibility of your Sales Director and sales team.

Learning activity

Produce a plan setting out:

* Key dates in the winding up of the business.

* Key responsibilities for winding up the company, who will take particular actions e.g. the Financial Director in producing the final accounts, the Company Secretary in informing shareholders etc. of winding down procedures, the Sales Director in informing customers, the Human Resources Director in informing and paying off employees etc.

* When and how creditors will be paid off.

* When and how the final dividend will be distributed among shareholders and share capital repaid to shareholders.

give our sales force something to work towards. The achievement of sales targets is often related to sales bonuses for successful performance.

7.4 Winding up your company

A company does not die. To terminate it for whatever reason, it has to be wound up. It is necessary to understand the function and effect that winding up has on the company, its employees, shareholders and assets.

Effective planning for winding up

There are two ways that a company can be wound up.

1   *Compulsory winding up by the courts.* Shareholders, creditors, the official receiver and government officials can seek a petition to wind up a company perhaps because it has run up too many debts, because it is not pursuing the activities set out in the Memorandum, or some form of mismanagement.

2   *Voluntary winding up.* This occurs when the business comes to the end of its working life. In the case of your enterprise when the members of your group split up perhaps to prepare for exams it makes sense to wind the company up.

The importance of winding up is to make sure that the company comes to the end of its life in an ordered way, so that nobody feels badly done by and everyone knows what to expect.

Key things to plan are:

* the date the company will finally cease to exist as an entity

* the date the company will stop trading

* the date the company will stop manufacturing

* how the company will ensure that it meets its obligations to customers

* how the company will meet its obligations to employees

* how the company will meet its obligations to shareholders.

Relevant documentation and reporting

Registered companies that cease trading will as a formality inform the Registrar of Companies that

DOCUMENT	WHO RESPONSIBLE FOR PRODUCING
Final set of accounts	Financial Director
Company report	Managing Director and Directors
Letter to shareholders	Company Secretary
Newsletter for employees	Human Resources Director
Letter to suppliers	Purchasing Manager

FIGURE 7.40 *Documents required when trading ceases*

they no longer intend to trade so that they can effectively be deregistered.

The most important documents to prepare when you want to cease trading are shown in Figure 7.40.

The Company Report is very important and should give an overview of:

* The business strategy – i.e. the plan that you pursued

* Key business successes

* Financial highlights

* A brief summary from the Chair of the company

* A brief summary from the Managing Director

* A set of financial accounts – the final balance sheet, and profit and loss account

* Notes to the accounts if relevant.

If you can produce these reports in a well-ordered

and structured way you will be able to show that you have an excellent understanding of business and all of its key aspects. You will have no fear of setting up a business enterprise of your own at some stage in the future.

Closing down trading activities

It is very important that when you close your company down that you maintain the hopefully excellent relations with wider stakeholders that you maintained during the period of running the enterprise.

Closing down trading involves:

* ending buying operations

* ending selling operations.

The Purchasing Director should write to all of the major suppliers that you have used on an ongoing basis thanking them for their support and explaining that you are ceasing trading.

The Sales Director should notify all customers well before the winding up date when you will cease trading. You need to make sure that you have met all outstanding orders so that nobody is left unhappy and frustrated that they have not received their orders.

Distribution of assets

During the course of running your business you will have acquired a number of assets, e.g. stocks of materials, and capital equipment. It is important to realise that these assets belong to the owners of the company, not to the employees.

You must sell off these assets for the highest price that you can receive for them. The revenue earned can then be used to add to cash reserves for paying back shareholders and distributing a final dividend.

Profit and Loss Account for Young Entrepreneurs Ltd as at 31 December 2004

	£
Turnover of assorted products	1040.50
Cost of sales	520.50
	————
Gross profit	520.00
Expenses (including wages)	320.00
Operating profit	200.00
Nominal tax charge at 20%	40.00
Profit after tax	160.00

FIGURE 7.41 *Final profit and loss account*

Financial implications

Hopefully when you come to wind up your enterprise, you will have made a profit. For example, consider the profit and loss account for a small enterprise (see Figure 7.41). Because the business will not be continuing the profit of £160.00 can be distributed to shareholders.

If the company started off with 500 £1 shares, i.e. £500 worth of share capital, then each £1 share is entitled to an 80p dividend (the £160 divided among £500 worth of £1 shares). Each share will receive the £1 initial capital back plus a further 80p in dividend.

However, it is also possible that your company might have made a loss – perhaps because it paid out too much in wages, or because it was not able to sell some of the products that it made.

Assuming that the same company makes a loss of £100, then each £1 share would have deducted from it a 20 pence loss. So, each shareholder instead of receiving their £1 nominal share value would only receive 80 pence.

The maximum loss that the shareholder is expected to pay is the value of their shares.

Learning activity

Work out how much profit your company has made and then calculate the amount of dividend accruing to shareholders. When will they be paid and who will be responsible for paying them?

Learning activity

Given the example shown in Figure 7.41, how much would:

a Sunil Patel who has 20 shares in the company receive in dividends?

b Brian Jones who has 5 shares in the company receive in dividends?

Impact of and on external factors

The winding up of your business will have a knock on effect on the wider business environment. For example, there will be an obvious impact on other stakeholders:

* Competitors will benefit from not having to compete with you.

* Customers will lose out from a loss of a suppliers.

* Suppliers will lose out from loss of sales.

* The community will lose out from not having an exciting and interesting enterprise working with it.

At the same time, external factors may impact on the winding up of your company, for example:

STAKEHOLDER GROUP	IMPACT ON OUR WINDING UP	HOW AFFECTED BY OUR WINDING UP
Customers		
Suppliers		
Competitors		
Wider community		

FIGURE 7.42 *Factors affecting and being influenced by winding up the business*

* Suppliers may put pressure on you to pay up or to return borrowed items.

* Customers who have paid in advance may demand delivery from you, etc.

Learning activity

Carry out an audit to assess which external stakeholders will exert pressures which affect your winding up and which external stakeholders are influenced by your winding up. Set it out in a table like the one shown in Figure 7.42.

UNIT ASSESSMENT

The assessment for this unit is based on written work and an oral presentation about an enterprise that you worked with other students to set up and run. Your work for the assessment should consist of the following four elements:

1 A personal diary or journal showing evidence of your participation in the launch, planning and running of the company and an evaluation of your own contribution. You should write up your diary/ journal every week outlining the key events in the life of your company and the part you played in setting up and running it.

2 An individual report on all the other roles and responsibilities in the launch, planning and running of the company and an evaluation of those roles and their contribution to the enterprise i.e. the roles of Chair, Managing Director, Marketing Director, Financial Director, other key Directors and the Company Secretary.

3 A group presentation and report explaining the planning and preparation which went into launching the company and product/service and which assesses the issues involved in the day-to-day running and monitoring of the business, its financial performance and the winding up of the business. The group presentation must include individual contributions.

4 An individual report reviewing and evaluating the success of the whole enterprise.

Resources

Books

Barrow, C., *Setting Up and Managing Your Own Business*, Sage, Kensington, 1998
Burch, G., *Go it Alone*, Capstone, 2003
Butler, D., *Business Planning; A Guide to Small Business Start-up*, Butterworth Heinemann, 2000
Clayton, P., *Forming a Limited Company*, Kogan Page, 2001
Impey, D., *Running a Limited Company*, Jordans, 2001
Macmillan, D., *Be Your Own Boss*, Kogan Page, 2002
Stone, P., *The Ultimate Business Plan*, How to Books, 2002
Williams, S., *Small Business Guide*, Lloyds TSB, Press Vitesse, 2003

Websites

Access these through www.heinemann.co.uk/hotlinks (express code 1149P, then go to Unit 7).

Business Links
British Chambers of Commerce (BCC)
BTG (company that develops novel technologies)
British Venture Capital Association
Companies House
Department for Trade and Industry (DTI)
Inland Revenue
HM Customs and Excise
DTI small business site
Lloyds TSB business site

Other information

Forms for the setting up of a limited company can be obtained from Purchasing, Companies House, Crown Way, Cardiff CF14 3UZ, or on the web through www.heinemann.co.uk/hotlinks (express code 1149P, then go to Unit 7).

The National Business Register offers free information, advice and support in setting up a new business, new company, trademark or brand and domain name. See them on the web through www.heinemann.co.uk/hotlinks (express code 1149P, then go to Unit 7).

Glossary

Accounting	Identifying, measuring, recording and reporting information relating to the activities of an organisation.
Ad hoc fees	Fees charged when an advertising agency contracts to carry out one specific task for a specific fee.
Advertisements	Paid ongoing non-personal communications from a commercial source such as a manufacturer or retailer.
Advertising Standards Authority (ASA)	Independent body that exercises control over all advertising in the UK.
Aim	A business aim is the general end purpose that it is working towards, e.g. our aim is to become the UK's Number 1…
Ambient media	Media designed to be mobile or meet consumers in their own territory.
Ansoff	H. I. Ansoff was born in Vladivostock in December 1918 with an American father and a Russian mother. He went on to become a leading US industrialist. He further developed his career as a university professor and became famous for his work upon business strategies.
Appraisal	Interview between a manager and a subordinate/colleague to establish priorities and targets for the future as well as to review previous and current performance.
Articles of Association	Set of rules governing the internal workings of a company.
Assets	Things that an organisation owns, as well as other items that may be owed to the business.
Auditing	Making lists and keeping records. For example, an environmental audit records all processes, activities etc that have an impact on the environment.
Auditors	Professional accountants who provide independent scrutiny and report on an organisation's financial position.
Augmented product	Going beyond the product offering to provide something which, although less tangible, is just as important.
Authorised capital	The value of shares that a company is allowed by law to sell in total.
Balance sheet	A snapshot of what an organisation owns and owes on a particular date.
Board of Directors	Group chosen by shareholders to represent their interests. The Chair of a company is the main representative of the shareholders.
Break-even point	The point at which sales levels are high enough not to make a loss, but not high enough to make a profit.
Bricks and mortar	A traditional business that does not engage in electronic trading, e.g. a high street store that does not have an Internet presence.
British Rate and Data	General lists of media and details of their basic rates.
Browsing	Viewing the Internet by entering it through a web viewing program such as Internet Explorer.
Budgets	Financial plan that helps businesses to set targets and control expenditure.
Capital	This is provided by the owner of the business and is therefore deemed to be owed to the owner by the business.
Cash	Liquid asset that enables an organisation to buy the goods and services it requires in order to add value to them.
Charity	An organisation set up for a particular charitable purpose e.g. for educational or religious purposes. The organisation is overseen by a group of trustees. It does not make a profit although it can make a surplus.

Clicks-and-mortar	A business that combines a traditional physical presence (e.g. retail shops) with Internet buying and selling.
Coach	Someone who provides help and guidance to a less experienced colleague by monitoring and assessing their performance in a constructive way.
Code of Practice	A written set of requirements setting out how activities will be carried out.
Communication	The process of establishing a commonness or oneness of thought between a sender and a receiver.
Company	An organisation that is a corporate body in law and which is owned by shareholders.
Company inertia	People's reluctance to alter what they are doing and their inability to see any need to change.
Consumers	People who use/consume a product.
Consumer protection	Laws, bodies and actions whose purpose is to look after the interests of consumers.
Contribution	Selling price per unit less variable costs per unit.
Control	Control refers either to the act of managing and making decisions in a business or to keeping an organisation on plan or working to previously decided programmes.
Controllable methods	Paid-for promotional methods that are carefully directed to achieve the objectives of an organisation.
Core product	This is what a product does and its main characteristics, functions and features.
Corporate Social Responsibility (CSR)	CSR is the process of making sure that an organisation (a corporate body) looks after the community and wider society e.g. through charitable work.
Corporation Tax	The first charge on profits paid to the Inland Revenue.
Cross-functional team	A team within an organisation made up of people from a range of specialisms.
Culture	The typical pattern of behaviors that characterize working relationships in an organisation e.g. friendly or cold, bureaucratic or laid back etc.
Current assets	Sometimes called 'circulating assets', these are short-term assets because the form they take is constantly changing.
Current liabilities	Debts a business needs to repay within a short period of time (normally a year).
Curriculum vitae	A specially prepared list of a job applicant's qualifications, previous job history, experience, etc
Customers	People who buy a product.
Customer care programmes	These are designed to improve the experience for customers and to encourage them to become advocates and repeat-purchasers.
Customer perceptions	The general public will have an overall impression of the level of service they expect an organisation to provide.
Customer satisfaction	A product's performance relative to a buyer's expectations.
Customer service	Process that provides time and place benefits for the customer pre-transaction, during the enjoyment of the product and post-transaction.
Database	Large amount of information stored on a computer in such a way that it can easily be found, processed and updated.
Deed of Partnership	A legal document setting out the relationship between partners in a partnership e.g. how profits will be distributed.
Demographics	Characteristics of people such as age, gender, marital status, etc., which are used by marketers to segment the market as a whole.
Desktop mapping	Way of viewing and analysing data geographically, with information superimposed in layers on digital maps.

Development	Identifying and seeking to meet the needs of individuals in the workplace, e.g. by providing them with opportunities to expand their job role.
Direct dialogue	Interactive two-way communication, for example between an e-seller and an e-customer.
Direct marketing	First-hand way such as direct mail or telephone marketing to reach and promote products or services to consumers.
Diversification	Spreading interests over a variety of products/activities.
Dividend	A share of the company's profit paid to shareholders.
Empowerment	Giving more decision-making responsibility to those lower down in an organisation.
Enterprise/Entrepreneur	Taking risks by running an enterprise.
Ethics	Moral principles or rules of conduct – getting things 'right'.
Executive Director	A company director involved in ongoing decision-making e.g. the Managing Director.
External customers	These may include individuals from different organisations working in business-to-business markets (B2B) as well as individual customers.
External written communications	Communications sent outside an organisation.
Financial accounting	Concerned with the recording of financial transactions and the preparation of financial reports to communicate past financial performance.
Firewall	A security system protecting a computer system against external threats such as viruses and hacking.
Fixed assets	These tend to have a life-span of more than one year. They comprise items that are purchased and generally kept for a long period of time.
Flat organisation	An organisational structure that has relatively few layers of command.
Focus groups	Small groups of customers who are able to discuss their needs in some depth.
Fringe benefits	Additional benefits on top of pay e.g. a company car or other perks.
Function	A specialist component of an organisation e.g. the marketing function of a company.
Gap analysis	Tool for analysing what is happening in the business environment.
Gap in the market	Opportunity provided by lack of competition in a particular sector of the current market.
Global warming	The raising of air and sea temperatures as a result of pollution, the emission of greenhouse gases, etc.
Good	The term used to describe something which gives a consumer value e.g. a physical good such as a bread roll or a curry. The term 'good' is sometimes used just to include physical items with the term 'service' being applied to an intangible provision of benefits.
Government department	A body set up by the government to run a particular activity or service. It is staffed by government officials known as civil servants.
Human Resource Management (HRM)	Involves seeking to help individuals to meet their own work needs while at the same time helping the organisation to achieve its objectives.
Hyperlink	A 'hotspot' on a page which when clicked on takes you somewhere else – known as the destination of the link.
HyperText Markup Language (HTML)	Language for creating web pages.
Induction	The process of introducing an individual to the workplace, to work routines, to colleagues and processes.

Information highway	A term used to describe the Internet where browsers can move around (surf) to find out the information they want down a variety of channels.
Informative advertising	Conveys information and raises consumer awareness of the features and benefits of a product.
Innovation	The addition of an additional step or advance to an existing idea or product.
Internal customers	Within an organisation these would include all colleagues, ranging from support roles such as delivering post within the organisation, to jobs at the top of the organisation.
Internal written communications	Communications within an organisation.
Internet	A worldwide network of computers, each of which has its own address known as a URL (Universal Resource Locator).
Internet Service Provider (ISP)	An organisation which provides Internet services like e-mail and access to the world wide web.
Issued capital	The value of shares that a company has issued at any one time. This will typically be less than the authorised capital.
Job analysis	The process where an employer looks at what is required within the current job. This can be done in a number of ways including looking at the job description, observing someone in the job or through a questionnaire.
Job description	The list of working conditions for a job, e.g. pay, hours and duties.
Legislation	Laws – often created by Acts of Parliament.
Liabilities	These include anything that an organisation owes.
Liquidation	This occurs when a business can no longer pay its debts.
Liquidity	Being able to meet financial obligations.
Long-term liability	Sometimes called a deferred liability, this is not due for payment until some time in the future.
Management accounting	Involves looking to the future using a knowledge of past performance, where relevant, to aid the management of the business.
Market	The range of means by which consumers can buy a particular product or alternative to it.
Market penetration	This involves making more sales to customers without changing products in any way.
Market positioning	The location of a firm in the market in terms of key criteria such as price and quality.
Market research	'The systematic gathering, recording and analysis of data about problems related to the marketing of goods and services.' (American Market Research Association).
Market segment	The result of dividing up large heterogeneous markets with similar needs into smaller markets (segments) according to shared characteristics.
Market segmentation	Dividing the customers within a market into groups, each of which has distinctive needs and expectations.
Market share	The percentage of sales within a market that is held by one brand or company.
Marketing	'The management process responsible for identifying, anticipating and satisfying customer requirements profitably.' (Institute of Marketing).
Marketing mix	A series of variable factors such as the four Ps (product/price/place/promotion) used by an organisation to meet its customers' needs.
Marketing objectives	The targets that the organisation seeks to meet through its marketing activities.

Marketing plan	A plan that uses the marketing mix to identify and then meet consumers' requirements.
Marketing strategies	Long-term plans designed to enable an organisation to identify and meet the wants and needs of its customers.
Matrix	Type of organisational structure in which a particular unit or individual is accountable to more than one line manager or function.
Memorandum of Association	Document setting out the nature of a company when viewed from the outside (by people outside the company).
Mentor	An individual that provides advice, guidance and support to a colleague in the workplace.
Method study	Examining the way in which work is carried out to try and ascertain superior methods for carrying out such work.
Mission	Sets out the long-term purpose of an organisation and helps to emphasise why the organisation is there.
Modern Apprenticeship	Government funded scheme combining education, training and the development of practical skills for work related occupations.
Monitoring	Recording and keeping an eye on activities.
Motivation	The personal drive to achieve targets and get things done.
Municipal enterprise	A government body that runs a particular activity on a local level and is usually financed by some form of taxation or government grant.
Navigation	Movement around a web page, web site or the Internet itself.
Non-controllable methods	Marketing messages communicated by word of mouth, personal recommendations and a consumer's overall perception of a particular product or service.
Non-verbal communications	Communications based upon body language.
Objective	A component part of an overall business aim. Sometimes objectives are quantified (numbers are attached to the objective e.g. to increase production by 10% this year).
Ofcom	The regulator for the UK communications industries with responsibilities across television, radio, telecommunications and wireless communications services.
Office of Fair Trading (OFT)	A government body set up to look after the interests of consumers and traders.
Opportunity to see (OTS)	Measure the coverage the media can offer through figures identifying the number of people who have an opportunity to view an advertisement once.
Overtrading	Expansion that damages cash flow.
Ownership	The act of being a part owner of a business e.g. shareholders are the owners of a company.
Performance Related Pay (PRP)	Pay that is tied to the achievement of targets, objectives and other measurable outcomes.
Person specification	List of attributes needed by a person to perform a job, such as personality type or experience.
Personal selling	Face-to-face communication between sales representatives and customers.
Persuasive advertising	Concerned with creating a desire for the product and stimulating purchase. It is used with established and more mature products.
Pilot	To gauge the market reaction before a test is viable.
Positioning	Placing a product within the overall market e.g. at the 'no frills' end or at the 'luxury' end of the market.

Post-sale surveys	Aspect of a customer care programme used as a means of identifying the levels of satisfaction experienced by customers who have recently made a purchase.
Potential product	Aspects that may become part of the product offer for the future, e.g. new games for a Playstation.
Primary information	Information that an organisation compiles by its own efforts perhaps commissioning a specialist market research agency.
Printed media	Media that includes all newspapers and magazines, both local and national, as well as the trade press, periodicals and professional journals.
Private sector	That part of the economy that is owned by private individuals e.g. one person businesses, partnerships and companies.
Probing	Finding out the prospect's needs and where his or her priorities might lie.
Process	An activity involved in turning raw inputs into more finished outputs.
Product knowledge	The ability of staff to deal with any queries or issues that arise about products or services on offer.
Product life cycle	Key stages in the life of a product e.g. launch, introduction, growth, maturity, decline.
Promotional budget	Budget allocated between the different elements of the promotional mix.
Protection pressure groups	These may be set up to fight a specific issue, such as the closure of a plant or the increased traffic on a road as a result of a local business.
Prototype	A trial version of a good or service.
Public company	An organisation owned by shareholders. The shares can be bought and sold openly through the medium of the Stock Exchange.
Public relations	The development and maintenance of positive relationships between an organisation and its publics, achieved through activities designed to create understanding and goodwill.
Public sector	That part of the economy that is owned by the government on behalf of citizens.
Qualitative	Research associated with consumer responses, feelings, attitudes and descriptions, usually from a limited number of respondents (people).
Quality circles	These provide a valuable opportunity for employees to meet together and think of ways in which they can improve how they work and how they meet both internal and external customer needs.
Quantitative	Research associated with figures or numbers that help to make the research more objective, usually from a large number of consumers.
Questionnaire	Systematic list of questions designed to obtain information from people about specific events, their attitudes, their values and their beliefs.
Recruitment	Taking on employees.
Recycling	Making use of material and 'waste' products so that they can be used again.
Registrar of Companies	Individual responsible for listing, recording and approving the details of companies. Companies House is located in Cardiff.
Regulations	Rules.
Reinforcement advertising	Concerned with reminding consumers about the product, and is used to reinforce the knowledge held by potential consumers about the benefits to be gained from purchase.
Rights issue	A cheap way of issuing new shares by giving existing shareholders the right to buy them.
Routine response behaviour	This describes what happens when customers frequently buy items of low value that requires little thought.

Sales forecast	A calculation of likely future sales based on previous evidence such as last year's sales figures and rises in consumer demand.
Sales promotions	Inducements designed to encourage a response from a customer.
Sample	Questioning a selection of respondents from the target market.
Search engine	A database of extracts from the web that can be searched to find references.
Secondary information	Published data collected by another organisation and not specific to the project in hand.
Selection	Choose employees to take up a position from a number of possible choices.
Self-regulation	Individuals, organisations, and industries controlling the way they behave rather than responding to external pressure/laws. For example, the advertising industry in this country regulates advertising through the Advertising Standards Authority.
Server	A computer (on a network) that provides services to users sitting at desktop (or laptop) computers such as Internet services.
Service	There are two main types of services: **1** Services to people – i.e. intangible benefits such as hairdressing, watching a film at the cinema, receiving personal insurance cover. **2** Services to businesses such as the transport of goods, the insurance of business items, etc.
Sex Discrimination Act	Legislation setting out how the two sexes can be treated equally (in a non-discriminatory way) in the workplace.
Shortlist	A list drawn up which selects the best possible candidates from all the candidates who have applied for a post.
Situation analysis	Study of the broad trends in the external factors which affect the business, such as the economy, and a detailed analysis of markets, consumers and competitors.
Social marketing	Linking the actions of organisations to the interests of consumers in social, ethical and environmental issues.
Sole trader	A one-person business. The one person may employ others but he or she is the sole owner.
Sponsorship	Providing opportunities for organisations to connect with a range of activities by providing financial supporting for events.
Spreadsheet	Table of numbers which can be organised and altered on a computer according to preset formulae.
Stakeholder	A person or group with an interest or concern in something.
Stock Exchange	A market for shares that have already been issued to shareholders. They can then sell off existing shares and buy others. Typically the work of the Stock Exchange today is carried out by means of computer screen trading.
Strategic choice	Setting out a menu of strategic options, comparing the options provided by the menu and choosing the best option from the menu.
Strategic implementation	Putting the chosen marketing strategy into action.
Suggestions box	A way of collecting customer feedback.
Surfing	Clicking around the Internet by following links between pages.
Tall organisation	An organisation with lots of layers in it.
Tangible	Something that you can touch and see – i.e. a physical good.
Target audience	The population on which an organisation's marketing effort is focused.
Target market	Sector of the overall market that a company targets its marketing activities at, including products and promotions.
Targeting	Developing strategies for particular segments.

The Data Protection Act	Regulation of the storage of information through a registration process to protect individual consumers and businesses.
The Sale of Goods Act	Ensure that sellers provide goods that are of 'merchantable quality' – that is, they must not be damaged or broken.
The Trade Descriptions Act	This attempts to ensure that the description given of the goods forms part of the contract the buyer makes with the seller.
The Weights and Measures Act	This ensures that consumers receive the actual quantity of a product they are buying.
Total Quality Management (TQM)	Philosophy based upon quality that shapes relationships between suppliers and customers.
Trade union	Body set up to represent the organised rights of labour in the workplace. Being united (a union) gives individual employees greater strength to bargain with employers than if they were working on their own.
Trading account	Shows how gross profit is arrived at (Net sales – Cost of sales = Gross profit).
Training	Activities designed to help an individual work more effectively within an organisation depending on their training needs.
Training needs analysis	Way of identifying the dimensions required for a new customer service strategy.
Unique Selling Proposition (USP)	Features that are unique to a product or service.
Variance analysis	A process of analysing where actual performance differs from budgeted performance.
Verbal communications	Speaking in a way that is acceptable to customers.
Voluntary organisation	An organisation managed and staffed by unpaid voluntary workers.
W3C	The World Wide Web Consortium, made up of academics and industry representatives who work together to create common standards for the World Wide Web.
Web pages	Documents that contain text, pictures and other visuals and sound which are brought together by a 'web browser' application.
Web server	A computer which is linked to the Internet. The server stores web pages and sends them out when browsers access them.
Website	A collection of pages, graphics and folders which form an integrated site area. The site is typically stored on one or more directory on a web server.
Working capital	This shows how easily the business can pay its short-term debts and is the ratio of current assets to current liabilities.
World Wide Web (www)	Section of the Internet concerned with storage and delivery to your computer screen of 'web pages'.

Index

Page numbers in italics refer to illustrations and diagrams.